Echoes of Detroit's Jewish Communities

A History

Irwin J. Cohen

Echoes of Detroit's Jewish Communities: A History
©2003 by Irwin J. Cohen

All rights reserved under the International and Pan American Copyright Conventions. No part of this book may be reproduced in any manner whatsoever without written permission from the author, except in the case of brief quotations embodied in reviews and articles.

Printed in the United States of America

08 07 06 05 04 03   5 4 3 2 1

ISBN 0-9677570-1-0

Published by City Vision Publishing
in cooperation with Boreal Press, Inc.
P.O. Box 40
Laingsburg, Michigan 48848
www.borealpress.com

DEDICATED
TO THE
GREATEST PARENTS
AND GRANDPARENTS

Contents

1 1760-1839: The Early Years 5

2 1840-1859: A Community Is Born 8

3 1860-1869: The Civil War Era 13

4 1870-1889: Synagogues Are Built 21

5 1890-1899: Hardship and Helping Hands 27

6 1900-1909: New Century, New Immigrants 34

7 1910-1919: A Time of Growth 49

8 1920-1924: Zionism and Anti-Semitism 68

9 1925-1929: From Boom to Crash 86

10 1930-1934: The Depression Years 111

Contents (cont.)

11 1935-1939: Before the War..134

12 1940-1945: War and Sacrifice...156

13 1946-1953: The Postwar Years..188

14 1954-1959: The Community Spreads..224

15 1960-1969: The Sixties...240

16 1970-1979: Detroit Becomes a Memory..274

17 1980-1989: The Shift to the Suburbs..295

18 1990-1999: Century's End..315

19 2000: The New Millennium..330

About the Publisher

City Vision Publishing is dedicated to helping Great Lakes regional authors publish books with artistic and historical merit and find their way through the complex world of the book industry. Services include database registration, editing, layout, design, printer liaison services, distribution, and targeted marketing.
For more information, write:

    Editor
    Boreal Press, Inc.
    P.O. Box 40
    Laingsburg, Michigan 48848
    www.borealpress.com

Cover Photos:
Front Cover: top left—page 26; top right—page 40; center—window from Congregation Mogen Abraham on Farnsworth, used until 1939, salvaged by Reconstructionist Congregation of Detroit. Bottom left—inside Congregation Shaarey Zedek; center—Congregation Ahavas Zion, Holbrook and Beaubien.

Back Cover: top: 1939 Detroit River at Woodward, courtesy of Michigan Views; bottom—Joe and Harry Dorfman inside Dorfman Drugs in 1934 (page 133), courtesy of Gail Zimmerman.

About the Author

Irwin J. Cohen worked as a photojournalist for national baseball publications, which led to interviewing numerous celebrity superstars including Hank Greenberg. Cohen also worked in the front office of the Detroit Tigers and earned a 1984 World Series ring. More than a nationally recognized baseball historian, Cohen, who has authored several history books, is available for speaking engagements.

Acknowledgments

Thanks go to many of the names and organizations listed in the index and to those in parenthesis under the photo captions,

Special thanks to Sylvia (Cottler) Cohen, Dexter-Davison historian; Benno Levi for his total recall and use of his diaries; Mrs. Fayga Weiss of the Holocaust Memorial Center, and Jim Grey, president of the Jewish Genealogical Society of Michigan and past president of the Jewish Historical Society of Michigan.

Being born and raised in the Twelfth Street and Dexter neighborhoods helped propel this book. However, a couple of years of visiting the past via the Burton Historical Collection of the Detroit Public Library were needed, as were numerous visits to the Leo M. Franklin Archives of Temple Beth El, ably managed by archivist Holly Teasdale.

A sincere, much-appreciated thank you goes to Arthur Horwitz and the staff of the *Jewish News*. I loved doing research there and getting to be on a first-name basis with the names listed in the JN masthead. Administrative assistant Rita Geiringer taught me how to research via microfilm, and others shared working space, copy machine tips, paper, and good conversation.

Getting to know the great, creative people at the *Jewish News* gave me an idea. We should have a "Community Connection Day" every two years or so at the West Bloomfield Jewish Community Center. Folks could go along rows of tables and get a chance to meet staff from the *Jewish News*, the Federation, Jewish organizations, Jewish day schools, and synagogues.

Well, I've got a lot more to say, but I'd like to do it in front of your group. We could talk about the past, present, or future. So give me a call at 248-968-5314.

FOREWORD

I spent my infancy in an apartment on Blaine just east of Twelfth Street and some pre-nursery school years in a larger apartment on Blaine just west of Woodrow Wilson.

My early memories, however, were based on Tuxedo between Dexter and Wildemere. I shared a bedroom with my younger brother and sister, and the other two bedrooms were occupied by my parents and my mother's parents. The seven of us shared one bathroom, a kitchen and a small front room and dining room in the lower flat. The front porch served as our family room in good weather.

Around 1951, our house became one of the most popular sites in the neighborhood. A fire destroyed our garage and my father salvaged some wood to build benches and bleachers. He painted foul lines and bases on the cement and we called our newly enlarged play area "Keystone Stadium."

Now we had the footage from the back of the house to where the garage used to be and the alley behind it to the back fence of the two-flat on Elmhurst.

Our little, mostly cement baseball park was in constant use in good weather. The only off days were Saturdays and Jewish holidays. When we wanted more room to roam around, we trekked two and a half blocks east up Tuxedo and crossed Linwood to Central High's ball field.

With Dexter just a half-block away, it became the street we walked on almost daily. When Detroit passed its 250th birthday in 1951, Dexter had many varied establishments. Some had close competitors and some had none in the area.

From Tuxedo heading south on Dexter's east side, we'd pass the Hi-Diddle-Diddle Children's Clothing shop; Midwest Shoe Repair; Margolis Kosher Meat & Poultry; Goldfarb Dairies & Groceries; Dexter Fruitland; Lefkofsky Delicatessen; Dexter Bakery; Plastic Apron Shop; Lilly's Fish Market; Goldin Meat Market; B'nai B'rith Youth Organization; Linden Super Market; Fine's Lingerie, and the Eagle Dairy Products on the corner of Webb. Crossing Webb we'd come to Cunningham's Drugs, and just south of that was S.S. Kresge's, Maurice's Ladies Wear, Philip Bricker Furs, Brody's Knee-Hi Children's Shoppe, and the large Dexter Theatre on the corner of Burlingame.

On the other side of Burlingame was the enticing

The author lived in the lower flat at 3318 Tuxedo, between Dexter and Wildemere.

show windows of Dexter Chevrolet, almost directly across the street from the imposing B'nai Moshe synagogue.

While walking north on Dexter didn't offer a chance to gaze at the movie murals of coming attractions or to view the latest colorful Chevys, it was where we bought baseball cards, candy, comics, magazines, and other important stuff.

A right turn down the block from Tuxedo to Dexter, passing Serlin's Drug Store and crossing Elmhurst, was Don's Sweet Shop. You could buy all kinds of little goodies for pennies by putting a penny in a machine and turning a dial. A sepia postcard-sized baseball or movie star would fall in your hands.

Crossing Duane and Monterey would lead to Danny's Confectionery. While I never sat at the soda fountain, I often stood in front of Danny while he held a box of Bowman baseball cards and I picked out a couple of packs.

Crossing Richton, George V Drug Store was the best place to check out the latest Superman, Batman, Captain Marvel, and Lone Ranger comics and baseball magazines. George Victor was a nice man and provided a large area for us to browse.

We'd pass those places going to and from our school-—the Yeshiva Beth Yehudah on the other side of Dexter at Cortland. We'd also enjoy the sights and sounds of other mom n' pop places.

The window display of American Savings & Loan Association on the east side of Dexter and Cortland had a clock flanked by large Associated Press pictures of current events. A couple of doors south was the window display of Spitzer's Hebrew Book Shop. On the way to Borenstein's Book & Music Store on the corner of Duane some two blocks south, we'd pass several food related stores, including one that had a large tank filled with live fish that would become someone's next meal.

You'd whiff the salami from several delis and the leather from the shoe shops and the fresh baked goods from Mayer's Bakery & Pastry Shop between Duane and Elmhurst.

There were always old ladies stationed outside the bakery shaking and jingling the tall round JNF and Yeshiva charity boxes. We'd get nice Yiddish words hurled at us for dropping in a penny, and our grandparents would hear about it.

Everything we needed or wanted was on Dexter or three blocks east on Linwood. The bus lines on the two streets took us to the ballpark and downtown.

Sometime during the transition from radio to television, the neighborhood began to change. By 1956 we moved a half-mile north to a single home on Leslie, and four years later it was on to Wisconsin, three blocks east of Wyoming and a half-block south of Curtis.

The '67 riots speeded the death of the neighborhood and most of the city, and by June of '68 we were residents of Oak Park. The old Dexter, Linwood, Twelfth Street, and Hastings Street neighborhoods are dead but the memories still live.

– Irwin Cohen

The Cohens model their favorite hats in 1950. The author is at lower right, with his younger brother, sister, parents, and grandparents.

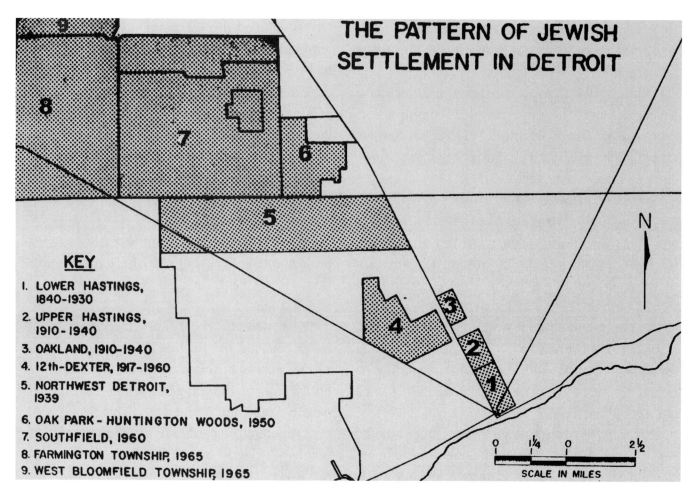
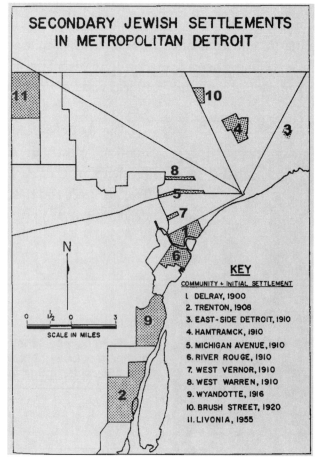

1
1760-1839
THE EARLY YEARS

In 1760, after 59 years of French rule, Detroit was surrendered by the French to the English during the French and Indian War.

The following year, 76 years before Michigan would be formally admitted to the Union as the twenty-sixth state, Ezekiel Solomon became the first Jew in what would eventually become known as the Upper Peninsula.

Solomon was soon joined by four partners from the same Montreal Jewish community seeking opportunities in the lucrative fur trade. One of the partners, Chapman Abraham, became Detroit's first recorded Jew in 1762 when he ventured along the Detroit River for trading purposes.

In May of 1763, Abraham was overseeing five boatloads of goods destined for Detroit. At the time, Abraham was unaware that Chief Pontiac was leading Indian attacks against the British and other whites in and around the fort at Detroit. The Indians captured Abraham and prepared to torture and burn him at the stake.

An account of the events that transpired was preserved by Rev. John Heckewelder:

Tied to the stake the fire burning by his side, his thirst from the great heat became intolerable, and he begged that some drink might be given to him. It is a custom with the Indians, previous to a prisoner being put to death, to give him what they call his last meal; a bowl of pottage or broth was therefore brought to him for that purpose. Eager to quench his thirst, he put the bowl immediately to his lips, and the liquor being very hot, he was dreadfully scalded. Being a man of very quick temper, the moment he felt his mouth burned, he threw the bowl with its contents full in the face of the man who handed it to him. "He is mad! He is mad!" resounded from all quarters. The bystanders considered his conduct as an act of insanity, and immediately untied the cords with which he was bound, and let him go where he pleased. This fact was well-known to all the inhabitants of Detroit from whom I first heard it, and it was afterwards confirmed to me by Mr. Chapman [Abraham] himself, who was established as a merchant at that place.

Abraham maintained a residence in the little village of Detroit, which numbered 678 exclusive of the garrison, in 1768. He dabbled in the selling of furs, gunpowder, liquor, real estate, silver works, snuff and tobacco.

Abraham died in 1783 when Detroit numbered around 2,200 residents in the entire settlement. He was buried in the cemetery of Montreal's Shearith Israel.

Ezekiel Solomon was successful in the Mackinac region and founded a general store there in 1779, believed to be the first department store in the United States. He moved to Detroit in 1789 and was involved in the fur trade.

In 1793, ten years after the Treaty of Paris awarded Detroit to the United States, the British were still in Detroit and refused to leave. President George Washington decided to force a settlement and sent troops

Thirty-foot-long freight canoes made of birchbark were used by traders such as Chapman Abraham to transport goods from Montreal to Detroit.
(Courtesy of Burton Historical Collection, Detroit Public Library)

Detroit in 1794 when Moses David often crossed the river from Canada.
(Courtesy of Burton Historical Collection, Detroit Public Library)

under the command of General Anthony Wayne. Wayne battled his way to Detroit and a new treaty was signed in 1794.

Also in 1794, Moses David, a Jewish trader from Montreal, lived in Sandwich (now Windsor) and often crossed the river to trade in Detroit until his death 24 years later.

The flag of the United States flew over Detroit for the first time on July 11, 1796. Two years later the name of Isaac Moses appears in the records of Detroit's first Masonic Lodge.

In 1805 all but one of Detroit's 300 structures were destroyed by fire. Ezekiel Solomon died in Detroit sometime between the time of the fire and 1808. Even though he married out of the faith, his body was brought back to Montreal for burial in Shearith Israel cemetery.

A few Jewish sounding names appeared occasionally in various Detroit records over the next several decades. In 1837 the first Directory of Detroit was published. Not one of the 1,330 names listed can be safely claimed as Jewish.

The second City Directory was published in 1845. It contained 2,800 names and two Jewish firms; one Jewish individual was listed.

The arrival of seven to ten steamboats a day, bringing new residents to Detroit, was common in the 1830s and 1840s.
(Courtesy of Burton Historical Collection, Detroit Public Library)

2
1840–1859
A Community Is Born

German Jews from Bavaria came to America in the 1840s to escape persecution. Jews were heavily taxed and lived under harsh laws governing their place of residence and occupation. Other restrictions limited the times when Jews could marry and how many could apply.

Word spread that many German non-Jews lived in Michigan's Washtenaw County, as it was the state's best area for farming and its related industries. Jews wouldn't have to worry about a language barrier and could farm or earn a living as craftsmen or peddlers until they could establish themselves in other professions.

By 1845, three of the five German Jewish Weil brothers were living in Ann Arbor, and they established Michigan's first *Minyan* (a religious service comprised of ten or more males who are at least thirteen years of age).

Another Weil brother arrived the following year and the fifth came in 1848. Early in 1850, the brothers sent for their parents. Prior to their departure, the elder Weils purchased a *Sefer Torah* in Prague. Joseph Weil piously bore the Scroll of Law all the way to Ann Arbor.

Detroit's population more than doubled in a decade. In 1840, Detroit counted 9,102 residents; by 1850 21,019 and some Jews from Washtenaw County moved to Detroit.

Isaac and Sarah Cozens and their five daughters moved to Detroit from New York early in 1850 and took up residence near the corner of Congress and St. Antoine. Cozens, and his wife were born in Germany and their daughters were born in New York. Mrs. Cozens attended services on a regular basis in New York and urged her husband to seek out other Detroit Jews interested in establishing religious services.

After a series of meetings, Orthodox services were held at the Cozens' home under the direction of Marcus Cohen, who received a religious schooling at an early age in Bavaria.

Joseph Weil was reunited with his five sons in 1850.
(Courtesy of Rabbi Leo M. Franklin Archives, Temple Beth El)

Marcus Cohen conducted Beth El's first religious services.

The home of Isaac and Sarah Cozens on Congress near St. Antoine where Detroit's first religious services were held.

Left: Sarah Cozens.
Right: Isaac Cozens.

(All photos on this page courtesy of Rabbi Leo M. Franklin Archives, Temple Beth El)

The estimated Jewish population at the time in Detroit was 60, with about 50,000 in the United States. Twelve Detroit Jews of German background formed the Beth El Society on September 22, 1850, and Beth El conducted a "Hebrew-German-English School," an all day school where children received a secular and religious education. Rabbi Samuel B. Marcus came from New York to serve as spiritual leader of the small Orthodox congregation. His other duties included cantor, teacher, *mohel* (circumciser) and *shochet* (ritual slaughterer).

Jacob Silberman, who was in the cigar manufacturing business, was elected president of the new congregation. The following year, Charles Bresler, in the fur and wool business, was elected president of Beth El's first society to visit the sick and dying. A few months before Bresler's election, Beth El purchased a half-acre of land on Champlain (now Lafayette) to use as a cemetery.

Beth El had eighteen members in 1852, and religious services were moved from the Cozens' home to a room above Silberman & Hirsch's cigar store on Jefferson east of Woodward.

It was easier to get to Detroit as rail lines reached New York and Chicago. Regular ferries went to Windsor, and a telegraph cable was laid across the Detroit River.

Detroit's Jewish population reached 113 in 1853 and Beth El charter member Joseph Freedman wanted to do his part to increase the numbers. Freedman, a native of Frankfurt, Germany, wanted to marry. His three brothers and two sisters had come to Detroit in the past few years, but Joseph wanted his own family. Joseph, his brothers, and brother-in-law Benjamin Goodkind were operating Freedman & Goodkind, the largest dry goods establishment in Detroit.

The last building on the left was the second site of Temple Beth El. It was above the store of Silberman & Hirsch on East Jefferson. The site today is in front of the Coleman A. Young Municipal Building, the former City County Building.

(Courtesy of Rabbi Leo M. Franklin Archives, Temple Beth El, Bloomfield Hills, Michigan)

Joseph wrote to Rabbi Isaac Leeser of Philadelphia, one of America's Jewish leaders and the editor of *The Occident*, a national Jewish monthly, to seek his help in finding a wife.

Joseph Freedman's letter to Rabbi Leeser, dated June 7, 1853, is as follows:

> *In addressing the following few lines to you concerning a private affair I hope you will excuse my trespassing upon your time and to be brief I will be plain. Would you have the kindness in case I should during the course of the summer visit Philadelphia of introducing me to some Jewish females of respectability and worth? My object is not business but to form another connection. Could you introduce me to some that are American by birth and education or so by manners and language? It seems to me there must be a large number of Portuguese or others of that class in Philadelphia than at any other place.*
>
> *I have a large business acquaintance in New York but, none to avail me in this respect.*
>
> *Such excursions would not be requisite for us did we not mean to adhere to faith. Otherwise, both gold and beauty would be within our reach.*
>
> *Though rather a delicate matter I am writing about I am encouraged to do so by confidence in you as a gentleman. and that no unworthy use will be made of.*
>
> *Respectfully,*
> *Joseph Freedman*

A cholera epidemic ravaged Detroit in 1854, claiming Rabbi Marcus among its victims. The saddened Beth El group turned once again to Marcus Cohen for religious leadership while a new rabbi was sought. Upon the advice of Dr. Isaac Mayer Wise of Cincinnati, who trumpeted Reform Judaism in America, Liebman Adler was hired.

Dr. Liebman Adler was a recent arrival from Germany. He assumed all duties held by Rabbi Marcus at an annual salary of $360. While he preached in German, he also preached less tradition and more reform.

While Adler was welcomed, the Jewish community and the town said goodbye to Detroit's first elected mayor. John R. Williams, who lived to be 72, became the first mayor in 1824. To distinguish himself from the other John Williams in town, he asked everyone to refer to him as John R.

Beth El had 25 members in 1855 and Rabbi Wise visited Detroit the following year to support Rabbi Adler and his ideas of reform. Some members voiced concern over the removal of *Selichos* (prayers of supplication) on fast days and some traditional prayers on Friday nights and Saturday mornings.

Rabbi Isaac Leeser was also a visitor to Detroit that year and was kindly received by Adler, even though they differed on the level of religious belief for Jews in America. Two months after his Detroit visit, Leeser wrote about the changes in the Beth El prayer service in the September issue of *The Occident*:

> *We trust that for the sake of the public peace, no more alterations will be attempted; for it is one thing to have order, but quite another to force measures on a part of the community which would necessarily provoke resistance.*

Beth El members organized Pisgah Lodge No. 34 of the Independent Order of B'nai B'rith. Its first president was Jacob Silberman, who was also Beth El's first president seven years earlier. Another active member of Beth El, Edward Kanter, who was one of the founders of the Republican party a year earlier, was elected to the state legislature as a Democrat after a

Liebman Adler was the second salaried spiritual leader of Beth El.

(Courtesy of Rabbi Leo M. Franklin Archives, Temple Beth El)

campaign filled with anti-Semitic attacks on him.

Kanter's was an interesting story. Born to prominence in Breslau, Germany, Kanter became fluent in German, Greek, French, English, Hebrew and Latin. Adventure overtook his senses and he ran away from home to Paris. Stories about America piqued his interest and Kanter sneaked aboard a ship and made his unpaid way to America, landing at New Orleans. Penniless and a victim of yellow fever, he was cared for by a group of New Orleans Jews dedicated to helping the sick. One of the men in the group soon moved to Detroit, and a restless Kanter followed later and worked his way through St. Louis and Chicago.

In 1844 at the age of twenty, Kanter came to Detroit but soon moved to Mackinac Island. He worked as an interpreter for a fur company and picked up several Indian dialects, then returned to Detroit in 1852 and opened a general store.

Jews in Detroit and around the country still talked about the plight of Syrian Jewry. In 1840, thirteen adults in Damascus and sixty-five children were arrested, starved, tortured and forced to confess. It all started with a false, vicious rumor. A leader of a Damascus monastery disappeared and the monks accused the Jews of killing him to use his blood in the preparation of unleavened bread for Passover.

Jews in America at the time held protest meetings while newspapers in Europe picked up on the rumor and fed it to the masses as truth. Rabbi Leeser of Philadelphia rallied American Jewry to speak out and write the government. The Secretary of State answered Leeser's pleas and the United States appealed to Syria. Months later, the Jews who hadn't died under the terrible conditions were released, but anti-Semitism in the middle east and Europe was unleashed.

In 1858, word spread to America that Edgar Mortara, a six-year-old Jewish boy who lived in Bologna, an area ruled by the Pope, was kidnapped by Papal guards and brought to a convent to be raised as a Catholic. The boy's former nurse claimed she secretly baptized the youngster while he was sick. Now, in the eyes of the church, he was Catholic and had to be raised as one.

Rallies were held in Jewish communities around America but this time without success. The United States government refused to get involved, saying it was an internal matter in another country. The Jews in Detroit and America were gravely disappointed but more unified.

Beth El held a meeting to protest the kidnapping of Edgar Mortara. The young child's cause was championed by Liebman Adler in the *Detroit Free Press*, but letters and protests from Jewish communities were no match against the power and will of the Catholic Church.

Dr. Adler turned his attention to a new synagogue for Beth El in Detroit, and a synagogue building association was formed with Edward Kanter as president. In the meantime, Beth El rented larger quarters at 39 Michigan Avenue (now Cadillac Square, between Bates and Randolph Streets) on the second floor above Scherer's Drug Store facing the large market house.

Edward Kanter was active in many fields.
(Courtesy of Rabbi Leo M. Franklin Archives, Temple Beth El)

3
1860-1869
THE CIVIL WAR ERA

Detroit's 1860 population of 45,619 included more than 200 Jews. Beth El had forty members. The five observant Weil brothers in Ann Arbor continued holding religious services in one of their homes. Their tannery firm was growing and would eventually employ more than a hundred men.

Beth El purchased its first building in 1861. The three-story structure on Rivard between Monroe and Lafayette was formerly a French Methodist Episcopal church. Shortly after the purchase of the building, Liebman Adler left for a higher paying position at a Chicago temple.

Scherer's Drug Store, in the center, rented its upper floor to both Beth El and Shaarey Zedek.

(Courtesy of Burton Historical Collection, Detroit Public Library)

Left: Temple Beth El on Rivard Street.

Below: Main floor and gallery of Beth El's Rivard Street Synagogue.

Facing page: The impressive interior on Rivard Street.

(All photos on these two pages courtesy of Rabbi Leo M. Franklin Archives, Temple Beth El)

Detroit had over 47,000 residents when President Abraham Lincoln proclaimed a state of war on April 17, 1861, and called for volunteers. Michigan answered and more than 90,000 men from the state served in the Civil War, 6,000 of whom were from Detroit. The war called on Michigan's Jewish families as 181 Jewish soldiers—more than one per family—served.

There were fewer Jewish men around on Friday, August 30, 1861, when Beth El dedicated the Rivard Street synagogue.

Detroit's leading papers covered the event as Rabbi Abraham Laser, who replaced Liebman Adler, made a striking appearance. A slim man with an Abraham Lincoln-style beard, Laser wore a black silk robe, white silk scarf and a velvet turban. Six little girls followed behind Laser bearing silver candlesticks in which long red wax candles burned.

The *Free Press* noted the impressive service with a front page report:

The children with the candlesticks walked around the altar three times, singing a hymn adapted for dedicatory occasions. When they ceased singing, Dr. Laser stepped up to the altar and sang the regular hymn. Then alternated singing, chanting by the priest, prayer, reading and marching around the altar, after which the parchments were deposited. The male portion of the congregation were seated in the body of the church, the women in the galleria. There was no uncovering of the head, men retaining their hats.

Like the *Free Press*, the *Detroit Tribune & Advertiser* was impressed with the dedication ceremonies and guest speaker Dr. Isaac M. Wise of Cincinnati. The *Tribune & Advertiser's* lengthy article concluded with:

The whole was very impressive, the ceremonies very imposing—and the whole proved that the race of the prophets—the offspring of the Divine bards—is not yet extinct.

Organ music and a mixed choir didn't sit well with

May 13, 1861: The First Michigan Volunteer Infantry heads off to war from Campus Martius as relatives and well-wishers say goodbye.

(Courtesy of Burton Historical Collection, Detroit Public Library)

some members when introduced four weeks later. When the choir occupied space in the gallery and some of the women had to sit on the main floor with the men, seventeen men had finally had enough of the reforms introduced at religious services.

The seventeen renounced their membership and formed the Schaarey Zedeck Society, now Congregation Shaarey Zedek. They rented the space previously used by Beth El above Scherer's drug store in Cadillac Square.

Even though they had seventeen fewer men worshipping with them, Beth El's Hebrew-German-English Day School had an enrollment of seventy-four children. Mark Fleischman was only ten years old but wanted to serve in the Union Army. He became a water boy in 1862 and for two years carried water and food at the train depot, serving soldiers waiting to depart for the battle front.

Beth El members departed further from traditional Judaism when they voted to use the prayer book of the Reform ritual of Dr. Isaac M. Wise. Also abolished was *aliyos* (calling up to the Torah), wearing the *talis* (prayer shawl), and separate seating for men and women. Services were also shortened by the introduction of the three-year cycle of reading from the Torah, instead of the one-year cycle.

Shaarey Zedek's Orthodox membership increased from seventeen to forty-four in about a year, and enough funds were raised to purchase their own burial grounds, the Smith Street Cemetery, now located within the General Motors Cadillac plant parking lot. Detroit's Jews were serving nobly in the Civil War but were disappointed in General Ulysses S. Grant. Grant had been stationed in Detroit just before Beth El was founded when he was commanding officer of the Detroit barracks. Often drunk in public, Grant didn't endear himself to Detroit's citizenry. Now, though, his anti-Semitism was out in the open.

Cotton speculators had secret partnerships with many of Grant's officers. Most of them weren't Jewish, but Grant referred to all of them as "Israelites" or in anti-Semitic terms.

Grant issued General Orders #11 in December of 1862, expelling all the Jews "as a class" from the military department under his command. Against Grant's will, President Lincoln revoked the order when it was brought to his attention.

Rabbi Laser organized the Detroit Hebrew Ladies' Aid Society for the support of widows and orphans in July of 1863. Even though it was under the auspices of Beth El, Shaarey Zedek's members contributed and were pleased by the support given to widows and or-

Left: David Marx, founding member of Congregation Shaarey Zedek and Detroit's first kosher butcher, with his family. Right: The first building owned by Shaarey Zedek, formerly St. Matthew's Episcopal Church, at Congress and St. Antoine Streets.
(Courtesy of Archives of Congregation Shaarey Zedek)

Jews and other Detroiters mingle at Campus Martius memorial for slain President Lincoln.
(Courtesy of Burton Historical Collection, Detroit Public Library)

phans in the Jewish community.

Around this time, Henry Ford was born. Detroit had about 400 Jews and the United States Jewish population numbered less than a quarter million.

In August 1864, Dr. Isidor Kalisch succeeded Rabbi Laser as Beth El's fourth spiritual leader. Kalisch would be the first Michigan Rabbi to deliver a sermon in English.

At this time, Shaarey Zedek had over fifty members and a spiritual leader—Laser Kontrovitch—and like Beth El, it operated a Hebrew-German-English day school.

A former church at Congress and St. Antoine was purchased and dedicated on September 23, 1864. Dr. Kalisch of Beth El and its choir was invited to speak and perform. Dr. Kalisch spoke in English and the dedication attracted Detroit's mayor, many aldermen, and a prominent judge.

Mail was extremely important to families waiting to hear from men serving in the war. In October 1864, free mail delivery by carriers began in Detroit. Iron letter boxes on lampposts of grocery and drug stores were introduced to Detroiters for outgoing mail.

Meanwhile, back at the warfront, Ulysses S. Grant, famous for losing many private battles with alcoholism, was gaining a reputation for winning military battles. President Lincoln appointed him commander-in-chief of all northern armies.

Lincoln's advisors didn't think it was a good idea to promote Grant because of his drinking problem. Lincoln rose and addressed them:

"Gentlemen," Lincoln said as he stood and looked

at those present, "find out what Grant drinks and send all the generals a case."

The Civil War ended on Sunday, April 9, 1865, when Lee's armies surrendered at the Appomattox Courthouse in Virginia. Detroit celebrated with huge bonfires and fireworks the following day.

Four days later, on April 14, President Abraham Lincoln was shot by John Wilkes Booth at the Ford Theater in Washington. Lincoln died shortly after dawn April 15. The country and Detroit mourned, and all houses of worship scheduled memorial services at noon on Wednesday, April 19.

The 63 members of Shaarey Zedek and other Detroit Jews were urged to attend a service at Beth El's Rivard Street synagogue, hosted by Rabbi Isidor Kalisch.

> "A great national calamity has called us together to meet in this place of worship at an unusual hour. Our bleeding hearts cry to God, and our eyes shed bitter tears at the unexpected death of our late President," Kalisch addressed the capacity crowd of mourners in English.
>
> "In the fifty-seventh year of his age, in full manly vigor, after four years of heroic labor, trouble, and struggle to preserve our sacred Constitution and to restore Union and Peace, and shortly after the wicked rebellion received a decisive blow, he, the true champion of national rights, the powerful and successful advocate of universal freedom, the upright and true patriot, was suddenly snatched from our midst.
>
> "It is trice that he shared the same fate of Moses, the deliverer of Israel from Egyptian bondage, who was not permitted to lead the freed men to the promised land, and could only see it from the top of the Mount of Nebo; so could he perceive only from the gigantic mountain of glorious victories over the enemy the revived power and the renewed glory, of our blessed Union.
>
> "But it is not only his early demise which fills our breasts with sadness, but also the manner in which he found his death especially grieves us to the core of our hearts. It is this that makes millions of men inconsolate. The faithful and righteous, sitting at the side of his amiable lady, was killed by a base villain.
>
> "Why, they moan with heartbreaking anguish, should such a horrible end be the reward of innumerable noble deeds?
>
> "But as a servant of our holy religion, I must remind you of the principle of our sages, that the reward of the good is not always given in this life. The real reward begins when the man ceases to be a member of this world. And the memory that he leaves in the hearts of men, the affection and deep emotions which follow him, are the reflected splendor of the heavenly reward that flashes upon the earth.
>
> "So will the name of our late President be perpetuated in the hearts of the great, glorious nation of the Union, and will shine forever among the most distinguished names in the records of all civilized nations. All this, however, is only a shadow of his great reward in the realms of eternity.
>
> "Let us, therefore, submit to the Divine Providence, Whose ways, although a great mystery to us, yet are just, and let us pray that the soul of our late President shall be bound up in the bundle of life in the blissful regions of light for ever and ever. Amen."

Isidor Kalisch departed for financially greener pastures in 1866 and was succeeded by Rabbi Elias Eppstein. The latter brought reform to a congregation in Jackson and came to Detroit at an annual salary of $1,500. Eppstein loved literature and chess playing and helped to organize the Polemia Club in Detroit devoted to his hobbies.

In 1867, Detroit's Jewish community numbered about 400 and Shaarey Zedek organized its societies for visiting the sick and burying the dead. Beth El was looking for larger quarters and moved west of Woodward for the first time. The new location was the former Tabernacle Baptist Church.

On August 30, 1867, the Washington Avenue Temple as it was called, on the southwest corner of Washington Avenue (now Washington Boulevard) and Clifford was dedicated. Dr. Isaac M. Wise of Cincinnati came to town for the ceremonies.

Accounts of the dedication appeared in lengthy front page stories in the *Detroit Free Press*, the *Detroit Tribune & Advertiser*, and *The Israelite*:

The *Tribune & Advertiser* wrote:

Previous to the dedication, prayers were offered up in the old place of worship; then the scrolls of the law were removed to the basement of the new building. Three o'clock p.m. the doors were opened and people holding cards of invitation were admitted. Four o'clock p.m. precisely the ceremonies commenced, and were conducted until half-past six, including the regular service of Sabbath eve. It was all done in the best style. Twelve girls dressed in white

Beth El on Washington Avenue and Clifford.
(Courtesy of Rabbi Leo M. Franklin Archives, Temple Beth El)

and bearing flower wreaths and bouquets preceded the bearers of the Law, the rabbis and officers followed. The choir discoursed classical music in a very fine style, and Rev. Mr. Eppstein led in excellent taste, and with a splendid voice.

The *Free Press* said:

Just within the middle of the altar rail is the desk for the scrolls of the law when in use. From this rise semi-circular steps, upon the fourth of which, in rear of the first desk, is that of the minister, and upon either hand stands a highly ornamented candelabrum, each with the seven candlesticks bearing lighted candles. Upon the summit of the pyramid of steps, which are carpeted with crimson, stands the "Ark of the Covenant," enclosed by double columns on each side and concealed by a crimson veil in front, heavily ornamented with gold. The columns support an arch, beneath which is a circular stained glass window, upon which are represented the two tables of stone bearing the ten commandments in the Hebrew tongue. The veil of the ark also bears in inscription in the same characters. High above the ark depends from the ceiling a lamp, where within a blood-red globe burns the "perpetual light." The five distinctive colors used in the ornamentation, viz.: orange, blue, red, purple and green, are shown in the circular openings above the windows, and also in the highly gilt and embroidered coverings of the five books or scrolls of the Mosaic law.

Rabbi Eppstein introduced late Friday evening services the following month and the following year published Confirmant's Guide to the Mosiac Religion, the first book of Jewish interest published in Michigan.

By 1869, Beth El and Shaarey Zedek discontinued their day schools and only operated religious schools after public school hours. Detroit's children were now receiving free public school education, and black children were admitted for the first time.

Dr. Kaufmann Kohler was brought in from Germany as Beth El's sixth rabbi, to succeed Rabbi Eppstein who left for a larger congregation in Milwaukee. Beth El and Shaarey Zedek organized the Gentlemen's Hebrew Relief Society (which later became the Beth El Hebrew Relief Society), Detroit's first Jewish philanthropic agency operated under one umbrella.

4
1870-1889
SYNAGOGUES ARE BUILT

In 1870, Detroit had 540 Jews among a population of 79,577, and the city bragged it was the eighteenth largest in the United States. Beth El had seventy members, and Dr. Kohler abolished the observance of the second day of religious festivals and the wearing of the *talis* (prayer shawl) by the rabbi.

Dr. Kohler left for a Chicago pulpit in October 1871 and Beth El hired Rabbi Emanuel Gerchter the following month. The congregation approved English instead of German as the language of instruction in the Religious School.

Edward Kanter, who had given up his mercantile business three years earlier to open a private banking firm, founded the German American Bank on West Larned. The building was called the "Kanter Building" and the Guardian Building now occupies the site.

A bit north of Kanter's Bank on the same side of Griswold, the magnificent City Hall opened. Michigan passed a compulsory school attendance law requiring children between eight and fourteen to attend at least twelve weeks a year.

A new congregation was formed in 1871. B'nai Israel, then known as Beinei Isroel, conducted its first services in a rented house on Montcalm and Hastings. Isaac Weinstein, a foreman at a rags and metals establishment, was the acting rabbi. The small congregation purchased a burial ground the next year adjacent to Beth Olam and Shaarey Zedek.

In 1872, Detroit's first elevator was installed in the Moffatt Building on the southwest corner of Fort and Griswold. Detroiters of privilege went to the top of the building to view the ceremonies dedicating the Soldiers and Sailors' Monument on Woodward and Campus Martius. Many Jews were among the throngs of Civil War veterans and their families beaming proudly at the monument honoring the sacrifices of Michiganders during the war.

Since Jews were excluded from Detroit's privileged clubs, German Jews founded their own elite club. The Phoenix Social Club was established and met in Edward Kanter's building on Griswold. The Independence Social Club, another group started by Jews, began the following year in 1873.

Beth El had its eighth rabbi that year as Dr. Leopold Wintner assumed the pulpit. Rabbi Gerechter remained as cantor and teacher. Dr. Frederick Hirschman, a member of Beth El, was the first Jewish physician to have attended the Detroit College of Medicine. In 1873 he was practicing and living at the corner of Adams and Brush—just beyond the bleachers at Comerica Park today.

By the end of 1874, Rabbi Gerechter accepted the pulpit of a Grand Rapids temple and Martin Butzel was elected president of Beth El. Butzel, in the clothing and men's furnishing business, was a tough-minded man and strongly urged Dr. Wintner to preach in German. By the September Holy Days of 1875, Butzel ordered Wintner to preach in German only. Butzel's decision was upheld by the congregation members at its annual meeting.

ECHOES OF DETROIT'S JEWISH COMMUNITIES

The Phoenix Club moved to Woodward and Duffield to accommodate its increased membership. Besides staging plays, dramas, debates, and other forms of entertainment, the club maintained a collection of newspapers, magazines and other reading materials for members. Beth El made another change in spiritual leadership. Its ninth rabbi, Dr. Heinrich Zirndorf from Germany, took the pulpit in September 1876.

Detroit officials took a twenty-year lease on most of Woodbridge Grove for a much-needed wood and hay market. The area around Michigan and Trumbull streets was cleared of trees and shrubbery and paved with cobblestones. Farmers now had a large market to bring lumber and hay to on the western edge of the city.

Shaarey Zedek experienced a steady growth in membership and appealed to Detroit's Jewish community for financial assistance to help build a new synagogue. It was decided to use its present site. The church Shaarey Zedek had bought in 1864 was razed and groundbreaking for Detroit's first structure to be built for synagogue use was held July 4, 1877.

A festive atmosphere prevailed as hundreds of people gathered to watch the ceremonies. The mayor and city council members, along with the crowd, watched as a tin box containing the names of Shaarey Zedek's 68 members, along with other information on the synagogue and Beth El was deposited in the cornerstone. Also included in the tin box were copies of the country's Jewish papers and the Detroit dailies of the previous day, the United States and B'nai B'rith Constitution, and a current silver Jewish and American coin.

While the building was going up, contributions to finance the project weren't meeting expectations. Lack of funds led to lack of harmony among committee leaders and soon led to accusations of incompe-

Looking east down Michigan Avenue. The new City Hall between Woodward and Griswold opened in 1871. The old city hall in the center, in front of Cadillac Square, was torn down in 1872.

(Courtesy of Burton Historical Collection, Detroit Public Library)

tence. Some claim that the infighting was more due to disputes over ritual rather than construction.

In any event, a split ensued and the defectors went to the existing B'nai Israel and the recently founded Beth Jacob, which met at the Kinsell home on Gratiot near Hastings. Shaarey Zedek was left with thirty-five members and B'nai Israel and Beth Jacob totaled eighty members.

While Shaarey Zedek was going downhill, B'nai Israel dedicated its new synagogue on Macomb Street, between Beaubien and St. Antoine, in 1878. It was a stately structure with large columns adorning the front of the building.

While many Shaarey Zedek members weren't talking to each other, more Detroiters were talking on the phone, and the city's first phone directory listed 124 customers in 1878.

In 1879, Detroit's telephone customers were the country's first to be assigned phone numbers to facilitate handling calls. Conversations among Shaarey Zedek's remaining members centered around ways to continue payment to the contractors. The ideas and funds soon ran out and the building was repossessed on April 1, 1879. The downsized Shaarey Zedek then operated out of Kittelberger's Hall on Randolph Street.

In 1880 the Jewish population in the United States reached 250,000. Detroit had 665 Jews out of a city population topping 116,000. Detroit's economy was booming. Fueled by its tobacco, stove, and pharmaceutical industries, the business section of downtown was pushing north of Campus Martius.

The Detroit Stove Works boasted it was the largest stove factory in the world and made 30,000 stoves per year. Thirteen hundred workers produced 700 models of stoves at the company's ten-acre site near Belle Isle.

Eleven-year-old Albert Kahn came to town from Germany with his family, and seventeen-year-old Henry Ford left his family in Dearborn and found a job at a Detroit machine shop for $2.50 a week.

Shaarey Zedek received more bad news. On a July night an explosion rocked the new unoccupied synagogue and caused considerable damage. Windows were shattered and sections of the gallery and ceiling

Groundbreaking for Detroit's first structure built for synagogue use was held Friday, July 4, 1877.
(Courtesy of Burton Historical Collection, Detroit Public Library)

and part of the roof fell in. Vandals left an open gas pipe in the basement and caused the blast, according to police reports.

Ten months later the building was auctioned and the new owners planned on demolishing it and replacing the parcel with houses. A determined Reuben Mendelsohn, president of Shaarey Zedek, rallied the membership to raise the needed funds to rent the damaged synagogue and even hired a new rabbi to replace Rabbi E. Rosenzweig, who left after five years.

In 1882, Beth El organized the Hebrew Ladies' Auxiliary Relief Society (later known as the Hebrew Ladies' Sewing Society). The group assisted Detroit's Russian Jewish immigrants.

Detroit's new residents brought tales of horror from Russia. Authorities and church officials blamed the Jews for social and economic ills. Gangs attacked Jews at will while police did nothing to assist the vic-

The B'nai Israel on Macomb Street, between Beaubien and St. Antoine, was dedicated in 1878. Henry Wicker, a tailor who operated out of his home, lived next door. Today the site is in the heart of Greektown.

(Courtesy of Burton Historical Collection, Detroit Public Library)

tims. Laws were passed ordering Jews to crowd into small districts. Occupations, areas of residence, and school attendance were severely restricted.

Immigrants came to the United States in large numbers. Most stayed in the East. Detroiters heard of a young woman by the name of Henrietta Szold, a writer for Anglo-Jewish magazines and a religious school teacher. In Baltimore she organized evening schools for immigrants to learn to read and write English. Miss Szold taught American history and civics to help people pass the test to become citizens.

With the addition of some Russian immigrants, Shaarey Zedek's membership grew to seventy and the building was repurchased by the congregation. The synagogue began to operate a Sunday and afternoon school around this period. Beth Jacob moved a couple of blocks north up Hastings Street and dedicated its small synagogue on Montcalm. At the end of 1884, Rabbi Louis Grossman became Beth El's tenth rabbi.

Grossman, a recent graduate of the Hebrew Union College, was the first to be schooled in America.

Beth El held a memorial service for former United States President Ulysses S. Grant in August of 1885. Many Detroit Jews were suspicious of Grant's attitudes toward Jews but respected the office he held. The day after Grant's memorial service, Beth El held one for Sir Moses Montefiore. Ten months earlier, there had been a service in honor of the distinguished English philanthropist and statesman's hundredth birthday.

The community pointed with pride to Dr. Edward Sloman. He became the first Detroit-born Jew to graduate from the Michigan College of Medicine. Sloman continued to live with his parents on Adams near St. Antoine (today near the southern entrance to Ford Field).

On January 17, 1886, Shaarey Zedek rededicated its impressive building. After a musical rendition, Mr. Ginsburg, one of the trustees, addressed the congre-

The Detroit Opera House in Campus Martius had space for rent in 1887 after Hudson's vacated and moved around the corner to the west side of Woodward.

(Courtesy of Burton Historical Collection, Detroit Public Library)

gation, and his feelings were captured by a *Detroit Tribune* reporter and printed in the following day's paper.

> The old saying that there is a silver lining to every cloud we now appreciate and accept. Nine years ago, after a terrific struggle, we succeeded in erecting this structure, and we then felt that we had accomplished an almost impossible task. We took great pride in the fact that we had one of the finest structures for an Orthodox congregation in the United States. Time rolled on, and about five years after we dedicated it came a vast amount of trouble and anxiety. The sources from which expected to realize the desired help failed us entirely, and we then found ourselves drifting on the sea of debt. Our rudder was broken, and no sail on the future's horizon cheered our hopes. We felt that all was gone, that all our struggles for years had come to naught. Instead, however, of abandoning hope, we came to the determination to make still another effort. I congratulate you, Mr. President, on the rededication of this, our old, "shule," to be held by us forever and forever.

The following year, J. L. Hudson moved his growing business from the ground floor of the Detroit Opera House to the west side of Woodward between Michigan Avenue and State Street.

There was a parade through the streets to Woodward as the Detroits—the city's pro baseball club—won the National League championship. The team played at Recreation Park on Brady between John R. and Brush—where Harper Hospital is today. There was no such thing as a World Series as the American League wouldn't be born until the turn of the century.

Tobacco tycoon Daniel Scotten owned the corner of Washington Boulevard and Michigan Avenue. The site had seen several hotels since 1836, and Scotten decided the time was ripe in 1888 for a larger one. He named the new 200-room, six-story hotel the Cadillac, after the city's founder.

While the Cadillac hotel was going up, Detroit's Jewish population was rising. The 1888 Detroit City Directory listed thirty-three Cohens, twenty-three Levys, fourteen Cohns, and nine Livi's. The Phoenix Club was the site of the twenty-fifth anniversary celebration of the "Ladies Society for the Support of Hebrew Widows and Orphans," Detroit's first philanthropic society. Mrs. Emil S. Heineman was still president, membership reached 169, and the official language was changed from German to English.

At this time many Jewish families lived on the site of what is now Comerica Park. Secretary of Beth El and B'nai B'rith president, Moses Cohen, whose father Marcus oversaw religious services at the founding of Beth El, lived where the left fielder roams today.

Starting pay for Detroit's public school teachers in 1889 was $30 per month. After nine and one-half years, teachers earned the maximum $70 monthly. Belle Isle had its first bridge. Prior to the opening of the bridge, riding the Belle Isle ferry was a favorite pastime. For ten cents one could ride back and forth all day, which some people did on hot days.

Rabbi Aaron Ashinsky came to Detroit as spiritual leader of Shaarey Zedek, Beth Jacob and B'nai Israel. Posters announced which synagogue he would be at mornings and evenings. Beth El choir girls began sewing for children of Russian refugees. The girls soon became teachers and passed on their knowledge to the children, which led to the organization of the Self-Help Circle to assist the new arrivals from Russia.

Rabbi Aaron M. Ashinsky came to Detroit in 1889.
(Courtesy of Archives of Congregation Shaarey Zedek)

Shaarey Zedek rededicated its impressive building in 1886. Samuel Tuke, treasurer of Home Knitting Works, operated his business out of the home fronting on St. Antoine.
(Courtesy of Burton Historical Collection, Detroit Public Library)

5
1890-1899
Hardship and Helping Hands

The Jewish population was estimated at 1,200 out of Detroit's 1890 population of 205,876. The city had gained 160,257 in only thirty years. Streetcar drivers received a raise to $1.50 a day, and barbers raised the price of a shave to 15 cents. Albert Kahn, now a twenty-one year old apprentice in an architectural firm, earned a $500 scholarship to study architecture abroad.

The Woman's Club of Temple Beth El was founded in 1891 to assist young women, in particular with social and economic help. The club motto was, "Giving is Receiving." Classes were given in literature, music, language, and the arts.

Shaarey Zedek organized the Jewish Relief Society and broke away from a similar group it belonged

Congregation B'nai Israel dedicated its synagogue on December 6, 1891.

(Courtesy of Rabbi Leo M. Franklin Archives, Temple Beth El)

to with Beth El. The Young Men's Hebrew Association—YMHA—signed its first bylaws. They called for a program of physical fitness, social cultivation, an employment bureau, and classes in Jewish learning.

The B'nai Israel congregation proudly invited the entire Jewish community to be present at the ceremony for the dedication of their new synagogue on Mullet Street, between St. Antoine and Hastings, on Sunday, December 6,

On May 9, 1892, eleven Jews of Russian origin founded Beth David (later known as B'nai David) in a rented hall the northwest corner of Gratiot and Hastings. The congregation was known as the "Russische Shul" (Russian Synagogue).

Only a day after the founding of Beth David, Beth Abraham (now one of the synagogues that led to Beth Ahm) was formally established. The congregation met on the second floor of a private home on Hastings and Winder.

1892 marked the twenty-fifth anniversary of Beth El in its Washington Boulevard location. A regular Beth El worshipper unskilled in many social graces was the popular and outspoken Emanuel Wodic. He was a real frontiersman who had served in the Civil War and then signed up for postwar service as a scout in Indian country. Before returning to Detroit he was a farmer in Utica, Michigan.

In 1892, Jewish settlers were living in Bad Axe, Michigan. The community, known as the Palestine Colony, wasn't having much success with farming despite philanthropic assistance. Wodic volunteered to help the farmers, and spent the spring and summer teaching the proper methods of sowing, cultivating and harvesting. Wodic also acted as communal leader and arbiter of disputes, besides being the cultural advisor.

Temple Beth El displayed products of the Jewish farmers during the Succoth holidays. It was the first exhibition of farm products raised by Jews in America.

Around this time, a cholera epidemic prompted President Benjamin Harrison to issue an order for twenty days' detention of all immigrant ships. Many blamed the influx of Russian Jews on the spreading of the disease. The press in Great Britain gave voice to the anti-Semitic outcry. The *Detroit News* of September 11, 1892, published a front page story of the "Dreaded Danger" with a London dateline:

> *It was feared that the influx of Russian Jews, regarding which the people of Great Britain are already impatient, would be directed altogether to Great Britain and that the larger cities to which these people invariably throng, would be overcrowded with them. A well-known statistician says that the movement of the Russian Jews was the most dangerous immigration known to history since the days of Attila, and that in some respects it was infinitely more to be dreaded by civilized communities. All sorts of deception has been resorted to in order to get these miserable refugees into England and America without exciting public suspicion.*
> **Ways That Are Dark.**
> *They were sent in batches to Glasgow, to Liverpool, and other places in order that the volume of their emigration by way of Hamburg, which was*

Former Civil War veteran and frontiersman Emanuel Wodic was a colorful and valuable member of Beth El.

(Courtesy of Rabbi Leo M. Franklin Archives, Temple Beth El)

their port of departure, should not attract too much attention. They were told to call themselves, Austrians, Prussians, or Germans or anything but Russian Jews. They were instructed to represent themselves as desirous of working on farms in order the allay the apprehensions of people in the cities, but not one in 10,000 had any idea of remaining on a farm...What they really want is to crowd into the cities and live as peddlers or street merchants.

They Brought the Plague

Everybody is convinced here of the correctness of Prof. Koch's statement, made after thorough examination, that the Russian immigrants brought the cholera to Hamburg, and there is little doubt that they brought it also to Liverpool. Many of those who have gone to America by way of Liverpool are indescribably filthy. Their clothes appear to have been worn for months, and sometimes it is difficult to tell whether the wearer are black or white. In this conditions they received into lodging houses, carrying with them the seeds of the plague. It is always necessary to whitewash and scrub after Russian Jews have left a lodging house.

The Jews Must Go

The opinion is everywhere expressed that the immigration of Russian Jews must be stopped, if western Europe and America are to be saved from the plague. It is pointed out that the czar has a vast and largely fertile country in Siberia and that if he does not want the Jews in Russia he ought to give them land in Siberia. As immigrants to western Europe they are a pestilence and a nuisance.

In 1893, Beth El allowed the Detroit High School to use their facilities after a fire destroyed the school building near the northern end of Griswold. The Temple opened a Sunday and afternoon school for poor children and those belonging to congregations where a school of religious studies didn't exist.

A community mutual aid society, the Hebrew Protective Association, was formed. Its purpose was "to unite fraternally acceptable Jewish persons, to provide for the relief of distressed members, visitations of the sick, burial of the dead, and similar benevolent and worthy purposes and objects."

Around the same time, the Hebrew Peddler's Association was organized. Jewish peddlers were targets of young thugs of mostly Polish and Irish extraction. In some cases the victims were killed. Peddlers united in their own defense, as they thought police did too little to ward off the attacks.

The Detroit Bureau of Police appointed the first policewoman in the United States and more Detroiters were using the phone and to farther destinations. The city had about 4,000 phones, and long-distance service began to Chicago and New York.

There were more peddlers on the streets in 1894 as the national economic crisis worsened. More railroads went broke, and more than 500 banks around the country failed, idling a quarter of all heavy industry. The depression of 1894 hit Detroit hard, and soon funds for many of the city's 25,000 jobless had run out.

Mayor Pingree urged real estate speculators holding vacant land to use their properties for the growing of potatoes and other vegetables. Pingree also appealed for funds to purchase gardening tools. He set an example by selling his favorite horse and using the funds to buy seeds and tools.

Soon Pingree's ideas and implementations were picked up by newspapers in other cities. New York papers dubbed Detroit's mayor "Potato Patch Pingree." More publicity meant more donations, and Detroit's real estate barons responded by lending their acreage. Mayor Pingree was often seen digging and planting, endearing him further to Detroit populace. Besides being fed, the poor and unemployed were kept busy digging, planting, harvesting, and distributing.

While the Detroit Jewish community experienced economic hardships, Beth El assumed the responsibility of maintaining several beds at the Children's Free Hospital on Fort Street near Seventh (Brooklyn).

Another form of aid was instituted in 1895 as the Hebrew Free Loan Association was officially incorporated. The aim of the society was to grant small loans free of interest to the needy among Detroit's Jewish community. The founders met in Selig Koploy's shoe store on Gratiot, and the office in back was open evenings to the public except on Friday and Saturday.

While Jews suffered economically, they also suffered indignities by being portrayed at times in newspaper articles and cartoons as comical, foreign-looking and -sounding. When Samuel Goldwater, a former president of the Detroit Council of Trades, an organizer of the Federation of Labor and former Detroit alderman, ran for mayor, he was caricatured as speaking with a Yiddish accent.

In 1896 the last horsecar operated on Detroit's streets and all streetcars were of the electric variety. A new form of transportation was seen on Detroit's streets as Charles Brady King and Henry Ford test drove their homemade automobiles. Another form of movement was shown as Thomas Edison demonstrated moving pictures on his Vitascope at the Opera House. Detroit's Western League ballclub moved from tiny Boulevard Park on Lafayette, not far from Belle Isle, to a new ballpark at Michigan and Trumbull.

Temple Beth El passed a congregational rule prohibiting the covering of the head of male members during services. Dr. Louis Grossmann—now in his twelfth year as spiritual leader—took a leading part in the fight to eliminate the use of *Reading from the Bible* from the Detroit Public Schools. Albert Kahn and Ernestine Krolik, both 27, married in 1896. The couple had met when the young architect was the chief designer of the firm commissioned to build the Krolik family home on Adelaide a few years earlier.

Rabbi Aaron Ashinsky, in Detroit for seven years as spiritual leader of Shaarey Zedek, B'nai Israel and B'nai Jacob, left for a Montreal pulpit. Rabbi Ashinsky was frustrated at the lack of support by the presidents of the congregations he served when trying to organize a communal afternoon school of religious studies.

The Sunday morning *Detroit News* of September 13, 1896, had an in-depth feature on "The Ghetto, Where the Jews of Detroit Congregate." Here's how an unnamed reporter described it:

> *In a rectangle formed by four streets, Monroe, Watson, Brush and Orleans, the larger portion, by far, of all the Jews in Detroit have made their homes. Of this whole district Hastings street is the business thoroughfare. Around that street and those that adjoin it pretty much all that is Orthodox and distinctive of the Jewish race in Detroit clusters. The wealthy Jews, those who have made their fortunes, have been gradually absorbed by their business interests and necessary social relations into the rest of the community. But the other, those who are poor and pious, "froom," as they say in their queer Yiddish dialect, live very close to Hastings street and the synagogue at the corner of Hastings and Montcalm.*
>
> *Over across the street from the synagogue, in*

Hastings Street in 1896.
(Courtesy of Burton Historical Collection, Detroit Public Library)

the little bookstore of Jacob Levin, at 363-1/2 Hastings street—where they sell books of strange device and Turkish cigarettes with the Russian label on them—a crowd was standing about all day discussing religion. Jacob Levin is a pale, thin man, said to be a scholar, and he keeps all sorts of writing in the Yiddish in his shop for the use of Hastings street. Some of the books are written in Yiddish on one page with an English translation upon the other for the use of the younger generation, who cannot all understand the tongue their fathers speak. He has in on his shelves all the books of the law and the scriptures and when some one on the heat of argument wants to cite history or tradition to establish their point they are in the habit of going over to this little bookstore for the information.

The character of Hastings street is determined by the fact that it is the business street of the ghetto, the one avenue of the city that is especially devoted to the traffic of Jews. Many of the wholesale notion houses are upon that street. It is the headquarters for the peddlers of the city and the surrounding country. All the junk and old clothes dealers are situated in the neighborhood of that thoroughfare. The three Orthodox synagogues are not any of them far from it. There is one synagogue on the street, another just off of it on Mullet and still another at the corner of St. Antoine and Congress. Friday evening at sundown or upon the holidays all the Jews walk down Hastings street to reach their synagogues. Meyer Jacobson, who lives a little farther up the street, is a man known for his "froomkeit."

Jacobson is the undertaker of the Ghetto. According to the custom of the Orthodox Jews it is one of the pious duties that belong to all Jews to assist at the burials of their neighbors. The synagogue furnishes the hearse and the burying ground and no Jew is so poor but he can find decent burial according to the rites of his church. The city never buries any dead for the Jews. It happens, however, that in the community there is one man who is known more than others and takes it upon himself the duty of caring for the dead, it being regarded as a mitzvah, a good deed. So it happens that Jacobson, the junk man, has become the undertaker and is held in high esteem among his people.

Among the other prominent men upon the street are I. W. Weinstein, who sells meats. He is the official slaughterer, a man learned in the lore of the faith. He is also the person who performs the circumcision.

Isidor Sweetwine, the grocer, is the teacher in the free Hebrew school, where those who are too poor to hire private teachers send their children to be taught in the doctrines and observances of the Jewish religion. Joseph Goldberg is another of these teachers. Phillip Sillman, the grocer, makes the larger portion of his business that of a maize factory; where he manufactures crackers for the passover and sells them over the United States.

Dr. Belsman, who lives on Hastings street, is the physician who is most popular in the Ghetto. He gives his services by the year, taking from each family what they can afford to pay, giving his services to the poor for less and to the rich for more.

Hastings street, which preserves the same prosaic exterior of other streets of the east side, has certain moments in the year, however, when it manifests something of the strenuous inner life of that smaller community within the larger one that we know and understand—the Ghetto.

Seven days later, the *Detroit Sunday News Tribune* carried a front page artist's conception of the Beth Jacob Synagogue as a prelude to a feature on Yom Kippur.

The article also described the exterior of the Beth Jacob on the southeast corner of Montcalm and Hastings:

From the outside the building seems to be the ordinary rectangular brick structure, but there is a reminiscence of oriental architecture in the circle of the doorway and of the windows, and in the curious, bulging domes that start up from the roof upon either corner of the facade. Within the building is constructed upon a plan not unlike the more primitive types of gothic architecture, with the galleries upon either side traversing the longitudinal length of the building, the suggestion of the pointed arch in the ceiling with the circular window in the clear space above the altar.

The Majestic Building was Detroit's tallest when it opened in 1896. Sightseers went to the fourteenth story and for ten cents could climb a flight of stairs to the observatory on the roof to view the growing city. Hazen Pingree enjoyed puttering around his mansion on Woodward and Farnsworth near where the art museum is today. Feeling a bit restless and somewhat smug about being elected Mayor of Detroit four times, Pingree ran for governor and won in 1896 while still mayoring. Pingree wanted to remain in both positions but the Supreme Court decided that the governor would have to choose which political office he wanted to work in. Pingree chose to govern the state but wanted the capital moved back to Detroit where there were more options for entertainment.

Central High School opened as an integrated school in an imposing new building on Cass and Warren. Decades later the structure would be known as "Old Main" in the Wayne State University complex.

In 1897, Rabbi Judah Leib Levin came from New Haven, Connecticut, to become spiritual leader of Shaarey Zedek, B'nai Israel and Beth Jacob. The thirty-five year old, Russian-born rabbi had his first American pulpit eleven years earlier in Rochester, New York.

A change of attitude among synagogue leaders led to the formation of an afternoon and Sunday school known as the Talaud Torah Institute. The religious school, located on Division Street, came into being principally due to the efforts of Shaarey Zedek members.

About a year after the death of its founder, Edward Kanter, the German American Bank moved to larger quarters at the western corner of Cadillac Square facing Campus Martius.

Sales were heating up for Detroit's several stove companies in 1898 as the economy improved. Over 3,000 workers produced 165,000 stoves. The average wage of all Michigan laborers at the time was $1.62 per day, while a pound of bread went for five cents. The city of Detroit declared an official day of mourning when Samuel Goldwater died. The well-known politician had been reelected to the Detroit City Council two years earlier.

Congress declared war against Spain after the U.S. Battleship Maine was blown up in Havana harbor. Many young Jewish Detroiters answered the call to arms, but the war was over in a few months as American forces quickly mopped up the enemy in Cuba and captured Puerto Rico without a fight.

Inside Beth Jacob in 1896.

(Courtesy of Burton Historical Collection, Detroit Public Library)

An old home was rented on the southwest corner of Brush and Montcalm (near the third base entrance of Comerica Park today) for various Jewish groups. The Ladies' Sewing Society did its stitching, the Self-Help Circle held classes, and the Jewish Women's Club immersed itself in culture. Soon the home evolved into a center of other community activities. The Philomathic Debating Club, began in 1898 by Jewish boys between the ages of fourteen and twenty-one, used a room there for three hours each Sunday before moving to a larger room in the Division Street Talmud Torah.

In 1899, Ransom E. Olds and his investors established the first factory in Detroit and the country to manufacture automobiles. The Olds Motor Works was located in a small building on the east side of Concord near Jefferson, near the Belle Isle bridge, where the Uniroyal plant stood in later years.

Also in 1899, Mayor William Maybury and a couple of well-heeled pals raised $15,000 to help Henry Ford form the Detroit Automobile Company. Ford became chief engineer and partner and quit his job at Edison.

When Rabbi Leo M. Franklin arrived early in 1899 and became the eleventh spiritual leader of Beth El, he found a Jewish community of about 5,000 and his congregation had 136 members.

Soon Franklin realized that there were many well-intentioned philanthropic societies competing for funds. After a series of meetings with the leaders of the groups providing duplicating services, Franklin oversaw the organization of the United Jewish Charities. Detroit's first central philanthropic organization was incorporated on November 21, 1899, and maintained its offices at Brush and Montcalm.

6
1900-1909
NEW CENTURY, NEW IMMIGRANTS

As the twentieth century dawned, the greater Detroit area had 304,132 residents. The city's population of 285,704 made the city the nation's thirteenth largest. Almost 12 percent couldn't speak English, and many were employed in Detroit's stove factories and breweries.

It was a new time for the electric trolley cars that rolled on the city's main thoroughfares. All streetcar lines were united into one system: the Detroit United Railway. The more comfortable, plush interurbans made 330 daily runs from the station at Jefferson and Bates to the far-flung suburbs and beyond.

Rabbi Jacob Ben Baruch, who had come to Detroit a year earlier, was the spiritual leader of Shaarey Zedek and teacher and principal of the Talmud Torah school. Baruch also made time to attend the Michigan College of Medicine and Surgery with hopes of becoming a doctor within three years when he would be thirty-nine years old.

The Talmud Torah was gaining students in 1900. A hundred and fifty were enrolled in the afternoon and 300 attended the Sunday School. Daily sessions began at 4 p.m. and lasted for three hours. The Daughters of Zion served food to the children during the winter and refreshments in the summer. While the number of students in the Talmud Torah seemed im-

Eight years after its founding, Beth David (later B'nai David) dedicated its first building. The location today would be in the northbound lanes of the Chrysler Freeway, about a half-mile north of the Madison exit.

(Courtesy of B'nai David)

ECHOES OF DETROIT'S JEWISH COMMUNITIES

pressive, even more impressive was that the Jewish community, which had numbered about 1,000 only twenty years earlier, was estimated at up to 10,000 in 1900.

After eight years in rented quarters on Hastings and Gratiot, Beth David dedicated its first building on Sunday, September 9, 1900. A band of musicians headed the procession going north up Hastings to the new location on Amelaide between Hastings and Rivard. Attending the ceremonies of the forty-member congregation were many community and city officials, including Mayor Maybury. It was announced at the dedication that until a full-time Rabbi could be engaged, Rabbi Yehudah L. Levin, chief rabbi of the Orthodox Congregations of Detroit, would serve the congregation on a part time basis.

Just hours before the start of 1901, letters from Detroit's political and community leaders relating the life and times of the city were deposited by Mayor William C. Maybury into a tin box and sealed. Instructions stated that the box should remain sealed until New Year's 2001 and opened by the Mayor and Common Council.

David W. Simons, well-known in Jewish, business, and political circles, was asked to describe the Jewish community to Detroiters a hundred years later. Simons titled his letter, "The Jewish People in Mercantile, Social and Professional Life in Detroit." Here are the contents of the letter:

To the Jewish People of the year two thousand, Greeting.

As the nineteenth century closes, the life of the Jew of Detroit as regards business and the professions is marked by no peculiar phenomena. In his choice of a pursuit, there is little to distinguish the Jew of today from other citizens of the community. There has been a decided breaking away from the old trend which led so many of the race into the same fields of industry. In almost every branch of trade and commerce the Jew is represented, and in most of them he has taken a very high place. A prominent bank is controlled exclusively by Jews, and the Jews are represented upon the Board of Directors of a number of other large banking institutions. One of the largest tobacco houses in the country, located here, is a Jewish institution. Jews control large manufacturing plants here in clothing, brushes, matches, corsets, liquor, cigars, potato flour, evaporated vegetables and drugs. The wholesale trade is the field of operation for many Jewish firms, notably in tobacco, liquors, clothing, dry goods, paper, paper stock, iron and steel. Many of the very large retail establishments of the city are operated by Jews, though not the largest as is true of some cities, and every branch of the retail trade of the city is the legitimate field for larger or smaller Jewish merchants. Real estate, and Insurance claims the attention of a number of active Jewish young men.

In the professions the Jew is everywhere, though in most of them his entrance has been comparatively recent. Detroit has about fifteen Jewish lawyers, most of them still young men and almost an equal number of physicians, several of them of high rank in the profession. Two or three dentists have large practices. One of the leading firms of architects is headed by a Jew. The most clever of the caricaturists on the local newspapers is a Jew. There are many Jewish musicians of great promise, a few of the young men have achieved success in engineering, and the teaching staff of the public schools included a large representation of Jewish young women.

There are a great many active social organizations both among the men and women, some of which are composed primarily of the Reformed Jews, while the membership in others is largely Orthodox. During the last decade or two there has been a tendency among the younger men and women to mingle more or less with gentiles in a social way and if we may judge of the future by the trend of the present, it would seem that in time many of the social barriers will be swept away as have been those of mercantile, professional and political life.

It would seem to us here that at the end of the century about to dawn there will be almost nothing to distinguish the Jew of that day from the non-Jew. True, the Jew has maintained his social and religious exclusiveness for over three thousand years, but more has been done to abolish that same exclusiveness in the last fifty years in the more enlightened countries than was accomplished in all of the rest of the thirty centuries put together.

In behalf of the Jew of today I greet the Jew of two thousand.

– David W. Simons

While D. W. Simons painted a rosy picture of the Jewish community, there were many who needed financial assistance and many who worked long hours exposed to all elements of weather trying to earn a living. Their horse-drawn wagons plodded through alleys. Every so often a tin horn was blown to let householders know they were coming. They bought old newspapers, rags, and small pieces of scrap or other metal.

As Detroiters of all economic levels used horse-drawn carriages, they followed the progress of the automobile. Engineer Roy Chapin drove an Oldsmobile from Detroit to New York in seven and one-half days in 1901. The Henry Ford Automobile Company was formed but Ford soon dropped out and the company was dissolved. The Cadillac Company was incorporated as many auto-related companies arrived and departed.

A lot on Winder Street between Beaubien and St. Antoine was donated for the construction of a new Shaarey Zedek as the community was moving northward. The old building on Congress and St. Antoine was sold, and services were held in the Division Street Talmud Torah's small rented quarters.

Around the same time, in September 1901, the cornerstone was laid for Detroit's first building used exclusively for a Hebrew school. On Division Street close to the Talmud Torah, the new brick building would contain four school rooms, an assembly hall and a library.

Detroiter Solomon Goldsmith purchased a small Jewish weekly from Cleveland, which had been established in 1900. On October 18, 1901, the *Jewish American* began as a Detroit weekly with Rabbi Leo M. Franklin as editor and Goldsmith as publisher. While it carried some international and national news, it became the official organ of Temple Beth El.

About five weeks later, the Woman's Auxiliary Association of Temple Beth El began, with Mrs. Adolph Sloman as its first elected president. Twenty-one years later its name would be changed to the Sisterhood of Temple Beth El.

In 1902 the Industrial Removal Office sent seventy-five people to Michigan. The IRO was formed a

On November 25, 1901, groundbreaking ceremonies were held for the new Temple Beth El on Woodward and Eliot Streets.

(Courtesy of Rabbi Leo M. Franklin Archives, Temple Beth El)

year earlier in New York. Its purpose was to relocate immigrant Jews from crowded sections of New York to cities with less Jewish population density.

The new Hebrew Free School building on Division Street was dedicated in April, 1902. Mayor William Maybury gave an address of encouragement and congratulations to a large audience at the close of the ceremonial exercises of music, prayer, and psalms by students, teachers and religious leaders.

On Wednesday afternoon, April 23, 1902, under the threat of rain, the impressive cornerstone laying ceremony for Temple Beth El's structure on Woodward and Eliot was held. Rabbi Franklin addressed the assembled:

The more than fifty years that have sped by since they laid the foundations of our congregation have been years pregnant with victory. During that time the conditions of physical life have been revolutionized. The forces of nature that controlled men have been fettered by him and he commands them to do his bidding. They who founded this organization lived in the age of the stage coach, but we have passed it, and through the era of steam into that of electricity. But the century's triumphs have been more and greater than mechanical. It has been an era of intellectual and spiritual growth the like of which no age before has dared to dream of.

Less than two months later, the cornerstone for Shaarey Zedek's new sanctuary on Winder Street between Beaubien and St. Antoine was laid. It was a hot day in mid-June, but that didn't deter the hundreds of people dressed in their best. Many members of Temple Beth El also attended the event, and Rabbi Franklin delivered a congratulatory message from the platform, as did Rabbi Judah Leib Levin. Bernard Ginsburg and his wife, who donated the parcel on the south side of Winder, were given the honor of laying the cornerstone.

Dr. Franklin was invited to take part in community dedications and urged Temple Beth El members to attend. Beth El members looked down on the Orthodox community socially, and the Orthodox community looked down on Temple Beth El spiritually.

Dr. Bernard Drachman, a leader in New York's Orthodox community and a visitor and past speaker in Detroit, respected Dr. Franklin as a man but not his views as a spiritual leader. Drachman penned a lengthy letter to Dr. Franklin in the May 2, 1902, issue of the *Jewish American*, which read in part:

In the first place I wish to disavow any intention of being personally offensive to you or to any one who holds views different to those which, I, and with me the vast bulk of the Jewish people, consider eternally true and valid. I am broadly tolerant of all views, however much I may disagree with them, and cheerfully accord to all others the same liberty of opinion which I demand for myself; neither do I find it all difficult to live in harmony and amity and even to entertain a high personal regard for those to whose religious and other opinions I may be entirely and absolutely opposed. This does not, however, deprive me of the right to express myself with entire and outspoken frankness concerning the defects and demerits of the system which these gentlemen represent, or any disqualifications which, in my humble opinion, exist in the religious or scholastic equipment of the gentlemen themselves. This is a right which I could not surrender, nor would you, I imagine, be willing to relinquish your right to give open expression to your sincere convictions concerning any phase of Judaism and its representatives.

Reform Judaism has deliberately sought to obliterate all specifically Jewish characteristics and to make us undistinguishable from the Gentile, substituting for the rich and overflowing Judaism of our ancestors an emasculated worship and a colorless morality. How, then, it can be maintained that Reformed Judaism has not been a destructive system is hard to comprehend. As for the claim that Reform represents the logical development of Judaism along historical lines, that is, in my opinion, an entirely baseless and unwarranted statement. The overthrow of a system cannot be its logical outcome. On this basis Christianity has an equal claim to be the logical outcome of Judaism.

Rabbis who eat Terefah [non-Kosher meat], congregations which hold no worship on the Sabbath but on the day consecrated to the Nazarene, other congregations which have removed the Sefer Torah from their temples, are these the logical development of Judaism? The fact is that the Reform movement is not, strictly speaking, a Jewish movement at all. It is "a strange branch" in our vineyard. It is the fruit of the spiritual disintegration wrought by the exile, it is the result of a lack of the moral courage necessary to remain loyal to the ancient flag of Israel amidst the pressure of alien environment.

A writer for the *Detroit News Tribune* visited Temple Beth El and summed it up in the June 22, 1902, edition by reporting

> *A strange Christian entering this place of worship as the service was about to commence would notice very little to distinguish it from an old-fashioned Presbyterian, Baptist or Methodist church. The seating is exactly the same. The people look the same, men and women, boys and girls all sitting together, men and boys bareheaded, women and girls with their ordinary street hats on. The rabbi sitting in a chair to the right of the pulpit, had neither vestment, gown or head covering of any kind—his whole appearance was that of a non-Episcopal American Christian minister.*

Fresh Air Society was organized to provide new American youngsters with summer programs of fun and nourishment. A streetcar was chartered, baskets of food were prepared, and volunteers accompanied the youngsters for a day in the fresh air, often to Belle Isle.

Detroit's Jewish youngsters already had their own method of obtaining fresh air. All they needed was fifteen cents. For a nickel they took a southbound streetcar to Jefferson; a free transfer on an eastbound Jefferson streetcar took them to the Belle Isle Bridge. After a walk across the bridge and the removal of some clothing, they were ready for a long, lazy day in the water; swimming and floating and lying at the river's edge.

A walk back across the bridge and just east of the intersection, one could purchase a strawberry sundae and fresh fruit for a nickel. The reverse streetcar journey home for the final five cents and an enjoyable day was had for three nickels.

The Jewish community lost a link to its past with the passing of Rebecca Cozens Schloss in 1902. A generous woman endowed with a sparkling personally, she had been married at age sixteen to Emanuel Schloss, who became president of Beth El in 1859. She was one of the five daughters of Isaac and Sarah Cozens and had witnessed Detroit's first Jewish religious service in the Cozens home in 1850, out of which grew Temple Beth El.

University of Michigan law school graduate David Heineman, who went on to serve in the state legislature in 1889 and 1890, became a Detroit City Council member in 1902. Another U of M graduate, Charles Simons, son of David W. Simons, successfully ran for the state senate at the time.

The Division Street Talmud Torah was dedicated in 1902.

(Courtesy of Rabbi Leo M. Franklin Archives, Temple Beth El)

Dr. Franklin was instrumental in organizing laymen of three faiths to create the Interdenominational Thanksgiving Service in November. Years later the organization would evolve into the Detroit Round Table of Catholics, Jews and Protestants.

As 1902 came to a close, Detroit boasted forty-four millionaires among the various faiths. Carpenters proposed a minimum wage of thirty cents hourly, and house painters asked for $2.50 a day. Jefferson and Brush was the hub of automobile row—there were four dealerships near the corner. Detroit held its first auto show, and a few months later had its first auto accident fatality when well-heeled lumberman George Bissell's carriage was hit at Brooklyn and Lysander on the city's lower west side.

In 1903 the price of milk rose to seven cents a quart, and the Ford Motor Company was incorporated. The factory was located at Bellevue and Mack, and forty-year-old Henry Ford owned twenty-five percent of the stock. The new Packard plant attracted sightseers as designer Albert Kahn created the world's first reinforced concrete factory.

On Sunday, the first day of March in 1903, the newly erected Shaarey Zedek was dedicated. Twelve of the oldest members of the congregation marched around the synagogue holding the sacred scrolls of the Torah, which were then deposited in the ark. After the appropriate prayers, psalms, and singing by Cantor Moshe Rogoff and the boys' choir, the audience rose and joined in the singing of "The Star Spangled Banner." Mayor William Maybury then followed with a short address. Rabbi Judah Leib Levin stated, "We must always remember that these beautiful halls and this lovely building, lit by electricity…will be the garden in which will grow the fruits of Judaism."

The new synagogue was 60 feet wide and 85 feet in depth. The main auditorium was 57 feet square and 30 feet high. The main floor had 400 seats and there were an additional 300 seats in the balcony. The basement contained two large meeting rooms that could be used as one large room. The entire structure cost $20,000.

Beth El held its first service in the chapel of the

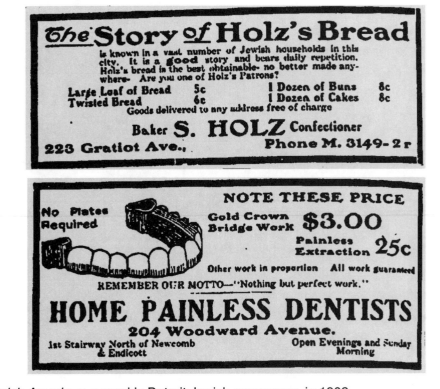

Advertisements from the *Jewish American*, a weekly Detroit Jewish newspaper, in 1902.

(Courtesy of Rabbi Leo M. Franklin Archives, Temple Beth El)

new temple on January 24, 1903, but the dedication of Beth El's first temple built by its members was spread over Friday night, September 18, through the next day. Both days featured organ music, solo and choir singing, and speeches. It was at this site that Dr. Franklin put into practice the unassigned seating of worshipers. Previously, pews were rented or sold by congregations to raise funds, and usually the best locations were held by the richest families, Services were also moved from Friday nights to Sunday mornings, a practice that would continue for another thirty-four years. Saturday morning services were also offered for those who wanted to pray on the same day held holy by traditional Jews.

The United Jewish Charities erected a building on the north side of High Street (now the Fisher Freeway, north of Ford Field), between St. Antoine and Hastings. The structure was devoted exclusively to housing philanthropic work. Albert Kahn donated his services as the architect of the two-story-plus-basement, red brick building.

The basement was equipped with a manual training school, cooking class, gymnasium, and showers and baths. The first floor had a large assembly room, a sewing room, offices, and two classrooms for kindergarten care. The second floor had a day nursery school and the self-help classroom and library.

At the dedication on the last Monday evening in September 1903, Seligman Schloss surprised the large gathering by announcing he would pay the entire cost of the building in memory of his wife, Hannah, who had been killed five years earlier in a train accident in Wisconsin.

Bernard Ginsberg furnished the nursery rooms in memory of his wife; they became known as the Ida E. Ginsberg Day Nursery. It was always Mrs. Ginsberg's wish that a nursery be established so young mothers seeking employment would have a proper place to leave their children.

Hung on a wall inside the Hannah Schloss Memorial Building were these words: "To Help the Poor to Help Themselves."

Designed by Albert Kahn, Temple Beth El on Woodward and Eliot opened in 1903.

(Courtesy of Rabbi Leo M. Franklin Archives, Temple Beth El)

The Free Press of May 31, 1903, featured prominent Russian Jews who were members of Shaarey Zedek. Top left: "S. Ginsburg, of Ginsburg & Son, is the head of a large iron business having contracts with the New York Central and other large railroad companies; Dr. N. E. Aronstam is a professor of the Michigan College of Medicine; D. W. Simons, formerly a member of the public lighting commission, is a well-known real estate dealer. William Saulson, secretary and treasurer of the Peerless Manufacturing Company of East Larned Street; Dr. Joseph Beisman and Dr. I. L. Polozker. Bottom left: M. Mitshkun is in the railway equipment business in the Chamber of Commerce building; Boris L. Ganapol, the well-known singer and teacher; Louis J. Rosenberg, attorney; A. Simon, a dealer in paper supplies." (Courtesy of Burton Historical Collection, Detroit Public Library)

Beth David elected Rabbi Jacob H. Scheinman as its spiritual leader. Scheinman, fifty-nine, received his Rabbinical ordination in Poland and had lived in the United States for the past twenty-four years serving several congregations. Before accepting the post with Beth David, Scheinman held a pulpit in Brooklyn.

Jacob Burstine, the founder and president of Congregation B'nai Israel, died at 60. The Russian-born Burnstine had come to Detroit in 1863 and became successful in the metal and rags business. As the community said goodbye to Burnstine, they welcomed the brilliant principal of the Talmud Torah as a doctor. Jacob Ben Baruch, who spoke more languages than anyone in the community, graduated from medical school and opened a medical practice.

In 1903, 21-year-old native Detroiter Isaac Rosenthal, who founded the Detroit Store Fixture Company, operated his furniture store on Gratiot, where he closeted himself for an hour each afternoon studying religious books. He married Minnie Kaufman in the family home on Columbia near Brush (now in the shadow of Comerica Park's large scoreboard). As

Native Detroiter Isaac Rosenthal became a successful businessman at a young age and spent an hour each afternoon studying in his store.

(Courtesy of Zelda Selmar)

the young couple, who would reside in Detroit the rest of their lives, stood under the wedding canopy, they had no idea of the effect they would later have upon the future of Detroit Jewry.

Jewish Detroiters were saddened to read about J.A. Detzer's opening account of his trip to Jerusalem in the *Jewish American*:

> *"The Jerusalem of today is only a mournful relic of the ancient city," Detzer reported. "Its former glory has departed. Blighted, bleak and barren, it now rests upon its crumbling hills—a city of ruins, rags and wretchedness. Jerusalem has no parks, public squares, promenades, driveways, boulevards, libraries or reading rooms."*

Jewish Detroiters were more concerned with reading about the situation in Russia, as many had family members there. Anti-Semitism raged across Russia in 1903, culminating in violence and murder. In April, during the Easter holiday, the 2,528 Kishinev Jews were terrorized, resulting in forty-seven deaths and hundreds of injuries. Fires and looters destroyed many possessions and the lucky ones fled. Later in the year in Warsaw, Poland, a holding of Russia, eighty Jews were seriously injured and many were slaughtered by mobs as authorities stood by. The pogroms would lead many Russian Jews to America. Some would come to Detroit.

William Saulson assumed the presidency of Shaarey Zedek in 1904. His immediate concern was the growing apathy of the younger generation. Saulson appealed to them by hiring an younger rabbi who would give sermons in English instead of Hebrew or Yiddish. Rabbi Rudolph Farber was given the pulpit and inaugurated Friday evening lectures and introduced more singing at religious services.

Rabbi Ezekiel Aishishkin became spiritual leader of B'nai David as Rabbi Scheinman, who had served the congregation for only one year, departed for an-

Ads from the *Jewish American* in 1904.

(Courtesy of Rabbi Leo M. Franklin Archives of Temple Beth El)

ECHOES OF DETROIT'S JEWISH COMMUNITIES

The Phoenix Club's new structure on John R. and Erskine opened in 1906.
(Courtesy of Rabbi Leo M. Franklin Archives, Temple Beth El)

other pulpit in the east. Rabbi Aishishkin, who was thirty-seven at the time, had come to America a year earlier as head of a religious school in New York.

In 1904, H. L. Goldman and his sons, Louis, Abe, and Harry, purchased the Reliance Motor Company and the Marvel Motor Company, which were merged into the Crescent Motor Company. Manufacturing began at Meldrum and Champlain (now Lafayette). At times, two Reliance automobiles and five Marvels were produced in a month. The Reliance had its motor under the center of the body, while the Marvel was one of the first cars to hide its motor under the front part of the hood.

In 1905 Michigan law required automobile drivers to pull over and stop if approaching horses appeared spooked by their machine. Movies were becoming more popular. The Casino, Detroit's first theater built exclusively for the showing of movies, opened on Monroe. People still preferred the live acts of vaudeville, as the movies were jumpy, without color and sound, and most immigrants had trouble reading the words on the bottom of the screen. Entertainment provided an escape, however, which was very important to Detroit's Jews who kept hearing reports of pogroms in Russia.

Because of the continued violence against Jews in Russia in 1905, a day of mourning was proclaimed in the Detroit Jewish community. Signs were posted in store windows along Hastings Street, and announcements were made in all houses of worship. All were urged to attend the B'nai Israel on Mullett Street on Monday, December 4, at four o'clock. The following Friday, the *Jewish American* reported the scene:

> When Rabbi Judah Levin, who conducted the services with the assistance of Dr. R. Farber, stepped to the altar, every seat in the synagogue was filled and hundreds were standing in the aisles while as many more at the doors were turned away.
>
> The rabbi told of the terrible atrocities of Odessa, of Kieff and other Russian cities; and as he alternately recited the tale of the horrors of the massacre and prayed for the safety of the living ones, the scene in the synagogue was heartrending. In the gallery were hundreds who have dear ones in Russia from whom they have not heard for weeks, or at best only tidings of suffering and death.
>
> At first there was only silent weeping among them, but, as the rabbi with tears in his own eyes bemoaned the fate of the victims of the massacre, the weeping became heart-broken wailing.

The Phoenix Club opened its new building on the corner of John R. and Erskine. It would stay at this location for the next thirty-six years. The structure of brick and stone was well adapted to the needs of a social club. The basement contained janitorial rooms, cold storage rooms, stock and wine rooms, a bar and stein room, a billiard room, bowling alleys, a laundry, and a large kitchen. The first floor featured a large dining room, card rooms, a library, and a private room for dining. The second floor had the large ballroom adjoined by eight roomy apartments for dressing.

On Wednesday, September 12, 1906, the Fresh Air Society closed its season when it took fifty children for an automobile ride around the city. Two large sightseeing automobiles were chartered to take children on their first automobile ride ever. During the summer, 325 children took advantage of Fresh Air's activities.

As the summer was coming to a close, a free dispensary opened to serve the Jewish poor on the corner of Hastings and Alfred Streets. About fifteen doctors offered their services.

The Ladies' Auxiliary (now the Sisterhood) of Shaarey Zedek was organized by Mrs. David W. Simons, who became its first president. Shaarey Zedek also organized its first Sunday school. At the same time, indifference led to the cancellation of Friday night lectures, to the disappointment of the congregation's officers and Rabbi Farber.

Jews beamed with pride when Oscar Solomon Straus became the first Jewish member of a presidential cabinet in 1906. Theodore Roosevelt appointed Straus as his secretary of commerce.

New residents kept coming in 1907, and there were plenty of employment opportunities as the railroad car industry was at its peak in Detroit and had about 9,000 workers. The auto industry had more competition and opportunity for employment as Charles B. King organized his own company. King designed the first automobile with the steering wheel on the left side and would produce autos using his many innovations.

Automobile Row, along Jefferson on both sides of Brush, had sixteen dealers in 1907. More autos meant more accidents, and Detroit had seven auto fatalities, prompting police to try to enforce an auto speed limit of eight miles per hour downtown and twelve miles per hour in residential areas. There was talk of replacing steam fire engines with motorized apparatus, and talk became fact when the fire chief had the fire department's first automobile.

The Jewish population was estimated at 12,000 in 1907, and Shaarey Zedek had 135 members when Rabbi Farber resigned. The congregation, trying to rejuvenate itself, wanted a graduate of the Jewish Theological Seminary of America. Its choice was Rabbi Abraham Hershman, twenty-seven at the time and single.

The congregation soon felt his impact. Rabbi Hershman established Shaarey Zedek's own afternoon

Abe Goldman and his sister Ray take a spin in the Goldman-produced Marvel auto.

(Courtesy of Leonard N. Simons Jewish Community Archives)

school and reorganized the Sunday school. A Young People's Society was organized, as well as the Kadimah Society for the study of Jewish history. The Friday night lectures were reintroduced and more people began attending services.

In 1907, sixteen people established a Detroit branch—Number 156—of the Arbeter Ring, the Workmen's Circle. The organization, formed seven years earlier in New York, focused on improved working conditions and benefits for its Jewish immigrant members. Later it turned its attention to implementing lectures and the establishing of schools based on its socialist beliefs.

In 1894 the Assembly of David and House of Shelter consisted of a devoted group of men who read psalms on behalf of the sick and provided burial for the Jewish poor. It soon rented a house on Columbia and Hastings to provide food and lodging for the homeless. The group bought a home on Adelaide near Rivard to also provide living quarters for families en route to other cities, or prior to their residence in Detroit. By 1907, the House of Shelter was based in a larger home on Division Street.

At this time, Jacob Levin was saddened by the plight of an elderly homeless Jew sleeping in the basement of the Beth Jacob synagogue on Montcalm and Hastings Streets. He rallied fellow members of the congregation's burial society who shared his sentiments and they purchased the home of banker Charles Kanter on Brush and Winder, where they provided kosher meals and lodging for the elderly. It was simply called "The Home." In time it would be referred to as "The Jewish Old Folks Home."

Jacob Levin, an Orthodox Russian Jew, was a busy man. He operated a tailoring business, became president of "The Home," and oversaw the incorporation of the Anshe Chesed Shel Emeth, which sprang from the organization formed two years earlier to visit the sick and arrange burials.

About twenty Jewish young men formed the Mutual Club in 1907. Its purpose was to promote good fellowship, socializing, and a spirit of fraternity among its members. Within six months of existence, almost a hundred members belonged. The club met in Duffield Hall, on Woodward and Duffield.

The established Phoenix Club's baseball team went to Buffalo to play the Apollo Club's team. Even though the Phoenix Club defeated the Apollo Club, the Detroiters were treated to dinner and a return engagement in Detroit was arranged.

Jacob Mazer, famous for his basketball playing ability, resigned from the Detroit Athletic Club over its rejection of a Jewish applicant's membership. Most Detroit Jews thought Mazer's athletic ability was the reason for his acceptance in the club.

Fresh Air Society took forty children on the boat to Belle Isle on its first weekly outing of the season. Each Wednesday, from nine in the morning until five in the afternoon, under the chaperonage of at least four young ladies, the children got fresh air and exercise and partook of bread, butter, eggs, fruits, snacks and refreshment.

Two new small congregations were formed in 1907: Nusach Ari, on Alfred Street, and Beth Hamidrash Hagodol, which met in the Hastings cor-

Ad from the *Jewish American* in 1907.
(Courtesy of Rabbi Leo M. Franklin Archives, Temple Beth El)

ECHOES OF DETROIT'S JEWISH COMMUNITIES

ridor and competed with Tifereth Israel (the future Beth Aaron), organized two years earlier.

The *Detroit Jewish Directory* of 1907 was published in Yiddish. Of the 2,145 working males listed, 334 or 16 percent were defined as peddlers. There were four policemen, one detective, two sheriff's deputies and one fireman.

David Heineman, the former Chief Assistant City Attorney of Detroit and Common Council president in 1907, designed the colorful flag consisting of four quarters and reflecting important phases of the city's history, that became the flag of Detroit.

D. W. Simons assumed the presidency of Shaarey Zedek in 1908, a post he would hold for the next twelve years. Simons, who was the first president of the United Jewish Charities (which became the Jewish Welfare Federation in 1926) continued to be active in the Chamber of Commerce and city politics.

Rabbi Hershman organized the Kadimah Zionist Society in 1908, which led to the Zionist Organization of Detroit. Its membership included business and professional men, and Rabbi Hershman served as president. Rabbi Hershman also assumed the post of principal of the Shaarey Zedek Hebrew School as it merged with the Division Street Talmud Torah.

The Hannah Schloss Memorial Building was enlarged in 1908, and a section of eight rooms were set aside in the basement for clinic purposes. Miss Louise Goldstone had the combined duties of administrator, social worker, and nurse. Seven doctors offered their services in the free dispensary.

The enlarged building also contained extensive

The Detroit Opera House in Campus Martius was the place to see well-known actors in the Yiddish theater.
(Courtesy of Michigan Views)

facilities for club rooms and a well-equipped gymnasium. There were football, baseball, and basketball teams in every age group. Detroit's best Jewish basketball player, Jacob Mazer, worked out there and offered tips to youngsters. The Homer T. Lane Club, named for the manual training instructor at the building, was popular with athletic and non-athletic youngsters. There were Boy Scout troops, as well as Girl Scout troops and other groups for females of all ages to join. Classes in English, American history, art, and music were available for youth and adults.

In 1908 the Fresh Air Society purchased a site at Venice Beach on Lake St. Clair. Eventually, the facility provided accommodations for 200 children.

The Grabowsky brothers—Max and Morris—who manufactured the first gasoline powered truck to be used in Detroit six years earlier, formed Grabowsky Power Wagon Company. Albert Kahn designed the truck manufacturing plant.

Solomon Goldsmith, the publisher of Detroit's weekly, the Jewish American, died at the young age of forty-eight. Goldsmith had worked in the newspaper industry in several cities before accepting the position of business manager of the *Detroit Tribune*. The opening article of the Friday, October 9, 1908, edition of the *Jewish American* told the story:

Ad from the *Jewish American* in 1908.
(Courtesy of Rabbi Leo M. Franklin Archives, Temple Beth El)

Seldom in the history of the local Jewish community has the death of a man carried with it such a shock as did that of Mr. Sol M. Goldsmith, which occurred at his home, 757 Brush street, early last Sunday morning. Greeting, as was his custom, the large congregation that gathered at Temple Beth El on Rosh Hashono, from his place at the entrance, comparatively few of those who spoke to him on that day could realize that ere the next day had dawned he had been stricken with typhoid fever, which from the first assumed a serious aspect. Physically weakened by his many labors, from which he seldom rested, and warned time and again by his friends and loved ones that he was overtaxing his strength, he felt no need of rest, and as a result he had little reserve power with which to combat the dread disease that terminated in his death.

Few men have ever lived in this community who meant so much to so many people as did he…He was brought into close contact with all classes of the Jewish public and…he was well known throughout the entire country. For the past seven years the faithful and efficient secretary of Temple Beth El, none was more conversant with its affairs or more loyal to its interests than he. He was devoted every Jewish cause, though his sympathies were by no means narrow or limited to denominational lines.

The personal traits of Mr. Goldsmith were such as to win the love, esteem and respect of all who knew him. The type of a gentleman by instinct, courteous always, innately refined, deeply sympathetic, an idealist of a high type, he stood out in any company as a man of obvious superiority.

He was not a man of two standards. His business integrity was as keen as his personal honesty, and his social standard was the standard that rules in his own home. He was the most modest of men and unselfishness was his central characteristic. Loyal to every good cause, faithful to every moral obligation, he was a man whom to know was a privilege and whom to have as a friend was an inspiration.

The funeral, which took place at Temple Beth El Tuesday afternoon, was largely attended by Jews and Christians. Rabbi Franklin, perhaps his closest friend, paid him eloquent and worthy tribute.

In his passing Detroit Jewry loses one of its foremost representatives and every worthy man in the community a friend who was loyal and true.

The 447 contributors to the United Jewish Charities in 1908 represented the first time the contributor list passed 400. Four years earlier, it had passed 300 for the first time. Beth Isaac was organized on the lower level of a frame home on Belmont near Hastings. Morris Rose was president and oversaw religious services of the new small congregation.

Automobile taxicabs with automatic fare registers made their Detroit debut in 1908. Detroit wasn't yet the auto capital of the world, but the industry kept growing locally as Ford Motor produced its first Model T, which sold for $950. William Durant founded General Motors around the Buick and Oldsmobile companies.

William Maybury, who held several political offices including mayor of Detroit, died in 1909. Maybury was widely admired in the Jewish and non-Jewish communities, and citizens quickly raised funds to erect a statue in his memory on the east side of Woodward at Adams.

Automobiles were getting heavier, going faster, and being driven farther. The first mile of concrete paved road in the country opened on Woodward from Six Mile to Seven Mile Roads.

Some Shaarey Zedek members traveled to New York in June 1909 for Rabbi Hershman's wedding at The Jewish Theological Seminary. Besides family and friends, many rabbis, Zionist leaders, and other active participants in the American Jewish community were present.

The Tigers won their third straight American League pennant and lost their third straight World Series. One of the games at Bennett Park drew a record crowd for Detroit baseball of 18,277.

William Rosenberg, thirty-six, a native Detroiter, was a telegrapher and supervisor for the Western Union Company. The Temple Beth El member attended every World Series game played at Bennett Park and relayed the play-by-play via his fingers.

7
1910–1919
A Time of Growth

In 1910 there were an estimated two million Jews in the United States. Figures differ on estimates of Detroit's Jewish population, but all sources put it at 10,000 or more.

Detroit claimed 465,766 citizens; 5,741 were black and 157,534 were foreign-born. New arrivals found they could earn some money even though they hadn't mastered English. The automobile industry had many foreign-born employees, as did the construction industry, and all types of stores. Other immigrants drove horse-drawn wagons through the streets for delivery and moving purposes.

More and more people were turning to automobiles for transportation, however. When the Highland Park Plant of Ford Motor Company began operation in 1910, there were 201 other makes of cars produced by an estimated 150 companies. Many were displayed at the 1910 Detroit Auto Show, held at the Wayne Gardens at Third and Jefferson.

Rabbi Hershman and Dr. Franklin addressed those

Edmund Street just west of Brush. North of Edmund are Watson, Erskine, Eliot, Rowena, and Brady. South of Edmund are Alfred, Adelaide, Winder, High (later East Vernor, now the east-west Fisher Freeway/I-75), and Montcalm (today the north end of Comerica Park and Ford Field.

(Courtesy of Michigan Views)

assembled to commemorate the sixtieth birthday of Temple Beth El on Sunday, October 23, 1910. The spiritual leader of Shaarey Zedek and his counterpart at Beth El had a deep respect for each other and often worked together on community issues. They differed on levels of religious observance and had opposing views on Zionism. Rabbi Hershman often spoke out for and brought more people under the umbrella of Zionism. Dr. Franklin often preached or said, "America is the new Palestine; Washington is the new Jerusalem."

The theme of the ceremony at the 310-member Temple Beth El that day was community unity despite the differences in religious application.

"Orthodox and Reformed Jews share many problems in common," Rabbi Hershman said. *"But not all, because our ideals as Orthodox Jews are not entirely your ideals, as Reformed ones. It was thought by those who instituted the Reform movement that such an upheaval would prove a panacea for the evils of Jewry. But anticipation is always greater than realization. There is a disparity, an incalculable distance between an idea and its embodiment. Today, there is a groping for unity among all Jews, a growing desire to approach one another on terms of equality. Tolerance comes too near indifference. Sympathy and respect are what is needed."*

Dr. Franklin said: *"Many of our co-religionists are included among the huge addition to population which made Detroit's growth a phenomenal thing during the last decade. The brain and brawn of these many have gone into the spiritual and material enrichment of the entire city, and we have benefited in our measure."*

The Beth Tefilo congregation was founded in 1910 (it would merge with Emanuel twenty-two years later) in a rented structure on Napoleon Street east of Hastings. Rabbi Joseph Eisenman, a thirty-six-year-old scholar from Poland, came to Detroit in 1910. He moved into an apartment on Winder near Hastings and became spiritual leader of Beth Tefilo and B'nai Jacob. Rabbi Eisenman would stay in Detroit for the next thirty-nine years, until his seventy-fifth birthday, and play an important role in many religious organizations.

Machpelah Cemetery was founded in 1910 on the site of a former saw mill on the west side of Woodward between Eight and Nine Mile Roads in Ferndale. One of the reasons for the establishment of Machpelah was that the Jewish community's other

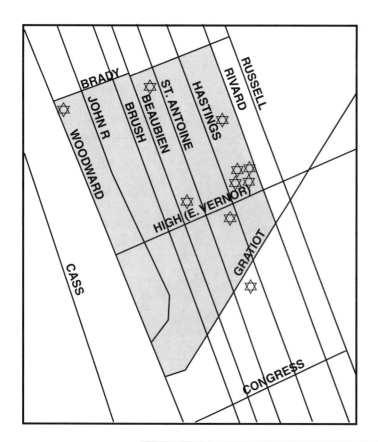

Distribution of Detroit's Jewish population in 1910. Shaded area indicates highest Jewish population density. Synagogues are indicated with a ✡.

(Map courtesy of Phillip Applebaum)

Shoppers walk on Winder Street east of Hastings to the Eastern Market in 1911.

(Courtesy of Burton Historical Collection, Detroit Public Library)

Hastings Street scene in 1911.

(Courtesy of Leonard N. Simons Jewish Community Archives)

main cemetery had limited burial space remaining. Beth Olam, founded in 1862, served members of Shaarey Zedek, B'nai Israel, and Beth Jacob. The Beth Tefilo congregation purchased eight and one-half acres for its members in 1910. Shaarey Zedek purchased a site on Brush and Willis for the purpose of building a new synagogue, and Hyman Buchhalter became the principal of the Division Street Talmud Torah.

The *Jewish American*, published weekly since October 5, 1900, ended its run unexpectedly with the May 12, 1911 edition. Shortly after its demise, a local attempt at a monthly, the *Reform Chronicle*, was short-lived.

Congregation Mogen Abraham was organized in 1911. Services were held at a home on Frederick Street, then moved to a store on the corner of Frederick and Rivard. The Elias Eincztg congregation was formed (six years later the congregation would be reorganized under the name of B'nai Moshe.) There were approximately one hundred Jewish families in Mt. Clemens in 1911, and Beth Tephilath Moses, an Orthodox congregation, was founded.

In March 1912, Rabbi Judah Levin led a march down Hastings Street calling attention to the need for a Jewish hospital. The group of Orthodox Jews carried placards reading, "Buy a brick to save the sick."

Dr. Franklin and the majority of the more affluent German Jewish community who were able to offer major financial support for the project, didn't feel the need to support a Jewish hospital offering food prepared according to the Jewish dietary laws. The hospital issue would simmer for another decade but would not gain support until the Reform community felt the need to provide positions for Jewish physicians.

Around this period in 1912, Dr. Albert Bernstein, a member of Shaarey Zedek and active in B'nai B'rith and the Zionist movement, headed a meeting of physicians, which culminated in the founding of the Maimonides Medical Society. Dr. Bernstein was elected president of the society, named after Rabbi Moshe Ben Maimon, known as Rambam (1135-1204). Dr. Jacob Ben Baruch suggested the name of the society, whose purpose was threefold: scientific, social, and the active promotion of a Jewish hospital.

In 1912 a weekend Yiddish school began in Detroit. The school met in rented rooms on High Street and moved down the block to the Hannah Schloss

Congregation Mogen Abraham's first building was on Farnsworth between Beaubien and St. Antoine.

(Courtesy of Archives of Congregation Shaarey Zedek)

Memorial Building.

Detroit went over the half-million population mark in 1912, and Michigan produced more cars than any other state. Ford more than doubled its production from the previous year, and in 1913, with Detroit home to forty-three automobile companies, Henry Ford initiated the assembly line in his Highland Park plant. Model Ts could now be produced in ninety-three minutes instead of in just over twelve hours.

Detroit boasted 70 moving picture houses and 14 variety theaters in 1913. The two-show-a-day vaudeville acts averaged 21,000 patrons weekly, while all 14 theaters amounted to 288,000. Moving pictures drew an estimated 300,000 weekly.

The Jewish Women's Club, formed by the women of Temple Beth El in 1891, had 550 members in 1913. The number of contributors to the United Jewish Charities passed 500 for the first time as 534 people made donations.

Congregation Mogen Abraham, founded two years earlier, built its first synagogue in 1913 on Farnsworth between Beaubien and St. Antoine. It would become known as the "Farnsworth Shuhl." The congregation built a Talmud Torah school next door

The Dime Bank Building on Griswold and Fort behind the City Hall was Detroit's tallest building in 1913.

The cornerstone laying ceremony for the new Shaarey Zedek building on Brush and Willis took place on November 13, 1913. Left to right: Rabbi A. M. Hershman, Rabbi Judah Levin (speaking), Dr. Leo Franklin (dark hat), David W. Simons (light hat, front), Harry B. Keidan, Isaac Shetzer, Isaac Saulson, and Louis Smith.

(Courtesy of Archives of Congregation Shaarey Zedek)

ECHOES OF DETROIT'S JEWISH COMMUNITIES

after the synagogue opened, under the supervision of its spiritual leader, Rabbi Judah Levin. Rabbi Levin also found time to serve other congregations on a part-time basis while pursuing his hobbies of mathematics and mechanics, resulting in the invention of an adding machine. The single model he built was never commercialized, and he kept it in his home on Ferry Street.

On Sunday, November 16, 1913, the cornerstone of the new Shaarey Zedek on Brush and Willis was laid. Rabbi Judah Levin delivered the invocation, and the children of Shaarey Zedek sang renditions from the psalms. David W. Simons, the president of the synagogue, Dr. Franklin of Beth El, and Rabbi Hershman addressed the assembled.

While the new Shaarey Zedek was under construction, the Winder Street synagogue was sold to Beth David in 1914. New congregations were established in various sections of Detroit as pockets of Jewish families lived close to their businesses.

The Beth Itzchok, a half-block north of Mack Avenue and a few blocks east of Van Dyke, was founded. The congregation met at 3836 Fischer street, a short walk north of Detroit's famed east side Indian Village neighborhood. On the west side of town, the Aaron Moshe rented a hall on Michigan Avenue and Vinewood, a bit over two miles from downtown. Way up Michigan Avenue in Inkster, a section of Westwood Cemetery was purchased by a subsidiary of Mishkan Israel and was known as Harmorean Cemetery.

In 1914, Dr. Franklin established the Jewish Student Congregation at the University of Michigan, the first Jewish collegiate religious organization formed in the United States. Similar congregations at leading universities were established and became the forerunner of B'nai B'rith Hillel Foundations. The 42-year-old Phoenix Club added a golf club and the Redford Country Club to its social holdings.

David T. Nederlander, who was operating a contract loan office on Monroe Avenue, purchased the old Detroit Opera House and offered vaudeville acts that featured such early show business names as W. C. Fields and Al Jolson. The Yiddish Theater opened on August 26, 1914, on Hastings Street. It was owned by the Schreiber Theater Company, with Joseph Optner as manager.

Ford Motor Company offered five dollars daily for an eight-hour shift, slicing an hour off the work day for almost double the money. The combination of jobs and money made Detroit a magnet. Fourteen thousand applied by mail, and many left homes and farms in all parts of the country and even other countries.

The Dodge brothers were getting rave reviews for an automobile with an all-steel body coming off the lines at their 20-acre Hamtramck plant. Neighbors on

The Beth Itzchok still stands on Fischer north of Mack. Jacob Lazaroff, father of Emma Lazaroff Schaver, was the congregation's first acting rabbi.

(Photo by author)

David T. Nederlander had his loan office on Monroe Avenue, where numerous houses of entertainment were located.
(Courtesy of Michigan Views)

East Boston Boulevard often saw John and Horace Dodge proudly sitting in the automobile bearing their name.

Two of Detroit's papers—the *News* and the *Journal*—merged in 1915. Detroiters were saddened to read of the burning of the Belle Isle Bridge on April 27.

The elegant Detroit Athletic Club opened on Madison Avenue in 1915. Albert Kahn, who designed the building, refused an invitation to the first luncheon to protest the club's policy of barring Jews from membership.

In 1915 a rented room in a home east or west of the Hastings street corridor averaged five dollars a month. Anything needed for daily existence could be purchased along Hastings Street. The largest furniture store was located on Hastings and High Streets (now the large interchange just north and east of Ford Field).

David Robinson and his five sons were the major operators of the huge Robinson & Cohen store. The store was closed on the Jewish sabbath. Long lines would form waiting for the doors to open as darkness fell on Saturdays.

The future B'nai Moshe—then known as Elias Einczig Congregation—purchased a house on the corner of Eliot and Hastings in 1915. The Agudas Achim rented a store on Hastings for its new congregation, and the Beth Yehuda congregation celebrated its first year in a home on Adelaide near Hastings, with Rabbi Eisenman as spiritual leader.

The huge Robinson-Cohen Company on Hastings at the corner of High carried a complete line of home furnishings. Ads boasted, "Our entire third floor is divided into a large number of rooms, where the suites are arranged just as they would appear in your own home."

Passers-by often stopped to chat in front of the Warsaw Bakery on Hastings and Winder.

(Courtesy of Burton Historical Collection, Detroit Public Library)

The imposing Shaarey Zedek on Brush and Willis. Today this location is in the heart of Detroit's Medical Center.
(Courtesy of Archives of Congregation Shaarey Zedek)

1915 was the second year of World War One, and the battles caused havoc in Poland, especially in areas inhabited by Jews. The Czarist regime accused the Jews of spying and sabotage to cover its incompetence in battle as it suffered military defeats. Jews left their villages and sought refuge in large cities such as Lodz and Warsaw. The plight of the starving, homeless refugees soon reached the American Jewish communities, and rescue committees quickly organized in America and Detroit.

The Progressive Literary Dramatic Club brought the great Yiddish writer and humorist Sholem Aleichem to a sold-out Detroit Opera House. Prior to the curtain raising, young ladies in white uniforms with red Mogen David-embroidered white kerchiefs on their heads walked through the aisles collecting funds for Hadassah in blue and white canisters. Joseph Bernstein started his first year of a 40-year career as managing director of the Detroit edition of *Forverts*, a Yiddish daily.

On December 15, 1915, Shaarey Zedek dedicated its large new synagogue on Brush and Willis. There were 1,432 seats in the large sanctuary, plus a 400-seat auditorium, seven classrooms, an impressive gymnasium, a kitchen, a dining room, and staff offices. Ushers dressed in black waistcoats and striped pants were in charge of maintaining decorum during services.

Rabbi Hershman wore black clerical robes but wore white on Yom Kippur. He began his sermons with, "Jews and Jewesses." Cantor Abraham Minkowsky, a biblical scholar who had studied at a Talmudical academy in Russia, was a graduate of the Imperial Conservatory of Music at Moscow and brought new vitality to the services via his own musical compositions.

In 1916, Henrietta Szold, founder of the new organization of Hadassah, visited Detroit and stayed with Bessie and Joseph Wetsman. Their daughter Sarah (the future mother of Bill Davidson), who taught at Shaarey Zedek's Sunday school, became an ardent supporter of Hadassah. The co-founder of the Detroit branch and its first elected president was Miriam Hershman, wife of Rabbi Hershman.

Miss Szold told of Hadassah going to Palestine to cure trachoma and to rid the swamps of malaria. She asked for funds, as sending nurses to Palestine, housing them, and providing them with supplies called for a considerable amount of money.

Since the aim of Haddasah was to improve the lot of Jews in Palestine, the supporters of the organization came from Shaarey Zedek and the Orthodox community. Members of Temple Beth El didn't support the Zionist cause of the return of Jews to their biblical homeland. The divine promise of the land of Israel wasn't part of the Reform brand of Judaism. The Reform clerical leadership had excised mention of the return to Zion from their prayer book. Women of the Reform movement were extremely devoted to helping Jews in their own communities and to the plight of Jews around the world, but not to the cause of the reestablishment of the Jewish state.

On March 3, 1916, the *Jewish Chronicle* (later the *Detroit Jewish Chronicle*) made its debut. Samuel J. Rhodes was the editor of the new weekly, and Anton Kaufman was general manager.

Four weeks later, Detroit Jews raised $110,000 for the relief of the war sufferers in Europe. About 2,000 Jews poured into a rented hall to hear reports from Europe. Community leaders and rabbis were seated in a semicircle on the platform facing the crowd as Dr. Franklin opened the program. The most impressive speaker, according to Anton Kaufman of the *Jewish Chronicle*, was Rabbi Stephen S. Wise

Here is Kaufman's account in the April 7, 1916, issue:

> Then the chairman announced the orator of the evening, and in answer to the outburst of applause which greeted his remarks, Rabbi Stephen S. Wise arose and with measured step advanced to the edge of the platform. A striking figure he made, standing there for a moment or two in silent contemplation of the assembled thousands. The squared shoulders were those of the athlete; and the firm stride massive build spoke of tremendous strength and reserve power. His remarkable personality was stamped upon every feature. The set, tenacious jaw denoted it. The keen, scrutinizing, almost frowning glance expressed it. The heavy, shaggy hair betokened it. The man looked every of what he is: the central figure among American rabbis, the foremost orator in the Jewish pulpit.
>
> He spoke and I can still hear his deep voice, full-throated and clear as a bell, resounding throughout the hall in the opening sentence of his eloquent address. I can still feel the shudder which ran through me as he vividly told of the sufferings of the Jews in the war zone, of the wretchedness of their condition, and of the horror and misery of their existence. A great wave of tenderness engulfed every fibre of my being, and my heart went out in one great outburst of pity to my stricken brethren in Europe's sacked cities and bloody fields. All about me women were sobbing openly. The man at my right was winking strangely, and the grimy hand of his neighbor was wiping away a furtive tear.
>
> Then a sharp note of appeal crept into the speaker's voice, and I thrilled in response to its magnetic quality. He was arousing American Jews to a sense of their duty. He was calling upon them to come to the rescue. I looked about me to note the effect of his words. People were straightening perceptibly in their seats. Their faces were becoming tense, and in their eyes there was shining the light of a great resolve.
>
> The speaker's tones grew louder, more compelling, more resounding. Towering above his audience, his countenance transfigured by the depth of his emotions, he reminded me of the historic figures of the ancient Hebrew Prophets. His language and utterances now were brilliant. And after a final moment during which he rose to the most sublime heights of eloquence, he concluded.

There were conflicting figures on the number of Jews in Detroit in 1916. According to the Funk & Wagnalls Jewish Encyclopedia, Detroit had 30,000 Jews in 1915. However, the April 23, 1916, issue of the *Jewish Chronicle* claimed Detroit's Jewish population had jumped from five or six thousand to 60,000 in 25 years.

Whatever the figure, the Orthodox community was worried about the future, as boys stopped their religious education around the age of 13. Rabbi Levin rallied business and community leaders for the purpose of providing advanced Jewish studies to a select group of boys of post-Bar Mitzvah age.

The first class of five was taught by Rabbi Abraham T. Rogvoy, with Rabbi Levin the principal, and Isaac August the first president. The Yeshivah, as it would become known, met in the school building attached to the Mogen Abraham Synagogue. Among the founders and funders was Isaac Rosenthal, who would also become a founder of the Yeshivah when it would become a day school, neighborhoods and decades later.

A new arrival to Detroit was Reb Hersch Cohen. Reb Hersch thought the yeshivah was a step in the right direction but only a very small step. Reb Hersch, a native of Minsk, Russia, was an imposing figure. A tall, strong man with dark hair and deep blue, piercing eyes, he had been living in the Brownsville section of Brooklyn and working as a carpenter when he wasn't immersed in advanced Jewish studies.

Reb Hersch Cohen was convinced that Detroit and America needed Jewish day schools.

His aunt, who had immigrated to Detroit a few years earlier, heard that he was living somewhere in Brooklyn and began a house-to-house search in certain areas. Not too many immigrants looked and acted as Reb Hersch did, and he already had gained a certain degree of fame for saving a family from a fire engulfing their residence. His strength and long legs allowed him to gain entry through high windows, and he carried youngsters to waiting hands below.

Reb Hersch's aunt wanted him to move to Detroit. Carpentry jobs shouldn't be hard to find with all of the construction going on, she reasoned. Besides, there were many shuls (synagogues) in which to worship. But, she stressed, she wanted him to be a mentor, a teacher to her sons, Wolf and Isadore Cohen.

Reb Hersch, his wife, and his three daughters and two sons moved to Detroit by train and settled near his aunt on Medbury Street (now the I-94 service drive) near Hastings.

Reb Hersch was taken to various shuls for services. After a few days, his younger cousin asked for his impressions. "I'm not impressed," he said. "Where are the youth?"

Reb Hersch stressed the need for a day school with a whole morning devoted to Jewish studies. He would urge his cousins, Wolf and Isadore Cohen, to help bring about a day school. A few decades later, they would.

Fresh Air Society volunteers, when not busy with camp duties, served as aides in the clinic at the Hannah Schloss Building on High Street. They helped with home care for the ill and aged and dispensed medicines, milk and proper foods. By 1916, the United Jewish Charities set up a small operating room in the clinic to perform minor operations, which saved hospital expenses. Fresh Air Society supervised the operation of the clinic and assumed its financial obligations.

For the first year time since its founding 14 years earlier, Fresh Air Camp was conducted along strictly kosher lines. Meats were brought from Detroit, and two sets of dishes were used. Authorities in charge made every effort to adhere to the dietary laws and guidelines set up by Rabbi Judah Levin.

Abraham Levin, the 19-year-old son of Rabbi Levin, president of the Michigan Menorah Society and vice-president of the Michigan Zionist Society, was elected to membership in the Phi Beta Kappa Fraternity at the University of Michigan. His brother, Isidore, three years older, was accorded a similar honor at Harvard in his junior year. As a sophomore, Isidore was chosen to Harvard's debating team and the following year was named captain.

In 1916, Beth David, based in the former Shaarey Zedek on Winder street, had a membership of 178 families. The First Hebrew Congregation of Delray formed in a house on Burdeno, just north of Jefferson and west of Fort Wayne. The Ahavas Achim organized and dedicated its synagogue at 9244 Delmar, about three-quarters of a mile east of Woodward and three-quarters of a mile north of Grand Boulevard. The newly formed Beth Yehudah Congregation held its first service in a frame dwelling on the corner of Adelaide and Hastings.

The Jewish Home for the Aged purchased a home at 318 Edmund Place, today about five blocks north of the northern entrance to Ford Field. Detroit's Branch No. 156 of the Arbeter Ring, the Workmen's Circle formed nine years earlier, became the largest in the United States and Canada. Former state senator Charles Simons, the son of Shaarey Zedek president D. W. Simons, was appointed as a Republican presidential elector. The Detroit Library Commissioners named a branch library after Bernard Ginsburg, former head of the Detroit Library Board.

President Woodrow Wilson appointed Louis D. Brandeis an associate justice with the Supreme Court, a position he would hold for the next 23 years. Brandeis, a native of Kentucky, was the first Jew to sit on the court. There were Jews in Detroit and around the country who fought against the appointment. Some thought Brandeis was too liberal, while others worried that if he made an unpopular move, all Jews would be blamed.

Detroit mourned the death of the great Jewish humorist Sholem Aleichem. Memorial services were held in most cities with sizable Jewish populations.

In 1916 you could buy a Ford for $440 or the most expensive model for $975. Ford Motor Company produced half of America's automobiles and 40 percent of the world's.

Detroit's black population reached 8,000 in 1916. The city had its first registered Girl Scout troop and the Albert Kahn-designed Detroit News Building opened on Lafayette.

Ford produced its first truck in 1917, and more cars were seen in the streets. To relieve congestion, Mayor Oscar Marx promoted the idea of a subway, while the Free Press suggested an elevated monorail system.

To help direct traffic, the city installed an elevated platform supporting a policeman responsible for regulating traffic flow on Woodward Avenue. It provided a sense of security for pedestrians and reduced reckless driving.

Jews wondered about and argued about the number of Jews residing in Detroit in 1917. Community leaders estimated the figure at 35,000. Besides places in which to worship, there were many houses of amusement in 1917. Along three blocks on Monroe Avenue, running eastward from Campus Martius, there were eleven theaters. Six presented live talent, and five were devoted to showing movies. There were many opportunities for employment in the auto industry, as 23 companies manufactured automobiles in Detroit.

Abe Rosen and his father, Sam, opened a branch of the Warsaw Bakery north of Grand Boulevard in the Westminster-Oakland area. Abe was responsible for many innovations. He placed bread on racks behind the counter so ladies couldn't pinch the bread on countertops to test its freshness. Abe sold rolls as a bakers dozen. Customers now got 13 instead of 12. He installed a container of string in the ceiling dropping down for quick, handy use. Abe Rosen's window displays of cakes for all occasions were well known. What wasn't well known, however, was that the enticing-looking cakes were made of cardboard. Abe's brother, Dave, had another Warsaw Bakery, a half-mile east of Oakland on Joseph Campau in Hamtramck.

On June 5, 1917, two months after the United States entered World War I, Detroit's males between

The Queen Anne Soap Merchandise store on the west side of Woodward near Jefferson was popular with housewives. Soap buyers saved their wrappers and redeemed them for merchandise.

the ages of 21 and 30 had to register for the draft. Boys in senior classes were presented with their diplomas early to allow them to graduate before they volunteered for service. Fort Wayne saw action by housing battalions of troops, and 65,000 of the city's men and women would serve in the armed forces.

Jews constituted only three percent of America's population in 1917. However, almost five percent of those serving in the armed forces were Jews. Eighteen percent of the serving Jews were volunteers, which also was above the national average. By the time the war ended almost 18 months later, more than 60 Detroit Jews would die while in uniform.

In August 1917, the Jewish Legion was organized by the British government. Its purpose was to drive the Turks, which had joined the Central Powers (Germany, Austria, and Hungary) out of Palestine. Joseph Sandweiss was the first Detroiter to sign up at the Hastings Street recruiting office.

Norman Cottler, who would become well-known years later for his Dexter-Davison markets, also enlisted in the Jewish Legion to fight for the liberation of Palestine from the Turkish yoke. Cottler became a corporal and served in the same battalion with David Ben-Gurion, who would become Israel's first prime minister.

British Prime Minister David Lloyd George and his Foreign Minister, Arthur Balfour, were sympathetic to the right of Jews to return to their biblical homeland and to the establishment of a Jewish state. The men were friends of Chaim Weizmann, head of the Zionist movement. Weizmann requested and received a statement from the British government supporting the establishment of a Jewish homeland in Palestine. The statement, drafted by Arthur Balfour, was delivered on November 2, 1917, and became known as the Balfour Declaration. It stated:

> *His Majesty's government view with favor the establishment in Palestine of a National Home for the Jewish people, and will use their best endeavors to facilitate the achievement of this object, it being*

clearly understood that nothing shall be done which may prejudice the civil and religious rights of existing non-Jewish communities in Palestine, or the rights and political status enjoyed by Jews in any other country.

Word of the Balfour Declaration swept across the Jewish world. Jews celebrated and danced in the streets, including in Detroit. The Reform community didn't share the excitement engulfing many others. For years, leaders of the Reform movement—including Dr. Franklin—had encouraged Jews to Americanize, not to adopt the Zionist cause, and to shed the antiquated dietery laws and other levels of observance. Dr. Franklin spoke out against Jewish soldiers based at Fort Custer, near Battle Creek, for requesting kosher food. After all, Franklin stated, they weren't in the army as Jews, but as Americans.

Joseph Papo, the first known Sephardic Jew in Detroit, arrived in 1911. Five years later, Jacob Chicorel arrived from Turkey and found a job working at the Ford Motor Company. In 1917 the Chicorels held the first high holiday services in their home for Sephardic immigrants.

Visitors from Saginaw told of a community of 1,000 Jews in 1917. Shaarey Zedek claimed a membership of 400 in 1917, but synagogue attendance was far less as many families were moving west of Twelfth Street. Through the efforts of its president, D. W. Simons, Shaarey Zedek purchased 50 acres on 14 Mile Road near Woodward, and Clover Hill Park Cemetery was established.

Business at Binyomin the Blacksmith and at Able Gross's Harness Shop and Feed Store on Hastings was declining as more Detroiters were opting for automobile use. The House of Shelter acquired a 15-room house on the corner of Winder and Brush. The new home formerly served as the Old Folks Home. Individuals or families needing temporary shelter had adequate sleeping quarters, a synagogue, reading room, and library.

Nate S. Shapero, a 26-year-old Navy Pharmacist's mate stationed in his hometown, used a borrowed $4,500 to open a drug store on the ground level of a Detroit rooming house on Cass and Ledyard. He named his new enterprise, "Economical Drug Store No. 1." The optimistic Shapero would live to a ripe old age, but would collect more stores than birthdays under the banner of Cunningham.

Abraham Levin, Fresh Air Camp's first head male counselor in 1916, graduated from the University of Michigan in 1918 and headed to camp, located about five miles from Mt. Clemens on Lake St. Clair.

Isadore Levin, Abraham's brother, rose to the rank of captain in France. His father, Rabbi Judah Levin, beamed with pride when he learned of his son's writing of the Artillery Officer's Manual, which was issued in five volumes and distributed to every artillery officer in France.

Jack Minkowsky, the son of Shaarey Zedek cantor Abraham Minkowsky, was stationed in the army in Georgia and rose to the rank of sergeant in only two months—a feat rarely accomplished. Cozzy Gottsdanker was an illustrator and cartoonist prior to his enlistment in the Navy. Jewish organizations often relied on his talent for posters prominently displayed in neighborhood stores. His talent was also put to good use by the Navy Recruiting Office on Griswold, where Gottsdanker was stationed, as his poster illustrations were distributed throughout the metropolitan area.

Max Madison, who enlisted in the Marines in April of 1917, became Detroit first Jewish war casualty a year after his enlistment. Madison crossed the Atlantic four times while aiding convoys of troops before succumbing to pneumonia. His body was shipped back to Detroit where a funeral was held from his home on Russel Street. With Rabbi Hershman officiating, a squad of soldiers from Fort Wayne accompanied the body to the Smith Street Cemetery, where the formal three volleys were fired over his grave and the bugle sounded taps.

While many Detroit men were serving in the armed forces, the women of the Jewish community did their part. The Jewish Women's Club Unit at the Phoenix Club often met on behalf of the Red Cross, as did the sisterhood of Shaarey Zedek. Rooms in the synagogue's basement were converted into hospital sewing rooms, where bandages or other items for Red

The Chesed Shel Emes would be in its Brewster Street location for five years. It would dedicate this large remodeled home on Frederick Street between Beaubien and St. Antoine in 1923.

(Courtesy of Leonard N. Simons Jewish Community Archives)

Cross use were prepared.

The Wetsman sisters were active on behalf of Hadassah projects in Shaarey Zedek and in private homes. They cut, sewed, packed and shipped items needed for the war effort.

In May 1918, about 200,000 women in Wayne County over the age of 16 registered for war work. Because of the war, jobs previously held by men were available, and women became streetcar conductors and letter carriers.

The Chesed Shel Emes, formerly the Jewish Free Burial Association, organized and purchased a home on Brewster west of St. Antoine. Land for a cemetery at 14 Mile Road and Gratiot also was purchased. The El Mosha Congregation, named after its founder, Morris Cohen, moved from the home it had been using to its first synagogue building on 29th Street and Michigan Avenue. The El Mosha was the first Jewish house of worship on Detroit's west side.

Nine Hungarian immigrant families had founded their own congregation in 1911. They worshipped in a hall on Winder and Hastings and a year later moved to the Hannah Schloss Building. In 1913, the congregation—known as Beth Eliyah or Elias Einczig, after one of its most ardent supporters—moved into a rented hall on Brewster and Hastings. In 1917, after moving into a home it purchased on Eliot near Hastings, the congregation's 70 families, under the leadership of Herman Eichner, undertook the building of its first synagogue on Garfield and Beaubien and sought funds from its members to complete the project. The four oldest of Moshe (Morris) Gunsberg's sons and his three daughter pledged $45,000, half the cost of the structure. (The pledge also was made in the hopes of a safe return of one of the sons in the army at the time.) Naming rights went to the Gunsbergs and they honored their genial, benevolent, 68-year-old father by naming the synagogue B'nai

The B'nai Moshe on Garfield and Beaubien was dedicated on March 3, 1918. Today the site is in the Medical Center.

(Courtesy of Manning Brothers HIstoric Photographic Collection)

Moshe. Membership reached 300 families by the time dedication took place on Sunday, March 3, 1918. Speakers included Detroit's leading Orthodox rabbis and Dr. Franklin of Temple Beth El. The main auditorium of 700 was filled to capacity, and the 300 spaces in the balcony were almost filled.

Dr. Leo M. Franklin was vice president of the Central Conference of American Rabbis. In their annual convention held in Chicago in June 1918, the Reform rabbis issued a statement regarding their reaction to the Balfour Declaration. The gist of it was:

> *We are opposed to the idea that Palestine should be considered THE homeland of the Jews. Jews in America are part of the American nation. The ideal of the Jew is not the establishment of a Jewish state—not the reassertion of Jewish nationality which has long been outgrown. We believe that our survival as a people is dependent upon the assertion and maintenance of our historical religious role and not upon acceptance of Palestine as a homeland of the Jewish people. The mission of the Jew is to witness to God all over the world.*

The present Detroit city charter went into effect in 1918. The ward system was abolished, and the elected nine-member Common Council was adopted. Seventy-year-old James Vernor—founder of the Ginger Ale Company—was the oldest councilman, and David W. Simons, the well-known public lighting commissioner and president of Shaarey Zedek, was the first Jewish member of the council.

Jewish Detroiters joined thousands of others swarming around Campus Martius to celebrate the end of the war on November 11. The festivities were tempered by the fact that 1,360 Detroiters, including more than 60 Jews, were killed serving their country.

Detroit's Jews were also pained to learn about the pogroms taking place in Poland. The December 6, 1918, *Jewish Chronicle* carried a front page report based on a series of cables received by Zionist organizations:

> On November 23rd, after all the wine cellars of the city had been looted, the massacres began. At first Legionaires slew several Jews walking in the streets. Afterward they drove the Jews into their homes and slaughtered whole families. Several families were entirely exterminated. Several hundred men and women who had fled into the synagogues, hoping the Poles would respect these holy places, met death in the flames to which the Legionaires consigned the synagogues. The number of victims in the synagogues was over a hundred.
>
> The whole Jewish quarter was cut off by the Legionaires and every house systematically destroyed by fire and bombs. People who fled from the burning houses were driven back by Legionaires using bayonets. They were either burned or slain.

In February 1919, the *Jewish Chronicle* changed hands as Joseph J. Cummins and Nathan J. Gould assumed control from Anton Kaufman, and within the year the paper would be renamed the *Detroit Jewish Chronicle*.

Max Milgrom and Jacob Soberman were part of a committee that oversaw the purchase of the Beth Yehuda Cemetery near 14 Mile Road and Gratiot in Mt. Clemens. The two immigrants, with five years of experience as house painters, borrowed money and opened a small paint and wallpaper store on Hastings Street. The business would eventually lead to the manufacture of paints and the establishment of the Mercury Paint Company.

James Couzens, one of Henry Ford's early partners, sold his Ford stock for over $29 million in 1919. Besides becoming one of the city's wealthiest men, Couzens became mayor of Detroit. Detroit's five largest stove companies employed almost 5,000 workers in 1919, and Dr. Franklin was elected president of the Central Conference of American Rabbis (Reform) and founded Temple Beth El's Men's Club. Jews pointed with pride to Meyer L. Prentis. Eight years after he began employment with General Motors and became chief accountant and auditor for the corporation, he was elected treasurer.

The Tifereth Israel Congregation was formed on Cameron Avenue, a block east of Oakland and less than three-quarters of a mile north of Grand Boulevard. The Detroit Stars of the Negro National League began playing their games at Mack Park. The shabby little wooden ballpark had 6,000 seats and was located on Mack and Fairview, a half-mile east of the Fischer Street shul.

Detroit's Jewish Legionnaires received a $25 bonus upon their return from the Zionist Organization of Detroit. Captain Mose Weingarden won a promotion to battalion chief for 27 years of meritorious service with the Detroit Fire Department. The Jewish Women's Club purchased a home on Rowena Street to be used as a center for Jewish working girls. The purpose was to establish a place with homelike surroundings where women could meet each other and strangers to the city could interact with Detroit's working women.

Captain Isadore Levin was ready to leave military service in France and return home to Detroit and begin a law career. Approached by Zionist leaders on the eve of his departure, Levin accepted their plea that he stay in Paris to help draft and give counsel on a

Isadore Levin

system of laws for the proposed Jewish state in Palestine.

Levin was looking forward to seeing friends and family in Detroit. In a letter he penned his emotions and it was printed in the April 25, 1919, issue of the *Detroit Jewish Chronicle:*

I am in truth very happy to be able to do a little in the way of a direct contribution to our cause. We are today face to face with an opportunity the like of which has not come to the Jewish people in two thousand years. Now is the time for everyone to help in the task of making the best of this extraordinary opportunity. The realization of our centuries old dream is close at hand, and with some effort on the part of all of us it can be brought to pass.

The United Hebrew Schools organized as a religious-educational institution. The first branch was located at Wilkins and Hastings. It became known as the Wilkins Street Talmud Torah and Kindergarten and opened with 625 students, 30 in the kindergarten class. Ten instructors were under the direction of Bernard Isaacs, and Rabbi Ezekiel Aishishkin led the Board of Education. Esser Rabinowitz, the well known Hebraist, became president, and officers included Isaac Rosenthal. The opening of the Wilkins Street School resulted in the closing of a single old home being used on Columbia and Hastings as a Talmud Torah for 40 overcrowded students.

The aim of the organization was to create a system of institutions that would serve the needs of the community as a whole, not merely of one locality. The parochial department, where Hebrew was taught in the morning and English subjects in the afternoon, had an enrollment of 50 students. The remaining 545 pupils attended sessions after public school hours. After the first week of sessions, Sabbath morning services were inaugurated for the youth of the community, a forerunner of junior congregations.

While Fresh Air Camp opened near Lake St. Clair, Fresh Air Society equipped and opened a dental clinic in the basement of the Hannah Schloss Building on High Street near Hastings. Dr. Benjamin Welling, a dental surgeon, volunteered his services two mornings per week and was assisted in operating the clinic by five other dentists.

In June of 1919, Sholom Asch, the world famous Yiddish writer, returned to New York after touring the stark conditions of Jews in Lithuania and painted a heart-rending picture of starvation and destitution that was published in the Yiddish and English Jewish press:

They had lived there for hundreds of years, and in one day and one night they were uprooted, not

The first branch of the United Hebrew School was on Wilkins and Hastings.

(Courtesy of United Hebrew Schools)

only the healthy, but the sick. The beds had to be carried out of the hospitals with their sick occupants, and when they died they had to be left on the road without burial. When the Russians stopped fighting, 50 to 70 per cent of the Jews returned to the site of their homes. In the smaller towns the percentage was even smaller. The rest of them are in Russia, Siberia, and heaven knows where. Thousands have perished of hunger, cold, and disease.

Those that got back found their property destroyed, stores entered, homes devastated. In the interval between the departure of the Russians and the arrival of the Germans, the local Christian population took advantage of the Jews and carried away all their property. Even furniture, bedding, doors, and windows were stolen.

President Woodrow Wilson sent a mission in September 1919 to investigate atrocities against Jews in Poland and Russia. Almost immediately upon entering Minsk, they became eyewitnesses to another pogrom resulting in the death of 31 Jews and the destruction of over 500 homes and shops. Besides the murder of five children, scores were wounded and mutilated.

Rabbi Nathan Krass of New York spent three months as a representative of the American Jewish Relief Committee touring parts of Europe to help alleviate conditions of the suffering Jews. Rabbi Krass was known to Detroiters through his fund-raising efforts. His letter to the *Detroit Jewish Chronicle* in October 1919 stirred emotions:

When the people heard that I was from the United States, they crowded around me, trying to kiss my coat and begging me to ask my country to keep them from starvation," Dr. Krass said. "I saw hundreds of orphans on the streets, wasted children who were either too weary to cry or who cried as grownup people do, turning away their faces to hide their tears. I saw thousands of starving mothers who were desolate, not on their own account alone, but because they had no food to give their children. I saw people living on one cup of soup a day who saved some of that to give cripples who could not go after their own.

There are thousands and thousands of starving Jews in Rumania without shoes, almost without clothes. In Vienna, alone, there are between 30,000 to 40,000 refugee Jews, living on the plate of soup and the piece of bread that they get every day from the Jewish relief stations. They cannot yet return to their homes."

While Detroit's Jews were worried about relatives and fellow Jews in Poland and Russia, they failed to see the growing menace in Germany. Berlin was being flooded with anti-Semitic literature as magazines, weeklies, and monthlies carried numerous anti-Jewish articles. The situation in Hamburg was worse as leaflets were distributed urging gentiles to boycott Jewish establishments.

It was during this period that a world famous Russian pianist, whose Jewish identity was known only to a select few besides his wife, moved to Detroit to become conductor of the Detroit Symphony Orchestra. Ossip Gabrilowitsch was married to soprano Clara Clemens, the daughter of writer Mark Twain.

Ossip Gabrilowitsch, a Russian Jew, conducted the Detroit Symphony Orchestra when Orchestra Hall opened in 1919.
(Courtesy of Burton Historical Collection, Detroit Public Library)

8
1920-1924
ZIONISM AND ANTI-SEMITISM

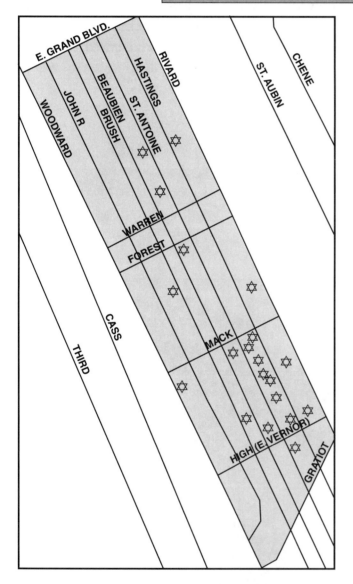

The Hastings Street area's Jewish population in 1920. Shaded area indicates highest Jewish population density. Synagogues are indicated with a ✡.

(Map courtesy of Phillip Applebaum)

In 1920, Detroit's population of 993,678 was ranked fourth in the nation. In only 20 years the population had increased by over 700,000, and in ten years the population had increased by about 528,000. 290,884 of Detroit's 1920 residents were foreign born.

The black population grew by 611 percent in only ten years, from 5,741 to 40,838, or 4.1 percent of Detroit's 1920 total. According to the New York-based Conference on Jewish Relations, a Jewish population study claimed that Detroit had 51,000 Jews. The U.S. Centennial Census of 1920 placed Detroit's Jewish population at 40,000. Detroit's community leaders put the figure closer to 35,000.

Most of the Jewish population was condensed along the Hastings corridor north of Adams and extending north of East Grand Boulevard. Some families were becoming part of the small Oakland community about a mile north of East Grand Boulevard.

Streetcars running down Hastings Street were crowded with young men and women on summer Sundays. A transfer to the Jefferson car and a walk across the bridge to the area in back of the Belle Isle Casino was known as "Yiddish Territory." Young people would congregate to see and be seen and to discuss current events. Hebrew and Yiddish melodies would be sung, along with the latest popular songs in English. Most of the youths would be back the following Sunday and the social ritual would be repeated.

D. W. Simons stepped aside as president of Shaarey Zedek after a long reign and was succeeded by Joseph Wetsman. Wetsman's daughter, Sarah, married Ralph Davidson in the family home on Virginia Park. They would become the parents of well-known industrialist and Pistons owner Bill Davidson.

The Detroit Hebrew Orphan Home was established. Men and women served on the board until squabbling caused a split along gender lines. The women formed a Hebrew Ladies' Baby Day Nursery, and both institutions operated on Rowena Street. The Talmud Torahs on Division and Wilkins Streets

Jewish Congregations in 1920

Bais Moshe	High Street west of Hastings	Rev. David Golden
Ben Jacob	Brewster Street west of Hastings	Rabbi Joseph Eisenman
Beth Abraham	Winder between Hastings and St. Antoine	Rabbi Jacob Thumin
Beth David	Winder between Beaubien and St. Antoine	Rabbi Ezekiel Aishishkin
Beth Hamedresh Hagodol	Wilkins between Beaubien and St. Antoine	Rabbi Joseph Eisenman
Beth Jacob	Montcalm between Hastings and St. Antoine	Rabbi Judah Levin
Beth Tephilo	Napoleon between Beaubien and St. Antoine	Rabbi Joseph Eisenman
B'nai Israel	Ferry between Beaubien and St. Antoine	Rabbi Judah Levin
B'nai Moshe	Garfield and Beaubien	Rabbi Joseph Thumin
El Moshe	Twenty-Ninth north of Michigan Avenue	Rabbi Raphael Spalter
First Hebrew Congregation of Delray	Burdeno north of Jefferson	Rev. Abraham Rubenstein
Mishkan Israel	Benton and St. Antoine	Rabbi Gabriel Zacutta
Mogen Abraham	Farnsworth between Beaubien and St. Antoine	Rabbi Judah Levin
Nusach Hari	Alfred east of Hastings	Rabbi Ezekiel Aishishkin
Shaarey Zedek	Brush and Willis	Rabbi Abraham Hershman
Tiferes Israel	Wilkins west of Hastings	None
Temple Beth El	Woodward between Erskine and Eliot	Dr. Leo Franklin

Some of Detroit's rabbis in 1920. From left: Rabbi Judah Levin, Rabbi Abraham Hershman, Rabbi Jacob Thumin, and Rabbi Ezekiel Aishishkin.

(Courtesy of Archives of Congregation Shaarey Zedek)

merged and the name United Hebrew Schools of Detroit was formally adopted. Temple Beth El outgrew its facility on Woodward and Eliot, and plans were unveiled for a larger structure about a mile and a quarter farther north on the northwest corner of Gladstone and Woodward.

Congregation Beth Moses bought 10 acres of land on Masonic Boulevard and Little Mack near Gratiot in Mt. Clemens as a cemetery for its members, then resold five and one-half acres to other congregations. Mt. Clemens dedicated the new building of eight-year-old congregation Beth Tefilath Moses. Congregation Mogen Abraham, located in the heart of Detroit's Jewish community on Farnsworth near Hastings, had 243 members in 1920.

Membership in the Phoenix Club and Redford Country Club were growing, and the Jewish social organizations that were operating under the banner of the Phoenix Club, at John R. and Erskine, decided to elect separate boards of directors and governing heads. Shaarey Zedek trustee Harry B. Keidan, former attorney and assistant prosecutor of Wayne County, was appointed by the governor as one of the judges of the newly created Municipal Court.

A Frankfort newspaper claimed that "Jews in Germany may become extinct." The article claimed that with the closing of the doors of Germany to Jewish immigration, the Jews of Germany would disappear as "birth control, baptism, and the high intermarriage rate would cause the complete annihilation of German Jewry."

News of violent activities by Polish soldiers outraged Detroit's Jewish community. Graves in the Vilna Jewish Cemetery were desecrated. According to reports, soldiers broke the fence and tombstone at the grave of the "Vilna Gaon" (Outstanding Scholar). Worse, however, was what the soldiers did to the living. Jews were arrested on the pretext that their passports must be examined for irregularities. All of the arrested, from children to old men, were taken to barracks and mercilessly tortured by Polish soldiers. Young Jewish women suffered indignities and brutal flogging at the whim of the soldiers.

A British commission was sent to investigate the conditions in Poland and found that 348 Jews had been killed in the pogroms and a far larger number were injured. The report concluded that the Polish masses believed that Jews required the blood of Christian children for ritual purposes.

In 1920, in a place called San Remo, a resort town

Rabbis and dignitaries were part of the estimated 10,000 Detroit Jews participating in a joyous demonstration on Memorial Day 1920.

(Courtesy of Archives of Congregation Shaarey Zedek)

in Liguria, northwestern Italy on the Riviera, a handful of the world's leaders met to draw up articles that would give Jews their long-promised homeland.

Detroit's Jews came together all too often to lament the situation in Europe. Memorial Day, 1920, provided another chance to get together. The demonstration, though, would be a joyous one as the promise of the future and remembrances of the past would come together.

The celebrants were estimated at 10,000, and marchers included the community's elder statesmen and children of all ages attending the Talmud Torahs. Jewish Legionnaires and war veterans headed the impressive parade that began from the Shaarey Zedek on Brush and Willis. In one of his earliest bylines in the *Detroit Jewish Chronicle*, 24-year-old Phillip Slomovitz wrote:

> *Everywhere the blue and white of the Jewish flag mingled its folds with the Stars and Stripes and the Union Jack. Nearly two thousand years of mourning were forgotten by the 10,000 Detroit Jews who signified by this demonstration their determination to perpetuate their ancient traditions on the soil of their fathers, and to lend their support to every project making for that end.*
>
> *More than three miles in length, the line of march took over two hours to pass a certain point. headed by Capt. Herman Waiss, the grand marshal, who rode on horseback, the line of march started from Willis avenue and Brush street at 2 p.m., going west to Woodward to Adams avenue and returning through Hastings street. Capt. Waiss was followed by the bearers of the American, British and Jewish banners, the Jewish colors being carried by Private Bookstein, who fought with the Jewish Legion in Palestine. Then came approximately 200 veterans of the World War and an additional 55 members of the Jewish Legion.*
>
> *The Jewish Legion members were followed by several members of the Zionist District Board of Detroit, including Rabbi A. M. Hershman and Mr. Fred M. Butzel, these being followed in turn by the Rabbis Levin, Aishishkin, Eisenman and Thumim. Then came the second of the 70-odd divisions in the parade, a division which has been named by a number of people who witnessed the parade as "The Hope of the Jewish People." Never before in the history of Detroit's parades was there a division so beautiful, so impressive, and the memory of this part of the line of march will ever live with those who have seen it.*

In its November 5, 1920, issue, the *Detroit Jewish Chronicle* told of its move from the Book Building on Washington Boulevard to its own building on High Street and Grand River. The *Chronicle* issued a lengthy front page statement, part of which read:

> *With the recent census report and city directory statistics came the realization that more than 80,000 Jews had made Detroit their home. Without seeking to differentiate between Reform and Conservative, Zionist and Anti-Zionist, Jews of the old world or Jews of this, the new, the Detroit Jewish Chronicle endeavored to record the activities of all and to find something of interest to all in the Jewish news of the city, the state, the nation and the world.*

While many didn't agree with the *Chronicle's* estimate of Detroit's Jewish population, even fewer Detroiters agreed with the articles being published under Henry Ford's name. Starting in 1920, Ford used his weekly *Dearborn Independent* newspaper to blame Jews for the world's social and economic problems.

Henry Ford

(Courtesy of Michigan Views)

The Ford International Weekly
THE DEARBORN INDEPENDENT

$1.50   Dearborn, Michigan, September 3, 1921   Ten Cents

The Peace Dove's Chances in Washington

The Peril of Baseball—
"Too Much Jew"

The First of Two Articles

What Do You Know About Muscle Shoals?

William Allen White, Editor, Politician and Novelist
A Forty Million Dollar Bridge at 'Frisco Bay
Borrowed Stimulants Keep Austria Alive

Mr. Ford's Page   Editorials   Briefly Told and Many Other Interesting Features

---

Jews Are Not Good Sportsmen

AND this is not of our own choosing. Baseball is a trivial matter compared with some of the facts that are awaiting publication. Yet it is possible to see the operation of the Jewish Idea in baseball as clearly as in any other field. The process is the same, whether in war or politics, in finance or in sports.

To begin with, Jews are not sportsmen. This is not set down in complaint against them, but merely as analysis. It may be a defect in their character, or it may not; it is nevertheless a fact which discriminating Jews unhesitatingly acknowledge. Whether this is due to their physical lethargy, their dislike of unnecessary physical action, or their serious cast of mind, others may decide; the Jew is not naturally an out-of-door sportsman; if he takes up golf it is because his station in society calls for it, not that he really likes it; and if he goes in for collegiate athletics, as some of the younger Jews are doing, it is because so much attention has been called to their neglect of the sports that the younger generation thinks it necessary to remove that occasion of remark.

And yet, the bane of American sports today is the presence of a certain type of Jew, not as a participant but as an exploiter and corrupter. If he had been a sportsman for the love of sport he might have been saved from becoming an exploiter and corrupter, for there is no mind to which the corrupting of a sport is more illogical and even unexplainable than the mind of the man who participates in it.

Exploiting and Corrupting Clean Sports

Above left: Each issue of Henry Ford's *Dearborn Independent* carried an anti-Jewish headline.

Above right: The Henry Ford sponsored publication blamed Jews for the world's social and economic ills, including supposed corruption of America's national pastime.

Right: This box appeared in the *Dearborn Independent* for several weeks in 1921.

(All photos courtesy of Burton Historical Collection, Detroit Public Library)

VOLUME two of this series of Jewish Studies is now off the press. It is entitled "Jewish Activities in the United States," being the second volume of "The International Jew," twenty-two articles, 256 pages. Sent to any address at the cost of printing and mailing, which is 25 cents.

Besides being sold on the street, the paper reached all corners of the country, as all Ford agencies carried the publication.

Over a span of 91 consecutive issues, Ford published four brochures, each containing articles compiled from the *Dearborn Independent* and retitled, "The International Jew." Foreign anti-Semites translated the articles into most European languages.

Jewish weeklies around the country, as well as some of the leading dailies, editorialized against Ford's views. Ford, though, was unfazed.

WWJ (then known as 8MK), operating out of the Detroit News Building on Lafayette and Second, became the country's first commercial radio station. An estimated 100 to 300 people listening with homemade sets heard announcer Frank Edwards give the station's call letters, followed by a phonograph recording of "Roses of Picardy," followed by "Taps." Women felt more liberated in the new decade as they voted for the first time in a general primary election, after serving as jurors for the first time the previous year in county courts.

A few blocks west of the heart of the Jewish community, the white Vermont marble Italian Renaissance-style Main Library opened on Woodward at Kirby in 1921. A few blocks north on Grand Boulevard, the Albert Kahn-designed General Motors Building was completed.

Assembly line mass production reduced the price of Model Ts from $850 in 1908 to $260 in 1921. The Detroit Police Department boasted it had the world's first radio-equipped car, a Model A Ford, to help patrol the streets.

The Agricultural Society gave the state of Michigan 164 acres on the east side of Woodward south of Eight Mile Road to host the annual Michigan State Fair.

In May 1921, an estimated crowd of 25,000 welcomed Dr. Chaim Weizmann, president of the World Zionist Commission, and his associates on their visit to Detroit. A crowd of admirers swarmed the large lobby of the impressive Michigan Central Depot, and most followed the group as it went to City Hall and on to Shaarey Zedek, where the children of the combined Hebrew schools sang and paraded with flags. Mayor Frank Couzens issued the following proclamation:

> *Because of the eminent character of this Zionist leader, and whereas, a great portion of our population is of the Jewish race and exceedingly interested in the national aspirations of the Zionists, I*

In May 1921, Dr. Chaim Weizmann was met by a large crowd at the Michigan Central Depot.

(Courtesy of Michigan Views)

respectfully call upon all citizens of Detroit who are in sympathy with this splendid work to decorate their buildings with American colors and flags of Zion on this day, and to assist in extending a hearty welcome to the distinguished visitor.

The *Detroit Jewish Chronicle* published pictures of European Jewish children orphaned in pogroms and World War One. Heart-wrenching biographies of the children were given to urge readers to donate funds. The *Chronicle* claimed, "It costs $100 a year to care for one Jewish war orphan or about two dollars a week. And there are more than 200,000 of them!"

The *Detroit Yiddish Daily—Der Weg* (The Way)—folded in its second year of operation. Readers of Detroit's Jewish papers were following the progress of 16-year-old Emma Lazaroff, who studied at the Detroit Conservatory of Music and the Julliard School of Music. The future Mrs. Schaver made her debut at the inaugural performance of the Detroit Civic Opera Company in 1921.

Tigers owner Frank Navin donated the use of Navin Field free of charge to B'nai B'rith for a Sunday afternoon game between teams from the Detroit and Toledo B'nai B'rith lodges. Fifteen hundred children from various Detroit orphanages were guests of B'nai B'rith as funds were raised for charitable purposes by charging spectators fifty cents.

The Ohel Moshe School, on Twenty-Ninth off Michigan a mile and a quarter up Michigan Avenue from the Tigers' ballpark, affiliated with the United Hebrew Schools. The Ahavas Achim Talmud Torah also joined United Hebrew Schools, as did the Hebrew Free School of Congregation Mogen Abraham on Farnsworth.

Congregation Ahavath Zion was organized on the southeast corner of Holbrook and Brush. Rabbi Samuel Fine was installed as spiritual leader. A few blocks north, the small Atereth Zvi congregation was established on Cameron near Mt. Vernon. Rabbi Isidore Strauss was in charge of religious services.

Edwin G. Pipp, former editor of the *Detroit News*, became one of the founders and editors of the *Dearborn Independent*. Pipp later quit in protest when the paper adopted its anti-Semitic stance and started his own publication, *Pipp's Weekly*. In a May 1921 issue, Pipp claimed that Henry Ford arranged for eleven men to go to Europe and search for materials with which to prove accusations that being made against the Jews were true. Part of Pipp's editorial read:

The Ford paper started out a year ago to prove that there was an international conspiracy among the Jews to bring on war to their own profit.

I personally have heard Mr. Ford say he could prove it.

He and his men have had a whole year in which to prove it, and have failed miserably.

They have looked into the character and personal acts of hundreds of American Jews and found nothing to prove their charge.

They have had detectives, experts hired away from the government, go over the country in search of anything that would give a semblance of truth to their anti-Semitic campaign, and could prove nothing.

The Ahavath Zion on the southeast corner of Holbrook and Brush was built in 1921.

They have had the business manager of their paper and others gumshoe the country to get stuff with which to discredit the Jew, and have gotten nothing but a libel suit.

Not satisfied with getting prejudice from European sympathizers who have brought old world hatred here, and from one who was convicted and sentenced to prison for serving the enemies of our government in time of war, they are now going to the seat of anti-Semitic propaganda.

Sleuths are to scour the old world for hatred that may bring more bitterness to our own country.

"Get the stuff, or you will be brought back and others sent in your place," these muck-rakers are told.

I should like to ask Mr. Ford if that is running the paper along the lines that he was he was going to run it when we started it together?

Is that going to lead to kindness among neighbors?

The Detroit Fire Department was entirely motorized by 1922, and the police department had several radio-equipped cars to receive messages. WWJ had two wires extended 290 feet to the Fort Shelby Hotel, increasing its broadcast range. On February 15, 1922, Ossip Gabrilowitsch, the Detroit Symphony Orchestra, and WWJ teamed up to broadcast the country's first concert on radio. The city added another radio station on May 4, 1922, when WCX began broadcasting. It soon merged into WJR.

Eleven-year-old Hy Horenstein started his deli career as a busboy and dishwasher at the original Boesky's, for owner Sam Boesky, on Hastings and Farnsworth. Twenty-two year old David Wachler moved to Detroit and started a downtown jewelry business. By the next century, nine Wachlers would work at the suburban David Wachler & Sons. Seven-

Hastings Street between Kirby and Frederick in 1922. Farnsworth was a block south, and the large Hebrew school on Kirby and St. Antoine was a block west.

(Courtesy of Manning Brothers HIstoric Photographic Collection)

teen-year-old soprano Emma Lazaroff was the star soloist for the Hebrew play *Samson & Delilah* at Orchestra Hall. Newspaper critics had praised her previous operatic work at the age of 16. The Phoenix Club celebrated its fiftieth anniversary in 1922 with gala balls and other celebrated events.

Entering its second year, the Workmen's Circle Yiddish School merged with the Peretz School. Students received a Jewish secular education. An impressive parade of automobiles and 500 students from the United Hebrew Schools began from the Wilkins Street Talmud Torah to Kirby and St. Antoine on Sunday afternoon, July 21, 1922, for the cornerstone laying ceremony of the school's new headquarters. After 21 years of existence as the Women's Auxiliary of Temple Beth El, its name was changed to the Sisterhood of Temple Beth El.

The family of Isaac Agree organized a congregation as a memorial. Services were held in a home on Rosedale Court, four blocks north of Boston Boulevard near Brush. It would evolve into the Downtown Synagogue. The Shaarey Tephilah Congregation, at 1227 Eastlawn between Jefferson and Kercheval, was chartered in 1922.

The country's Jewish leaders had formed the Industrial Removal Office in 1901. Its purpose was to relocate immigrant Jews from New York to cities with smaller Jewish populations. The organization sent over 3,000 men to Detroit between its formation and its liquidation in 1922.

Most Jewish youngsters in Detroit were avid baseball fans. Their fathers, many still uncomfortable with the English language, attended ballgames with their sons at Navin Field, even though the Tigers didn't have a Jewish player in 1922. In fact, most teams didn't have a single Jewish player, and very few franchise owners were Jewish.

That didn't stop Henry Ford, however, for blaming Jews in two lengthy articles in the *Dearborn Independent* for problems afflicting baseball, from unruly fans to gambling on games. Ford summed up his opinions by stating:

If fans wish to know the trouble with American baseball, they have it in three words—too much Jew. Get rid of the Jews and their money-grubbing character and baseball and the world in general would be a better place.

The Tigers didn't participate in the 1922 World Series, but WWJ made news and friends by broadcasting results after each inning. The station had loud-

A patrolman directs traffic at Woodward and Congress in 1922. The country's first overhead suspended light at Woodward and Michigan is visible in the center of the photo.

(Courtesy of Burton Historical Collection, Detroit Public Library)

speakers set up in Grand Circus Park, and crowds gathered to hear the latest score from the game in Yankee Stadium.

The University of Detroit faculty announced it had purchased a large site at Livernois and Six Mile Road for a new campus, including an athletic stadium. John C. Lodge became acting mayor of over a million Detroiters on December 5, 1922, when Mayor James Couzens resigned to become a United States Senator.

In 1922, two small vacated kosher poultry stores at Westminster and Delmar were transformed into a clinic managed by the Fresh Air Society. It marked the beginning of the North End Clinic.

After 18 years of holding Sunday services, Temple Beth El continued the practice in its new edifice on Woodward and Gladstone. Three days of special programs and services marked the dedication of the new building in November 1922. Emanuel Wodic, who had served in the Civil War and came dressed in his military uniform, was given the honor of lighting the perpetual light and reciting the appropriate verses from the bible. The 18-foot-high Aron Kodesh (Holy Ark), which had served Temple Beth El in its three previous structures, was sold to Congregation Tephilath Moses in Mt. Clemens, and installed in its new sanctuary.

Close to 2,000 people packed the hall of the new United Hebrew Schools headquarters on Kirby and St. Antoine for its dedication in January 7, 1923. *Detroit Jewish Chronicle* reporter Philip Slomovitz was very moved by Rabbi A. M. Hershman's keynote address. In a front page story in the January 12, issue, Slomovitz wrote:

Rabbi Hershman pointed out in his address, which was perhaps the most inspiring lecture ever heard in this city, that the education of the Jewish youth is the most important problem affecting our people. He said that the education of youth stood first and continued:

"We turn to the young to help us perpetuate the Jewish spirit. The Jewish boy is the father of the Jew to be. If we want Jews and Jewesses who should be spiritually Jewish through and through, we must begin with the child. There are hundreds of young men whom we may call disloyal, but who will have a perfect right to turn to us and charge us with the responsibility of having kept them ignorant of Jewish things and Jewish ideals."

Referring to the growth of materialism, Rabbi Hershman said that what the world will condone in the non-Jew it will condemn in the Jew and the with the lack of education in the Jewish youth, materialism will increase to the detriment of the entire people. "Jews have no right to be materialists," Rabbi Hershman declared. "What a minyan good Jews accomplish will be undone by half a minyan of bad

Temple Beth El member Albert Kahn designed the impressive structure on Woodward at Gladstone, which opened in 1922.

(Courtesy of the Rabbi Leo M. Franklin Archives of Temple Beth El)

The Kirby Street United Hebrew Schools building opened in 1923.

(Photo by author)

Jews, and bad Jews don't need a minyan.

"Our slogan should be 'Back to the Bible.' We Jews will disappear and will suffer without the Bible. Without our Isaiah and our Jeremiah, without our prophets and the Bible we cannot exist and ought not to exist.

"Your children may not attend this school, and the children of your friends may not attend it. But as long as Jewish children attend the school you should support it, because it is your work. In Moscow the education of the young is done in secret and in dug-outs because religious training is forbidden in Russia and the parents nevertheless forego food and starve in order to be able to educate their young. Here we have the opportunity of freely offering the young a good Jewish education and we ought to show our appreciation of this privilege and thank God for it by supplying the schools with the means of existence. In return for your money you will receive something vastly greater—the satisfaction of knowing that your future is assured."

The new building, the largest Talmud Torah in the country, contained 14 classrooms and a large auditorium. A popular feature of the new building was the children's synagogue, where students would conduct services every Saturday morning under the supervision of the teachers. The new Talmud Torah also served as a communal center for local organizations, and was available for Bar Mitzvahs and other celebrations.

With the opening of the Kirby Street building, the 700 students assigned there, the 400 at the Wilkins school, and 350 students farther north in the Delmar-Westminster district comprised the main branches of the United Hebrew Schools.

The Hebrew Free Loan office moved to the Kirby street UHS building and the Benevolent Loan Association was formed by the Ladies' Auxiliary of B'nai B'rith. The organization planned to place boxes bearing the inscription, "A penny a day keeps sorrow away," in every home, creating the foundation of the fund. The object of the new organization was to offer interest-free loans to needy families.

In a survey of the Detroit Jewish community of 1923, it claimed a population of 34,727, of whom approximately sixty percent were foreign born. Ben Canvasser relocated his kosher meat market from Hastings Street to Twelfth Street at Gladstone as more families were moving into the area. The University of Detroit conferred an honorary doctorate upon Rabbi Leo M. Franklin. Temple Beth El published the first issue of the *Bethelite*, the newspaper of the Religious

Saul Rabinowitz, founder and first president of Beth David (now B'nai David).

The impressive front edifice, on the Taylor Street side, of the large Congregation Emanuel synagogue. The synagogue would become known as the "Taylor Shul."

(Author's collection)

The Beth Abraham opened on Palmer Street in 1923.

(Photo by Joe Kramer)

School. The Yeshiva (forerunner of the Yeshiva Beth Yehudah) moved from its Farnsworth Talmud Torah Building next to Congregation Mogen Abraham, to rented rooms on Rosedale Court near Oakland. *The Ten Commandments* opened in Detroit movie theaters. The Yiddish Theater of Detroit opened its season at Orchestra Hall with the comedy, *Woman's Secrets,* starring Boris Tomashefsky.

In 1923 the original stands along the foul lines at Navin Field were double-decked, and a press box was built on the roof. Detroiters dialed their own local calls for the first time, and a new police headquarters went up on Beaubien between Clinton and Macomb. The new Belle Isle Bridge, measuring 2,356 feet long, opened. The Detroit Automobile Club, forerunner of Automobile Club of Michigan, installed Detroit's first stop signs.

In 1923 the Workmen's Circle, or Arbeter Ring, claimed nearly 800 dues-paying members. Outsiders considered them strong supporters of socialist causes. The Workmen's Circle schools instructed the children in Yiddish, and the curriculum focused on Yiddish literature and Jewish history. For the second time in two years, Detroit greeted Dr. Chaim Weizmann. A luncheon was held at the Wolverine Hotel on Witherell near Montcalm. In the evening, the world Zionist Jewish leader addressed a mass meeting in the auditorium of Temple Beth El.

In August 1923, Detroiters and Jews around the world were saddened by the death of President Warren G. Harding. The 57-year-old Harding, in the waning months of his presidency, was vacationing in San Francisco when he was felled by a heart attack. Harding was eulogized as a friend of the Jews and a strong, vocal supporter of a Jewish national homeland. In a recent statement on the subject, Harding had said:

> *It has seemed the definite assurance to the Jewish people that their long aspiration for reestablishment of Jewish nationality in the homeland of this great people is to be definitely realized. This is an event of notable significance, not only to the Jewish people but to their friends and well-wishers everywhere, among whom the American nation has always been proud to be numbered.*

Sol Rabinowitz, the founder of the Beth David Congregation on Winder Street and its president for many years, died at the age of 68. At the time of his death, Rabinowitz was president of the Agudath Achim Synagogue on Hastings Street and president of a local Talmud Torah. Leopold Wineman, the president and founder of People's Outfitting Company, died at the age of 71 at his home on Kirby.

The Chesed Shel Emes, formerly the Jewish Free Burial Association, moved from Brewster Street and ceremoniously opened its new building on Frederick Street, between Beaubien and St. Antoine. The Beth Abraham moved from Winder and Hastings and dedicated its new building on the northeast corner of Palmer and Beaubien. Ground was broken for Congregation Emanuel's new synagogue on the corner of Taylor and Woodrow Wilson in the northwest Twelfth Street section. Congregation Shaarey Zion organized and held its first services on Indiandale Avenue between Linwood and Twelfth, south of Davison.

An imposing reception met 44-year-old, Hungarian-born Rabbi Moses Fischer and his family on Sunday, August 26, 1923. After serving Chicago's largest Hungarian congregation for 20 years, Rabbi Fischer assumed the pulpit at the B'nai Moshe, at Garfield and Beaubien, and the Delray Hungarian Congregation on Burdeno.

Leading members of both congregations met the Fischers at the Michigan Central Depot and escorted Detroit's new residents to their home at 448 Ferry, west of Beaubien. Later in the afternoon, most of the membership of both congregations, along with community leaders and rabbis, escorted Rabbi Fischer east on Ferry to Beaubien and then south to Garfield. Rabbi Fischer entered the B'nai Moshe Synagogue under a hand-held canopy escorted by almost a hundred men. A large American flag was carried behind the canopy.

Henry Ford's compiled anti-Semitic articles in the *Dearborn Independent* were sold throughout Switzerland. Publicity over Ford's summer visit to Switzerland spurred sales.

Detroit's Jews were constantly reminded of Henry Ford's activities. This was the editorial in the August 17, 1923, edition of the *Detroit Jewish Chronicle:*

The Ford Method

From November, 1920, to may, 1922, there appeared in the Dearborn Independent a series of abusive and vituperative articles on the International Jew. These articles were subsequently collected and reprinted in book form: vol. 1, The World's Foremost Problem; vol. 2, Jewish Activities in the United States; vol. 3, Jewish Influences in American life; vol. 4, Aspects of Jewish Power in the United States. These articles aroused such protests of indignation and hostility that Mr. Ford was compelled to defend himself. In his defense, which was broadcasted all over the United States, he assured the people of the country that he was not an anti-Semite and that his only purpose was to arouse the "boob gentile" from his lethargy and indifference.

The outstanding characteristics of the articles were their violent bitterness and uncontrolled emotionalism. There was no attempt to appeal to the intelligence of the readers. His appeal was to the "pogromshchik" hooligan prejudices.

Despite Mr. Ford's recantations, apologies and protests, we are convinced that Mr. Ford is the arch anti-Semite of America. He discovered that he could not continue his open attacks upon the Jewish people, so he has merely changed his method of attack. Instead of employing the crude Russian anti-Semitism which appealed to the basest passions of the drunken peasants, Mr. Ford and his editor, Mr. Cameron, decided that the German anti-Semitism, the intellectual method, although not so sensational, would be much more effective and would bring even more satisfactory results.

Instead of titles (picked at random), "How Jews Gained American Liquor Control," "The Jewish Associates of Benedict Arnold," "The Jewish Element in Bootlegging Evil," etc., Mr. Ford continues his attack upon the Jew in this fashion: "Einstein Theory Declared Colossal Humbug," "Proving the Case Against Abrams and Era," "A Modern Disraeli," "Fur Ring Linked With U.S. Threatens All Seals."

On the surface, these titles would not indicate any anti-Jewish animus. And even the reading of the articles would not arouse any special animosity against the Jews, but the impression is nevertheless subtly created which leaves the reader with the feeling and with the idea that Jews are fakers, liars and parasites.

The special method employed is that of the dishonest lawyer who wishes to deceive the court. He presents a brief, citing authorities not in their entirety, but takes sentences and paragraphs out of context, which sentences and paragraphs are frequently the very opposite of the opinion itself.

The people of this country, lacking adequate analytical minds, accepting at face value any explanation offered, have been all too ready to take Mr. Ford's denial of his anti-Semitism. These shrewd gentlemen know these facts concerning the average mentality all too well. They realize that it would be a dangerous precedent to continue the vicious, malignant attacks that formerly appeared. However, they have not the slightest intention of discontinuing their anti-Jewish fulminations.

As we view it, the old method was comparatively harmless, for it spent itself in emotional outbursts. The present method is a most noxious one. It builds up a body of ideas seemingly innocent, but by their constant repetition, the cumulative effect leaves the reader with a definite picture that the Jew is a dangerous menace to American life and institutions. We view the present anti-Jewish activities of Henry Ford with much more trepidation than his former crude, pureile efforts. Every article written in the past six months has been in disparagement of the Jew. They have all cast odium upon him. Every criticism has been an adverse one. We do not believe in abridging the freedom of press or of speech. We believe in open, frank and free discussion of every question. We hold that every people and every subject can and should be criticized. But we cannot be persuaded that the continuous, repeated fault-finding, which has characterized every article concerning the Jews, can emanate from any other than a thoroughly poisoned anti-Semitic mind. The Jew has become an obsession to Henry Ford. He conjures up in his mind all sorts of fantastic dangers and catastrophes when he thinks of the Jew.

So, when Mr. Ford discontinues to mention the Jew in any connection whatsoever, will we be persuaded that his anti-Semitic complex is receding. Until such time we must insist that his propaganda is more dangerous than ever and that Ford is an anti-Semite.

Detroit's Jews felt powerless against Henry Ford's press and money. They silently protested by not buying Ford products. Not so silently, they told Henry Ford jokes:

Henry Ford goes to a fortune teller. "I see," says the fortune teller as her hand slowly glides over the crystal ball, "that you are going to die on a Jewish holiday."

"Which Jewish holiday, ?" Ford anxiously asks. "Is

it their New Year's? Is it their Day of Atonement? Is it their Passover? Is it their Chanukah? Another one? Which one?"

"Mr. Ford," says the fortune teller, "any day you die will be a Jewish holiday."

While Jews around the country were shunning Ford products, Hollywood's Jewish moviemakers thought about using a Ford in their movies only when a comedian would kick an auto and it would fall in a heap of parts, or when the script would call for brakes to fail.

During this period, Adolph Hitler was beginning his rise to power. While serving eight months in jail for helping to engineer the Nazi Party takeover of the government of Bavaria, Hitler spent much of his sentence writing most of *Mein Kampf.*

While Hitler was jailed, Jews in many parts of Europe suffered brutal pogroms. Anti-Semites were celebrating in the little Polish town of Ksionz-Posen as all Jews were driven out and the synagogue was turned into a motion picture house. Jewish funerals in Warsaw were attacked, mourners injured and dispersed, and rabbis ridiculed. Pogroms and famine ravaged Jewish quarters in the Ukraine, resulting in thousands of deaths. Jewish sections were considered living tombs. Starving children reduced to skeletons dressed in rags, were barely breathing and unable to move.

Jewish students were severely attacked in the University of Bucharest. Rioting mobs of Roumanian students beat Jews and threw them down stairwells In the Jewish section of Berlin, windows were smashed and gardens uprooted. Bombs were placed in the Jewish cemetery. In Nuerberg, a mob killed four well-known Jews, and many shops were destroyed. In many cities of Germany, the press was becoming increasingly anti-Semitic.

Hitler's fame was increasing as many referred to the roving bands of anti-Semitic looters and killers as "Hitlerites." The European Jewish press said, "The Hitler spirit controls not only the government, but also all public opinion."

The situation worsened in November as the first pogrom in the history of Berlin took place. In a lengthy front page story on November 16, 1923, the *Detroit Jewish Chronicle* stated:

> *No Jew was safe on Berlin streets Monday and it is too early to say that greater security prevails at this time. Jewish passersby were stopped at every turn, were searched, maltreated, robbed of their possessions, and stripped of their clothes, some being left only in their undergarments.*
>
> *Homes of Jews were searched for food and money, owners offering the least resistance being severely beaten.*
>
> *Shops owned by Jews were plundered of their contents which were hurled through the windows smashed by the hooligans in order to gain entrance. Jewish tenement dwellers were dragged from their beds and driven to the streets in their night clothes.*

World Jewry lost a great friend with the passing of former President Woodrow Wilson. While in office, Wilson vetoed three restrictive immigration measures. He didn't hesitate to say he thought them to be aimed principally at the Jews. Wilson was also remembered for appointing Louis D. Brandeis to the Supreme Court bench.

Many windows of opportunity to European Jewry were slammed shut with the passage of the American anti-immigration legislation of 1924. Before the law was enacted, 140,000 Jews came to America in one year. After its passage, only 10,000 a year were permitted to enter. Detroit Jews despaired over the situation. Many realized they would never see their European relatives again.

The situation worsened in Europe in 1924 as more pogroms injured Roumanian Jews. Jewish homes were bombed near Hanover, Germany, and mobs estimated at 30,000 attacked Jews in Berlin. Fifty Jews in Lodz were badly beaten by Polish police and forced to pay huge ransoms for their release. The noose was tightening around European Jewry. In Detroit and around the world, the same question was asked, "Why are the leaders of the church silent?"

In 1924, the *Dearborn Independent* began another series of anti-Semitic articles under the banner of "Jewish Exploitation of Farmer Organizations." Henry Ford targeted prominent Chicago attorney Aaron Sapiro,

The Philadelphia-Byron branch of the United Hebrew Schools opened in 1924.
(Courtesy of Leonard N. Simons Jewish Community Archives)

who produced a standard contract for cooperative farmers. Ford accused Sapiro of cheating the farmers. Sapiro sued Ford for a million dollars. Four years and many articles later, the battle would end in a Detroit courtroom.

On April 27, 1924, the day immediately following the last day of Passover, the newest branch of the United Hebrew Schools opened on the northwestern corner of Philadelphia and Byron Streets. The location, approximately a quarter-mile north of Grand Boulevard and a quarter-mile west of Woodward, was considered the northwest section of the city.

The Talmud Torah Beth Sefer moved from its lower Hastings-Columbia location to Rosedale Court, north of Boston Boulevard between Woodward and John R. The auditorium also was built to accommodate a synagogue for daily, Sabbath, and holy day services. Rabbi Fischer inaugurated a Sunday school for B'nai Moshe. It opened with close to a hundred students and seven female instructors.

In 1924, Miss Rose Meyers was the new Fresh Air Camp director. She earned $350 for the season. Well-

Noted soprano Emma Lazaroff married Morris Schaver in 1924.
(Courtesy of Emma Lazaroff Schaver)

known soprano Emma Lazaroff married Morris Schaver in the home of her parents. Schaver had enlisted in the United States army in 1918 and saw action in many battles in Germany. As a young man in his native Poland, he was a member of the *selbstchutz*— the Jewish self defense against pogromists.

Girl Scout Troop No. 28, Detroit's first Jewish Scout Troop, was organized by Temple Beth El. The Temple also celebrated the Silver Anniversary of Dr. Franklin as its spiritual head in 1924. In only 12 years, Hadassah's worldwide membership numbered 18,500 in 186 chapters, exclusive of the 91 Junior Hadassah groups and 547 sewing circles. Joseph Chagai became managing editor of the new Yiddish weekly edition of *Der Tog*.

Judge Harry Keidan, chairman of the board of Congregation Shaarey Zedek, served in the recorder's court and became a judge in the circuit court in 1924.

Judge Harry B. Keidan earned the respect of Jews and non-Jews.

Keidan was a celebrity of sorts. It was well known in Jewish and law circles that if his judicial services were necessary on a Saturday, the highly observant Keidan would walk downtown, regardless of the weather.

Congregation B'nai Israel broke ground for a new synagogue on Ferry Street, adjacent to the one used since 1913. As its membership was moving farther northward from its Winder Street location, the Beth David Congregation purchased a site on Owen near Oakland Avenue. The B'nai Zion organized and built a synagogue on Humphrey and Holmur, one block east of Dexter and a few blocks south of Chicago Boulevard. Barely enough families to organize a minyan formed the Etz Haim Congregation on Englewood in the Westminster-Oakland area. In the area between Grand River and Livernois, Warren and Tireman, the West Side Hungarian Congregation was formed on Begole Street. Detroit formed a branch of Young Israel in the basement of the Mogen Abraham on Farnsworth. Young Israel, a national group organized in New York 12 years earlier, sought to strengthen the commitment of young people to Zionism and religious practice.

Cantor Minkowsky, also known as a great musician and composer, died at the age of 56. In his eight years at Shaarey Zedek, he wrote and produced two Hebrew operas performed at Orchestra Hall and wrote

The B'nai Israel congregation moved from Mullett Street to the south side of Ferry between Beaubien and St. Antoine in 1913 and built this building replacing the older structure in 1924.

and oversaw plays performed by Talmud Torah children. The 609 members of Shaarey Zedek felt the loss of Minkowsky but approved the selection of Samuel Vigoda to succeed him.

Since the march on Hastings Street 12 years earlier calling attention to the need for a Jewish hospital in Detroit, the more affluent Reform community was at odds with the more observant community over the hospital issue. Reform Jews had no need for a hospital conforming to Jewish dietary laws. By 1924, with more doctors experiencing discrimination in finding positions, more Reform Jews were willing to compromise if it would help bring about a Jewish hospital. In its November 28, 1924, edition, the *Detroit Jewish Chronicle* reported in a front page story that a local Jewish surgeon in a high position in a Detroit hospital felt that all Jewish physicians would be excluded from the hospital staff in a matter of time.

Dr. Lee Cowen, president of the Maimonides Medical Society, felt "anti-Semitic influences about us" were helping to build support for a Jewish hospital. Cowen was bothered by "the gross insults we have seen offered to Jewish patients by ignorant hospital employees and even by physicians and nurses."

While Jews were troubled by the hiring and admitting policies of Detroit's hospitals, they also experienced anti-Semitism in the workplace. It wasn't unusual to see newspaper ads advertising positions excluding Jews from even applying:

"Stockman—Wanted, good opportunity for advancement. Gentile. Apply F. W. Woolworth Co.";
"Girls of good Christian character to work in a store which has a reputation for friendliness and helpfulness...S.S. Kresge Company."

The community mourned the passing of Hyman Buchalter. A resident of Detroit for 35 years, Buchalter touched the lives of adults and children. He had received rabbinical ordination in his native Russia, helped establish the Division Street Talmud Torah, became its first principal, and helped bring about the United Hebrew Schools.

One of the most memorable Bar Mitzvahs in Detroit history took place in 1924, and the *Detroit Jewish Chronicle* thought the young man and the event worthy of a front-page story in its December 5 edition:

Samuel Reshevsky at six years of age contended with chess masters in European capitals. At nine he toured the United States, showing vast audiences how one may conquer opponents at the chess board.

Samuel's bar mitzvah, celebrated at Shaarey Zedek Synagogue last Saturday, nevertheless, was unique. Not only did he read the Prophetical portion in a charming voice, free from hackneyed style, in a manner which suggested that he thoroughly understood Prophet Malachi's message, and which was replete with musical emphases that are original and instinctive, but he did more. He occupied the cantor's desk for the Musaph, or additional service. And there was a large congregation present.

Samuel, of the melodious, finely developed voice, was as signally successful as he has been in the thousands of chess games from which he emerged the victor. After two or three hours of preparation with Cantor Samuel Vigoda of Shaarey Zedek Synagogue, the lad recited the service in a manner which suggested not only that he is a devotee o the art of the famous Cantor Josef Rosenblatt, but, musically speaking, that he possesses the creative spirit. For he sang several songs which he himself had conceived. Worshipers at Shaarey Zedek never before had attended so unique a service as last Saturday's.

Reshevsky would gain further international fame in the coming years as a chess master.

9
1925-1929
From Boom to Crash

Detroit had 85,000 black residents in 1925, an increase of 77,000 in only nine years. Blacks were moving into the Hastings Street area north and south of Warren, near the B'nai Moshe, Shaarey Zedek, Mogen Abraham, B'nai Israel, and Beth Abraham synagogues.

Walter Percy Chrysler, who absorbed the Maxwell and Chalmers Company and incorporated the Chrysler Corporation in 1925, introduced a popular car with a high-compression engine and a price tag of $1,395. The 5,000 seat Michigan Theater on Bagley, the former site of the home where Henry Ford worked on his first automobile, was nearing completion. The Bonstelle Theater opened in the former Temple Beth El on Woodward.

The Carmel Kosher Restaurant, located on Broadway near Gratiot, announced it would be open for Passover with "strictly kosher Pesach meals," under the supervision of Rabbi Judah Levin. Lillian Rein Sherman and her husband Fred founded Sherman Shoes and opened their first store on East Jefferson. Rabbi Leon Fram left Chicago to become assistant rabbi of Temple Beth El and founded Beth El's College of Jewish Studies, one of the first adult evening schools in America. WWJ radio began carrying weekly broadcasts of services. From radio's beginnings in

In the 1920s, double-decker buses ran on Woodward to Jefferson, then east to Belle Isle. Many Jewish singles took the bus on weekends.

(Courtesy of Burton Historical Collection, Detroit Public Library)

America in 1920 with Detroit's WWJ, the city now boasted five more stations by 1925.

Civil War veteran Emmanuel Wodic died at the age of 89. According to a personal request penned years earlier, Wodic was wrapped in an American flag prior to burial. Wodic was considered one of the most colorful members of Detroit's Jewish community. He had enlisted in the United States Army in 1856 and was honorably discharged in 1861, but re-enlisted on the same day and eventually saw action in many battles, including Gettysburg and Bull Run. After being wounded several times, Wodic was honorably discharged in 1864 and took up farming before moving to Detroit 21 years later. After joining Beth El, he became warden of the temple's cemeteries. In 1921, when Beth El held its ground-breaking ceremonies on Woodward and Gladstone, Wodic was given the honor of turning the first sod with the same shovel he had used in 1901 for the temple's previous edifice.

The estate of Leopold Wineman donated $75,000 to the United Jewish Charities toward the establishment of an outpatient clinic. Mrs. Eleanor Ford was hired to direct the agency, Jesse Hirschman became president, and the North End Clinic was born. The Fresh Air Society, which previously oversaw the clinic, turned its full attention to camping activities.

The Hebrew Free Loan office at the United Hebrew School Kirby Center was robbed. Jewelry and other valuables were taken from the safe. The stolen articles represented the collateral put up by persons who made loans. The robbery deeply disturbed the community and donations far exceeded the estimate of what was stolen.

Recently returned from a trip to Palestine, Detroiter Robert Marwil addressed the Detroit district of the Zionist Organization of America at the Philadelphia-Byron Talmud Torah. "We are turning wilderness into a beautiful country," Marwil said. "Every Jew who can afford to do so should visit the Holy Land and he will become inspired with the ideal."

Three days later at the same location, Henrietta Szold, national president of Hadassah and vice-president of the Zionist Organization of America, inspired the audience with a stirring report on activities in Palestine. Miss Hattie Gittleman was unanimously re-elected president of the Detroit chapter of Hadassah and the organization sought to increase its membership from 800 to a thousand in 1925.

The *Detroit Jewish Chronicle*, in its February 13, 1925, edition, reported that 2,000 children were enrolled in the "various grades conducted by the five branches of the United Hebrew Schools of Detroit." Rabbi Franklin urged support of U.H.S. by stating:

> *The United Hebrew Schools are established for the benefit not only of the Orthodox Jews of Detroit, but for the Reform Jews as well. There can be no lines of demarcation in the work they are doing. Education is the keynote to the salvation of Jews of America today.*

The U.H.S. hired Isadore Rosenberg as principal of the high school department. Rosenberg, who studied at a rabbinical seminary in Kovno, Poland, had a master's degree from Columbia University and held

In 1925 the Mishkan Israel Congregation built its synagogue on Blaine, just west of Linwood.

The First Hebrew Congregation of Delray dedicated its building on Burdeno Street near Jefferson in 1926.

a position in Rochester, New York, before coming to Detroit.

U.H.S. opened evening classes for adults at the Kirby and Philadelphia-Byron locations. In addition to Bible and Hebrew classes, adults could learn to speak Yiddish and take courses in Jewish history.

Rabbi Judah Levin was still principal of the afternoon yeshivah when it moved to the Emanuel Synagogue, known as the "Taylor Shule." Young Israel of Detroit, which began its existence a year earlier when it established religious services in the basement of the Mogen Abraham, moved to the U.H.S. at the Philadelphia-Byron building.

The 12-year-old Mishkan Israel Congregation moved from Benton and St. Antoine to its newly built synagogue on Blaine, just west of Linwood. Rabbi Isaac Stollman would be its spiritual leader. The First Hebrew Congregation of Delray, which had held services in a home for eight years, dedicated its brick structure adjacent to the previous site. Rabbi Solomon H. Rubin was named rabbi. The B'nai Jacob built a synagogue on King Street east of Oakland. Rabbi Joseph Eisenman was installed as spiritual leader.

The Beth Israel Congregation organized in 1925 and dedicated its synagogue at 15700 Muirland and Midland, north of Fenkell. Reverend Benjamin Moldawsky, also a well-known cantor, was in charge of services. The two-year-old Shaarey Zion Congregation moved from Indiandale Avenue to a store on Linwood at Highland, between Cortland and Sturtevant. Shaarey Zedek purchased a site for a new synagogue on Chicago Boulevard at Lawton. To accommodate many of its members moving into the area, Shaarey Zedek began looking for a site nearby in which to hold supplementary services on the High Holy Days.

Temple Beth El was celebrating its 75th anniversary and paid tribute to its oldest member, Samuel Heavenrich, who joined Beth El in 1861 at the age of 21. Heavenrich would go on to hold every office in the temple, including the presidency twice.

Temple Beth El claimed the largest congregation of Jews that ever worshipped under one roof in America, on Sunday night, September 27, 1925, for Yom Kippur services. Five auditoriums and assembly halls were filled as the congregation's rabbis conducted services. Beth David closed its Winder Street synagogue and moved all religious articles into the John R. and Owen building, which previously had served as a branch.

In 1926, Plotkin's Hebrew Book Store, on Hastings between Theodore and Warren, was losing business as families were moving from the area. Most were relocating to the Twelfth Street neighborhood. Baker-

Some ads from the *Detroit Jewish Chronicle* in 1925.

ies, delicatessens and other businesses opened, solidifying Twelfth Street as the major center of Jewish activities.

The Warsaw Bakery opened on Twelfth Street near Pingree under the proprietorship of Louis Buchbinder. The New York Bakery, under the management of L. Zeman, opened a bakery on Twelfth Street between Blaine and Gladstone. Soberman and Milgrom, distributors of wallpaper and paint, opened their new store at 8675 Twelfth Street near Blaine. Morris Subar opened his new Hebrew Book Store on Taylor off Twelfth Street. The Manuel Urbach Monument Company moved from Winder Street to Twelfth and Delaware.

Seven local Zionist organizations—Keren Hayesod, National Fund, Zionist Organization, Junior Hadassah, Senior Hadassah, Young Judea and Mizrachi—formed the Zionist Council of Detroit. Each organization appointed three delegates to the council offices in the Majestic Building, which became the headquarters of all Zionist activities.

In 1926 the North End Clinic opened its first building built exclusively for the health agency at 936 Holbrook near Oakland. It would serve as a Jewish health center for the indigent, and more than forty doctors and six dentists donated their services. Fresh Air Camp on Blaine Lake in Brighton had a full time nurse for the first time instead of a volunteer. The Young Women's Hebrew Association Camp opened its second season at Jeddo, Michigan, 14 miles north of Port Huron.

Little Billy Davidson, dressed in white satin, was the ringbearer at the wedding of his aunt, Mary Wetsman, to Dr. Jack Uhr of New York. Rabbi

The Soberman and Milgrom wallpaper and paint store opened on Twelfth Street near Blaine in 1926. It would later evolve into the Mercury Paint Company.

(Courtesy of Manning Brothers Historic Photographic Collection)

ECHOES OF DETROIT'S JEWISH COMMUNITIES

The estate of Leopold Wineman donated $75,000 to the United Jewish Charities for the establishment of an outpatient clinic. The North End Clinic opened in 1926 on Holbrook near Oakland.

Hershman officiated at the ceremony, held in the Wetsman home on Virginia Park. Benny Friedman, a hero to Detroit's Jewish kids, was starring at quarterback for the University of Michigan football team and was named the Big Ten's most valuable player in 1926.

Rabbi Judah Levin was suffering from a severe cold that developed into bronchial trouble as he was readying for Passover. As Friday night service began in the area around Ferry Street, word quickly spread that Rabbi Levin had passed away just before the Sabbath began. He was 64.

Eight thousand mourners gathered in the streets for the funeral on Sunday morning. The procession, led by police on motorbikes, began from Rabbi Levin's home on Ferry, proceeded to Farnsworth past the Mogen Abraham Synagogue, and turned onto Brush to the Shaarey Zedek.

Thousands overflowed the sanctuary and halls of Shaarey Zedek. Those who weren't crammed inside crowded outside. "We come to give public expression to our grief at the passing of a great sage, a great scholar, and a faithful and conscientious worker," Rabbi A. M. Hershman addressed the crowd.

A long motorcade escorted the body to Clover Hill Park Cemetery for burial. At the time of his passing, Rabbi Levin was the head of the United Jewish Orthodox Congregations of Detroit, which comprised 30 Orthodox congregations. The day after the funeral, Passover began. It was the first Passover in 30 years in Detroit without Rabbi Levin.

Morris Stol came to Detroit with his family in 1926, and the Stol family attended services at the Beth Yehuda Synagogue on Pingree and Woodrow Wilson. To learn English and prepare himself for citizenship, Morris attended night school at Northern High School on Woodward near Temple Beth El.

A fellow student suggested that he would learn a

Rabbi Judah Levin, the leader of Detroit's Orthodox community, died in 1926.

(Courtesy of Archives of Congregation Shaarey Zedek)

Pisgah Lodge Community Center opened on East Ferry Street in 1926.

(Courtesy of B'nai B'rith)

proper, scholarly English by listening to Rabbi Franklin. Morris, who was and remained Orthodox, attended Sunday morning services at Beth El for several years in order to master the new language without a trace of an accent, as he furthered his career as an insurance agent for Metropolitan Life.

Pisgah Lodge Community Center opened at 275 East Ferry Street. It was the only lodge in the District to own its own building. The 75-piece B'nai B'rith Symphony Orchestra practiced there, and it was the home of many activities and classes. Myron "Susie" Schechter learned basketball at the Hannah Schloss Jewish Center while growing up. In 1926 he led City College (now Wayne State University) to a championship. To celebrate the election of rabbi for life, Congregation Beth David honored Rabbi Ezekiel Aishiskin with an elaborate banquet at the Kirby U.H.S. Building. On Sunday, July 4, the cornerstone laying for the new Yiddish playhouse on Twelfth Street and Seward was held. Rabbis and community leaders mingled with entertainers and well-wishers of all ages. Until construction was finished, performances were given at the Majestic Theater on Woodward.

Congregation Emanuel (Taylor Shule) installed Rabbi Aaron Ashinsky, for the past 25 years one of Pittsburgh's foremost rabbis, as spiritual head in a ceremonial dinner attended by over 300 people. Prior to the dinner, Rabbi and Mrs. Ashinsky and their four daughters were met at Michigan Central Depot by a committee of prominent Jews and escorted to their new home.

Young Israel of Detroit raised funds for the Yeshiva, which until 1926 was supported by members of Congregation Mogen Abraham. Irving Schlussel, Abbe Levi, and Miss Naomi Buchhalter led the campaign to distribute charity boxes and make the community more aware of the needs of the school. The Young Israel moved religious services from the basement of the Mogen Abraham to the Jewish Center at 31 Melbourne, just east of Woodward. The Beth Aaron V'Israel Congregation purchased land for a cemetery

Central High School, along Tuxedo between LaSalle and Linwood, opened its new building on February 1, 1926.

ECHOES OF DETROIT'S JEWISH COMMUNITIES

The Shaarey Torah synagogue and branch of the United Hebrew School was the first Jewish house of worship and religious school to locate north of Six Mile Road.

(Courtesy of Leonard N. Simons Jewish Community Archives)

on Gratiot at 16 Mile Road. Edmund G. Lewis, who established the first Jewish undertaking parlor in 1920 with his brothers on John R. near Ferry, established his own mortuary business at 604 Delaware and Second Boulevard.

With the passing of Rabbi Levin, the Yeshiva was renamed "Yeshivath Beth Judah(or) Yehudah" in his memory. Rabbi Ezekiel Aishiskin took over the leadership of the institution and also assumed Rabbi Levin's duties at Congregation Mogen Abraham. The Ladies' Auxiliary of the Yeshiva was organized, with Mrs. Shifrah Stollman as president. A new school, known as the Folk-shule Geselshaft (People's School Society), opened with two branches, one in the Twelfth Street area, and the other farther north around Fenkell. Temple Beth El reached 1,400 members in 1926 and leased a two-story building at Fenkell and Wildemere to use as a branch religious school. The United Hebrew Schools started construction on their Fenkell area branch at Parkside and Midland. Wyandotte had its first synagogue with the founding of the Orthodox Beth El Congregation. Rabbi A. Davis was hired as resident rabbi.

Shaarey Torah organized in 1926 and started construction for their new synagogue and Hebrew school on the corner of Brush and Minnesota, north of Six Mile Road. This was the first synagogue established north of Six Mile. Rabbi Joseph Rabinowitz, from the eastern European town of Berezno and a relative of the Berezner Rebbe, was brought to America to conduct High Holy Day services in Baltimore. Natives of Berezno now living in Detroit contacted Rabbi Rabinowitz and offered him the post as their spiritual leader. After Rabbi Rabinowitz was assured that he would have almost complete control, the Rabinowitz family moved to Detroit and settled in an apartment above a store on Twelfth Street at Taylor next to the apartment where religious services were held.

Fred Butzel chaired a meeting of leaders representing various Jewish organizations in the United Jewish Charities office in the Penobscot Building. The meeting led to the formation of the Detroit Jewish Welfare Federation.

The editorial of October 1, 1926, in the *Detroit Jewish Chronicle* welcomed the Jewish Welfare Federation of Detroit:

The much discussed and long awaited Federation of Jewish Philanthropies has become an actuality. At a meeting held on Tuesday, Sept. 21, in the offices of the United Charities in the Penobscot Building, definite action was taken in the form of a charter application and the election of provisional officers.

Henry Wineman was chosen president; Samuel Summerfield and William Friedman, vice-presidents; David W. Simons, treasurer; Morris D. Waldman, secretary and director; Fred M. Butzel, chairman of the executive committee.

Two boards of governors were chosen: one known as governors at large, composed of David A. Brown, Fred M. Butzel, Rabbi Leo M. Franklin, William Friedman, Bernard Ginsburg, Nathan M. Gross, Judge Harry B. Keidan, Julian Krolik, David W. Simons, Milford Stern, Samuel Summerfield and Henry Wineman.

The other board consists of representatives of the constituent organizations and includes: Esser Rabinowitz, representing the United Hebrew Schools; Walter Fuchs, the United Jewish Charities; Melville S. Welt, Jewish Social Service Bureau; Milton M. Alexander, Jewish Centers Association; Edith Heavenrich, Fresh Air Society; and David S. Zemon of the Hebrew Free Loan Association.

The purpose of the federation is explicitly set forth in the charter application as follows: "To raise and collect funds, acquire and hold property by purchase, gift, devise, bequest, or otherwise; and to distribute and apply the same of the use or income thereof, directly and through others presently existing or subsequently organized agencies for the advancement of the social and cultural welfare of the Jewish community and for the promotion of any other philanthropy and to bring about co-ordination and co-operation among Jewish welfare and relief organizations in Detroit."

The new organization is to be known as the Jewish Welfare Federation of Detroit.

This organization is a long step from the original Jewish charities agencies created in this country. Even the word charities is deleted and not because of any special aversion to the word charity or sentimentality, but because the major activities are social and cultural and not charitable. Detroit Jewry is fortunately not faced with any serious charities problem due to the general prosperity, while at the same time our late comers have accommodated themselves to American life and are able to take of their financial and economic affairs.

It was at one time a current belief that with the solution of the economic problem of the immigrant, there would be a disintegration of the Jewish group as a distinctive entity, but the fact is that a whole host of problems have emerged which tax the capacity of cultural and social leadership to a much greater extent than did the financial and economic ones. One would be foolhardy to maintain that the problems of European Jewry have not had an integrating and coalescing influence upon American Jewry. Few events have happened in the history of Detroit Jewry which have unified it more than did the United Jewish Campaign. The momentum given by the overseas drive crystallized loose sentiment which gave birth to Detroit Service Group. From the Detroit Service Group to the Jewish Welfare Federation of Detroit was but a short step.

The Welfare Federation has before it, for immediate action, the building of a Jewish Hospital and a representative "Y". The social and cultural matters to which it will have to give its attention have been cared for by existing agencies in a satisfactory and adequate way, but yet the federation can widen the scope of these activities to a degree not visioned heretofore.

We are hopeful that the federation will be able to take over the administration of all relief drives affecting the Jewish people everywhere in the world. This does not mean that the groups forming the federation will be deprived of their autonomy or initiative, but merely means that greater economy and efficiency will be had in the administration of those activities which call for common action.

We welcome the federation. We know that the cultural and social life of Detroit Jewry will attain to a higher level, while all philanthropic undertakings will receive the attention they merit.

The Nash dealer on Twelfth Street and Glynn Court sold many 1926 automobiles to residents of the Jewish community.

Grave reports from Europe in 1926 saddened Jewish Detroiters. Many Polish Jews were starving, and some resorted to suicide. A heart-wrenching letter was sent to American community leaders by the editor of Warsaw's Yiddish daily:

Lodz is dying. Grondo is in agony. The streets of Wilna swarm with children begging for food. The two great teacher seminaries in Wilna, pride of Polish Jewry, have closed their doors.

The lengthy letter went on to describe harsh conditions and poverty brought on by government factories expelling Jewish workers, resulting in the severe economic conditions among Jews.

Harry Houdini was in great pain as he finished his scheduled performances in Montreal and boarded the train to Detroit for his next appearance on October 24, 1926. With his distraught wife at his side, Houdini retold the events leading to his abdominal discomfort. A university student had asked him if it was true that Houdini was immune to blows to his midsection. Before Houdini could tense his muscles and verify the claim, the young man delivered sharp blows to Houdini's abdomen. The pain didn't let up on the way to Detroit as Houdini arrived and checked into his room at the Statler Hilton on Washington Boulevard.

The audience at the Garrick Theater on State Street waited for "The Great Houdini" to appear, at first patiently, then whistling and stamping their feet Houdini heard the noise of the crowd but was lying down as his temperature rose to 104. A doctor examined the magician, diagnosed appendicitis, and advised immediate hospitalization. Houdini agreed to go, but only after the audience got what they came for.

It would be the last performance of Houdini's life. He apologized to the audience for being late and gave an entertaining two-and-a-half hour program curtailing absolutely nothing. The audience responded with a tumultuous ovation. Houdini couldn't take a bow as the pain was too great. As the curtain descended, the world's greatest magician fell to the floor. He was rushed to Grace Hospital on John R. where surgery was performed to remove his ruptured appendix. Houdini managed to hang on for five more days before death claimed him at the age of 52. Surgeons at the scene felt Houdini's greatest trick was to live as long as he did under the circumstances.

Detroiters gained a National Hockey League team of their own when the Detroit Hockey Club bought the Victoria Cougars, who became the Detroit Cougars. The first season began on November 19, 1926, in the Windsor Border Cities Arena, as Olympia Arena at McGraw and Grand River was still under construction.

When Moses Weingarden became a Detroit fireman in 1892, fire apparatus was pulled by great horses. Firemen worked nine consecutive days and rested the tenth. In 1904 Weingarden became a lieutenant; in 1913 a captain; and in 1919 he was promoted to battalion chief. After 35 years of service, Weingarden retired at the age of 56 in 1927. At the time of his retirement, he was the only Jewish battalion chief in the country.

The 1927 baseball season was the first time Tigers fans heard play-by-play on radio. Since most families still didn't have radios, kids flocked to the tire store on Twelfth Street between Collingwood and Glynn to catch firsthand reports.

Jake Mazer, who gained national attention in basketball as a player and coach, celebrated his fiftieth birthday by shooting 50 consecutive free throws. Ma-

Harry Houdini's 1926 performance at the Garrick Theater would be his last.

zer founded the Cadillac Athletic Club in 1927 at First and Lafayette Streets.

The Jewish community came together in appreciation to celebrate the fiftieth birthday of Fred Butzel. While not a practicing Jew in the religious sense, Butzel gained the respect of the observant community by being a friend, mentor, contributor, and organizer to anyone or any organization in need.

Twenty-nine-year-old Dr. Harold August, who had begun his practice in the Macabees Building on Woodward and Warren a year earlier, was named attending psychiatrist at the North End Clinic in 1927. Dr. August would live to be 100 and play an important role in the Jewish community.

The Knollwood Country Club, organized three years earlier, opened its new clubhouse on Maple and Town Line Roads, two miles west of the Oakland Hills Golf Club. Membership in Knollwood was limited to 300, and in 1927 the club had 215 members.

Governor Fred Green signed a "Kosher Food Law."

Battalion Chief Moses Weingarden.

(Courtesy of Alan Bennett)

Any products sold as kosher not in accordance with the Jewish dietary laws, was punishable by a maximum fine of $500 or four months in jail. The law applied to butchers, delicatessens and restaurateurs, and other store owners. Rabbi Aaron Aishinsky was the moving force behind the bill.

Solomon Chesluk came to Detroit from Poland, taught at the afternoon Yeshiva, and gave private lessons in Talmud. Chesluk wanted to combine his love of religious Jewish books with his interest in business, so he bought religious books from Poland and sold them out of his residence. He also placed books on consignment with Detroit's three Jewish bookstores. As Oakland Avenue, three-quarters of a mile east of Twelfth street, was also developing into an area of Jewish commerce, Chesluk opened a store on Oakland near Westminster.

Mrs. Joseph Ehrlich was elected head of the Detroit Chapter of Hadassah. Rabbi Judah Cohen, known in Detroit as "the Chassid," was hired by Congregation Agudath Achim at Hastings and Ferry Streets as their spiritual leader.

Samuel Sandweiss, one of the organizers of the Chesed Shel-Emess, the Jewish Free Burial Association, passed away. He had served as the society's president for a number of years and stayed in a leadership capacity until his last days. Sandweiss was known for being a tireless worker and for calling on people to raise funds.

Young Israel branched out and held services at three locations: the United Hebrew School Kirby Building, Mishkan Israel at Blaine and Linwood, and the Jewish Community Center at Melbourne and Woodward. The Young Israel Yeshiva (the future Yeshiva Beth Yehudah) had 32 students studying for the rabbinate at the Emanuel synagogue on Taylor and Woodrow Wilson. The Young Israel also had an active sports program with one of the top Jewish basketball teams and an employment bureau for Sabbath observers, whose purpose was to help secure positions in Jewish or Gentile firms.

Harry Keidan, who began his political career in 1912 as an assistant prosecutor, was appointed to the Wayne County Circuit Court bench in 1927. Keidan, who married Kate Levenson in her home on Taylor near LaSalle that year, took an active role in supporting Jewish education. Before the couple left on their honeymoon in the northern part of Canada and the West Coast, Judge Keidan lent his support to the Yeshiva.

> We have been having a great many drives for relief, both foreign and local, and we have met all appeals with promptness and generosity," Keidan stated. "But we have done very little for our own future. The traditional Yeshiva is a revival of Judaism, a renaissance of Jewishness. It is not a parochial school, as some people believe, but even if it were I would see no objection to that. The Catholic parochial schools are constantly turning out men who become distinguished in all fields. I see in the Yeshiva idea a happy solution of the problem of Jewish education in America.

Detroit's Yeshiva was often referred to as the Yeshiva of Young Israel, as the young men and women of the youth oriented Young Israel movement were the main volunteers for raising funds and other support. School hours in 1927 were from 10 a.m. to 1 p.m. on Sundays and 3 p.m. to 8 p.m. Mondays through Thursdays.

In 1927, 157 Jews graduated from the University of Michigan. Fifty-three were from Detroit, four from Highland Park, and 21 from elsewhere in the state. Albert Kahn was commissioned to build the new Shaarey Zedek synagogue at Chicago Boulevard and Lawton. Ground was broken on March 3, 1927, the twentieth anniversary of Rabbi Hershman's position as spiritual leader.

Fresh Air Camp opened its new 55-acre camp on Blaine Lake in Brighton in 1927, and two new small Orthodox congregations were born. The Adoth Yeshurin opened on Tyler west of Linwood and quickly became known as the "Tyler Shule." Around the same time, Petach Tikvah also dedicated its synagogue on Petoskey west of Dexter, between Chicago and Boston boulevards. For the rest of the decade, Rabbi Mendel Zager served both congregations as spiritual leader. People called Petach Tikvah the "Petoskey Shule" and didn't pay attention when Petach Tikvah changed its name ten years later to Beth Tikvah.

The Aaron Moshe on 29th Street just north of Michigan Avenue—west of the Tigers' ballpark—remodeled their nine-year-old building. An estimated 300 families were living around East Jefferson and the Grosse Pointe section in 1927. The Shaarey Tephilah congregation reached 75 members and had 30 children in its day school, while 60 children were enrolled in the Sunday school at 1227 Eastlawn between Jefferson and Kercheval, some nine blocks west of the Grosse Pointe boundary.

Beth Abraham celebrated its 35th year of existence and announced plans to construct a new synagogue in the northwestern Linwood area. Over 300 members belonged to the synagogue at Palmer and Beaubien. Three hundred members of Congregation Beth David attended the cornerstone ceremonies of

The Adoth Yeshurin organized in 1927 and dedicated its synagogue on Tyler that year.

the new synagogue at the southwest corner of Fourteenth and Elmhurst. Rabbi Ezekiel Aishiskin, head of the congregation for 20 years, was the main speaker.

Abe Nusbaum had been conscripted into the Austro-Hungarian army when he was 14. Shot while trying to desert, Nusbaum recuperated in a field hospital and was forced back into uniform. He deserted and spent the rest of World War One staying one jump ahead of the authorities. In 1925, leaving his wife and daughter behind, Nusbaum came to the United States with the dream of working hard and bringing his family to America. After working for a relative in the rug business, he opened a small linoleum and scatter rug business on Joseph Campau in Hamtramck in 1927. Nusbaum named it the New York Linoleum and Rug Company. After all, New York was the number one impressive city and the place people around the world dreamed of coming to.

There were several other Jewish businesses near Nusbaum's on Joseph Campau. The Finks operated the Pure Foods Markets, Max Ankerman had a department store, Jacob Bielfield was a well-known clothier, the Shapiros had a furniture store, Dave Stoller's R & S Clothes was nearby, the Davidsons had Federal Department Store, Barney Sommer and Morris Lantor had competing clothing stores, and Louis Margolis had another furniture store.

Tuvia Berman (Tom Borman) opened a meat market on Twelfth Street and Forest. His brother Avrham (Abe "Al") joined the business when a second store opened. More stores would eventually lead to the Farmer Jack supermarket chain.

After his historic solo transatlantic flight in May 1927, Charles A. Lindbergh was welcomed home at the Ford airport in Dearborn. Lindbergh, who had been born on West Forest Avenue 25 years earlier, was the grand-nephew of Mayor John C. Lodge. The pioneer pilot's mother was the mayor's niece and a chemistry teacher at Cass Technical High School. Detroiters cheered the whole family at a parade for America's newest hero, who also was honored with ticker tape parades in New York and Washington.

A year after the first dial telephones were available in residential sections, the first transatlantic call

Above: The Beth Tikvah organized and built under the name of Petach Tikvah on Petoskey.

Right: The Aaron Moshe remodeled its nine-year-old synagogue in 1927.

from Detroit was made to London.

Detroiters were surprised to see the headline on the front page of the July 8, 1927, *Detroit Free Press*:
"FORD ADMITS JEW CHARGES
ARE NOT TRUE"
The automaker asked forgiveness for printing "gross forgeries against the Jews."

It had begun in 1924. Ford's *Dearborn Independent* spent most of the year attacking Aaron Sapiro. Ford tried to link Sapiro, a lawyer and agricultural cooperative movement leader, to an alleged plot headed by international speculators and communists to cheat farmers and American consumers.

Ford claimed Sapiro and his colleagues would grow wealthy by charging higher prices and paying farmers at lower rates for their goods. Ford's investigators spent enormous sums of time and money trying to dig up evidence to back his theories. The multimillionaire hired top orator and lawyer James Reed, who was at the time a United States Senator. Reed, a democrat who had eyes on occupying the White House, was joined by two other top Ford attorneys. When all the papers were filed and the legal ducks in a row, the trial began on March 15, 1927.

Sapiro used a local trial attorney, William Henry Gallagher, an Irish Catholic. Gallagher argued that the attack against Sapiro was motivated by Ford's anti-Semitism. Ford's defense team succeeded in delaying the trial, but as the legal wrangling progressed, the auto manufacturer sensed public opinion wasn't on his side. Neither was his son. Edsel Ford had always distanced himself from the controversial newspaper articles printed by the *Dearborn Independent*.

While Ford was getting more publicity, the company was selling fewer cars. General Motors was taking more and more of the market share. Ford settled the lawsuit out of court and even paid Gallagher's fee. Ford's apology claimed he was unaware of the content of the anti-Semitic articles. "I would have forbidden their circulation without a moment's hesitation," Ford said. Settling out of court meant Ford didn't have to take the stand and open himself up to questioning.

Detroit's Jewish community followed the lengthy

Aaron Sapiro

saga through the daily papers and local Jewish publications, which often featured the goings-on on their front and editorial pages. Detroit's prominent Jews were very forgiving.

Fred Butzel: "I am very glad the statement has been made. I hope that the Jewish people in general will accept it at its face value and forget the entire incident."

Rabbi Leo M. Franklin: "The Jews of the world should be glad to grant to Mr. Ford the forgiveness which he seeks at their hands. They should accept his word that he has been misled in the information upon which he has based his accusations against them. It is my thoroughgoing belief that Mr. Ford will do all in his power to prove the sincerity of his repentance. It is the part of the Jew to forgive. It requires a man of courage to admit his errors. Mr. Ford in this instance has shown himself to be a thoroughly courageous man."

Rabbi Abraham M. Hershman: "All that we ask of Mr. Ford is a change of policy. The Jewish people have always had an abiding faith in the ultimate triumph of truth and justice. Mr. Ford may be assured that the Jewish people harbor no spirit of vengeance against anybody."

B'nai Moshe left its Garfield location in the spring of 1927 and rented stores at the corner of Linwood and Claimount. The main auditorium of the Jericho Temple on Joy Road near Linwood was used for the

Cantor Yussele Rosenblatt performed in the historic first "talking picture."

High Holidays to accommodate members and their families while plans were proceeding to occupy the new synagogue on Dexter.

In the eight years since its inception, membership in Jericho Lodge No. 490 grew from 18 members to nearly a thousand, making it one of the largest all-Jewish fraternal organizations in the state. Jericho Temple undertook the building of its large, three-story structure on Joy Road in 1927 to serve the community.

A new Jewish weekly—the *Detroit Jewish Herald*—began to rival the eleven-year-old *Detroit Jewish Chronicle*. Philip Slomovitz, who left his position as editor of the *Chronicle* to edit the *Palestine Pictorial* in New York, returned to Detroit as editor of the *Jewish Herald* effective with the September 2, 1927, edition.

The Isaac Agree Memorial Building opened at 121 Rosedale, between Woodward and John R., four blocks north of Boston Boulevard, on Sunday, September 18, 1927. The remodeled home served as a synagogue and school and charged no tuition for students. The 35-member congregation invited the community to join them for High Holy Day services.

Young men who followed the exploits of Benny Friedman bought tickets to University of Detroit Stadium on Sunday, October 9. Friedman had many duties with the Cleveland Bull Dogs since he left Michigan. He was the manager, coach, captain and quarterback. Maurice J. Caplan, head of Metropolitan Moving Pictures Company, owner of the Detroit Cougar football team, and director of the new Olympia Stadiums, oversaw the event.

The new Yiddish playhouse—Littman's Peoples Theater—located on Twelfth Street at Seward, made its debut Wednesday evening September 7, 1927. The rich, colorful, Assyrian style interior dazzled over a thousand theater goers. The lobby was lined with flowers sent by friends and well-wishers.

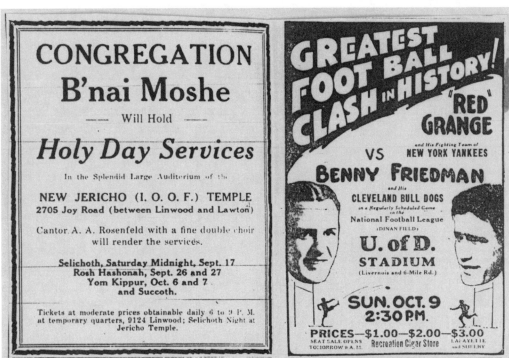

Ads from the *Jewish Chronicle*.

Detroit's beautiful Yiddish playhouse opened in September 1927.

Forty-six-year-old Abraham Littman operated the Yiddish playhouse on Hastings and Alfred Streets for three years and leased the Majestic Theater for a season as the original location was no longer the center of Jewish activities. Littman, who was in his thirtieth year in the profession as an actor and manager, said:

> I have gone hungry many times. I have worn shoes with shined tops when the soles were worn thin and torn. Even the building of this house was not always smooth sailing. There were terrible obstacles to overcome and many times it looked as it the project was doomed to failure. We are depending on the Jewish public of Detroit to prove by its steady patronage that our struggles have not been in vain. With the help and appreciation of Detroit Jewry the Peoples theater will become a real institution in the Jewish life of our city and a force for intellectual and cultural betterment.

People's Confectionery, one of the stores on the street level of the theater, was a popular stop after the last curtain for drinks and cigarettes.

Detroit had several other openings in 1927. The Detroit Institute of Arts building on Woodward opened, as did Olympia Stadium and City Airport. Until then the Ford airport, now the company's proving ground, was considered Detroit's aviation center. A few weeks later, regular air passenger service began from Detroit to Chicago.

October was designated "Month of Education" by concerned Jewish leaders. In an editorial in the *Detroit Jewish Herald's* October 7, 1927, edition, Phillip Slomovitz warned of dire consequences Detroit's future Jewish community would face if more children did not receive more of a Jewish education.

> *The present state of affairs, with regard to the training of the Jewish youth is so deplorable that to fail to notice it would be nothing short of criminal neglect of the education of our boys and girls. It is true that in the past four or five years a noticeable improvement marked our Hebrew school system as well as the progress of enrolling more and more pupils for the study of the history, religion and language of their people. But the progress was not marked enough to alter the existing sad situation.*
>
> *Perhaps we can best prove our point by means of figures. The result of the most recent census showed that there are approximately 65,000 Jews in Detroit. It has been accepted that of these the number of boys and girls of Hebrew school age is 13,000. The enrollment in the United Hebrew Schools in Detroit approximates 2,000. There are an additional 2,000 who attend private Chedarim and the Sunday Schools, making the number of our youth receiving any sort of Jewish training about 4,000, against about 9,000 who are receiving no Jewish education whatsoever.*
>
> *In the figures above quoted we listed among those receiving a partial Jewish training about 2,000 Detroit Jewish boys and girls attending the Sunday Schools. The education of this number is crammed into about 50 hours a year. True, even the extremest adherents of the Sunday School system are admitting to the failure of an education reduced to about an hour and a half or-two hours a week, and gradual extensions are planned. But it is such training that is dominating our Jewish life in America. It is such*

a minimum of Jewish learning that endangers our existence and threatens our cultural progress.

On Tuesday night, January 10, 1928, the burning of fiery crosses could be seen throughout Detroit. Earlier in the day, John C. Lodge was inaugurated as Mayor of Detroit. Police records confirmed at least 25 or more blazing crosses in Detroit that night. One cross burned in Campus Martius, opposite the City Hall, where the new council met in its first session, and two other flaming crosses lit up Grand Circus Park. It was the practice of the Ku Klux Klan to "adopt" candidates without their knowledge or consent.

"If I were adopted by an organization with intolerance as its fundamental I should repudiate my foster parents with great gusto," Lodge firmly stated. "No man in Detroit ever grew up in a more tolerant environment than I. No man hates that sort of stuff more than I. I not only have no sympathy with it, but I hate it."

While Jewish Detroiters admired Lodge's comments and felt good about their future, they despaired over the fate of their relatives in Europe. Attacks on Jews were commonplace. Many Jewish businessmen committed suicide as their establishments were boycotted, damaged, and destroyed. Jewish students were hounded, beaten, and robbed in Poland and Hungary. Jews of all ages were thrown off trains in Russia by hooligans. Christian university students in Budapest staged strikes and barred doors calling for government expulsion of Jewish students. In Bucharest, 95 percent of pupils of the Jewish High School were declared by the Rumanian committee overseeing examinations to have failed. Parents were worried about their depressed teenagers committing suicide.

Detroit's Jewish teens were elated over the opening of Central High School's Linwood/ LaSalle campus within walking distance of most of the student body. There were plenty of after school activities at the newly remodeled Jewish Center on Melbourne just east of Woodward. Young Judean leader Irwin Shaw, who would go on to a long career as executive vice president of the Jewish Center, became the first paid field secretary for the Young Judean movement in Detroit.

In a front page statement in its January 20, 1928, edition, the *Detroit Jewish Chronicle* announced its consolidation with the *Detroit Jewish Herald*. Phillip Slomovitz, former manager of the *Chronicle* and editor of the *Herald* during the previous five months of its 14 month existence, returned to the *Chronicle* as editor.

Mrs. Joseph H. Ehrlich was re-elected Detroit president of Hadassah for a second term The organization claimed 101 new members over the previous year. Miss Henrietta Szold, national president of Hadassah, came to Detroit on behalf of the organization she founded and stayed at the Pallister Avenue home of Mr. and Mrs. David W. Simons. Days of meeting and dinner gatherings were capped by a luncheon at the Statler Hotel celebrating the thirteenth anniversary of the founding of Hadassah.

Detroiters also welcomed Zionist leaders Goldie Meyerson (Golda Meir) and Dr. Chaim Weizmann in 1928. At the Appeal for Palestine dinner at the Statler, Joseph Ehrlich, chairman of the Detroit Palestine Appeal, presented Dr. Weizmann, president of the World Zionist Organization, with a check for $25,000 as Detroiters raised $110,000 for the purchase of property in Palestine and other avenues used to rebuild the Jewish homeland

The Hebrew Free Loan office relocated from the Kirby United Hebrew School building to a store on Twelfth Street and Clairmount, closer to the heart of Detroit's Jewish population.

The nine-year-old United Hebrew Schools had many branches serving the Detroit area in 1928. The schools were located at 609 E. Kirby (east of Woodward and south of Grand Boulevard), 1245 W. Philadelphia (east of Twelfth Street), 9243 Delmar (Oakland district), 15705 Parkside (northwest), 17750 Brush (north of Six Mile) and 528 Tuscaroda Street in Windsor.

Rabbis Aishishkin, Ashinsky, Fischer, and Hershman spoke at the cornerstone laying ceremony of the seventh United Hebrew School branch at the northwest corner of Tuxedo and Holmur. The United Hebrew Schools graduated the first high school class on July 31, 1928.

The Tuxedo-Holmur branch of the United Hebrew Schools opened in 1928. In later years it would be known as the D. W. Simons Branch.

(Courtesy of Leonard N. Simons Jewish Community Archives)

Forty young men and women received their certificates of graduation from Temple Beth El High School. The valedictorian of the class was Miss Josephine H. Stern, daughter of temple president Milford Stern. Miss Stern was selected for the honor because of her perfect attendance record extending over eleven years, from the Kindergarten class to the Senior High School.

The Isaac Agree Memorial Society, which was organized during shiva (week of mourning) following the death of Alexander A. Agree in November 1921, purchased a small structure at 123 Rosedale, between Woodward and John R., for use as a Hebrew school. The remodeled building contained classrooms and an auditorium.

Rabbi Arthur Ginzler became spiritual leader of Congregation Shaarey Tefilah on Eastlawn near East Jefferson. Ginzler stayed with the congregation for only a few months before moving to Flint's Beth Israel, also known as the Jewish Community Center of Flint. A Detroit family relocated to South Haven and helped that Jewish community establish the first Hebrew Congregation on Broadway in 1928.

The Beth Yehuda Congregation relocated from the corner of Adelaide and Hastings to their first synagogue structure at 1600 Pingree at the corner of Woodrow Wilson. Rabbi L. Landau served the congregation during its entire 12-year existence, but was succeeded by Rabbi Solomon Kleimplatz in its new location. The El Moshe Congregation on 29th near Michigan Avenue engaged Rabbi Samuel Novak as spiritual leader.

On August 26, 1928, a 50-piece band led more than a thousand parading participants from the branch synagogue of Beth David at Owen and Brush to the new building at Elmhurst and 14th. Thirteen Torahs were carried in the parade as it wound its way from Owen, west on Clairmount to 14th, then north on Elmhurst. Rabbi Ezekiel Aishiskin led the Torah procession and the privilege of carrying the other Torahs was auctioned off by Ralph Paul, who purchased the privilege of opening the front door for $250.

September 11, 1928, marked the opening of the Hebrew school and Beth Mordechai Synagogue on Wendel Street near Vernor Highway in southwest Detroit. The building, the only Jewish public building in the neighborhood, also served as a Jewish Center where all Jewish activities in the area were centered.

Al Saltsman was born on Montcalm east of Hastings in 1908 and experienced life in and around the Hastings corridor. In 1928 the 20-year-old Saltsman played Sunday football for an all-Jewish team in a Detroit Parks and Recreation League. Saltsman's team played an all-Polish club for the De-

The magnificent Beth David Synagogue at Fourteenth and Elmhurst.

(Courtesy of Burton Historical Collection, Detroit Public Library)

troit City Championship but lost the contest by two points. While they lost the game, Saltsman and his mates gained the respect of the winning team. "They called us Bennies," Saltsman recalled. "After Benny Friedman, who was the great quarterback at Michigan." Friedman was in the Detroit spotlight in 1928 as he spent the football season playing for the Detroit Wolverines before moving to New York.

Nate Shapero celebrated Economical Drug Stores' tenth birthday in 1928. The chain grew from one to 31 stores in the ten year period. The best known store in the Detroit chain was located in the General Motors Building and was famous for its malted milks. While Shapero's chain was growing, Stanley Winkelman's father and uncle entered the ladies apparel business on Woodward, south of the General Motors Building. The store would evolve into the Winkelman chain.

Isaac Weinstein, a biblical looking man with a full, almost white beard, was honored by Congregation Shaarey Zedek for 40 years of service as Baal Kore (reader of the Torah). Weinstein's retirement was marked with a gold watch presented by leaders of the congregation. Only a few months later, Weinstein's peaceful retirement was shattered when his daughter, Rose, died suddenly in the home they shared on Hazelwood near Fourteenth. Miss Weinstein's death shocked the Detroit Jewish community as she was known in many circles for her many charitable activities. She was a member of the board of directors of Detroit Hadassah and was employed by the Hupp Motor Car Corporation as secretary to the chairman of the board.

Benjamin Oppenheim, one of the original members of Shaarey Zedek and B'nai Israel, died at the age of 80. A well-known, successful businessman in one of Detroit's first wholesale dry goods and notions establishments, Oppenheim was a cantor in several Orthodox congregations and active in many charities.

Emma Lazaroff-Schaver interrupted her operatic studies in Chicago to star in the third annual Halevy Choral Society's program of Jewish music at Orchestra Hall. Ossip Gabrilowitch was the pianist and Pablo Casals, cellist, in a sold out joint recital at Orchestra Hall. The four levels of tickets ranged from $1.10 to $2.75. Some folks came by bus from Chicago, paying four dollars each for a one-way ticket to Detroit.

Followers of jazz often went to Harvey Harry Koppin's Koppin Theatre, at Gratiot near Beaubien, to see and hear top classic blues performers. At Woodward and Warren, the Graystone Ballroom was owned and operated by Jean Goldkette, the well-known

At the dedication of the Beth David Synagogue, Ralph Paul (top) auctioned off the keys to the two main entrances of the synagogue. Mr. Paul and Mrs. Louise Gladstone were the highest bidders for the privilege of opening the doors. The synagogue's spiritual leader, Rabbi Ezekiel Aishiskin, wore a top hat for the ceremonies.

(Courtesy of Burton Historical Collection, Detroit Public Library)

French Jewish bandleader.

Brothers Ben and Lou Cohen opened the beautiful 4,000-seat Hollywood Theater at Fort and Ferdinand, close to the small Jewish community of Delray in southwest Detroit. The Gillman brothers built the 1,500-seat Piccadilly Theater at the northeast corner of Fenkell and Petoskey. The structure also had space for five stores, four flats, and three offices.

The luxurious Avalon Theatre opened on Linwood and Davison. The lowest admission price was fifteen cents. The Avalon had 1,972 seats and was owned by Joseph Wetsman. His grandson, six-year-old Billy Davidson, became a frequent visitor and sat in many of the seats. Internationally famous cantor Josef Rosenblatt came to Detroit to perform Hebrew, English, Yiddish, Spanish, and Italian songs at the newly opened 2,078-seat Oriole Theater on Linwood and Philadelphia. The theater also featured a first-run movie before and after Rosenblatt's performances. George Jessel, who recently had celebrated his thousandth performance as "The Jazz Singer," starred in the play at the Lafayette Theater. The United Artists Theater and building opened on Bagley next the two-year-old Michigan Theater.

The changing Hastings Street neighborhood had several movie houses within easy walking distance of each other. Little Marvin Schlossberg's mother often took him from Schlossberg's Hardware store on Hastings near Farnsworth, a few doors down to the Warfield Theatre. "My mother knew the movie schedule and I was more than happy to go and see the same movie over and over," Schlossberg (the future Sonny Eliot) recalled. "My mother would just leave me there and go back to help my father in the store. The Warfield was my baby-sitter. When the movie ended, she would pick me up and we'd go back to the store or around the corner where we lived."

The Beth Mordechai on Wendel Street in southwest Detroit opened in 1928.

Plotkin's Book store, on Hastings between Theodore and Warren, served the area near the Warfield Theater, south of Grand Boulevard, and offered the largest assortment of greeting cards and books in Hebrew and English. Plotkin's had machzerim (High Holy Day prayer books) translated in English, German, and Hungarian. Jacob Lazaroff, father of famous soprano Emmma Lazaroff Schaver, opened a Jewish book store on Westminster near Oakland.

Lieberman's Kosher Restaurant opened on Twelfth Street at Taylor and offered chicken dinners on Sundays for 75 cents. The Morris Restaurant opened a kosher cuisine establishment on Linwood and Taylor while it continued to operate Blaine Lunch on Twelfth Street. David Goose, who operated a market on Westminster near Oakland, opened his kosher meat, poultry, and live fish market in the new Dexter area at

Left: The Oriole Theater featured a huge raised stage, offering audiences a chance to see live performances, as well as movies.

Below Left: The lobby of the Avalon Theater became a popular destination for young singles on Saturday nights.

(Photos courtesy of Manning Brothers Historic Photographic Collection)

Left: The Warfield Theater on Hastings near Farnsworth.
(Courtesy of Manning Brothers Historic Photographic Collection)

Above: The Warfield served as a babysitter for little Marvin Schlossberg, who would grow up to be known as Sonny Eliot.
(Courtesy of Sonny Eliot)

Skyscrapers sprouted near City Hall in the late 1920s. This 1929 view shows a forest of warehouses and small factories closer to the riverfront.

(Courtesy of Michigan Views)

ECHOES OF DETROIT'S JEWISH COMMUNITIES

the corner of Dexter and Boston Boulevard.

The Albert Kahn-designed, 28-story Fisher Building, featuring stylized mosaics and colorful frescoes, opened. Dazzled visitors wandered around the lobby and crossed the street to drink in the exterior of the 440-foot high structure. The building was visible from the Jewish neighborhoods around Hastings Street, Oakland Avenue, and Twelfth Street.

The Detroit Zoo opened in 1928, four years after the Detroit Zoological Society presented Detroit with 100 acres of land in the area. Horace Rackham, president of the Zoological Park Commission, donated an additional 22 acres, while the *Detroit News* donated the popular miniature railroad.

In 1929 Detroit added another jewel in its downtown skyline as the Guardian Building opened. The latter part of the "Roaring Twenties" saw the completion of the Book Tower and the Book-Cadillac Hotel on Washington Boulevard; the Barlum Tower (now the Cadillac Tower) in Cadillac Square; the David Stott Building and the Penobscot Building on Griswold.

In 1929, Detroit industry had 330,000 workers. More than 30 percent of Detroiters were employed in factories. Besides the auto industry; major employers were steel, copper, tobacco, pharmaceuticals, and meat packing.

There were opportunities on the other side of the law, too, as prohibition banning the sale of intoxicating beverages for the past decade created the bootlegging industry. Illegal alcohol was produced and found its way to Detroit by air, ground, and water from Canada. Thousands of illegal drinking establishments, known as "speakeasies" and "blind pigs," sprang up in Detroit. Providing illegal alcohol made many criminals rich and gave birth to several gangs. These were mostly populated by thugs comfortable with other thugs of the same ethnic background. At times they were allied with other gangs or national crime syndicates.

The Purple Gang, made up of Jewish mobsters who loved to sport expensive gray suits, controlled much of Detroit's illegal activities on the west side. The newspapers often called them rum-running racketeers, but some Purples were involved in killing rival

1929 ad from the *Jewish Chronicle*.

gang members who had designs on their west side activities.

Exactly how the Purple Gang got its colorful name is not known. Some remembered how as youngsters they enjoyed swimming together wearing purple trunks. Others said they idolized a shady character named Sammy Purple, while a neighborhood shopkeeper referred to them as "tainted," or "rotten meat."

Besides profiting from prohibition, the Purple empire included arson, drugs, extortion, and gambling. The Purples did perform good deeds and charitable acts, and in some cases even served as protectors of fellow Jews by members of other gangs. The Purple Gang hung around the Cream of Michigan Cafe on Twelfth Street where around the corner young men attended the yeshivah on Pingree.

Esser Rabinowitz, president of the United Hebrew Schools since its founding ten years earlier, passed away suddenly on June 12, 1929. While the 62-year-old Rabinowitz had no children, he had an enormous interest in children and their Jewish education. Rabinowitz was a noted collector of Hebrew books, and his home on Virginia Park near Twelfth Street contained the most valuable collection of Hebrew volumes in the city. Rabinowitz's funeral was one of the largest ever held in Detroit. The service began at the Philadelphia-Byron Talmud Torah, where leading rabbis delivered eulogies, and the procession

The B'nai Moshe Synagogue in 1929.

(Courtesy of Manning Brothers Historic Photographic Collection)

continued to other branches of the schools before internment in Clover Hill Cemetery.

For the first and only time in its history, a mother and daughter were among the United Hebrew Schools graduates. Mrs. Isaac Rosenthal and her 13-year-old daughter, Sarah, were classmates and fellow-graduates. The Rosenthals were star pupils at the Philadelphia-Byron branch on Kirby. Mrs. Rosenthal, who enrolled in the school in 1924, completed the full seven-year course in five years and delivered an address in Hebrew at the graduation.

Abraham Grace, well-known in the Oakland district, passed away at the age of 52. The Russian-born Grace was in the flour, grain and sugar business on Delmar and was one of the founders and the first president of the Ahavath Achim Synagogue on Delmar and Westminster. The newly-formed River Rouge Jewish Congregation advertised it was holding services in a hall on Jefferson and Henry Street. Cornerstone laying ceremonies were held for Windsor's Shaar Hashomayim Synagogue, at the corner of Goyeau Street and Giles Boulevard.

The imposing B'nai Moshe Synagogue on Dexter and Lawrence was dedicated on Sunday, July 26, 1929. The principal address was delivered by spiritual leader Rabbi Moses Fischer. Other speakers included attorney and community leader Fred Butzel, Dr. Leo M. Franklin of Temple Beth El; Rabbi A. M. Hershman of Shaarey Zedek, and Rabbi Ezekiel Aishishkin of Beth David.

13,502 Jews were admitted into the United States in the fiscal year ending June 30, 1929, but in Ann Arbor, Jewish college students were denied housing in certain areas. "Jewish non-sorority women are compelled to go from house to house in search of lodging, being refused on one pretext or another," Rabbi Adolph C. Fink of the Hillel Foundation claimed. "For the crime of being Jewish, Jewish students are subjected to spiritual and mental humiliation."

Jews were concerned about the continuing pogroms in Europe and were shocked and saddened by the events in Palestine. According to a front page story in the *Detroit Jewish Chronicle*, the Jewish Telegraphic Agency reported:

Arab mobs, organized and inflamed to fanaticism by political intriguers working on the religious fury of the ignorant, attacked the scattered Jewish settlements and murdered and plundered wherever no resistance was offered. In Hebron the inmates of the Rabbincal College, innocent youths who never handled weapons in their lives, were butchered in cold blood. In Safed the same fate befell the rabbis, their wives and children. Recently some Arabs raided a Jewish orphan settlement, where, the pathetic remnants of the great Russian pogroms had found a haven of refuge. It is not amazing that the orgy of such primitive brutality upon a peaceful population has been utilized by a certain section of the British press for a campaign of propaganda directed not against the authors and instigators of these brutalities, but against their victims?

In Hebron, 59 Jews, including 24 yeshivah students, were slaughtered by Arabs with knives and axes. Among the dead were twelve American students studying for the Rabbinate. Some Detroiters were frantic, as they had relatives in Hebron. Mrs. Isidore Cohen, a Palestinian married to a Detroiter living on Kirby near Brush, had a brother and three cousins studying in the yeshivah.

A 1929 report of the Jewish doctors serving the North End Clinic claimed, "90 percent of the doctors do not have staff appointments in the better hospitals, and therefore must refer their hospitalized patients to other doctors." The report strengthened support for the cause of creating a Jewish hospital.

Governor Green appointed Henry Butzel as Associate Justice of the state Supreme Court. Butzel filled a vacancy caused by the death of Justice Fellows, becoming the first Jew to sit on the state Supreme Court. Judge Charles C. Simons, who was appointed by President Warren G. Harding to the United States Circuit Court of Appeals in 1929 by President Herbert Hoover.

The Marx Brothers played to many full houses in a three-week engagement in the play, "Animal Crackers," at the Cass Theater. Abie's "Irish Rose" played at the Garrick Theater for five months. Tickets ranged from 50 cents to $2.50. A two-week stay for a child in Fresh Air Camp in 1929 was $17. The American Palestine Line, operating out of New York, offered a 15-day each way round-trip fare ranging from $325 to $850.

Leonard Simons and Larry Michelson worked together at an advertising agency and in 1929 the pair formed the Simons-Michelson Company Advertising Agency. It marked the beginning of a lifelong part-

Looking south from above Grand Circus Park in 1929. The beautiful landscaped areas of Washington Boulevard are on the right.

(Courtesy of Michigan Views)

nership and friendship. Mrs. Ralph Davidson was elected president of Detroit Hadassah, succeeding Dora Ehrlich, a founding member. Mrs. Ehrlich and her husband Joseph were one of the marquee couples in the Jewish community and active in many circles.

Besides holding High Holy Day Services at its synagogue on Brush and Willis, Congregation Shaarey Zedek also held services at the Oriole Theater at Linwood and Philadelphia. Days after Greenfield Village opened, the stock market began its heavy decline. By the end of October, the New York Times Industrial Average of selected stocks plummeted from 452 to 38, wiping out 75 percent of the value of all securities.

Many Detroiters put their financial woes aside and cheered the dedication of the 1,850-foot long Ambassador Bridge, the longest suspension bridge in the world at the time, on November 11, 1929. The Armistice Day crowd estimated at 100,000 swarmed over the new International Gateway to get a closer look at the 363-foot-high steel towers.

For the fourteenth consecutive year, Nate Shapero, operating out of his drug store chain, distributed 500 baskets of food to Jewish and non-Jewish needy on Thanksgiving. Non-Jews had baskets containing chicken, while Jews were given fish in baskets tied with yellow ribbons to distinguish the dietary difference.

Unfortunately, the ranks of the Jewish and non-Jewish needy would increase as the "Roaring Twenties" ended with an economic bomb that would mushroom across the world.

Jewish Detroiters living around Congregation Beth Itzchok, on Fischer Street just north of Mack, took the streetcar from Cadillac Square home.

(Courtesy of Burton Historical Collection, Detroit Public Library)

10

1930-1934 THE DEPRESSION YEARS

Detroit was the fourth largest American city in 1930 with a population of 1,563,662, an incredible increase of 1,362,958 in only 30 years. New residents came from all parts of the country and from many other countries, looking for opportunities. Black people came mainly from the south looking for employment in the factories, giving Detroit a black population of 120,066, 7.7 percent of the city's total.

1930 should have been a great year for Detroit. The city had a new skyline, an international bridge, and a tunnel nearing completion. There were two cars for every horse in the city, while ten years earlier it was two horses for every automobile. However, the Great Depression deepened and fewer customers around the country were willing or able to purchase a new automobile. Unemployment, which stood near 1.5 million in America in October 1929, rose to 4 million by the following spring.

Because of the automobile industry and its related businesses, Detroiters felt the pains of economic hardship sooner than in most areas of America. For 14 consecutive days early in the year during specified

The east side of Twelfth Street looking south from Clairmount. Taylor was a block down and Boesky's was two blocks down at Hazelwood.

(Courtesy of Manning Brothers Historic Photographic Collection)

hours, the Boesky brothers—William, Samuel, and Harry—helped the unemployed by feeding the hungry free of charge at their restaurant on Twelfth and Hazelwood.

Boesky's fed 600 daily and more than 7,500 were helped during the two-week period. No questions were asked of those seeking meals, and 86 were fed at each sitting. The Boesky brothers were touched by the letters and cards of thanks—some signed and some unsigned. "It was a heart-rending scene to watch," said Sam Boesky, speaking on behalf of his brothers. "To see some of those poor, penniless, and half-starved men, many of whom are without homes, veritably dive into the meal. To some it was the first meal they had in days. We want it distinctly understood that this is not a commercial proposition done as an 'advertising stunt.' It was merely our bit to those unfortunates who are in dire need of the bare necessities of life. We have been amply compensated with the knowledge that we have brought some sunshine into their hearts."

Attorney George Stutz was a young man of 26 and active in many Jewish organizations in 1930. He helped organize the community-wide appeal for food, coal and clothing housed in a block of stores on Twelfth Street and in the basement of the Shaarey Zedek at Brush and Willis.

Stutz, representing the overwhelmed volunteers, met with Federation leaders at his Twelfth Street law office. The meeting with Fred Butzel, Julian Krolik, and Abe Srere gave birth to a relief committee within the Jewish Social Service Bureau to be known as the Jewish Unemployment Relief Council. Stutz became an active board member of JSSB and was elected president eight years later.

Isaac Rosenthal, president of the Hebrew Hospital Association, told a group of Jewish physicians and interested laymen at a meeting in his home that the treasury of the association had $41,785 available for a future Jewish hospital in Detroit.

The Rosenthal home at Edison and Fourteenth was the scene for meetings for several organizations. Mrs. Rosenthal served as an officer in the Women's League of United Hebrew Schools, and her husband helped organize the Federation of Orthodox Jewish Congregations in 1930 under the direction of Rabbi Aaron Ashinsky.

The new organization oversaw the application of Kosher laws and standards among buyers and sellers of meat and other products, and it also decided which out-of-town charities would be sanctioned to appeal for funds in local synagogues.

Detroit's Jewish population was estimated at 75,000 in 1930, and the United Hebrew Schools had five constituent schools with 1,443 pupils and four affiliated schools with 370 students. The Philadelphia-Byron branch had 572 pupils. The second largest was on Delmar in the Oakland area with 261. The pay rate for UHS teachers ranged from $1.09 to $2.84 per hour. Yeshivah Beth Judah bought a home

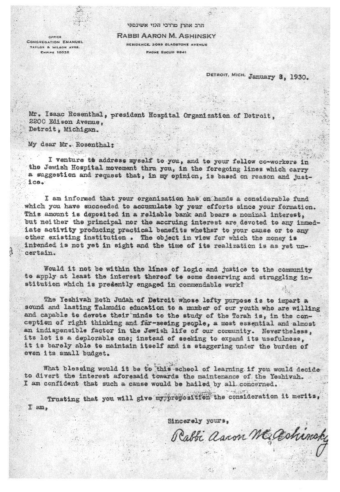

Rabbi Aaron Ashinsky, Principal of Yeshivah Beth Judah and spiritual leader of Congregation Emanuel (the Taylor Shule), sent a letter to Isaac Rosenthal, president of the Hospital Organization of Detroit, seeking funds to help the Yeshivah operate, as many parents couldn't pay tuition.

on Pingree near Twelfth Street to house its afternoon and Sunday classes.

Abraham Rogvoy, the first teacher when the yeshivah opened in 1916, died at the age of 53. He was a noted Talmudist, and was secretary of the United Hebrew Schools and secretary of the Hebrew Orphan Home. Affiliated with the Jewish Old Folks Home, House of Shelter, and Mizrachi, he taught the Talmud to a group of men Saturday afternoons at Congregation Emanuel.

Nathan Bielfield, president of the House of Shelter for 25 years, past president of the Hebrew Orphan Home, and a board of directors member of the Jewish Old Folks Home, died at the age of 72. Bielfield was active in several synagogues and was one of the founders of the Beth Jacob Synagogue.

One of Detroit's oldest active businessmen, Samuel Heavenrich, died at the age of 90. In 1862 he started a dry goods store with his brother, Simon, and at the time of his death he was active in the life insurance business. Heavenrich was an officer in Temple Beth El and was the only surviving charter member of the Phoenix Club.

World Jewry mourned the death of Lord Balfour. The author of the historic Balfour Document which he issued on behalf of the British government in 1917, died in London at the age of 81. Arthur James Balfour, a non-Jew, was considered Jewry's greatest friend and often spoke and wrote about the right and cause of Zionism.

Morris Schaver was chairman of the 1930 Detroit Gewerkschaften (the United Hebrew Trades Movement). To raise money for Histadrut for the purchase of land by the Jewish National Fund, the group met in the social hall at Littman's Theatre on Twelfth Street.

Emma Lazaroff Schaver was receiving rave reviews for her starring role in an all-Yiddish opera in New York. Max Blatt started a Yiddish radio program in Detroit, but because of the Depression, enough advertisers couldn't be found and the program went off the air after six months. While unemployment was increasing, Max Fisher graduated from Ohio State University and joined the Keystone Oil Refining Company, his father's oil recycling business in Detroit.

Charles Meltzer built the Oakland Bathhouse on Oakland and Clay in 1930. Customers called the establishment "The Schvitz." Schvitzers came from both sides of Woodward and both sides of the law. Purple Gang members were some of the colorful regulars. Besides a steam room and other appurtenances to induce relaxation, the Detroit Oakland Bathhouse was famous for its Porterhouse steak.

The Schvitz lost a few customers in July as 28 mobsters were killed by rivals in gang wars in the first 22 days of the month. Mob violence was the major news as the first regularly scheduled news reports began on local radio.

Sam's Kosher Meat Market, formerly at Twelfth and Cortland, opened on Dexter and Webb. Kraemer's Restaurant on Twelfth and Blaine offered lunches at sixty-five cents. The strictly kosher establishment, supervised by the Vaad Hakashruth of Detroit, adver-

Ads from the *Jewish Chronicle* in 1930.

Rabbi Joseph Isaac Schneurson, the Lubavitcher Rebbe, visited Detroit in 1930.

tised, "it pays to pay fare to come to Kramer's." Jacobs and Pearlman relocated their meat store from Hastings and Eliot to Dexter and Monterey, while the Modern Delicatessen opened nearby on Dexter between Burlingame and Webb.

Representatives of many of Detroit's synagogues and admirers gathered at the Michigan Central depot to greet Rabbi Joseph Isaac Schneurson, known throughout the world as the Lubavitcher Rebbe. A parade of automobiles departed for the depot from Linwood and Davison, and returned with the Rebbe along Vernor Highway to Wabash, to Ferry Park, to Twelfth Street, to Taylor and Woodrow Wilson, where a formal reception was held at Congregation Emanuel. During his stay, the Rebbe spoke at several synagogues, including Ahavath Achim on Westminster, and Delmar and Beth David on Elmhurst and Fourteenth.

When his father died in 1919, Rabbi Schneurson was clothed with the mantle of Lubavitcher dynasty. Eleven years later he was arrested and endured harsh prison conditions. Charges included the Rebbe used his widespread influence to create rabbinical seminaries and Hebrew schools, and that he imposed taxes upon religious Jews to maintain the institutions. Foreign public opinion mixed with influential diplomatic intervention led to the death sentence being changed to a prison sentence and later to three years in exile. Large demonstrations by followers of the Rebbe led to his freedom after ten days in exile.

The Detroit Hebrew Orphan Home, which opened in 1918, and the seven-year-old Detroit Hebrew Infants' Orphan Home, merged in 1930. The Young Women's Hebrew Association (YWHA) had 1,700 members in 1930, an increase of 1,495 in eight years.

Because the Depression impacted on the ability of many Shaarey Zedek families to pay dues, Rabbi Hershman asked for and received a salary reduction, which helped to defray some construction costs as Shaarey Zedek continued with its plans for a new synagogue. On May 26, 1930, the cornerstone of the new structure was laid on Chicago Boulevard and Lawton. Earlier in the month, Shaarey Zedek left its Brush and Willis location to rented quarters above a Detroit Edison substation on Twelfth Street and Clairmount. Shortly after the first Shaarey Zedek—Detroit's first structure built as a synagogue—on Congress and St. Antoine was razed, membership reached 625, and on the High Holy Days services were also held in a building owned by the Westminster Church at Hamilton and Glynn.

With many families moving from the area of B'nai Israel on Ferry and St. Antoine, the synagogue also conducted services in a leased store on Linwood near Cortland. After seven years on Frederick between Beaubien and St. Antoine, the Chesed Shel Emes, formerly the Jewish Free Burial Association, dedicated its new building on Joy Road near Lawton.

Morris Gunsberg, after whom the B'nai Moshe congregation was named, died at the age of 83. He was president of Yeshivah Beth Judah, active in several Jewish causes, and known for his benevolence. By November Detroit had an underwater link with Canada as the Detroit-Windsor Tunnel opened. The toll for the international crossing was 25 cents per car. Thirty new buses operated through the 5,160 foot tunnel.

In 1931 city officials estimated about 41,000 people had left Detroit in the past year in search of jobs in other parts of the country. It was estimated that 20 percent of Detroit's work force was idle. Auto-

The cornerstone laying for Shaarey Zedek's Chicago Boulevard building was held on May 26, 1930. The congregation's president, David W. Simons, is on the left, and on the right side of the youngster holding the sign is Rabbi Abraham M. Hershman.

(Courtesy of Archives of Congregation Shaarey Zedek.)

mobile production was down, plummeting from 5,337,687 in 1929 to only 1,331,860 in 1931. Thousands of Detroiters were out of work, out of money, and out of credit. Jobs were hard to find and hard to keep.

Lawbreakers were part of the times and crooks even wore Detroit police uniforms. Detroiters were shocked when 50 members of the Police Department were indicted for various crimes by a grand jury in 1931.

Gangsters, called the Little Navy Gang because of their rum-running activities on the Detroit River, were cutting into the profits of the Purple Gang. Truce talks were arranged in Apartment 211 at 1740 Collingwood near Fourteenth. The three Navy guys arrived unarmed, and a peaceful meeting was held. Ray Bernstein left, started his car, and revved the engine. It was the signal for the three remaining Purples to end the small talk, pull out their revolvers, and empty the contents into the Navy guys. The four Purples were caught and one testified against the other three. The squealer went on the lam while his three former crooked friends went to the slammer for life. The "Collingwood Massacre" and the ensuing trial was the talk of the town for months.

On one day in 1931 there were reports of four suicides in the Jewish community of Berlin. Because of the harsh economic times and the Hitlerites, many Jews were being evicted from their homes. Jews in Poland were the target of widespread economic boycotts by local citizens, even though the number of physical beatings were less than the previous year.

While the number of Jewish cemeteries desecrated in Germany approached a hundred, Chancellor Bruenning assured the correspondent of the Jewish Telegraphic Agency in the course of an interview, "The present government has the situation strongly in hand and there need be no fear that the Nazi forces will seize the power."

At a meeting of the Hebrew Sheltering and Immigrant Aid Society (HIAS) at the Astor Hotel in New York, the subject was legislation reducing immigration from European countries by ninety percent for the next two years. It was adopted by the House of Representatives. New York Mayor Fiorello LaGuardia emphatically stated that "the State Department joined with Congress and the Ku Klux Klan to back a bill which is especially designed to block Jewish immigration.

"There is a prejudice against you there that has become an obsession," LaGuardia continued. "There are men there gloating over having separated some of your people from their families."

While LaGuardia was speaking, 19-year-old, Swedish-born Raoul Wallenberg lived on Madison Street in Ann Arbor while attending the University of Michi-

Many billboards in and around the Jewish community had this reminder to help.

(Courtesy of Leonard N. Simons Jewish Community Archives.)

Gertrude Wineman (left), co-chair of special gifts and chair of the Women's Division in 1931, and Dora Ehrlich, active in the Federation and Hadassah, often worked together on behalf of the community.

(Courtesy of Leonard N. Simons Jewish Community Archives.)

gan. In 1931 the House of Shelter moved to 77 Alger, between Woodward and John R. and affiliated with the Federation. The 26-year-old Jewish Old Folks' Home also became a member agency of the Jewish Welfare Federation. Because of the Depression, the number of contributors to the Allied Jewish Campaign dropped by 401, from 5,047 in 1930 to 4,646 in 1931.

The Jewish Children's Home, the merged Detroit Hebrew Orphans Home, and the Detroit Hebrew Infant's Home had a newly built structure, funded by the United Jewish Charities, at Petoskey and Burlingame on the west side of the Dexter section.

Hyman Altman began "Altman's Jewish Radio Hour" on radio station WJLB on Sundays. It would continue for nearly 33 years. Jack Cinnamon opened the Linwood-Euclid Market, aptly named for its location. The meat and fish market also featured bakery goods, fruits and vegetables, groceries, and a delicatessen. William, Sam and Harry Boesky opened another Boesky Brothers Restaurant and Delicatessen downtown near Hudson's, Kern's, and Crowley's, at Library and Gratiot. In 1931, Nate Shapero's Economical Drug Stores, which had 43 stores in its chain, assumed control of the floundering Cunningham Drug Stores.

Nate S. Shapero, active in Jewish causes, took control of Cunningham's in 1931.

Mr. and Mrs. Adolph Sloman, both native Detroiters, celebrated their golden wedding anniversary with a reception for their friends and relatives at the Belcrest Hotel on Cass. Mr. Sloman, one of the oldest members of the American, Detroit, and Michigan State Bar associations, also served as a professor of law at the University of Detroit. Mrs. Sloman was the first president of the Temple Beth El Sisterhood and president of the State Federation of Temple Sisterhoods.

Ephraim Wolfson, the sexton of Congregation Mogen Abraham for over two decades, died at the age of 76. He was widely known as "Ephraim Der Shammes" and lived next door to the synagogue on Farnsworth. A member of many charitable organizations, his well-attended funeral was officiated by eight rabbis from the community.

Lillian (Goldman) Cohen, who started high school at Central High when the building opened in 1928, graduated in June 1931 along with 365 other seniors. While there was only one African American in the class, 55 percent of the graduates were Jewish.

Robert Marwil was elected president of the United Hebrew Schools. While the Depression affected UHS as teachers salaries were cut, no Jewish child desiring an education was turned away. The problem America faced, according to Phillip Slomovitz in an editorial in the September 4, 1931, *Jewish Chronicle*, was apathy.

Figures on the numbers of Jewish youths in Jewish schools in the thickly populated Jewish centers in this country reveal that not more than 16 to 20 percent of the Jewish boys and girls receive any sort of Jewish training. Those who retain the memory of the days when Jews actually were "ready to suffer and to starve, if necessary" for the sake of attaining Jewish knowledge must feel a sense of deep concern and extreme regret over the sad plight of the cause of Jewish education in this country.

In our own community we are fortunate to be blessed with a system of Hebrew education and a group of schools of which we may justly feel proud. It is unfortunate that this system, without doubt the finest asset in our Jewish community, should be compelled to suffer many handicaps on account of the existing crisis. But we are not concerned at this time with financial problem, as much as we are with the human element. These schools, in spite of their perfection, are still caring for educational needs of a small minority of the Jewish children in this community as it is everywhere else.

Lilian (Goldman) Cohen lived in an apartment on Twelfth Street between Taylor and Hazelwood, above a grocery and butcher store. To go to Central High, she took a streetcar on Twelfth Street a mile and a half north and walked carrying books west along Tuxedo almost three-quarters of a mile. The hike in all kinds of weather wasn't made easier when the "rich kids" from Boston Boulevard and Chicago Boulevard were dropped off by chauffer-driven limousines.

Ad from the December 1931 *Jewish Chronicle*.

Rabbi Aaron M. Ashinsky, spiritual leader of Congregation Emanuel for the previous five years, returned to Pittsburgh in 1931 to assume the post of chief rabbi of the city's nine United Orthodox Congregations. Later in the year, Congregation Emanuel merged with Beth Tephila to form Congregation Beth Tephila Emanuel. Despite the merger, most of the community continued to call the synagogue the "Taylor Shule" because of its location on Taylor and Woodrow Wilson.

Rabbi Joseph Eisenman, spiritual leader of Beth Tephila for the previous 20 years, was retained as the rabbi of the merged synagogues. In 1925 Beth Tephila had relocated from Napoleon Street to a rented hall on Twelfth Street and Taylor. Rabbi Joseph Rabinowitz moved to an apartment on Twelfth Street and opened Congregation Beth Shmuel next door.

Clara Clemens, Mrs. Ossip Gabrilowitsch, released a biography of her famous father titled, *My Father: Mark Twain*. Two paragraphs appearing on pages 203-204 were of particular interest to Jewish readers.

> Father had always been a great admirer of the Jewish race and now had the opportunity in Vienna to test and prove the soundness of his good opinion of that great people. For, in every walk of life there were large numbers of successful Jews, so much so that one frequently heard the complaint: "Everything

Clara Clemens
(Mrs. Ossip Gabrilowitsch)

Ads that appeared in 1932 in the *Jewish Chronicle*.

in this city is owned by the Jews—newspapers, banks, high professional offices and the successful shops." It was perhaps largely due to this fact that there existed an extremely strong anti-Semitic feeling in Vienna; because aside from any religious prejudices, there were certainly evidences of much jealousy on the part of Christians, and particularly of Catholics. Arguments as to the virtues or non-virtues of the Jews were often the topic of discussion in our drawing-room, and father always grew eloquent in defense of Christ's race. Indeed, so often were his remarks on this subject quoted that it was rumored at one time father himself was a Jew.

About this time he wrote his article, "Concerning the Jews," in which he states he considers them "the most marvelous race the world ever produced." He used also to say that the difference between the intellect of a Jew and that of a Christian was about the difference between a tadpole's intellect and an archbishop's. Many of the talented and cultivated Hebrews were invited to call on us, adding much grace to every occasion.

General Motors laid off 100,000 of its work force in Detroit by the end of 1931. In 1932 about 40 percent of the city's work force was idle. There was a serious fiscal crisis, salaries of city employees were reduced sharply, and there was a drastic cut in welfare expenditures. For those lucky enough to still have jobs in the auto industry, average weekly earnings fell from $35.14 in 1929 to $20 in 1932.

Thousands of demonstrators began their march in downtown Detroit in an attempt to reach Henry Ford's Dearborn office with demands for better working conditions and union representation. As they reached Dearborn, local police unleashed tear gas and gunfire, killing four marchers and injuring scores in the ensuing melee. Detroit police arrived and helped to disperse the marchers short of their goal.

"Unions are organized by Jewish financiers, not labor," Henry Ford wrote about his feelings regarding unions long prior to the march. "A union is a neat thing for a Jew to have on hand when he comes around to get his clutches on industry."

Because of the high unemployment rate and the Hitlerites, hundreds of Jewish families made their way from Germany to France. Phillip Slomovitz warned of the Hitler menace again early in a 1932 editorial in the *Jewish Chronicle*.

> *Recent reports that two-thirds of the German students are National Socialists, the virtual exile of thousands of Jews from German cities, the attacks upon Jewish synagogues and the desecration of cemeteries add to the tragic situation. There are some who are inclined to minimize this danger. But the manner in which the wild fires of hatred are spreading, and the seriousness with which the situation is becoming more aggravated by the economic problems, give reason for anxiety rather than optimism.*

Charles Coughlin, the priest who was assigned to the Shrine of the Little Flower in Royal Oak in 1926, began giving Sunday morning sermons on radio station WJR in 1930. Two years later, Coughlin created his own network of eleven to eventually 49 stations around the country.

David W. Simons died at the age of 75. The former president of Shaarey Zedek was well known in the business, civic, and religious life of the area. In 1922 Simons had gone to Palestine and donated a site for the Hebrew University Library on the Mount of Olives, and he donated a parcel of land in Palestine seven years later in memory of his daughter. She was a talented musician associated with Ossip Gabrilowitsch's Detroit Symphony Orchestra.

Milford Stern, serving his third term as president of the Detroit Jewish Welfare Federation, suffered a heart attack in front of the Penobscot Building a few minutes after leaving his office. The former president of Temple Beth El died two days later at the age of 50.

The number of contributors to the Allied Jewish Campaign dropped for the second year in a row to 4,302. One of the contributors, Max Fisher, donated five dollars. Fisher arranged a joint venture between Aurora Gasoline and Keystone Oil that year to refine crude oil in Michigan. The Guardian Glass Company was born in 1932. It would become more widely known decades later under Bill Davidson.

The Jewish Community Center purchased farm property at Woodward and Holbrook. An apartment and a house on the site were planned to be part of the Center. The Jewish Old Folks Home celebrated its 25th anniversary. The home on Edmund Place and Brush housed 46 residents in 1932. Downtowners rejoiced when the new library opened on Gratiot, just east of Hudson's. The old library had stood on the same site from 1877 to 1929. Rabbi Leo M. Franklin served as director of the Detroit Symphony Orchestra and was elected president of the Detroit Public Library.

University of Michigan quarterback Harry Newman was named Outstanding College Football Player of 1932. The Detroit native was Michigan's quarterback starting in 1930. Another Jewish Detroiter, Abe Eliowitz, was starring in football and baseball at Michigan State. Jewish baseball fans in Detroit followed the pitching exploits of Isadore "Izzy" Goldstein. The New York native's only season with the Tigers was in 1932 and he pitched in parts of 16 games, compiling three wins and two losses with a 4.47 ERA. It was back to the minors for the 24-year-old Goldstein. He never pitched in the major leagues again.

Harry Weinberg's "Weinberg's Jewish Radio Hour" moved from Monday nights to Sundays at noon. It

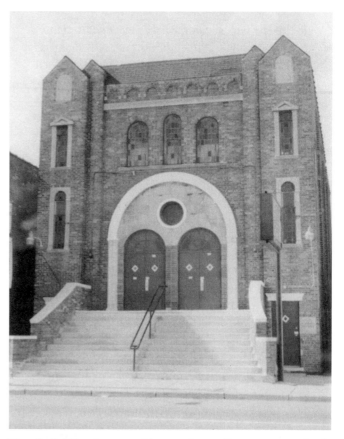

The Beth Abraham on Linwood was the congregation's third building and fourth location.

would run mostly on WJBK for close to 32 years. Irving Eisenman opened Eisenman's Pharmacy on Dexter and Burlingame, across from the Dexter Theater. Attorney Manuel Merzon announced his candidacy for the State Senate as a Democrat. Merzon sought to protect rights of Jews concerning laws of Kashruth enforcement and Jewish holidays conflicting with dates of public functions and elections.

In the midst of the Depression, 18-year-old Ralph Stone founded a small soap business on Ferry Street. Stone Soap would evolve into an international manufacturer of cleaning and wax products for the auto wash industry and a supplier of nursing homes, municipalities, and health clubs.

Abraham Levin, the youngest son of Rabbi Judah Levin and the first male counselor of Fresh Air Camp in 1916, went on to law school at the University of Michigan and practiced law in the firm of Butzel, Levin and Winston. Always having a love for the outdoors, Levin and his wife, Caroline, purchased the Franklin Cider Mill and adjoining property in 1932, where they raised their five children.

Herman Radner attracted national attention by providing three meals daily to hundreds of needy at his Walkerville Brewery, Ltd., in Canada, across the river from Detroit. In a period of only three months of the previous year, Radner had fed 110,000 people, including hundreds of children. Radner would be an active worker for Jewish causes for decades, and his trademark homily, "It's always something," would become nationally known thanks to his future daughter, Gilda, on television's "Saturday Night Live" in the 1970s.

Emma Lazaroff Schaver received an invitation to sing in Tel Aviv and in Jewish colonies in Palestine during her planned stay. The Schavers set sail from New York and also visited Germany, Poland, Russia, Austria, Switzerland, and England. Mrs. Goldie Meyerson, one of the most prominent woman labor leaders in Palestine, who would become one of Israel's Prime Ministers, visited America and Detroit for four days and addressed meetings under the auspices of the Women's Pioneer Organization for Palestine (Chalutzos).

Rabbi Samuel Fine, spiritual leader of Ahavath Zion on Holbrook and Beaubien, assumed the duties of principal and secretary of Yeshivah Beth Judah, replacing Rabbi Ashinsky. The school had 35 students at its Pingree location. Temple Beth El expected about 1,500 children ranging from pre-kindergarten to senior high school to enroll in its schools in 1932.

Dedication ceremonies featuring a procession of

The large amount of main floor seating at Shaarey Zedek accommodated a change in the 1931 bylaws allowing for mixed seating.

The Shaarey Zedek Synagaogue was dedicated in 1932.

Torah scrolls from Jericho Temple on Joy Road, Beth Abraham's temporary house of worship, to the new edifice on Linwood between Fullerton and Sturtevant, took place on Sunday, July 16. Rabbi Joseph Thumin, in his 17th year as spiritual leader, gave the dedication address. The community mourned the passing of Abraham Hersh Klein, after whom Congregation Beth Abraham was named. Klein, 68, was one of the synagogue organizers in the Winder and Hastings area in 1892. He was in the men's furnishing business on Oakland and active in charitable organizations.

Isaac Weinstein died days before his 81st birthday. He was honored by Shaarey Zedek four years earlier upon his retirement after 40 years as Baal Kore (Reader of the Torah). Weinstein continued to provide his services to the synagogue whenever he was needed.

Shaarey Zedek dedicated its imposing Chicago Boulevard synagogue on January 10, 1932. Rabbi Hershman summed up the feelings of many in attendance: "We rejoice that after years of anxious deliberation, arduous labor, painful experiences, disappointments and difficulties which at times seemed insuperable, this building stands forth bright and radiant—a graceful and noble structure."

At the end of the year, 500 people gathered at Shaarey Zedek's social hall to celebrate the festival of Chanuka, the 70th anniversary of Shaarey Zedek and Rabbi Hershman's 25th year as spiritual leader. Also in 1932, Rabbi Hershman inaugurated the first Junior Congregation in the city, and Cantor Jacob Soneklar succeeded Cantor Elijah Zaludkowsky.

The ongoing Depression was hurting almost everyone, and banks were feeling the financial pain, too. Many Detroiters couldn't pay their mortgages and loans. Governor Comstock feared that if big banks failed, smaller institutions in better financial shape might be pulled down. Government loans were sought to bolster Detroit's troubled banks, but after attempts failed, the governor declared a bank holiday. From February 14-21, 1933, Michigan banks were closed. President Roosevelt declared a national bank holiday on March 6, and by March 21 all solvent banks reopened. Two large Detroit banks weren't allowed to reopen and had to liquidate.

A new bank, National Bank of Detroit, opened on March 24, 1933, and thousands of Detroiters swarmed in carrying bags, briefcases, and bundles of cash and coin. By closing time that day, $12 million had been deposited, and by the end of the year NBD had 96,000 accounts and deposits of $189 million.

Edsel Ford and other founders opened Manufacturers National Bank in the Penobscot Building in August and took $11 million from depositors the first day. The S.S. Kresge Company was the first commercial depositor.

While Detroit's banks stabilized, the city treasury ran on empty. A cashless Detroit paid its employees in scrip in April, and in June the state raised money by passing a sales tax resolution. Mayor Frank Murphy resigned his office to accept President Franklin Roosevelt's appointment of governor-general of the Philippines.

Detroiters celebrated on April 7, 1933, as the newly created Michigan Liquor Control Commission authorized the sale of beer and wine and Prohibition was history. Blind pig and speakeasy operators applied for liquor licenses to legalize their establishments. Stroh's was ready to stock Detroit's shelves with beer. The only Detroit brewery licensed to produce near beer, Stroh's was able to get its machinery foaming quicker than the competition.

As Detroit was gripped by the Depression, movies provided escapism, and theaters offered two films for the price of one to lure customers. Many Detroiters didn't have the admission price for a double bill, however, so they stayed home and listened to the radio.

Detroiters needing escapism in 1933 found it on the local radio dial when the Lone Ranger began his 21 year ride. The masked rider of the plains and his Indian companion Tonto brought outlaws to justice three times a week.

George Stenius, who had local acting experience, won the audition to be the radio voice of the Lone Ranger. Stenius held the job only briefly as he had higher show business aspirations. He moved to Hollywood, changed his name to George Seaton, worked on Marx Brothers films, and gained fame as a writer-director and producer. Later Seaton would win Oscars for *Miracle on 34th Street* and *The Country Girl*.

Stenius was familiar to some Orthodox Jews as he was a "Shabbos Goy." Local synagogues would seek out the personable young man who took care of the lights and heat and performed other work duties religious Jews were unable to do on Saturdays. Stenius (Seaton) picked up on so many Jewish laws and customs that he invited the Marx Brothers to his Hollywood home for a Passover Seder.

Ads appearing in the *Jewish Chronicle* in 1933.

On January 30, 1933, Adolf Hitler, leader of the National Socialist German Workers Party, became chancellor of Germany. Soon afterward, Hitler employed terror tactics against political opponents to gain complete power. Hitler opened Dachau outside of Munich, a concentration camp built for political prisoners. Over time, it would become another concentration camp in which Jews were brutalized and murdered.

Paul Josef Goebels, head of the Nazi party in Berlin, called for a bloodless pogrom to expel Jews from government employment and from the country's economic life. Soon the pogroms became anything but bloodless. Jews were assaulted and robbed at will, and homes were invaded by Nazi hooligans. With only a day's notice, more than 8,000 Detroit Jews went to the Naval Armory on East Jefferson in March to protest the situation in Germany. Milton M. Alexander presided over the event and speakers. "Persecution is no new novel experience for us Jews," Alexander said in his opening remarks. "All too long and all too often we have felt the bitter sting of the bigot's lash. From Egypt—to Rome—to Spain—to Czarist Russia—the trial of the Jew through history has been of running a gauntlet of trial and suffering."

Orthodox leaders of the Detroit community called for prayers on May 10 at three assigned synagogues: Congregation B'nai Moshe, Dexter at Lawrence; Beth Tephila Emanuel, Woodrow Wilson at Taylor; and Ahavath Achim, Westminster at Delmar. Jews were urged to leave work in time for special prayers and addresses at 4 p.m.

On the same day in Germany, the Nazis vented their insane hatred by throwing books and manuscripts by Jewish authors into huge bonfires. In England, Winston Churchill warned the House of Commons that "the odious conditions now ruling Germany" would spread to Poland, "and another persecution and pogrom of Jews begun in this area."

Albert Einstein, who won the Nobel Prize for physics in 1921, moved to the United States in 1933 and became a professor at Princeton. In an address at the Sorbonne in Paris that year, Einstein said, "If my theory of relativity is proven successful, Germany will claim me as a German and France will declare that I am a citizen of the world. Should my theory prove

Jewish Community Center—1933.

untrue, France will say that I am a German and Germany will declare that I am a Jew."

In Detroit, Detroit Symphony Orchestra leader Ossip Gabrilowitsch, never a practicing Jew, had performed in Palestine four years earlier and began to take a strong interest in Zionism and other Jewish causes. In 1933, Gabrilowitsch denounced Hitler and wrote to fellow orchestra leader Arturo Toscanini, urging a public statement. "A decisive protest from you at this time would amount to a great historic fact," Gabrilowitsch said.

With politicians, celebrities, and some not-so-famous people making statements regarding the situation in Germany, John Haynes Holmes wrote in *The Sensible Man's View of Religion*, "If Christians were Christians, there would be no anti-Semitism. Jesus was a Jew. There is nothing that the ordinary Christian so dislikes to remember as this awkward historical fact. But it happens, none the less, to be true."

Revelations in the book *Hitler as Frankenstein* by a German known to have close contacts inside the Nazi movement, claimed that Henry Ford helped fund and fan the flames of German anti-Semitism by contributing large sums or money to a Nazi publisher.

During the critical financial period for many banks and individuals, Isaac Rosenthal, president of the Hebrew Hospital Association, announced that $10,000 has been loaned to the Jewish Welfare Federation in an effort to keep many of its institutions open. "In response to the many desperate efforts made by Federation officers to meet the present emergency, the loan from the Hebrew Hospital Association comes as a most helpful and encouraging act of cooperation," said Kurt Peiser, executive director of the Jewish Welfare Federation.

Operating expenses led to mergers in 1933. The Jewish Family Service and Resettlement Service merged into one office at the Community Fund Building on Warren, and the House of Shelter absorbed the Free Kosher Kitchen.

At a meeting at the home of Mrs. Isaac Rosenthal, plans were formulated for the Women's Auxiliary of the House of Shelter. The House of Shelter, at 51 Alger east of Woodward, was almost entirely dependent upon the Jewish Welfare Federation for financial assistance. During the previous year, 942 unemployed and transient individuals were helped with lodging, and 32,014 meals were provided.

The Vaad Ha-Ir, to be known as United Jewish Council of Detroit, was formed. Besides Orthodox synagogues joining the fold, Mizrachi and other organizations became part of the unified group. For every 50 members, each organization and synagogue placed one delegate to the council. Formation meetings were held at the home of Isaac Rosenthal. Besides the focus on unity, the organization prevented any conflicting community activities and overlapping groups.

There were 3,330 contributors to the Allied Jewish Campaign of the Jewish Welfare Federation in 1933, 972 less than in 1932. The Hebrew Free Loan Association made 1,585 loans the previous year. Almost 1,800 children were enrolled in the United Hebrew Schools in 1933.

The Jewish Centers Association and the Young Women's Hebrew Association merged to form the Jewish Community Center. The two groups had close to 4,000 members, and ground was broken at Woodward and Holbrook for the first building to be called the Jewish Community Center. Two existing buildings on the property were remodeled and joined with a lounge, and a combined auditorium and gymnasium was built in the rear.

Fresh Air Camp at Blaine Lake near Brighton boasted an enrollment of 200. The boys and girls were

Jacob Sklar passed away in 1933. 65 years later, his grandson, Robert Sklar, would become editor of the *Jewish News*.

given a physical exam at the North End Clinic on Holbrook before leaving from the Jewish Center. A 1933 Jewish Centers Association study put Detroit's Jewish population at 71,268. Ten years earlier, a similar study claimed the area had 38,221 Jewish residents. In 1927 the community was estimated at 64,400.

Jacob Sklar, one of the most well-known members of the Orthodox community, died at 68. Active in numerous organizations and in Congregation Beth Tephila Emanuel, Sklar also was a popular *mohel* (circumciser).

Max (Matisyahu Chaim) Milgrom was well known in the religious and business community. Milgrom, only 39 when he passed away, was the Baal Tefillah (Cantor) and Baal Koreh (Torah Reader) at Congregation Beth Yehudah (Pingree Shule). He was one of the organizers of the synagogue and part owner of the Soberman and Milgrom paint store on Twelfth Street. More than 2,000 mourners and numerous rabbis attended the funeral, which centered around the synagogue located on Pingree and Woodrow Wilson. In one of the longest funeral processions ever in the Detroit Jewish community, more than 200 cars accompanied the body to its final resting place at the synagogue's cemetery near Mt. Clemens.

Jews mourned the passing of the famed "Chofetz Chaim." Considered the spiritual head of world Jewry, Rabbi Yisroel Meir Kagan died in the small village of Radin, Poland, where he had spent most of his hundred years. *Chofetz Chaim*, the title of Rabbi Kagan's first book in 1873, dealt with the laws of *loshon hora* (derogatory gossip). Stories of his piety, humility, and ability to interpret and write religious books spread throughout the world during his life.

In 1933 the Junior Congregation of Shaarey Zedek conducted its first service in the main synagogue. The Junior League reelected Louis J. Gordon as president. Decades later, Lou Gordon would become one of Detroit's most well-known and controversial radio and television personalities. Also in 1933, Shaarey Zedek bestowed life tenure upon Rabbi Abraham Hershman and established its library and Adult Jewish School to serve its 629 members

Rabbi Joshua Sperka served congregations in Mt.

Advertisements appearing in the *Detroit Jewish Chronicle* in 1934.

Clemens and Ann Arbor and became associate spiritual leader of congregation B'nai David in 1933. The synagogue's religious school also started that year. Pontiac's nine-year-old synagogue changed its name from the Jewish Center of Pontiac to Temple Beth Jacob. Rabbi Joseph Rabinowitz, called by his countrymen the "Brezner Rebbe" after their hometown, led a march to Congregation Beth Shmuel's new location. The synagogue bought a home on Blaine east of Twelfth Street.

The First Hebrew Congregation of Delray on Burdeno brought Rabbi Benjamin Goldberg from Hazelton, Pennsylvania, to serve as rabbi and as principal and teacher of the synagogue's school. At the same time, the congregation extended the contract of Cantor Solomon Rubin, who had served in that capacity for the past six years.

Young Israel celebrated its 10th anniversary with a Sefer Torah presented by the Gendelman family. An automobile procession began from the Gendelman home on Gladstone and proceeded to the Young Israel's new building on Joy Road. The Gendelmans also were feted on the occasion of their 35th wedding anniversary.

The 25th anniversary of the Jewish Old Folks Home was observed in 1933. Jacob Levin, president of the Home almost since its inception, celebrated his 50th wedding anniversary the same year. The Old Folks Home had 28 male residents and 25 female.

Stanley Winkelman's father wasn't doing too badly in the ladies' apparel business during the Great Depression. The Winkelmans moved to a home costing $10,500 on Fairfield, just north of Six Mile, only a half block from the University of Detroit. Harry Mondry started an appliance repair business in a small store in Highland Park. The establishment would evolve into the appliance and electronic Highland Superstore Chain. Nathan "Toddy" Elkus wasn't deterred by the Depression either. Elkus borrowed $300 and opened Todd's on Randolph near Gratiot, in what would be the first in a chain of men's fashion stores.

Harper Furniture began in 1933. Founders Anna and Irving Goodman named the company after the store's Harper near Van Dyke location. Dexter Davison Markets got its start in a tent at that location by entrepreneur Norman Cottler in 1933.

Barney Broner wanted to be a history teacher, but family obligations after the death of his mother led him into business with his father. The elder Broner had a stand outside Ford's Highland Park plant catering to assembly line workers, selling snacks, supplies, and work gloves. After Ford moved its production to the Rouge Plant, Barney, then 21, and his father established the Broner Glove Company. It marked the beginning of a successful national supplier of gloves, hats, and safety items and operated into the next century.

Hank Greenberg had one major league at-bat with the Tigers in 1930 and came up to stay in the 1933 season. For Jews suffering economically in the Great Depression and following the news from Europe, Greenberg became an instant hero and his exploits on the field provided much-needed escapism. Greenberg hit .301 in 1933, the first of eight consecutive .300-plus seasons. Detroiter Harry Newman, who starred in college football at Michigan, had an out-

Hank Greenberg as pictured on a 1934 baseball card.

standing rookie season in the National Football League with the New York Giants. Newman led the team to a 11-3-0 record and its first title.

In October, an audience of 4,000 stood and cheered Emma Lazaroff Schaver's leading role performance in the opera *Faust*. Detroit's papers covered the event and gave the soprano high marks.

When Emma Lazaroff Schaver, in the prima donna role of Marguerite in the Opera "Faust," completed her first long aria in the garden scene, it was evident beyond any question that another local girl has made good.
Ralph Holmes in the "Detroit Times"

Detroit added a star of its own to opera Thursday night.
Herman Wise in the "Detroit Free Press"

Her whole garden scene was of the first order, vocally and as to acting, too.
Russell McLaughlin in the "Detroit News"

While Michigan was the first state to repeal its Prohibition statutes, cutting into the profits of the Purple Gang, the Purples remained colorful figures around Twelfth Street. For the most part, residents avoided contact with the group the press and police had labeled gangsters and hoodlums. Others had a different view.

"To me," Danny Raskin said, "they were swell guys. Always polite, never swearing, excellent dressers and complete gentlemen." Raskin, who would go on to a long career with the *Jewish News*, retained a vivid memory into the next century.

"We lived in an apartment on Pingree near Twelfth Street," Raskin recalled. "On the corner was the Cream of Michigan where a couple of fellows asked me to join them for some banana cream pie.

"Co-owner Johnny had just brought over our banana cream pies when a young boy ran into the Cream of Michigan crying…A truck had stopped on Twelfth Street and Philadelphia, he said, and the two fellows in it tried to grab his sister…When she ran away, they grabbed him, called the boy a damn Jew and slapped him hard across the face.

"The young gents I was with continued to eat their banana cream pie while the boy told them what had happened…Then they got up, asked the boy what the truck looked like, and were told that it was like a large wagon he used to deliver papers…The two fellows looked at each other and nodded their heads as if seeming to know about the truck…They asked the youngster to come with them and point out the truck if they should come across it…'C'mon, Raskin, take a ride with us.' …So I went.

"They seemed to know where to go…After driving up and down streets of the neighborhood they visited, the boy suddenly pointed and said, 'There it is!' …He was right about that wagon look…It had wooden slats with openings.

"We were told to stay in the car…The two young gents went into the bar in front of where the truck was parked and came out with armlocks on two men… "Are these the fellows?" the gents asked the boy…He said that they were.

"One of the young gents pulled out a gun, pushed it into the mouth of a wide-eyed and shaking fellow who had suddenly turned very white, took off the lock and pulled the trigger…Nothing, of course, happened …Just a click… "The next time you come to Twelfth Street, there'll be a bullet in it," he quietly remarked.

"The two fellows turned and ran away very fast.

"We drove back to the Cream of Michigan, where the young gents sat down and finished their banana cream pie as if nothing had happened … I asked what if there had been a bullet in that gun and the young gent never lifted his head as he continued eating the banana cream pie, softly exclaiming, 'There never is.' "

In 1934 Rabbi Hershman introduced Consecration classes for girls nearing the age of 15 at Shaarey Zedek. Graduates of the classes participated in an

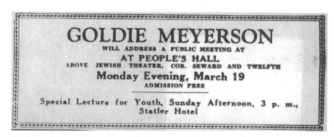

Goldie Meyerson, well-known Zionist labor leader and orator, would become Golda Meir and Israel's Prime Minister 35 years later, visited Detroit in 1934.

Hirsch Alper, sexton at Shaarey Zedek since 1920, chose Hank Greenberg for a Rosh Hashonah honor.

(Courtesy Archives of Congregation Shaarey Zedek)

impressive annual event at the synagogue. Despite the objections of many synagogue leaders, B'nai David allowed men and women to sit together in a designated section on the main floor. B'nai David Men's Club was formed, as was Boy Scout Troop No. 135. For the 12th consecutive year, Congregation Beth Itzchok, on Fischer Street north of Mack, reelected Rabbi Isadore Strauss. The B'nai Israel in Pontiac was organized and held its first services in a hall over a store on Saginaw Street.

Dr. Leo Jung, Rabbi of Jewish Center of New York City, came to Detroit to be guest speaker at Young Israel's 10th anniversary celebration banquet at the Statler Hotel. Rabbi Jung, a graduate of Canterbury University, England, authored several books including *The Jewish Library, Toward Sinai, Essentials of Judaism,* and *Living Judaism.* Jung was often quoted by rabbis. One of the many memorable phrases attributed to Jung was, "The Greeks say, everything that is beautiful is holy. The Jews say, everything that is holy is beautiful."

Henry J. Meyer, a researcher at the University of Michigan, claimed 33.1 percent of male Jewish Detroiters in 1934 were proprietors, managers, and officials and had a median income of $1,638. Non-Jewish Detroiters engaged in those professions earned a median income of $1,646 and accounted for only 10.4 percent of the local male population.

The Detroit section of the National Council of Jewish Women opened its first resale shop in 1934 on the first floor of 89 Rowena Street near John R. On his way to becoming a major labor leader over the next few decades, Isaac Litwak organized the Detroit Laundry and Linen Drivers Association. Isaac Rosenthal was unanimously elected president of the Mizrachi Organization of Detroit. A new 1934 Pontiac sold for $715, while a comparable Buick model stickered for $795.

Rose Phillips, a noted educator in the Detroit school system in the 1920s and 1930s, helped devise and implement the platoon system for elementary education, now used nationwide. Instead of one teacher for all subjects, the system provided a teacher for each subject. In 1934 at the age of 49, Phillips, the Detroit public school principal, married Israel Himelhoch, owner of the women's clothing chain. While Rose Phillips Himelhoch took a keen interest in her husband's business affairs, she remained in the Detroit school system early in their marriage.

Things were looking greener at the Franklin Hills Country Club. The banks foreclosed on the club's mortgage during the Depression, and Meyer Prentis saved it by paying the mortgage and buying the club. As the economy improved and new financing was found, Prentis sold the club back for the exact amount he paid, even though he could have made a substantial profit.

Detroit's baseball fans knew him as Patsy O'Toole, but his birth certificate read "Samuel Ozadowsky." He grew up to be a newsboy, boxer, liquor salesman, and ticket scalper and swapper, before becoming an errand boy for Mayor Frank Murphy.

O'Toole seemed to be present at all Tigers ball games at Navin Field. He was called the "Human Ear-

The finished product as it appeared in the paper.
(Courtesy Hy Vogel)

Detroit News caricaturist Hy Vogel draws Hank Greenberg in the Navin Field dugout in 1934.

ache," as his loud, booming voice could be heard around the ballpark at Michigan and Trumbull. To instigate a Tiger rally, O'Toole would climb onto the roof of the Tigers dugout and yell his usual rallying cry: "Boy, oh boy, oh boy, oh boy! Keep cool wit' O'Toole."

He called opposing players "bums" often and loudly. While O'Toole wasn't blessed with a high IQ, he was smart enough not to get close to the visitors dugout, as more than one opposing player tried to take a swing at him. Years of long, loud bellowing took its toll on O'Toole, and a throat operation silenced the loudest Jew and loudest Tiger fan of all time.

In the summer of 1934, many Jews were following baseball for the first time. Hank Greenberg, the 23-year-old Tigers first baseman, was in his second full season and rapidly becoming one of baseball's star players. The Jewish community embraced the tall, charismatic, Bronx-bred Greenberg.

As the summer wore on, Greenberg maintained his .300-plus batting average as the Tigers aimed for their first pennant in 25 years. As the season grew closer to Rosh Hashonah, Jews and non-Jews wondered if Greenberg would or could play on the Jewish New Year.

Greenberg turned heads as he appeared at Shaarey Zedek for services on the first day of Rosh Hashonah. The most accurate and best report of Greenberg's Holiday activities appeared in the September 14, 1934, edition of the *Detroit Jewish Chronicle*.

All eyes were on Hank. He was handed a Talith (prayer shawl), a Machzur (Holiday prayer book), and was even offered an honor: he was selected to go "Hagbah" to uplift the Torah following the Reading of the Law. But modest, at times shy, Henry Greenberg, refused. "I am only a ball player," he told venerable Hirsch Alper, the Shamess (Sexton). "Give it to some one else who really deserves it."

And when "Hank" walked out of the synagogue at 12:30 on Monday, there was a rush after him. Every boy in the place, and many a charming girl, followed him to wish him a Happy New Year. The next day on Tuesday, it was even worse. Everyone seemed to sense when "Hank" would rise to leave the synagogue, and again there was a rush after him. Henry was visibly embarrassed. He resented being given so much attention while in "shul" for Holy Day Services.

But we must not interrupt the sequence of our Greenberg Rosh Hashonah epic.

While "Hank" was at services on Monday, the newspapers hailed the news, in front-page, six-column streamers, that he was not to play on that day on account of Rosh Hashonah. "Hank" went back to his apartment and immediately a flood of telephone calls came to him—from Manager Mickey

Cochrane, from Frank and Charles Navin, the owners of the ball team, from teammates and leading citizens. "This is a civic duty," they told him. "If Detroit is to win the pennant you must play.

So "Hank" played. The Tigers won 2 to 1. Both runs were Greenberg's. Both were the results of home runs. It was a great day for the Tigers. It was a great day for Henry Greenberg. It was a great day for Detroiters, who got a thrill out of this one-man game by a Jewish boy who had already hammered in the winning runs in two preceding games. And it was a great day for the boys on Chicago Blvd., Rochester Ave., Boston Blvd., and the entire neighborhood bordering on the Shaarey Zedek synagogue. Worshipers on the way to services on Tuesday morning heard the word passed around by our boys on these streets: "Hank will be in shul today." And Hank was met by a cheering group as he came and left services on that day.

The Views of the Rabbis

But this is not the whole story. The rabbis have a place in it. Our newspapers could not pass up such a human interest yarn without consulting the spiritual leaders. Dr. Leo M. Franklin, Rabbi of Reform Temple Beth El, was asked for his view, whether Greenberg ought to play on Rosh Hashonah or not. Said Dr. Franklin:

"Mr. Greenberg, who is a conscientious Jew, must decide for himself whether he ought to play or not. From the standpoint of Orthodox Judaism, the fact that ball playing is his means of livelihood would argue against his participation in the Monday game. On the other hand, it might be argued quite consistently that his taking part in the game would mean something not only to himself but to his fellow players and, in fact at this time, to the community of Detroit."

So Greenberg played.

And the next day the Detroit News carried a statement which it accredited to Orthodox Rabbi Joseph Thumin. Rabbi Thumin was quoted to have gone to the Talmud, quoted Bitzo 8:12 under the heading of Tosofoth, where, the Detroit News Reported, it is said that ball was played on the streets on the Sabbath 900 years ago. He was reported as having quoted the Shulchan Aruch—and to have told the newspaper to tell Greenberg that he may play on the Sabbath and on Holy Days.

Now Greenberg has the Hechsher—and it will be recorded that he played and won a game on the first day of Rosh Hashonah.

Over the radio on Monday, Ty Tyson of WWJ, the Detroit News, continually emphasized that "Hank" made a sacrifice to play on Rosh Hashonah. And Ty Tyson's every announcement was followed by the statement: "But he is a swell fellow. He is a swell boy. He is a swell guy." And on Tuesday, as "Hank" came to bat, Ty Tyson paraphrased the popular song, "Bang, bang, bang, go the British," and declared that from now on, on Navin Field, it is:

"Bang, bang, bang, go the Yiddish."

Scholarly Rabbi Joseph Thumin, spiritual leader of Beth Abraham, was upset regarding reports that he granted Greenberg permission to play on Rosh Hashonah. Thumin issued a statement after the Holiday clarifying his position that was carried in the *Jewish Chronicle*:

In answer to many requests regarding the statements published in my name about Henry Greenberg's ball playing on Rosh Hashonah, I would like to make some explanations," Rabbi Thumin stated. "Mr. Greenberg did not play with my permission because I was not questioned by anybody concerning this matter before he played. On the second day of Rosh Hashonah, after Greenberg had played so spectacularly on the first day, reporters from the local papers came to me to inquire whether the Talmud dealt with the subject of ball playing on Rosh Hashonah or other holidays.

I was informed that people pointed out that Greenberg's violation of Rosh Hashonah was carried out with such success (Greenberg's two home runs accounted for the only runs needed as the Tigers defeated the Boston Red Sox 2-1) that this left a bad impression on light-minded young Jews. Since the question was not for any ruling on the subject, but only for information as to what the Talmud said about ball playing on holidays, I gave them quotations from the Talmud arid Shulchan Aruch on both sides of the question.

In Tosefeth of Tract "Baitzo" of the Talmud, page 12, it says "It is the custom among Jews to play ball on holidays. It is allowed because it is only enjoyment and exercise, which is not prohibited."

In Shulchan Aruch, which is the book of Jewish Statutes compiled by the two great authorities Rabbi Joseph Caro (1488-1575) and Rabbi Moses Isserles (1520-1572), when these two disagreed, Rabbi Isserles' ruling, coming later, is followed, section 308, paragraph 45 Hilchos Shabath. "There are two opinions," Rabbi Caro says. "It is prohibited to play ball on Saturdays and holidays." Rabbi Isserles commenting on this says, "Some authorities permit and this is what should be done."

Hank Greenberg
(Author's Collection)

In Hilchath Yom Tov Section 518 paragraph 1, it says, "It is permitted to play ball on holidays even in public places because it is only enjoyment and exercise." The commentary of Rabbi Solomon Luria (1510-1573) says, "It is a bad custom to play ball on holidays because this is not enjoyment for adults but for children."

In Shulchan Aruch Section 338 paragraph 5, it says, "A game which is played for profit and loss through winning or losing is comparable to buying and selling and is prohibited but nevertheless women and children ought not to be prevented from playing it." It is understood that this does not apply to a player who is on a salaried basis. Section 306 paragraph 4 deals with this question:

"If one is hired to do a work permitted on Saturdays and holidays, such as a watchman or a cantor, he may accept pay for his work on Saturdays and holidays if he is hired for a period of time such as a week or a month which includes these days. But if he is hired only for the holiday he is forbidden to take pay for it. An exception is made in the case of a cantor because of the mitzvah."

It must be understood that the foregoing about ball playing on Saturdays applies only in the European cities where there is an "airiv," streets enclosed in accordance with Jewish law or in places surrounded by a wall. On the open street, it is not even permitted to carry a ball.

Greenberg did not play on Yom Kippur as the Yankees defeated the Tigers at Navin Field. However, the Tigers remained in first place while Greenberg prayed in two places. Henry attended Kol Nidre services at Temple Beth El and returned to Shaarey Zedek for Yom Kippur Day, Wednesday.

Detroit poet Edgar A. Guest penned his sentiments for the *Detroit Free Press*:

The Irish didn't like it when they heard of Greenberg's fame
For they thought a good first baseman should possess an Irish name;
And the Murphys and Mulrooneys said they never dreamed they'd see
A Jewish boy from Bronxville out where Casey used to be...
In July the Irish wondered where he'd ever learned to play.
"He makes me think of Casey!" Old Man Murphy dared to say;
And with fifty-seven doubles and a score of homers made
The respect they had for Greenberg was being openly displayed.
But upon the Jewish New Year when Hank Greenberg came to bat
And made two home runs off Pitcher Rhodes—They cheered like mad for that.
Come Yom Kippur—holy fast day world wide over to the Jew,
And Hank Greenberg
to his teaching and the old tradition true,
Spent the day among his people and he didn't come to play.
Said Murphy to Mulrooney, "We shall lose the game today!
We shall miss him in the infield and shall miss him at the bat.
But he's true to his religion—and I honor him for that."

In an era of vicious anti-Semitism in Europe and not-so-subtle local anti-Semites, all of Detroit's Jewry stood taller because of the 6-foot-3-1/2 inch Greenberg.

While Hank Greenberg provided escapism for Detroit's Jews, future Detroiters living in Germany at the same time were worried about survival.

Benno Levi remembers the situation vividly:
I was eleven years old during the high holiday season of 1934. For 20 months Hitler had been in

power. What at first had been expected to be a brief interlude in the constantly changing German political scene now became to the country's Jews a daily escalation of terror.

The avalanche of evil enveloped the country. The boycotts became more vicious and the songs more virulent. One day, just after Yom Kippur, my father met me coming home from school to warn me not to react in any way to a picture of Adolf Hitler that our gentile tenant had put outside her door on the stairway leading to our apartment.

That same day he announced to my sister Ruth, my brother Ernest, and me that he had submitted our names to the German-Jewish Children's Aid Society in New York. Our community had been notified that this committee was anxious to help by placing youngsters with Jewish families in America. In November we received a letter from a cousin who had just arrived in New York with the first group under this program. His letter ignited a sense of excitement as he described the marvels of the biggest city on earth. I couldn't wait to be on my way.

There were still a few who urged my father not to take such drastic action. "Hitler will be gone in another six months," they assured him.

"So, when Hitler is gone the kids will come back and they will have learned to speak English and will have broadened their horizons," answered my father.

In early December we traveled to Stuttgart and were processed through the American Consulate. On the way home we stopped to say goodbye to our grandparents. We never saw them again. A week later a special delivery letter arrived confirming that on December 29th the three of us would be leaving on the S.S. New York of the Hamburg-American Line.

Once in New York, we were much too busy to be homesick. We were all housed as a group in the Jewish Orphanage on Amsterdam Avenue, across from Lewison Stadium. We were treated like royal guests. On our first evening, we were taken downtown by subway and shown the sights. I walked around and gaped with my mouth open—the subways, the skyscrapers, the cars, the people, the restaurants.

The committee was placing our group in homes all over the United States. My Father had specified that we were to be placed in an Orthodox home. Our destination, we were told, was to be DETROIT. I had never heard of it and couldn't even pronounce it.

We arrived in Detroit to be greeted by our new family. Ernest and I were to be with the Rosenbergs who immediately became Uncle Robert and Aunt Ella. Ruth was welcomed by the Friedmans, Aunt Ella's brother's family, Uncle Julius and Aunt Fanny. Compared to New York, I now felt that we were in a very small town. All I saw was Linwood, Dexter and vicinity. My glimpse of the big city—downtown Detroit—was yet to come. Now suddenly we were the epicenter of a very large family. We had instantly acquired dozens of cousins, aunts, uncles, and even a set of grandparents. It felt strange but also very good.

The committee's Detroit member, Fred Butzel, made regular visits to see that we were adjusting to our new surroundings without trauma. We wrote to our family in Germany on a regular basis and heard from them without fail. Homesickness was not one of our problems. Ernest and I were enrolled in Roosevelt Elementary School where we became an instant attraction as the first refugees from the Nazis. We were given special tutors who spoke German and in no time at all we were fluent in English and avidly following the Tigers and Hank Greenberg.

Joe Dorfman works behind the soda fountain of Dorfman Drugs on Joy Road at Quincy, west of Dexter. Hank Greenberg was one of the regular customers.

(courtesy Gail Zimmerman)

ECHOES OF DETROIT'S JEWISH COMMUNITIES

11

1935-1939
BEFORE THE WAR

Hank Greenberg turned 24 on the first day of 1935. Local Jews looked forward to the baseball season to see if Greenberg and the Tigers would play in the World Series again. The Tigers had lost the 1934 Series but the team started the '35 season on a winning note.

"Your Hit Parade" was a popular new radio program, and Detroiters were humming the new hits: "Begin the Beguine," "I Got Plenty O' Nothing," "It Ain't Necessarily So," "I'm in the Mood for Love," "Lullaby of Broadway," "Red Sails in the Sunset," The Music Goes 'Round and 'Round," and "Zing! Went the Strings of My Heart."

Estimates of Detroit's Jewish community ranged from 75,000 to 82,000. Either study put Jewish residents at more than 5 percent of Detroit's total. As Detroit pulled further away from the Depression, there were 8,063 contributors to the Allied Jewish Campaign in 1935, which was 3,311 higher than the previous year.

The Jewish Center on Woodward and Holbrook had 1,153 male and 1,076 female members. The Center operated 76 clubs, 36 classes, six mothers' clubs, a summer play school, day school, athletic, music and art programs, and employment and vocational guidance bureaus. The Jewish Children's Home at

Allied Jewish Campaign leaders in 1935: Seated: Ray Fisher, chairman; Fred Butzel, general chairman; Gus Newman, division secretary; Maurice Aronson, chairman of Team 1; Mrs. Joseph Ehrlich, president, Detroit Service Group; and Henry Wineman, chairman, Solicitation Committee.

Standing: Maurice Enggass, chairman, General Solicitation Committee; George Stutz, division secretary; Marvin Gingold, co-chairman, Team of Israel; Israel Himelhoch, chairman of Team 3; Irving Blumberg, co-chairman of Team 3; Simon Shetzer, co-chairman of Team 4, and Kurt Pieser, executive director.

Petoskey and Burlingame cared for 74 children—48 boys and 26 girls. Thirty-five were considered infants and 39 were between the ages of six and 18.

The combined enrollment of the United Hebrew Schools in 1935 was 1,600. A new branch opened at MacCullough Public School on Buena Vista and Wildemere. Central High School also housed a new branch of the UHS after public school hours. Isaac Rosenthal, president of the House of Shelter, said from 25 to 30 meals for transients were prepared daily in its kosher kitchen. Jacob Levin was elected president of the Jewish Old Folks Home for his thirtieth term. The Hebrew Immigrant Aid Society (HIAS) celebrated 50 years of service during which it had welcomed 2,382,093 immigrants.

Rabbi Joshua Sperka undertook an extensive survey of Detroit's synagogues in 1935. Sperka did not include Temple Beth El (Reform) and Shaarey Zedek (Conservative). Sperka, the spiritual leader of B'nai David, found the area had 44 Orthodox congregations comprising 2,497 members. Sperka broke the area down into four districts: (1) the east side, including the entire Oakland area; (2) the section from Grand Boulevard to Clairmount and from Woodrow Wilson to Linwood; (3) from Chicago Boulevard to Davison and from Twelfth Street to Dexter; and (4) outlying districts.

The first district contained 14 synagogues whose membership totaled 328. The second district had 725 members in its 10 synagogues. The third also had 10 synagogues but had 1,220 members. The fourth district had 224 members in its 10 synagogues. Only 11 synagogues of the 44 had permanent rabbis and only four rabbis received compensation sufficient to be considered a living wage.

Henry Meyer's *Jewish Social Studies* estimated that 44.2 percent of Detroit's Jewish population resided in the Dexter section in 1935, but many Jews lived in a neighborhood with only one small synagogue.

Sol Lachman and his wife set up housekeeping, like so many neighboring Jewish merchants, above their store on Michigan Avenue, three doors west of Junction. The Lachmans attended the Aaron Moshe, on 29th street just north of Michigan Avenue.

Sam Shevin owned three large theaters in the neighborhood: the Senate on Michigan west of Livernois, the Kramer on Michigan and Thirty-Fifth, and the Crystal on Michigan four blocks east of the Kramer. While many establishments were Jewish owned, the neighborhood mainly housed Polish Catholics.

The Ice Cream Parlor next to the Senate Theater was a popular hangout for all residents. Helen Kuperman recalls that her family's good friends, the

Many Jewish proprietors lived above their stores.

(Courtesy of Lachman & Co.)

Goldmans, lived in a flat above the Senate. Mrs. Kuperman, whose father had a jewelry store on Michigan and Central, fondly remembers the Jewish businessmen and women and their butcher, candy, shoe, linen, and dry goods shops, all a short walk from the 29th Street shul.

Edith (Kaner) Butrimovitz lived on the east side near Jefferson and Dickerson in a much more spread out area. Mr. Kaner operated a shoe repair shop, and Edith's playground was Waterworks Park near the Indian Village border. On Saturdays and Jewish holidays the family walked a long distance for services to the Beth Itzchok, on Fischer north of Mack. One route the Kaners could choose was to walk a mile north to Mack, then a mile and a half west along Mack to Fischer, and a half block north on Fischer.

Fueled by a merger with the Detroit Hungarian Hebrew Congregation, B'nai Moshe undertook to improve its synagogue on Dexter and Lawrence. The remodeling included an acoustic ceiling for the social hall and furnishings for the chapel, library, lobby and office. The merger and membership drive brought in 115 new members, bringing B'nai Moshe's total to 485.

Also in 1935, the Detroit Jewish Hungarian Congregation formed to provide another alternative for Jews of Hungarian background. The congregation used the Beth Tikvah Synagogue on Petoskey. A few blocks east, Shaarey Zedek opened its library and in western Michigan, the Jewish Center of Battle Creek formed and conducted services in a rented dwelling.

Because of the dire situation of European Jewry in 1935, the Central Conference of American Rabbis, the national association of Reform rabbis, repealed its policy of anti-Zionism. If Jews, the Reform leaders surmised, had a homeland, then they would have somewhere to go.

After 42,000 mostly German and Polish Jews had managed to enter Palestine the previous year, 61,000 Jewish immigrants came in 1935. Germany enacted the Nuremberg Laws, thus legalizing its anti-Jewish policies of confiscating businesses and property and removing Jews from their professions and public schools. Jews were stripped of their German citizenship and became further targets for murder and mayhem.

Nazis didn't need to pass laws or make excuses to attack Jews. On one warm day in 1935, Nazis barged into restaurants and places of businesses, hauling Jews to the streets and beat, robbed, and chased them. The Jewish Telegraphic Agency headlined the attack, "Bleeding Men and Women Driven Along Streets by Maddened Nazis."

Winston Churchill spoke and wrote about Hitler

Lachman's was on Michigan Avenue, three doors west of Junction.

(Courtesy of Lachman & Co.)

and the Nazi atrocities: "Even the wretched Jewish children" endured persecution in the national schools, Churchill informed his English countrymen. Falsely accused of treason in 1895, Jewish officer Captain Alfred Dreyfus died of natural causes in his 76th year in Paris, exactly 20 years after the Supreme Court of France had completely vindicated him.

Raoul Wallenberg completed his B.A. in architecture at the University of Michigan and graduated with honors. Wallenberg then left Ann Arbor and worked in Cape Town, South Africa, where he loved the scenery but not his position with a lumber and hardware firm. After six months in South Africa, Wallenberg traveled to Palestine.

Dr. Morris Fishbein, the eminent national authority on medical questions, came to Detroit to address the Temple Beth El Forum and surprised many in the audience with these facts: while Jews were only 3 percent of America's population, Jewish students in medical colleges accounted for 17 to 18 percent of enrollments in spite of discrimination in the selection of students.

The dismantling of the Purple Gang continued in 1935 due to infighting. Henry Shore, who represented the gang's "brains," disappeared without a trace after meeting one of the gang's "brawn" in a Twelfth Street restaurant.

David E. Heineman, who operated a successful law practice and served as a member and president of Detroit's Common Council as well as on numerous civic boards, died at the age of 70. Heineman had varied interests and 28 years earlier had designed what would become Detroit's official flag.

Aaron DeRoy, well-known Detroit auto dealer and sportsman, was killed when his automobile overturned in South Carolina. During the Depression in 1931, DeRoy, then 51, donated $10,000 to the Allied Jewish Campaign, and more than 3,000 workers were under his guidance in the drive that year. On a trip to Germany in 1925, DeRoy purchased two giraffes at $5,000 each and donated the pair to the Detroit Zoo. While en route to Detroit, the giraffes were in the news almost daily, and a contest was held to name the animals. DeRoy delegated a special army train to transport the giraffes, who were over 27 and a half feet tall, bypassing low bridges and tunnels.

The community mourned the loss of Rabbi Ezekiel Aishiskin, 69, who served B'nai David full time until 1933. An eminent scholar and sought-after speaker, Aishiskin often sprinkled his short addresses with humor. Funeral services were held in a jammed B'nai David, and the funeral procession marched past the main (Philadelphia-Byron) branch of the United

Interior of B'nai David at Elmhust and 14th. Rabbi Aishiskin stood at front right.

(Courtesy Walter P. Reuther Library, Wayne State University)

Hebrew Schools, as Aishiskin was active in Jewish education.

Former University of Michigan football star Benny Friedman, who had played professional football for seven years with four teams, became head coach at the City College of New York. Detroiter Harry Newman was starring in his second season in the National Football League with the New York Giants, but he was severely injured, forcing a premature retirement at the age of 25. Newman would return to Detroit and would operate a Lincoln-Mercury dealership at Van Dyke and Outer Drive. Joseph Wolf and John and Nate Lurie founded Wrigley Super Market in 1935. At the time, Tom and Al Borman were operating 10 food markets.

Two weeks after the Tigers won their first World Series in franchise history, Hank Greenberg was named the American League's Most Valuable Player on the strength of his league-leading 170 RBIs, 36 home runs (tied for league lead) and .329 batting average. Shortly after Greenberg's award, Tigers owner Frank Navin died and co-owner Walter O. Briggs assumed control of the team.

The Lions and Red Wings also won championships, and Detroit was known as the City of Champions. During the year, auto workers earned 76 cents hourly and the United Auto Workers union was organized. The Social Security Act made life easier by providing a pension for every worker starting at age 65.

The Detroit Chapter of Hadassah honored the first Lady of Zionism, Henrietta Szold, on the occasion of her 75th birthday by inviting members and friends to an Oneg Shabbat at Shaarey Zedek. Also in 1935, land was purchased on Mt. Scopus in Jerusalem and was donated to Hadassah by Joseph Wetsman and D. W. Simons. Wetsman's grandson, Billy Davidson, celebrated his Bar Mitzvah at the end of the year.

In 1936 *Fortune* magazine estimated that 90 percent of scrap metal dealer businesses in the country were owned by Jews. A study conducted earlier in the decade by Henry Meyer estimated that 25 percent of Detroit's laundry workers were Jewish and 90 percent of the city's linen and laundry supply businesses were owned by Jews.

Hank Greenberg, the American League's Most Valuable Player in 1935, was popular outside of the Jewish community too.

(Courtesy of collection of Jim Raetz)

Ossip Gabrilowitsch died in 1936 at the age of 58. He had begun conducting the Detroit Symphony Orchestra in 1918 and conducted radio's first complete symphony on WWJ in 1922. Gabrilowitsch created a weekly symphony program for radio in 1934 that went national a few months before his death. Mrs. Gabrilowitsch, the former Clara Clemens and daughter of Mark Twain, was at the famed conductor's bedside when he died.

Gabrilowitsch had visited Palestine eight years earlier and returned to become active in Zionist causes. He helped establish the Palestine School of Music. Gabrilowitsch once told Miss Ruth Bretman in an article in the *Detroit Jewish Chronicle*, "I regret that in my childhood I did not study Hebrew. To be able to read the Book of Books, i.e., the Bible, in Hebrew, is an accomplishment which has been denied me. It is fine and poetical, this language of our ancestors."

Philip "Cincy" Sachs turned 34 in 1936 and was named head coach at Lawrence Institute of Technology, then located on Woodward in Highland Park. The Sachs family had moved to town from Cincinnati in August 1917 and Sachs went on to become a basketball legend in the Detroit Jewish community.

Hank Greenberg started the 1936 season with a bang, batting .348 after 12 games. However, a broken wrist sidelined him for the rest of the season, breaking the hearts of many Jewish fans

Three hundred sixty-four Detroiters died in a July heat wave as the thermometer topped 100 for seven consecutive days. Mounted policemen poured buckets of water on their horses, and people wore cabbage leaves on their heads as they sought relief from the heat.

In 1931 Al Nagler had become publicity director at the University of Detroit at the age of 20. Nagler listened as candidates tried out for the job of broadcasting the school's football games. Nagler, a young, modest Jewish fellow, was confident he could do a better job and asked permission to try out. He won the position with WJBK radio and soon graduated to broadcasting Detroit Red Wings hockey. In 1936 he was behind the microphone for the longest hockey game ever played as Detroit and Montreal skated through six overtime periods and an exhausted Nagler worked from 8:20 p.m. to 2:30 a.m. "I couldn't speak for two days afterward," Nagler, who was the voice of the Red Wings for decades, recalled.

Many newspapers throughout the country reprinted an open letter to the Catholic Church published by the *Detroit Jewish Chronicle* urging that the Rev. Charles E. Coughlin's anti-Semitic campaign be halted. For several weeks in the summer of '36, pro and anti Coughlin parties vented their opinions. An anonymous woman caller warned the editor of the *Chronicle* that supporters of Coughlin, through the membership of the National Union of Social Justice, might organize a countrywide boycott of all Jews.

A letter from a Catholic from Indianapolis congratulated the paper for its stand and urged the *Chronicle* to keep up the pressure.

Dr. Ewart Edmund Turner, former pastor of the American Church in Berlin, toured parts of Germany and spoke with Jews, non-Jews, and Protestant and Catholic Church officials on a fact-finding mission.

"Jews in Germany still do not know what Hitler wants of them," Turner wrote in a lengthy article printed in many Jewish newspapers. "The latest move against the Jews got under way in Southern Bavaria in June when the police began refusing to renew the passports of Jews. In July the practice reached Berlin. This is not an announced Nazi policy, but a sufficient number of Jews have been refused passports to establish the fact that a new move is being launched to prevent Jews from leaving Germany."

The Black Legion, deeply prejudiced men clad in black robes and hoods emblazoned with a skull and crossbones who kidnapped, beat, and murdered people of minorities, was finally unmasked. The fascist group which operated almost at will in and around Detroit, Oakland, and Livingston counties in the

Rev. Charles E. Coughlin spewed anti-Jewish propaganda over the national airwaves.
(Courtesy of Burton Historical Colection of the Detroit Public Library)

National 1936 advertisement.
(Author's collection)

1936 Zuroff Furniture ad from *Detroit's Yiddish Forward*. Models; bedroom sets, $49, Dining room sets, $99, living room sets, $79.

(Courtesy Dr. Jack Belen)

1930s, were finally linked to a murder in 1936 of a Catholic who was accused of beating his Protestant wife. The Legion was also traced to hangings of blacks and killings of union organizers.

Legion members had plans to use typhoid germs in milk to poison Jews. The plot called for the poisoned milk containers to be distributed in stores in heavily populated Jewish areas. Among the thousands of Legion members were several high ranking police officials and others in public office.

After living and working in South Africa for six months, Raoul Wallenberg was working for a Jewish banker in Palestine, a friend of his grandfather from Holland. Wallenberg moved on to Sweden for what he hoped would be better financial opportunities, but he took with him memories of seeing once-prosperous Jews from Germany arriving in Palestine with not much more than the well-worn clothing on their backs.

Under the direction of former president Isaac Rosenthal and others, the House of Shelter moved from Alger, east of Woodward, to 1622 Taylor between Woodrow Wilson and Twelfth. A ladies auxiliary was organized, and the group raised funds for the building of additional rooms to accommodate those needing food and shelter. Medical care continued to be provided at the North End Clinic and Receiving Hospital.

The Jewish Community Council of Detroit was organized in 1936. Its main purpose was to have a central body composed of congregations and philanthropic and fraternal organizations. In September 1936, the United Hebrew Schools opened a branch in the Brady School at Joy Road and Lawton. Shaarey Zedek hired Janet Olender as their full-time librarian. The synagogue's library opened in 1935.

The late Miss Carrie Sittig Cohen willed the largest individual amount to date to a local Jewish institution. Fred Butzel, chairman of the 1936 Allied Jewish Campaign and vice-president of the United Jewish Charities, estimated the amount bequeathed would be in excess of $100,000. Miss Cohen was a member of Temple Beth El and eventually a branch of the United Hebrew Schools would be named in her memory.

After a three-month strike at General Motors and a one-month strike at Chrysler, the two companies recognized the United Auto Workers union. With agreements at Hudson Motor, Packard, Studebaker, and some parts companies, Ford was the UAW's next target. On May 26, 1937, Walter Reuther, a former Ford assembly line worker who became a UAW organizer, had a legal permit to distribute leaflets outside the Ford Rouge Plant in Dearborn.

Henry Ford was vehemently opposed to union recognition and allowed his hatchet man, Harry Bennett, to bolster security. Bennett hired former wrestlers and known hoodlums to stand guard at the plant gates. As Reuther, Richard Frankenstein, and a few union associates got ready to distribute their leaflets, they were ordered to leave. With tough-looking men approaching, Reuther and his party complied, but their exit was blocked by more of Bennett's men. The union men were rushed, beaten, kicked, and stomped by the Ford-Bennett thugs.

Photographers caught the violence on film and raced away before the Ford-Bennett gang—which also included some Dearborn policemen—could get at them and their cameras. When the photographs appeared in the papers, the union gained sympathy and public opinion turned against Ford. Because of the violence in what became known as the Battle of the Overpass, union membership picked up. By July 1937, the UAW had 200,000 members in Detroit and 370,000 nationwide.

Detroit had eight radio stations in 1937. The Detroit-born Lone Ranger program, on the air locally for four years, went national via the studios in the Maccabees Building on Woodward near the Main Library. Going nationwide meant the programs, which aired Monday, Wednesday, and Friday at 7:30 p.m., had to be performed twice more on those nights for the different time zones. The voices of Rube Weiss and Harry Goldstein could be heard coming out of the big old radios—sometimes they'd be good guys and sometimes they'd be bad guys.

Nate Shapero's Economical Drug Store chain of over 70 stores changed its name to Cunningham's in 1937. Shapero's office was way down Twelfth Street, two blocks south of Michigan, in a block-long warehouse. If the weather was nice, Shapero would take the pleasant stroll to Michigan and a couple of blocks east to check out Hank Greenberg and the Tigers.

Shapero tied in Cunningham's and the Tigers by providing 40,000 tickets to youngsters in a promotion, which resulted in more parents shopping at his stores.

Young Max Lapides and his father typically attended 50 to 60 Tigers games a year together. So Max wasn't a happy camper when a broken leg left him bedridden. He cried himself to sleep after he learned that Hank Greenberg would be nearby eating dinner with friends. Word was that the Tigers All-Star would shake hands with neighborhood kids. Young Max woke up when his father entered the room and turned on the light. He thought he was dreaming as Hank Greenberg towered over him and sat on the bed. Hank and Max chatted for a half hour or so, and Greenberg autographed Max's cast and favorite book before leaving. Max recuperated from his broken leg, and Greenberg recovered from his broken wrist the previous season by batting .337 with 40 home runs and an amazing 183 RBIs.

Dr. Salo W. Baron, professor of Jewish history, literature and institutions for the Miller Foundation at Columbia University, published a three-volume study of Jewish social and religious problems. Titled *A Social and Religious History of the Jews*, Baron claimed that the birthrate of the Jewish people in the world was dropping quicker than other races or religions. "If the population trend continues for five decades," Baron stated, "world Jewry will be threatened with a stationary population."

Goldie Meyerson, who would become Prime Minister of Israel in 1969 as Golda Meir, was a prominent leader of the Federation of Jewish Labor in Palestine (Histadruth) in 1937. Mrs. Meyerson was touring America as a representative of the new port of Tel Aviv and other maritime activities in Palestine and came to Detroit for a speaking engagement at the Jewish Community Center.

Approximately $300,000 was left to the United Jewish Charities by the estate of the late Joshua Cohen, who died in March 1937. The deceased was a brother of the late Carrie Sittig Cohen, who had willed her estate of approximately $150,000 to UJC in 1936.

Al Saltsman was operating a tire and battery shop when his father-in-law offered him twenty dollars a week, about five dollars more than he was earning at the time. "I gave the tire and battery place to my brother and went to work on my father-in-law's old truck, delivering around to different scrap yards," Saltsman recalled. "We often went through alleys, sounded our horn, and people would come to us with their scrap. Once we drove by a coal yard in the Russell-Six Mile area that was out with business and I suggested to my father-in-law that we should operate from there. After all, the yard had a long railroad track that ran through it. We bought it, fenced it, and I worked there for about ten years before I operated Factory Steel and Metal with the Carmen boys."

Veteran attorney Joseph Weiss died at the age of 80. Weiss graduated from Cass Technical High School in 1873 and was admitted to the bar in 1877. Weiss, a member of Temple Beth El who was politically well-connected, had a strong hand in drafting and reforming pension laws for Detroit police and firemen. A baseball enthusiast, Weiss was active in amateur baseball and was one of the founders of the Detroit Baseball Club in the 1880s when the team was a member of the National League.

Joseph Wetsman, well-known Zionist who was active in Shaarey Zedek and many Jewish causes, died in 1937. He had traveled to Palestine twice, spent several weeks in Soviet Russia, and planned another trip to the Jewish homeland at the time of his death. Wetsman was active in real estate and the theatrical business and imparted a love of the latter to his grandson, Bill Davidson.

A. Louis Gordon died suddenly at the age of 49 as he was preparing to leave his home on East Grand Boulevard for services at Shaarey Zedek. The former president of the congregation was credited with overseeing the building of the synagogue on Chicago Boulevard during the Depression. Decades later, his son, Lou, would be a controversial commentator on local radio and television.

Temple Beth Israel and Ahavas Achim merged, giving Grand Rapids a new congregation called Ahavas Israel. The present Orthodox synagogue, formerly occupied by Ahavas Achim at Second and Scribner Streets, housed the merged congregations. Pontiac's

Mrs. Goldie Meyerson, the future Prime Minister of Israel, visited Detroit serveral times on behalf of Jewish causes.

Orthodox congregation, the B'nai Israel, remodeled its house of worship and hired its first resident rabbi, A. E. Miller.

Shaarey Zedek celebrated its Diamond Jubilee and the thirtieth anniversary of Rabbi Hershman. Beth Israel reorganized and adopted Shaar Hashomayim as its new name as it continued to use its present structure at 15700 Muirland. The Joseph W. Allen Memorial Synagogue organized and used facilities in the new Jewish Home for the Aged on Petoskey. Temple Beth El held Sunday morning services in its present location since it opened in 1922. In 1937 services on Friday nights were reintroduced.

After nine years on Twelfth Street and Clairmount, the Hebrew Free Loan moved its office to Linwood and Blaine in a former bank building. Isaac Shetzer succeeded David Zemon as president. Simon Shetzer was elected chairman of the Detroit Chapter of the American Jewish Congress. Shetzer also urged the Jewish Welfare Federation to adopt the strategy of boycotting Nazi goods and services. The Federation responded and appointed Rabbi Leon Fram, who served as rabbi and educational director of Temple Beth El under Rabbi Leo Franklin, as head of the League for

Human Rights.

Fram was given a budget for an office and staff and publicized the growing menace of Nazism through educational materials and mass meetings. The group brought leading Christian clergy and many community leaders together to help spread the message. Volunteer shoppers went through stores, sought out German-made goods and convinced storekeepers to remove the items and not reorder.

Danny Raskin graduated from Detroit High School of Commerce and planned to pursue a career in sports writing. Danny had a job at the Jewish Community Center on Woodward as editor of the newspaper and enjoyed organizing and running the regular Holiday Hops. Danny suggested the Center should host dances more often and Social Inc. was born. "The Social Inc. events were so successful that we were forced to have them at restaurants with dance floors," Danny recalled. "It is the only dance or social that was finally disbanded because it became too successful. We couldn't find a place big enough to hold them."

Abraham Littman sadly closed his Littman's People's Theater on Twelfth Street. Littman cited attendance problems due to the dwindling Yiddish-speaking population and financial difficulties brought on by the Depression. Dr. Pearl Hauser opened her optometry practice in 1937 in Hamtramck. Sixty-five years later she would receive an award for being the oldest practicing optometrist in Michigan as she continued to average an eight-hour day, six days a week in her Hamtramck office.

In June 1937, 48 residents moved from the Jewish Home for the Aged on Brush and Edmund Place to the almost-completed new building at 11501 Petoskey. Within months the new 110-bed facility was filled to capacity. Mrs. Aaron DeRoy offered the board $100,000, payable over about ten years, according to Leonard Simons who was at the meeting to name the new building the "Aaron DeRoy Home for the Aged." The offer was rejected along with the DeRoy money (eventually $190,000), and the name went to the Jewish Center on Woodward and Holbrook.

Community leaders and well-wishers of all religions sent congratulatory messages to Fred Butzel on his 60th birthday in August. Isidore Sobeloff, experi-

Residents occupied the new Jewish home for the aged on Petoskey in June of 1937.

Rabbi M. J. Wohlgelernter came to Detroit in 1937.

enced in social work and as a newspaper reporter and editor, assumed his new duties as director of the Jewish Welfare Federation a few days prior to Butzel's birthday. The 9,908 contributors to the 1937 Allied Jewish Campaign raised $350,690, both record numbers.

The Ladies Auxiliary of Yeshiva Beth Judah under the leadership of Mrs. Pearl Rottenberg, raised the needed $1,500 to purchase and renovate a four-family residence on Elmhurst east of Linwood for the school's new quarters. Younger boys entered preparatory classes for the first time, and English became the language of instruction while Yiddish continued for the advanced classes. The Jewish Welfare Federation granted its first subsidy to the Yeshiva.

Isaac Litwak, who helped organize the Detroit Laundry and Linen Drivers Association in 1934, endured beatings and threats as he led the drivers to join the Teamsters Union. Morris L. Schaver traveled to Zurich as Poale Zion representative to the World Zionist Congress. Harry Millman, the lone surviving trigger man of the Purple Gang, was rubbed out in a hail of bullets while eating dinner in November 1937. Crime busters felt the Purple days were over.

Rabbi M. J. Wohlgelernter became spiritual leader of the Beth Tefilo Emanuel (Taylor Shule) on Chanukah in 1937. The leaders of the congregation were seeking a rabbi able to deliver a sermon in proper English.

Wohlgelernter was born in Poland in 1909 and went to Yeshivah in Warsaw at the age of 12. He emigrated with his family to Toronto in 1923 and received his rabbinical ordination at the Isaac Elchonon Theological Seminary in New York. After obtaining a Bachelor of Arts from City College, Wohlgelernter accepted the position of rabbi of Beth Jacob in Hamilton, Ontario. He moved to Seattle in 1933, where he was educational director of the Seattle Talmud Torah and took postgraduate courses at the University of Washington. Before moving to Detroit, he held the post of executive director of the Union of Orthodox Jewish Congregations of America in New York.

Father Charles Coughlin began radio sermons on WJR in 1926. By 1933, the "Radio Priest" had his own network of stations as he bought time with listener contributions. In 1936, listeners noticed a shift in Coughlin's ideas. Previously a supporter of labor unions and President Roosevelt, the priest from Royal Oak's Shrine of the Little Flower often criticized both. Coughlin brazenly called Roosevelt the "great betrayer and liar." By 1937, more church superiors openly rebuked Coughlin and his rhetoric.

In 1938, more Catholics in positions other than in the church criticized Coughlin and his opinions. Coughlin responded by becoming more defiant and offended even more people by delivering openly anti-Semitic broadcasts. While Hitler called for violence against Jews in broadcasts heard in Europe, Coughlin told his audience that Hitler stood as a "defense mechanism against the incursion of communism." Coughlin continued his support of Hitler and his anti-Jewish tirades, but most listeners were not in agreement and withdrew financial support.

Reports of terrible pogroms were reaching the Jewish communities in America. After Germany annexed Austria in March, scores of Jews were beaten, robbed, murdered and many were deported. Czechoslovakia was partitioned, and anti-Jewish laws were passed. Many Jews in Germany were starving as non-Jewish stores refused to allow Jews to purchase food. Jewish-owned stores were paint-sprayed, vandalized, and looted.

Because of the situation in Europe, Detroit rabbis declared a penitential day of mourning and condemnation of the anti-Semitic atrocities. Merchants and professional men were urged to close businesses and refrain from work from four to six in the afternoon of May 10. Three synagogues were designated as the gathering places: Congregations B'nai Moshe, Dexter and Lawrence; Beth Tephila Emanuel, Woodrow Wilson at Taylor; and Ahavath Achim, Westminster and Delmar. Cantors read portions of lamentations, and rabbis and lay leaders gave addresses and messages of hope.

In 1938 Detroit was the only major city in the top 100 population centers of the US without a Jewish hospital. Dr. Jacob Golub, director of the Hospital for Joint Diseases in New York, issued a report which broke down Detroit's 344 Jewish doctors by age and graduating school. "Detroit's Jewish physicians are as a whole young in age," Golub wrote. "Two hundred ninety-seven are under 50 years of age, 24 are between 50 and 64 years of age, and nine are over 64 years of age. No record could be obtained for 14 physicians.

"Out of the 344 physicians, 279 were graduated from Grade A medical schools in the United States. In that number are included 139 who were graduated from Wayne University College of Medicine, and 86 from the University of Michigan Medical School. A total of 225 physicians came from the two medical schools in Michigan. The remaining 54 physicians came from 23 other Grade A medical schools in the United States. In addition, 13 were graduated from three Grade A Canadian medical schools; 12 from six foreign medical schools and 13 came from 10 medical schools that are now extinct. Information was not available for 27 physicians."

Fred Butzel was chairman of the 1938 Allied Jewish Campaign, and the number of contributors increased by 3,466 over the previous year to 13,374 as $390,732 was raised. Irwin Shaw, director of Fresh Air Camp at Blaine Lake in Brighton, had Irving Rosen and Sara Stein head the list of 24 counselors, while Ben Chinitz, principal of B'nai Moshe Religious School, supervised the camp athletic program.

The United Jewish Appeal was formed in 1938. The UJA was a combination of the Joint Distribution Committee, responsible for overseeing overseas relief work, and the United Palestine Appeal, responsible for settling Jews in Palestine. The organization focused its efforts on trying to get Jews out of Nazi Europe. During 1937, the JDC enabled 1,600 refugees from Germany to emigrate to 48 different countries.

Rabbi Isaac Stollman was chairman of the Board of Education of the Yeshiva. The new board consisted of the Detroit Council of Orthodox Rabbis, along with some scholarly laymen. Twenty-five former students of the Yeshiva were attending yeshivas in New York and Chicago in 1938.

Rabbi Samuel Fine died suddenly at the age of 53, only a few hours after participating in evening services at Congregation B'nai Israel. The spiritual leader of B'nai Israel and Congregation Ahavath Zion, Rabbi Fine left Russia in 1923 and settled in Detroit a year later. Fine was an outstanding lecturer and writer and wrote books in Yiddish and Hebrew. Many of his articles on commentaries on the Bible and world affairs were translated into English. Rabbi Fine also took an active role in the affairs of the Yeshiva under its president, Isaac Rosenthal.

Heart disease claimed Rabbi Reuben Hurwitz at the age of 68. Rabbi Hurwitz was spiritual leader of Congregation Ahavas Achim at Westminster and Delmar for almost 20 years. Rabbi Hurwitz also was active in many Zionist causes, including the Allied Jewish Campaign and United Hebrew Schools.

Rabbi Szyjah Strauss, a founder of Detroit's Council of Orthodox Rabbis, passed away in 1938. A 1889 graduate of the Rabbinical Seminary at Szitomar, Poland, Rabbi Strauss had been a spiritual leader in Zakrocym, Poland, for 32 years before coming to America. At the time of his passing, Rabbi Strauss was affiliated with Congregation Beth Moses, which he had led for 17 years.

Rabbi Leizer Levin, his wife, and four children moved to Detroit in 1938 and took up residence on

Richton, a few blocks from Dexter. Rabbi Levin, trained in the famous yeshiva of Radin and other Torah academies, was an outstanding student of the famed "Chofetz Chaim." Rabbi Levin served as spiritual leader of Washki, Lithuania, for seven years before emigrating to the United States. Before coming to Detroit, he had served as a rabbi of two synagogues in Erie, Pennsylvania, for a year and a half. In his first year in Detroit, Rabbi Levin became widely known through study groups at the Tuxedo Talmud Torah Synagogue and the Beth Tikvah Congregation on Petoskey. He also was an active participant in the Vaad Hakashruth and the Yeshiva.

The River Rouge Congregation, organized in 1929 and holding services in a hall on Jefferson, built a small synagogue in 1938. The Congregation was located two miles south of the River Rouge Ford Plant. Its small membership couldn't raise enough funds to employ a full-time spiritual leader, so rabbinical students and visiting rabbis were employed on major holidays and for group study sessions. The Macziki Hadath, organized in 1918, disbanded in 1938 due to lack of attendance in the changing neighborhood. The congregation used a frame dwelling on Alger, west of Oakland.

The Jewish Community Center boasted that 360 of its members were playing on 30 teams in three leagues in 1938. Sunday games were played at the JCC, while Central High hosted Tuesday and Thursday games, and Northern High School was used on Mondays.

The Cincinnati Opera Company engaged Emma Lazaroff Schaver for several performances. The Detroit soprano also had a concert tour scheduled in Central America. Albert Kahn's architectural firm captured one-fifth of all designed factories in the United States in 1938. Max Fisher brokered a business deal with the Ohio Oil Company to supply Aurora with oil. Max celebrated on September 9 when his daughter, Jane Ellen, was born at Harper Hospital.

Pitcher Harry Eisenstat was well aware of the publicity Hank Greenberg had received regarding playing ball on Rosh Hashonah in 1934. The following year, Eisenstat, almost 20, was brought up from the minor leagues in September by his hometown Brooklyn Dodgers. Eisenstat posed the Rosh Hashonah question to a non-Orthodox rabbi, and the liberal spiritual leader gave his blessing. Eisenstat waited patiently

The River Rouge Congregation organized in 1929, built its small synagogue in 1938. It was two miles south of the River Rouge Ford Plant. The small congregation employed visiting rabbis and rabbinical students on a part-time basis.

(Courtesy of Joe Kramer)

in the Dodgers bullpen for his chance to pitch. One day late in the season, manager Casey Stengel brought him in with the bases loaded. It happened to be Rosh Hashonah. The young left hander's first big league pitch was smacked for a grand slam home run and the rival New York Giants scored four runs.

In 1938 the Dodgers dealt Eisenstat to the Tigers. Greenberg took the 22-year-old pitcher under his wing and introduced him to Detroit and the Jewish community. Eisenstat won nine games for the Tigers in 1938, two in one day. Brought in to relieve the starting pitcher in both ends of the doubleheader, Eisenstat was credited with the victories as Greenberg hit two home runs in one game and one in the other.

"Lock yourselves in your rooms tonight, fellas," joked manager Mickey Cochrane. "The Jews of Detroit will be going crazy." Greenberg homered often in 1938, the first year Walter O. Briggs, who lived in a Boston Boulevard mansion, called the remodeled

Harry Eisenstat pitched for the Tigers in 1938 and was introduced to Detroit's Jewish community by Hank Greenberg.

double-decked ballpark Briggs Stadium. By season's end, Greenberg totaled 58 home runs while batting .315.

Aviation pioneer Charles Lindbergh visited Berlin and accepted the service cross of the German Eagle, presented by Herman Goering at the direction of Hitler. On Henry Ford's 75th birthday in August 1938, Ford accepted the Grand Cross of the Supreme Order of the German Eagle, the Third Reich's highest honor for non-Germans. It was created by Hitler himself. Hitler's personal congratulations were read at Ford's birthday dinner in front of 1,500 celebrants.

The Jewish War Veterans of the United States planned a national convention in Detroit a few weeks after Ford's birthday. However, the organization only waited a few days after Ford's birthday to condemn Ford's acceptance of the decoration, calling it "an endorsement of the cruel barbarous inhuman action and policies of the Nazi regime." The protest was sent to Ford via telegram, and another wire was sent to Edsel Ford, refusing his offer to supply 75 automobiles for

Hank Greenberg became a national celebrity in 1938 as he hit 58 home runs, two shy of tying Babe Ruth's single season record.

(Courtesy of Ernie Harwell Collection, Burton Historical Collection of the Detroit Public Library)

convention delegates.

Herschel Grynszpan, a 17-year-old Polish Jew, attempted to kill an official of the German Embassy in Paris. Grynszpan, charged with attempted homicide by premeditation, told a French magistrate, "I regret my action but I obeyed a will stronger than myself."

Before being sent to prison to await trial, Grynszpan was questioned in German and Yiddish. He told of his parents who were deported from Germany in the expulsion of Polish Jews. Grynszpan's parents had previously been threatened with expulsion, and he had tried to help them by writing two letters to President Roosevelt, but to no avail.

"I did it because I loved my parents and the Jewish people who have suffered so unjustly," Grynszpan stated. The Nazi diplomat shot by Grynszpan died of his wounds, and the Nazis retaliated with a vengeance against the Jews. The *Detroit News* carried extensive United Press dispatches from Berlin and Paris on November 8 and 9, predicting dire consequences for the Jews.

On Wednesday evening, November 9, 1938, many Jewish families in Detroit gathered around the radio dial, fishing for news. Only snippets of information at the top of each hour—mostly on WWJ—told of the situation in Europe. Music filled the airwaves from most local stations: "Beer Barrel Polka," "My Heart Belongs to Daddy," "Thanks for the Memories," "You Must Have Been a Beautiful Baby," Kate Smith's "God Bless America," and other new hits of 1938. At times, local Jews were caught up in the programming, completely forgetting the plight of their brethren under Nazi rule.

The following day, the pain of local Jews and the violence in Europe was brought home. "NAZI MOBS BURN SYNAGOGS IN 6 CITIES" was the headline that ran across the *Detroit News*. "22 Jews End Lives in Vienna" was the subhead of the column on the far right of the front page. The dispatch from Berlin, which ran from the top all the way to the bottom of the page, told of the violence which would become known as Kristallnacht (the night of the broken glass), as plunder-bent crowds of Nazis raged through cities and towns in Germany and Vienna.

Elsie Simkovitz was a ten-year-old girl living in Europe when the horrific events unfolded. "I looked out of my bedroom window at the massive flames engulfing my Nuremberg synagogue," she recalled. "The German fire department stood by and watched the flames. They were there to see that the fire did not spread to German buildings.

"Hours later, the Nazis broke into our apartment. They were looking for my father. If he had been there, they would have taken him away to a concentration camp. We might never have seen him again. Disappointed that my father was not there, the Nazis began to destroy our furniture. They slashed an oil painting that was on the wall.

"Fortunately, my father had left for the United States five weeks before. Without visas, my mother, brother, and I were left in Nuremberg, the capital of Nazism. The U.S. State Department's consulate office played the quota waiting game; the lines of Jews seeking refuge grew longer."

Synagogues, Jewish establishments and many private homes were torched and vandalized. Many Jews were attacked, beaten, robbed, and killed, and thousands were hauled off to concentration camps. Children were thrown out of their beds as residences were ransacked. Jewish owned shops were looted and windows smashed.

Ironically, as Jews were beaten and killed and some committed suicide in Vienna, the Vienna Boys Choir was touring the United Sates and appearing in Detroit at the Masonic Auditorium. Detroiter Jay Kugel wondered how many fathers of the choirboys took part in the violence.

Some prominent Jews tried to rally Jews and non-Jews to the plight of European Jewry. Rabbi Leo Franklin conferred with Henry Ford in Dearborn. Ford was receptive to the rabbi of Temple Beth El and issued a statement which ran in Detroit's newspapers on December 1, 1938:

I believe that the United States cannot fail at this time to maintain its traditional role as a haven for the oppressed. I am convinced not only that this country could absorb many of the victims of oppression who must find a refuge outside of their native lands, but that as many of them as could be admit-

ted under our quota system would constitute a real asset to our country.

Because of their special adaptability in the fields of production, distribution and agriculture, they would offer to the business of this country a new impetus at a time like this when it is badly needed. Hundreds of Jewish men now employed in our plants show marked ability and loyalty and if the turnover among them is sometimes comparatively high, it is indicative of their justified ambition to improve themselves.

It is my opinion that the German people, as a whole, are not in sympathy with their rulers in their anti-Jewish policies, which is the work of a few warmakers at the top.

My acceptance of a medal from the German people does not, as some people seemed to think, involve any sympathy on my part with Nazism. Those who have known me for many years realize that anything that breeds hate is repulsive to me.

I am confident that the time is near when there will be so many jobs available in this country that the entrance of a few thousand Jews, or other immigrants, will be negligible.

I believe that the return-to-the-land movement is one of the ultimate solutions to our economic problems and in this movement the Jews of the old world can play a significant part. I am wholly sympathetic with the movement to give the oppressed Jew an opportunity to rebuild his life in this country, and I, myself, will do everything possible toward that end.

Soon after Ford's statement hit the newspapers, Fr. Charles E. Coughlin, pastor of Royal Oak's Shrine of the Little Flower, used his nationwide radio broadcast to charge that the statement was really Rabbi Franklin's words, not Ford's. However, Harry Bennett, personnel director of the Ford Motor Company, told the *Detroit News* that Ford "authorized Franklin to write the statement covering the points they had discussed. Rabbi Franklin did so, and it was submitted to Ford, approved by him and its publication authorized.

While most Americans were sympathetic to the plight of Jews and were willing to grant them asylum in the United States, thousands of Coughlin supporters in New York demonstrated against it. "Send Jews back were they came from in leaky boats," shouted demonstrators.

New York Mayor Fiorello LaGuardia, born to a Jewish mother and Catholic father, spoke Yiddish fluently and didn't hide it. LaGuardia also didn't hide his disdain for Coughlin and Hitler, and he used non-diplomatic language to describe the Nazi leader. The German press fired back, calling LaGuardia, "a dirty Talmud Jew,"…"a shameless Jew lout,"…and a "whore monger."

At a rally in Madison Square Garden publicizing the plight of the Jews in Germany, LaGuardia, in a voice choked with emotion, said: "I am unable to adequately describe to you the brutality of Hitler's government to my people. The Nazi regime is a great threat to world peace."

George Stutz was one of many Detroiters pained by Kristallnacht. Active in many causes and elected president of the Jewish Social Service Bureau in 1938, Stutz had come to America from Germany in 1916 at the age of 12 after the family leather business was destroyed by anti-Semitic arsonists. Benno Levi was grateful that his parents and sister got out of Germany and came to Detroit. As they became a family again,

Because of local, national and international news, Sammy Cohen, manager of the Triangle News Company, sold out of daily newspapers on his stand on Michigan Avenue and Griswold.

(Courtesy Michael Cohen)

some of their former friends' families were being torn apart.

As Detroit Jewry continued to agonize over the situation in Europe in 1939, Clarence Engass, chairman of the governors of the Jewish Welfare Federation, reminded the community: "While providing the necessary sums for relief and colonization of the tens of thousands of refugees, we must not overlook the fact that our present important drive is also to provide the necessary funds for the upkeep of existing local agencies."

As Britain was trying to disengage itself from the Balfour Declaration calling for a Jewish homeland in Palestine, United States Senator Arthur Vandenberg of Michigan was one of the most vocal supporters of the Jews' right to their biblical land. In a telegram to Philip Slomovitz, editor of the *Jewish Chronicle*, on May 19, 1939, Vandenberg stated:

"I believe today more than ever in the Zionist home in Palestine. As a member of the original Christian Pro-Palestine Committee, I thought I saw a great vision. It is clearer than ever today and the inhumanity of man makes it more logical and more essential than ever. I emphatically favor every cooperation that America can give to the…culmination of this promised Jewish homeland. The Balfour assurances should not default. The Jews of the world took them in good faith and have invested heart and fortune in them. They have a right to every international cooperation in behalf of this Jewish homeland. Count upon my interest to the limit."

Some Central High students rushed from the school to the Linwood streetcar on Tuesday afternoon, May 2, 1939. Their destination was Briggs Stadium, where the Yankees would be making their first appearance of the season. It was a chance to see Hank Greenberg and the visiting legendary Lou Gehrig.

The latter had participated in every Yankees game for almost 14 seasons—2,130 consecutive games. Everyone knew Gehrig was struggling and not playing with his usual zest and power, but the students were shocked to see Gehrig absent from first base by the time they arrived after the three o'clock game time. Gehrig felt he wasn't helping the club and had planned to bench himself even before the train arrived in Detroit. Players on both sides found out about the decision close to game time, but the less than 12,000 fans in attendance were shocked when Gehrig's name was missing from the pregame introductions. The Yankees battered several Tigers pitchers, including Harry Eisenstat, and the Central High students left before the final 22-2 score was posted.

A few hours later at the Jewish Community Center on Woodward, Henry Meyers was reelected president of the JCC. Other elected office holders were Mrs. Samuel Glogower, first vice-president; Saul Saulson, second vice-president; Mrs. Joseph Welt, secretary; and Saul H. Levin, treasurer. New directors were Mrs. Aaron DeRoy, Judge Harry B. Keidan, Mrs. Leonard Weiner, and Harvey Goldman.

Over the next few days, as Lou Gehrig underwent a battery of physical tests that would label his problem as amyotrophic lateral sclerosis, many Jews were frantically trying to get visas out of Germany. Jews who could leave Germany were only allowed to take ten Reichsmarks—worth about four American dollars. They were forced to surrender property, savings and valuable possessions.

Jules Lederer grew up with a knowledge of ladies' apparel. His father's business grew to manufacture

The Allied Jewish Campaign used heart-wrenching photos and advertisements on flyers and in publications in 1939.

(Author's collection.)

housedresses for the Kresge chain and other stores. Jules' father was killed in an auto accident and the business was eventually sold. As family funds ran out in 1933, Jules, then 16, went to work as a stock boy and unwrapped ladies' hats for Kern's Department Store.

Jules gained valuable experience and worked for other stores in other cities. A promotion took him to Sioux City, Iowa, where he fell in love with a customer named Esther "Eppie" Friedman. On July 2, 1939, Jules then 22, married "Eppie" in a Sioux City synagogue. His brother married her twin sister, Pauline. The two brides had three local rabbis officiate—Orthodox, Conservative, and Reform. It was a large wedding with 750 guests. No one, however, not any of the guests, or the grooms, or the brides, knew that the twin sisters would become the most famous women in America in the future.

In 1939, Temple Beth El honored its spiritual leader, Rabbi Leo M. Franklin, age 69, with a testimonial dinner celebrating his 40th anniversary with the temple. To better serve the needs of its members, Beth El bought its own cemetery on Six Mile in Livonia. Congregation Beth Shmuel (Blaine Street) purchased a half acre of land off Gratiot in Mt. Clemens for use as a cemetery. Congregation Ahavath Zion sold its Holbrook synagogue and rented a store on Oakland to use for religious services. Congregation B'nai Moshe honored its spiritual leader Rabbi Moses Fischer by electing him to life tenure.

Rabbi Morris Adler was hired by Shaarey Zedek as its first assistant rabbi in time to assist during the High Holy Days in 1938. Rabbi Adler was heavily involved in Jewish education and reorganized the synagogue's instruction and methods. The adjoining Kate Frank Memorial Building opened in 1939 for cultural and educational classes. Congregation B'nai Jacob moved from its previous King Street location east of Oakland to 12230 Linwood, between Richton and Cortland. Because most of its members had relocated to the Twelfth Street or Dexter areas, Congregation Mogen Abraham sold its Farnsworth Street synagogue in 1939. A small group of active participants met in private homes while relocation plans were considered. Observant Jews from Germany organized Congregation Gemilas Chasodim. Twenty families met for Sabbath and Holiday services at Lachars Catering Hall on Twelfth Street near Taylor. The Isaac Agree Memorial Synagogue rented two floors of a four-story building on Griswold near State. The congregation, which quickly became known as the Downtown Synagogue, began in 1922 on Rosedale Court east of Woodward and remained in that location for 17 years.

In 1939 it was estimated that less than 30 percent of local Jewish children received any kind of religious education from the United Hebrew Schools or other independent and synagogue schools combined. A financial gift from the David W. Simons family led to the remodeling of the Tuxedo-Holmur Talmud Torah. In appreciation, the branch was renamed the D. W. Simons Branch of the United Hebrew Schools. There was also a synagogue in the building served by Rabbi Leizer Levine. The Ladies' Auxiliary of the Yeshiva Beth Judah (Yehudah) bought the first bus to transport children to and from classes, easing parents' concerns about inclement weather and walking home after dark. Rabbi Isaac Stollman served as the first voluntary instructor at the Yeshivah as he taught an advanced Talmud class.

Dave Dombey graduated from Durfee and his parents gave him an expensive fifteen dollar Argus. His prowess with the camera led to a position as Central High's newspaper and yearbook photographer and a long avocation in photography. 1939 marked the fiftieth anniversary of the founding of Andrew Cunningham's drug store on Joseph Campau. In 1931 Nate Shapero's Economical Drug Company took over the Cunningham name and business, and eight years later there would be over 1,700 employees and 96 stores in the chain. Soberman and Milgrom opened another store at 14301 East Warren in 1939. The manufacturers of paints, flat paints, varnishes, and enamels already had stores on Twelfth Street, and on Livernois two blocks north of Fenkell.

Jake Mazer formed a pro basketball team, the Detroit Eagles. The team included Carl Bayer, who was a star player for Northern High School and a star player for a championship fast pitch softball team. Nathaniel Pieman moved his one-year-old Hebrew and Yiddish bookstore out of a home on Lawrence near Dexter to 9008 Twelfth Street between Taylor and Clairmount. Pieman, the father-in-law of Rabbi Joshua Sperka of B'nai David, carried religious oriented items and publications and some food products. Stanley Winkelman graduated from Cooley High School and from Temple Beth El. He spent most of the summer working in the blueprint room of Chrysler's Highland Park plant. Stanley spent the previous summers working in different areas of Winkelman's downtown warehouse learning different aspects of the business. Rose Himelhoch left the Detroit school system after 20 years of service to become vice president of personnel for her husband's women's clothing store chain.

Gertrude Berg received a million dollar five-year contract to star as "Molly Goldberg" and write the episodes of the national radio series. On April 3, 1939, Berg brought the plight of German Jewry home in an episode in which the Goldberg's Passover Seder was interrupted by a rock thrown through the window.

Over the course of the year, Berg had relatives of the Goldbergs in Europe trying to escape the Nazis. On September 3, 1939, two days after Germany attacked Poland, Britain and France declared war on Germany. Newsman Edward R. Murrow went to London to broadcast war news back to the states. Between Murrow's updates, dial-switchers often caught the two big hits of 1939, "I'll Never Smile Again," and Judy Garland's "Over the Rainbow." Movie audiences streamed to *The Wizard of Oz* and *Gone With the Wind*.

The skyline of Fresh Air Camp had more buildings in 1939. A bequest from the Carrie Sittig Cohen Estate brought the grounds dormitories, a dining hall, a 12-bed hospital, and other improvements. Later in the year, the Jewish Community Center at Woodward and Holbrook was remodeled, enlarged, and dedicated as the Aaron DeRoy Memorial Building. An assembly hall, cafeteria, 40 clubrooms, a gymnasium, library, and pool were among the additions.

After serving with the Jewish Legionnaires in Palestine in the same battalion as David Ben Gurion, Russian-born Norman Cottler came back to Detroit in 1920 after a four-year absence. He purchased a horse and wagon and began a fruit and produce business. Cottler's day began at 3 a.m. when he piloted his horse through the streets of Detroit. In 1930 Cottler operated an open-air fruit stand at the corner of Dexter and Davison. In 1939 he moved across the street to an enclosed store at 13301 Dexter. He named the new establishment "Dexter-Davison." The menorah (nine-branched candelabrum) became the store's symbol after the emblem on Jewish Legion caps when Cottler served.

As the decade was nearing its end, life for the unique Hungarian Jewish community still centered around the First Hebrew Congregation of Delray, on Burdeno one block north of Jefferson. The dark, plain-looking brick building, built in 1925, was the lone house of worship serving the families' social and spiritual needs.

Thriving Jewish-owned businesses dotted most of West Jefferson from Dearborn Avenue to Junction. The Lax brothers operated the only kosher meat market and grocery. Kalman was the butcher, and his brother, Sigmond, oversaw the grocery area. There were varied establishments such as Isaac Henig's dry goods and several furniture stores: Fox Furniture, Kollenberg Furniture, and the Wein Furniture Company. Nathan Goldman and Benjamin Lachman had jewelry shops, while the Klein and Liebowitz families had competing shoe stores. The Kleins also had a men's furnishings store, while the Zwiebacks had ladies' apparel. Harry Zalkower had a department store, and some other synagogue members operated a bowling alley, auto supplies, and beauty shop. Harry Greenstein was building up his Golden Valley Dairy Company as area residents could also shop at Cunningham's and Neisner's.

Charismatic Rabbi Harry Greenfield and his family saw to it that the small Orthodox synagogue had many activities for the women while the men kept long hours operating their businesses. The Greenfields instituted a sisterhood and girl scout troop, besides giving classes.

"The Greenfield family had an apartment in back of and adjoining the main sanctuary," recalled Shirley

The old Jewish Community Center on Woodward and Holbrook was a one-floor building connected on both sides to older structures.

The fire hydrant and tree on Woodward and Holbrook remained the same, but the new Aaron DeRoy Memorial Building was an impressive new JCC.

(Photos courtesy of Walter Reuther Archives of the Detroit Public Library)

(Greenstein) Gomezano, who grew up in the area. "Their doors were always open and often a haven to many. Besides the synagogue and a classroom on the main floor, there was a social hall downstairs and a small area for the women upstairs.

"The rabbi was also the shochet (ritual slaughterer)," Gomezano continued. "The backyard had a small ritual slaughterhouse for chickens. On Wednesday and Thursday evenings the rabbi slaughtered chickens for residents for the Sabbath."

Gomezano enjoyed strolling along Jefferson on Saturday evenings. "There were happy sounds of gypsies singing, dancing, and playing their violins, while wearing their native costumes. Stores would be open Saturday nights and bustling with shoppers, while limousines would arrive in front of Hungarian Village. Elegantly dressed couples would be out for an evening of Hungarian cuisine and entertainment.

"Young kids like myself would stand behind the Hungarian Village to listen for hours to the hauntingly beautiful gypsy orchestra. Saturday night was always greatly anticipated."

Jewish Houses of Worship in 1939

Adas Yeshurin – 2625 Tyler Ave.
Ahavath Achim – 9244 Delmar Ave.
Ateres Tzvi – 520 Mt. Vernon Ave.
Beth Aaron V Israel – 9550 Oakland Ave.
Beth Jacob – 655 E. Montcalm Ave.
Beth Joseph – 8607 Twelfth St.
Beth Moses – 588 Owen Ave.
Beth Shmuel – 1736 Blaine Ave.
Congregation Ahavath Zion – 446 Holbrook Ave.
Congregation Beth Abraham – 12517 Linwood Ave.
Congregation Beth Israel – 15700 Muirland Ave.
Congregation Beth Tefilo Emanuel – 1550 Taylor Ave.
Congregation Beth Tikvah – 9736 Petoskey Ave.
Congregation Beth Yehuda – 1600 Pingree Ave.
Congregation B'nai David – 2201 Elmhurst Ave.
Congregation B'nai Israel – 13101 Linwood Ave.
Congregation B'nai Jacob – 12230 Linwood Ave.
Congregation B'nai Moshe – 11401 Dexter Blvd.
Congregation Gemilas Chasodim – 8931 Twelfth St.
Congregation Nusach Ari – 8648 Linwood Ave.
Elim Chapel – 7361 Linwood Ave.
El Moshe – 3226 29th St.
First Hebrew Congregation of Delray – 8124 Burdeno
Ateres Israel – 9231 Cameron Ave.
Mishkan Israel – 2625 Blaine Ave.
Northwestern Congregational B'nai Zion Synagogue – 3841 Humphrey
Shaarey Torah – 17550 Brush St.
Shaarey Zedek – 290 West Chicago Ave.
Shaarey Zion – 12407 Linwood Ave.
Stollman Isaac Synagogue – 649 Belmont Ave.
Temple Beth El – 8801 Woodward Ave.
West Warren Congregation Atereth Tzvi – 6306 Begole Ave.
Young Israel – 2691 Joy Road

Jewish Organizations in 1939

Jewish American Business Men's Club		8739 Twelfth Street
Jewish Child Care Council Home	Mrs. Ida Lieberman, caretaker	581 Holbrook Avenue
Jewish Child Placement Bureau	Mrs. Edith Bercovich, director	51 West Warren Avenue
Jewish Children's Home	Louis Newmark, superintendent	4205 Burlingame Avenue
Jewish Chronicle Publishing Company	Joseph J. Cummins, president Harry L. Cummins, vice president Jacob H. Schakne, secretary-treasurer	525 Woodward Avenue
Jewish Community Center	Herman Jacobs, executive director	8904 Woodward Avenue and 11518 Dexter Boulevard
Jewish Community Council	William I. Boxerman, executive director	51 West Warren Avenue R307
Jewish Folk School	Morris Haar, principal	12244 Dexter Boulevard
Jewish Fraternal Club		8679 Twelfth Street
Jewish Fraternal Club Ladies' Auxiliary		8679 Twelfth Street
Jewish House of Shelter	Siegmund Bernard, manager	1620-22 Taylor Avenue
Jewish Metropolitan Club	Eli Altman, manager	1912 Taylor Avenue and 8836 Twelfth Street
Jewish Social Club		9036 Twelfth Street
Jewish Social Service Bureau	Harold Silver, director	51 West Warren Avenue
Jewish War Veterans Auxiliary		704 East Jefferson
Jewish Welfare Federation	Clarence H. Enggass, chairman of the board Fred M. Butzel, chairman of the executive committee Abraham Srere, president Israel Himelhoch, vice president Nate S. Shapero, vice president Mrs. Henry Wineman, vice president Isidore Sobeloff, secretary Maurice Aronsson, treasurer	308 Community Fund Building 51 West Warren Avenue

12
1940-1945
WAR AND SACRIFICE

While buildings and families were being torn apart in war-ravaged Europe, Detroit prospered as many families moved to the Motor City in search of a better economic life. Many southern whites moved to Detroit for the same reason blacks did: jobs. Black residents numbered 149,119 or 9.2 percent of Detroit's 1940 population of 1,623,452. Almost 20 percent of Detroit's population was foreign born and most were paying close attention to the events in Europe.

There were conflicting reports on the number of residents populating the local Jewish community. The 42nd annual volume of the *American Jewish Year Book*, issued by the Jewish Publication Society of America, claimed Detroit had 90,000 Jews, and 105,201 Jews resided in the entire state of Michigan. America had 4,771,000 Jews, according to the Year Book, or 3.69 percent of the country's population.

The *Detroit Jewish Chronicle* had its own take on the number of Jews in Detroit and published the following editorial in its November 8, 1940, edition.

> *The American Jewish Year Book for 5701, just published by the Jewish Publication Society of America, gives 90,000 as the figure of the Jewish population of Detroit, in the study of "Jewish Communities of the United States: Number and Distribution of Jews in Urban Places and in Rural Territory," prepared by Dr. H. S. Linfield.*
>
> *This figure will be seriously disputed. About 10 years ago, the estimate of the Jewish population of Detroit was 72,000. Last year, Henry J. Meyer's study of the economic distribution of Detroit Jews, made on behalf of the Jewish Welfare Federation and the Conference on Jewish Relations, estimated the Jewish population as being approximately 84,000.*
>
> *It is generally believed in well-informed quarters that there are about 85,000 Jews in Detroit. We are inclined to agree with this estimate.*

Large numbers of European Jews were forced into ghettos as the Nazis took control of Poland. Within

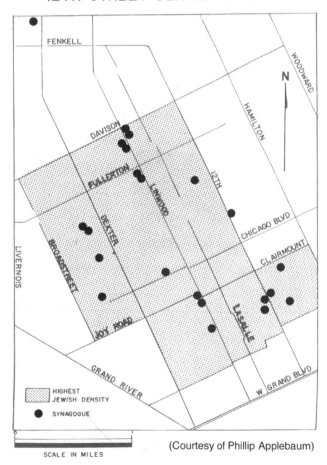

12TH STREET-DEXTER IN 1940

(Courtesy of Phillip Applebaum)

ECHOES OF DETROIT'S JEWISH COMMUNITIES

the walled areas, Jews were isolated from the rest of society. The ghettos soon had thousands of hungry and sick residents as food and medical supplies were cut off. Starvation and disease led to numerous deaths, and many were led off to concentration camps.

As western Europe was being overrun by the Nazis, Winston Churchill became premier of Britain in May 1940. The following month, Italy declared war on France and Britain, and around the time German planes started bombing Britain two months later, the first organized anti-Semitic demonstrations occurred in Paris. Jewish shops were looted, and owners and customers were beaten before police intervened. Demonstrators were arrested but released shortly after.

German planes targeted the heavily Jewish populated East End district of London. An estimated 2,000 planes virtually destroyed the Jewish quarter in one terrifying night. Many survivors loaded their possessions on their backs and sought shelter in central London's schools, hotels, and public buildings. In the same week, an Italian bombing mission destroyed many homes in Tel Aviv. The raid killed 112, 55 of whom were children, and wounded 151.

On the recommendation of the Jewish Child Care Council, a committee of the Jewish Welfare Federation, the Detroit Hebrew Orphan Home, and the Detroit Hebrew Infants' Orphan Home combined into the Detroit Jewish Children's Home in 1930. Two residences used since 1920, on Rowena near Woodward, were sold, and the children were moved into a new building on Petoskey. By 1937, 57 children called it home. Three years later, only 24 youngsters resided there.

In 1940. smaller children were placed in foster care and the older ones were reunited with their parents. The home became a day care center for children of parents serving in the war effort during World War II.

The Allied Jewish Campaign set a quota of $925,000 for 1940. The first week netted $550,000, but by the end of the drive, the 20,440 contributors accounted for $735,970. However, it marked the first time the number of contributors passed 20,000 and the amount raised passed $700,000.

The Center Symphony Orchestra made its debut under the direction of composer, conductor, and pianist Julius Chajes at the Jewish Community Center on Woodward and Holbrook. Benno Levi got a job as

Jewish Detroiters were among those waiting in line to see *Gone with the Wind* at the Adams Theater in 1940.

(Courtesy of Michigan Views)

a pin boy at the bowling alley in the JCC. He worked the three-hour shift to 10:30 p.m. and biked to work to retain more of his 60 cents an hour pay. Bowlers whistled the new tunes of 1940: "All or Nothing at All," "When You Wish Upon A Star," and "You Are My Sunshine." Harry Dermer, of the Blaine Kosher Restaurant, opened a kosher style eatery downtown in Cadillac Square. Al and Tom Borman split the operations of their food markets, with Al handling "Food Fair" and Tom overseeing "Lucky." Ira Kaufman, a former milk salesman and hardware store owner who went to night school to earn a license to operate a funeral parlor, opened the Ira Kaufman Chapel in a two-story flat on Dexter.

Temple Beth El's Sisterhood organized a Red Cross unit that became the largest of any congregation in Detroit. Beth El's membership was less than it was a decade earlier, though. In 1940 there were 1,613 members, 137 less than in 1930. Shaarey Zedek had 750 member families, while the 32 other Orthodox synagogues in Detroit had a combined membership of 2,977 families.

Rabbi Menachem Mandell Zager died at the age of 54. Rabbi Zager, who was born in David Horodok, Poland, had pulpits in Poland and Russia before coming to Detroit in 1925, where he served congregations Adas Yeshurin, Petach Tikvah, and Ateres Zvi. Organized in 1916, the Ahavas Achim on Delmar closed its doors in 1940 as its congregants moved farther north and west.

The Rose Sittig Cohen Building on Lawton and Tyler, housing the new branch of the United Hebrew Schools and the Jewish Community Center, was formally dedicated on Sunday, October 26, 1940. Abe Srere, president of Detroit's Jewish Welfare Federation, presided over the ceremonies, which included community dignitaries and rabbis. UHS pupils previously attending the branch at MacCulloch School were transferred to the new building.

Rabbi Dr. Samson R. Weiss, who led a teachers' seminary in Wuerzberg, Germany, and served the Ner Israel Rabbinical College in Baltimore as a professor, was hired as dean and principal of the Yeshiva Beth Yehudah (Judah). Rabbi Jacob Unger and Dr. Hugo Mandlebaum were added to the instructional staff of the school, which had 103 students and six grades in

The Yeshiva Beth Yehudah was located in a four-flat on the south side of Elmhurst, several houses east of Linwood.

(Courtesy of Yeshiva Beth Yehudah)

its Elmhurst location. A fire in a nearby house on Elmhurst east of Linwood led Detroit safety officials to condemn the four-flat the Yeshiva was using for school purposes.

A meeting of Yeshiva board leaders David I. Berris, Isadore Cohen, and Isaac Rosenthal, along with directors of Congregation Mogen Abraham, led to a merger consummated on the last day of 1940. The Mogen Abraham had sold its Farnsworth synagogue building the previous year and was looking for a site in the Dexter area, which also suited the needs of the Yeshiva.

As few Jewish residents remained in the Oakland area east of Woodward in 1941, a Federation study concluded that about 80 percent of Detroit's Jews lived in the Twelfth Street and Dexter neighborhoods. The two districts were almost one continuous area as six blocks separated Twelfth and Dexter, with Linwood three blocks east of Dexter. However, the Jews living closer to Dexter were in streets further north than those clustered closer to Twelfth Street.

Abraham Srere, active in Zionist and numerous other Jewish causes, was president of the Jewish Welfare Federation in 1941. Mrs. Abraham Srere headed the women's division of the Allied Jewish Campaign for the second year. The Jewish Vocational Service was organized in 1941; its job placement department had been around since 1926 when it was part of the Young Women's Hebrew Association. Years later the employment bureau relocated to the Jewish Community Center on Woodward. The Jewish Community Center also served as a USO center in 1941, and Gertrude Glowgower became the first woman president of the JCC. Only 12 children lived at the Jewish Children's Home on Petoskey in 1941, 41 less than had resided there five years earlier. By August the building was closed and the children were placed elsewhere.

Charles Lindbergh, who was awarded Hitler's Service Cross of the Order of the German Eagle on a trip to Germany in 1937, said in a speech covered by the New York Times in 1941 that "the Jews' greatest threat to this country [America] lies in their large ownership and influence in our motion pictures, our press, our radio, and our government."

More than 700 Jews were killed and over 2,000 wounded during a five-day pogrom in Rumania. Many thousands of other Jews were slightly wounded but didn't seek treatment as they feared reprisals. Hundreds of Jews sought and were granted shelter at the American consulate. Jews who tried to escape to Hungary were machine-gunned, as were others who tried to flee in small boats. Criminals were released from jails in Rumania by Iron Guardists to help butcher the Jews. The director of the Zionist Organization in Bucharest and his 36 employees were beaten and hauled to a suburban field, where they were murdered. When Nazi bombing squadrons targeted Belgrade in April, causing 700 Jewish casualties, Yugoslavia's Chief Rabbi, Dr. Isaac Alcalay, was among the victims. The rabbi was killed when a Nazi bomb completely demolished the synagogue where several hundred men, women and children also had taken refuge during the raid. The bombing mission also destroyed every other synagogue and the Jewish Community Center in Belgrade. Several hundred Jews who survived had been afforded protection during the air raids at the American consulate.

Six days later, Dr. Chaim Weizmann, president of the Jewish agency for Palestine and the World Zionist Organization, addressed a meeting under the auspices of the Jewish Welfare Federation at Cass Technical High School. The well-attended meeting served as a forerunner of the Allied Jewish Campaign. The following day, the Jewish quarter of London was destroyed by Nazi air attacks. Many women and children were buried under tons of debris from what had been homes, apartment buildings, and shops.

For the most part, Thursday, July 10, 1941, was a dismal summer day in Detroit. A partly cloudy morning gave way to scattered showers and thunderstorms. Used car salesmen weren't happy as the rain kept customers away from the lots along Livernois. The papers were full of used car ads for 1937 automobiles. A '37 Plymouth Coupe was advertised for $775, while a four-door sedan could be had for $219. Movie theater operators, however, loved the rain. The air-conditioned Royal Theater way out on Seven Mile and Meyers, had the best double-bill: James Stewart,

Hedy Lamarr, and Judy Garland starred in *Ziegfeld Girl*, and a "B" movie, *Angels with Dirty Faces*. The Mercury at Schaefer and Six Mile had Cary Grant and Irene Dunne in *Penny Serenade*, and Ralph Bellamy in *Ellery Queen's Penthouse Mystery*. The air-cooled Avalon on Linwood and Davison had Tommy Dorsey and his band featured in *Las Vegas Nights*, and Robert Cummings and Ruth Hussey in *Free and Easy*. The Dexter double bill didn't have much appeal to the ladies: *The Mad Doctor* with Basil Rathbone, and *The Man Who Lost Himself*, starring Brian Aherne.

For those who chose to stay home in the evening, WWJ was the popular station on Thursday nights. The Bing Crosby Show hit the airwaves at 8:00, followed by Rudy Valee an hour later, and Fred Waring and his band at 10:00. The variety programs provided listeners with a chance to hear the latest tunes of the summer of '41: "By the Light of the Silvery Moon," "Chattanooga Choo-Choo," "Deep in the Heart of Texas," and "You Made Me Love You."

Reading the paper in a big comfortable chair within good hearing range of the radio was how most older Detroiters relaxed. The newspapers that day didn't have much coverage on the happenings in Europe. There were still plenty of human interest stories on the All-Star baseball game that had been played in Detroit two days earlier. With Hank Greenberg in the army, though, the game didn't have the interest it would have had in the Jewish community.

Without thinking of events in Europe, Jewish Detroiters could go to bed humming the latest tunes. Sleep wouldn't come easily if Detroit's Jews knew what was transpiring in Jedwabne (Yadovneh) that very same day. Some of the Jews in the small Polish town were clubbed to death by shovels, hammers, and boards. Others were butchered with knives and axes. The rest were forcibly herded into a barn and burned alive. When the carnage of death ended, 1,600 Jews, numbering about 60 percent of the town's population, had been murdered—not by Nazis but by their former neighbors. When the Nazi killing squads arrived in town to do their work, they were amazed that their mission had already been carried out, and with such savagery.

After more than 42 years of leading Temple Beth El, Rabbi Franklin notified the board of his desire to retire from the active ministry. Many Beth El members hoped that Rabbi Leon Fram, associate rabbi and director of education for the past 16 years, would replace Rabbi Franklin upon his retirement. However, Rabbi Fram supported causes not popular with a large portion of the membership. Fram championed Zionism and civil rights and was in the forefront at a mass meeting calling for the unionization of auto workers. When it became clear that Dr. B. Benedict Glazer, senior associate of New York's Temple Emanu-El, would be offered Franklin's position, some Beth El members including former president Morris Garvett held

A "Horrors of War" card set, issued by Gum, Inc., of Philadelphia, with descriptive stories on the back of the card, helped educate youngsters of the generation to current events in Europe.

(Author's collection)

meetings to organize a new Reform congregation with Fram as its spiritual leader.

In its August 1, 1941, edition, the *Detroit Jewish Chronicle* reported on the birth of Temple Israel.

> At an enthusiastic rally of the founding members of the New Reform Jewish Congregation held Monday night, July 28, at Hotel Statler, the congregation decided to adopt the name "Temple Israel."
>
> The name was proposed by a committee consisting of Mrs. Milford Stern, Roy Sarason, Alexander Freeman, Rabbi Leon Fram, and Benjamin E. Jaffe, chairman.
>
> In a solemn ritual Rabbi Fram dedicated the congregation to its new name. The congregation recited the classic Jewish credo, "Hear, O Israel, the Lord Our God the Lord Is One," and the Rabbi pronounced the priestly blessing.
>
> Morris Garvett, who presided over the meeting, announced that the Rosh Hashonah and Yom Kippur services of the new Temple Israel would be held in the auditorium of the Detroit Institute of Arts, at John R. and Farnsworth. The Succoth services will be held in the smaller lecture hall of the Institute of Arts. In response to several inquiries the chairman stated that there will be a special service for the children on Wednesday afternoon, Oct. 1, and Rabbi Fram would follow his practice of the past 16 years, and tell the children a Yom Kippur story.
>
> It was announced that Miss Anna Oxenhandler, formerly assistant educational director at Temple Beth El, is now in the service of the new congregation. This announcement was greeted with an enthusiastic response.
>
> One hundred new members joined the congregation at this meeting. Temple Israel now has a membership of 200.
>
> Mr. Garvett announced that the religious school of the new Temple Israel will follow the curriculum and organization which made the schools formerly administered by Rabbi Fram and Miss Oxenhandler nationally famous. Members of their former teaching staff in the high school department, as well as the elementary school, who had raised the quality of their school to the highest standard in America, have spontaneously offered to follow their administrators into the new school.
>
> The new religious school will begin with a pre-kindergarten class and go on through the entire high school period, and continue with adult education. All boys and girls who are qualified for confirmation will form the charter confirmation class of Congregation Israel.
>
> Until a new Temple is built, or Temple Israel obtains it own quarters on the northwest side, the religious school classes will be held in the Hampton Public School at 18460 Warrington Drive.
>
> Before the next meeting of the congregation, the committees will be appointed for the organization of Temple Israel's Sisterhood, Temple Israel's Brotherhood, and Temple Israel's Youth League. A Temple Israel Boy Scout Troop is being organized. It was decided that the entire congregation shall constitute the membership committee.

On August 10, 1941, five weeks after German soldiers entered David Horodok, now in Belarus, local citizens assisted the SS Nazi killing squads in machine-gunning 3,000 Jewish men and burying the victims in a mass grave. Women and children were herded into a barbed wire ghetto to await their fate. As the German army advanced in Russia, SS killing squads followed behind with the mission of executing Jews. Tens of thousands were murdered. Within three days in September at Babi Yar, outside Kiev, more than 30,000 Jews were forced to undress before being shot to death.

After prayers on behalf of the Jews of Europe, the cornerstone ceremonies of the Yeshiva Beth Yehudah took place on Sunday, September 28, on the northwest corner of Dexter and Cortland. David I. Berris, chairman of the building committee, presided over the event and a large, spacious tent with comfortable seating was provided. Well before the 1:30 starting time, all seating inside the tent was filled to capacity and several hundred had to remain outside. The crowd was estimated at a thousand, and tears of emotion filled the eyes of Mrs. Beila Simon as she was given the honor of placing the cornerstone. The Simon children of the Simm's Cut Rate of Pontiac honored their mother and the memory of their father by donating a thousand dollars.

In addition to providing accommodations for the school's 115 students in six classes, the building would house a synagogue for Congregation Mogen Abraham. The Congregation turned over $20,000 of the $55,000 estimated cost of construction. The Ladies of the Yeshiva raised $10,000, while Young Israel of Detroit donated $2,000. A bequest from the D. W. Simons estate accounted for another large contribution.

The community was shocked to learn of the auto accident which took the lives of Ralph Davidson and his brother-in-law, Morse Saulson, in Troy Township. Well known in the Zionist and Shaarey Zedek circles and affiliated with many charitable organizations, Saulson, 56, left two sons, and Davidson, 57, left a daughter and a son, William, who would become one of the biggest entrepreneurs in the state of Michigan.

Henry George Hoch, the church editor of the *Detroit News*, covered Rabbi Franklin's farewell address in the November 8, 1941, edition of the paper.

"All I hoped to do has not been done. Only a small part of my early dreams have been fulfilled. But I have done, and I can say this honestly, whatever my feeble talents have permitted me to do."

This was Rabbi Leo M. Franklin's humble farewell to the congregation he has served and guided nearly 43 years, as for the last time he led his people in the prayers and responses of the Evening Service for the Sabbath at Temple Beth El Friday night.

As he left the pulpit at the end of a reminiscent sermon, he told them:

"I step down from this spot, which is more sacred to me than any other that I know, bequeathing to you such memories as you may wish to cherish, and maybe some inspiration.

"To my successor I bequeath, I am happy to believe, a strong, unified, warm hearted and enthusiastic congregation—a great opportunity for self-realization.

"May it be given to him who shall take my place to lead you a little nearer to the mountain top, and thus bring you closer to God and closer to each other."

When the final prayers had been chanted and the service was ended, there was a rush to the pulpit, and for nearly a half hour the friends of the congregation crowded around the retiring rabbi for personal and affectionate farewells.

Later many of them adjourned to the social hall of the temple, where there was an hour of fellowship, refreshments, and more farewells.

Rabbi Franklin has been elected rabbi emeritus by the congregation, and will continue to live in Detroit.

His successor, Rabbi B. Benedict Glazer, of New York, will take over the spiritual leadership of the congregation next week, and will be formally installed at the Sabbath Eve service next Friday night.

On December 5, Sgt. Hank Greenberg, less than four weeks away from his 31st birthday, was finally discharged from the army. Back in August, Congress had passed a law that men over 28 shouldn't be drafted. Greenberg was disappointed that he wasn't released in time to rejoin the Tigers for the last part of the season but was looking forward to resuming his baseball career in '42.

December 7, 1941.

Myron Milgrom, 13, went to the Avalon on Linwood near Davison to see Orson Welles in *Citizen Kane*. Benno Levi, 18, went swimming at the JCC on Woodward. Sammy Cohen, 30, got married at Congregation Beth Tefilo Emanuel on Taylor.

Arriving guests told the groom what they heard on the radio. Swimmers at the JCC went looking for a radio. Moviegoers exiting the Avalon scanned the newspaper stand. In large print, the headline and subheadlines read:

Superstar Hank Greenberg averaged 43 home runs and 148 RBIs in the previous four seasons. The morning after his 19th game in the 1941 season, in which he hit two home runs to help beat the Yankees, Greenberg was inducted into the U.S. army.
(Courtesy of Ernie Harwell Collection, Burton Historical Collection of the Detroit Public Library)

Japan Declares War on US & Britain After Attack on Hawaii & Honolulu.
Many Reported Killed in Attacks.
Battleship Afire.
US Army & Navy Put on War Bases Along Pacific Coast.
Roosevelt to Address Joint Session of Congress Tomorrow.

The following day, the United States declared war on Japan, and three days later, Germany and Italy declared war on the U.S., after which the U.S. declared war against them. The newspapers on December 15 told of the destruction eight days earlier:

Six Warships Lost & 2,729 Men Killed, 656 Wounded in Hawaii Attack on 12-7.

One of the 2,729 men killed at Pearl Harbor was Harold Eli Shiffman. The 27-year-old native Detroiter was a graduate of Central High School and enlisted in the Navy in 1940. He was stationed on the battleship *Arizona* as a radioman. After Pearl Harbor, Hank Greenberg decided to reenlist. He was the first major league player to join the army after the United States declared war.

In March 1942, Detroit had over 1.7 million residents, even though thousands of men were a world away serving in the Armed Forces. Followers of the news didn't rely on the city's seven radio stations but on the three daily newspapers—the *Detroit News*, *Detroit Free Press*, and *Detroit Times*.

There were no Jewish day schools, and while the Jewish Center was located on Woodward and Holbrook, Twelfth Street—slowly giving way to Dexter—was the heart of Jewish commerce, housing caterers, cleaners, delicatessens, jewelers, pharmacists, printers and apparel and furniture stores. The two stores dealing in Jewish books and other religious items—Pieman's near Blaine and Chesluk's near Clairmount—were a short walk from each other on Twelfth.

It was a difficult time to launch a new weekly publication in the Jewish community, though. Hundreds of Jewish men had recently departed to do their part in the war effort, and hundreds more were readying to join. Budgets were tight. But more importantly, there was already a Jewish weekly serving the community. For twenty-six years, since 1916, the *Detroit Jewish Chronicle* had reported on the happenings of Jewish interest.

Most people saw no need for another local Jewish weekly. However, several community marquee names, including rabbis, formed an advisory board and some provided financial backing behind well-known editor Phillip Slomovitz.

Slomovitz had emigrated from Russia in adolescence and mastered writing English in excellence. He began his journalism career as a night editor on the University of Michigan's student publication and graduated to the *Detroit News* copy desk as a reporter and editor. His interest in championing Jewish causes and issues led to editorships with the *Jewish Pictorial*, the Jewish Telegraphic Agency news service, and the *Detroit Jewish Chronicle*

Sgt. Hank Greenberg's photo appeared in the first issue of the *Jewish News*.

(Courtesy of Jewish News)

ECHOES OF DETROIT'S JEWISH COMMUNITIES

Small in stature, Slomovitz towered over others as a ferocious fighter for and defender of justice and Jewish causes. Slomovitz contacted Danny Raskin, then a young reporter with the *Detroit News*, to join the new publication. Raskin didn't think there was room for two local Jewish newspapers, but Slomovitz's determination soon melted Raskin's reluctance. Danny Raskin's first column in the first *Jewish News* on March 27, 1942, was titled: "Jewish Youth's Listening Post."

Benno Levi, 19, joined the office staff of the *Jewish News* on the 21st floor of the Penobscot Building as a copy boy at $17.50 per week. Si Weingarden, who had spent long hours at his newsstand in front of the Majestic Building on Woodward and Michigan since 1910, added the new weekly Jewish publication to his stock of papers and magazines.

Manuel Merzon, a well respected, observant attorney, published the *Detroit Jewish Review*, a bi-monthly religious oriented small magazine. Merzon, who often appeared in public wearing the yellow star arm band similar to those worn by the Jews in Europe, wanted to keep the plight of the Jews in the public eye. However, with two local Jewish weeklies on the scene and tighter economic conditions brought on by men off to war, Merzon had to cease publication.

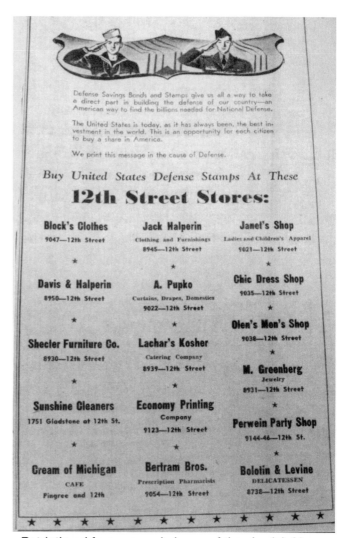

Patriotic ad from an early issue of the *Jewish News*.

(Courtesy of Jewish News)

Si Weingarden sold the Jewish News from his newsstand on Michigan and Woodward, a short walk from the new local weekly's office in the Penobscot Building.

(Courtesy of Si Weingarden)

The finishing touches on the exterior of the new Yeshiva Beth Yehudah and Congregation Mogen Abraham building were put on in 1942.

(Author's collection)

The week-long program of activities marking the dedication of the new Yeshiva Beth Yehudah building on Dexter and Cortland culminated on Washington's birthday while the first issue of the Jewish News was being planned. At the time, the United Hebrew Schools was headquartered in the Rose Sittig Cohen Building on Lawton and Tyler, and the system had a staff of 42 with almost 1,500 students spread around several school buildings. Samuel and Leah Bookstein donated $25,000 toward the purchase of the Professional Building on Linwood and Elmhurst to be transformed into Yeshivath Chachmey Lublin. Rabbi Moshe Rotenberg, a graduate of the institution in Lublin who had come to America earlier in the year, served as dean of the school, which temporarily used Congregation Beth Yehudah on Pingree and Woodrow Wilson.

In a 1942 board meeting, the Jewish Home for Aged reported that 146 residents had been cared for the previous year. One left the home voluntarily and 19 passed away. The average age of the deceased was 77 years and two months. There were 1,277 professional visits by doctors representing different areas of health. Herman Pekarsky, general administrative assistant of the Jewish Welfare Federation, compiled a report on the Jewish Aged of Detroit. Pekarsky estimated there were 4,140 Jews over 60, representing 4.6 percent of the total Detroit Jewish population of 90,000.

Henry Wineman, who was president of the United Jewish Charities for three years and became the first president of the Jewish Welfare Federation in 1926, was named chairman of the executive committee of the 1942 Allied Jewish Campaign. For the past four decades, Wineman had been considered one of Michigan's leading business executives as he was engaged in the family business, the People's Outfitting Company. To honor the memory of Joseph Wetsman, a $5,000 contribution to the Hebrew Free Loan Association was made by the Wetsman family. The contributing members of the family were Mrs. Joseph Wetsman, Frank Wetsman, Mrs. Ralph Davidson, Mrs. Morse Saulson and Mrs. Jack Uhr. According to census figures published by the Detroit Jewish Chronicle, 1,750,000 Jews among the 4,700,000 Jews in the United States stated that Yiddish was their primary and secondary language.

The Hebrew Hospital Association of Detroit went on record stating that it would pledge $42,000 to any group able to raise $150,000 toward a hospital within a year. The board of directors of the Jewish Children's Home agreed to turn over its vacant building and adjoining lots on Petoskey and Burlingame for a hospital, provided $200,000 was raised in 1942.

Newspapers called Gerald L. K. Smith "America's number one anti-Semite." An ordained Protestant minister and leader in the Ku Klux Klan in Indiana, Smith relocated to Detroit in 1939 as there were more opportunities to find supporters and to fund anti-Semitic activities. His popularity among anti-Semites was at its peak early in 1942. However, the federal government threatened Smith's activities as seditious. For the most part, the American public wasn't sympathetic to groups like Smith's as war casualties mounted, and eventually Smith refrained from stating his anti-Jewish views through the U.S. mail. Pressure from government officials suggesting charges of sedition also led Father Charles Coughlin to cease publication of his anti-Semitic *Social Justice* magazine.

Besides worrying about relatives and friends serving in the armed forces, Detroit's Jews were hearing about the heart-wrenching reports from Europe. Five thousand Jews from the Minsk ghetto were forced to stand beside a large pit and the children were thrown in. The adults were machine-gunned to death, falling on top of the children who ultimately died of suffocation. Reports from Greece confirmed that thousands of children had died of starvation since the Nazi occupation began. By May, it was learned that 1,500 Jews in Radom had starved to death and 13,300 Jews were murdered by Nazis in Lwow.

More than 16,000 Jews of Poniewiesch, in Nazi-occupied Lithuania, were massacred over a three-day period. The Nazis were converting thousands of Talesim (prayer shawls) into winter underwear for German soldiers. In Nazi-occupied White Russia, only attractive young Jewish women were spared from death, to be subjected to brutal indignities and enslavement by German soldiers. The Chief Rabbi of Kishineff was beheaded with an axe by Rumanians. His head was left in public view for days.

According to a letter dated August 11, 1942, 93 young Jewish women and girls of a Beth Jacob School in Warsaw, Poland, chose mass suicide instead of being forced into prostitution by German soldiers. The letter from a teacher, made public by Rabbi Leo Jung of the Jewish Center of New York City, stated: "It is good to live for God, but it is also good to die for Him. All of us have poison. When the soldiers come, we shall drink it. We have no fear."

In an effort to save ammunition, the Nazis herded about 500 Jews onto a barge and drowned them in a river near Minsk. The women and children of David Horodok (now in Belarus) were executed on September 10, 1942. They had been kept in a barbed wire ghetto for over a year after the men of the town were machine-gunned to death.

Rabbi M. J. Wohlgelernter taught a 12-hour course in air-raid instruction in Yiddish at the Beth Tefilo Emanuel on Taylor and Woodrow Wilson. Over 100,000 Detroiters received training as air raid wardens and as auxiliary fire and police. Practice blackouts were held, and lights were turned off in the city. Air raid wardens patrolled the streets making sure unauthorized citizens remained indoors.

By the summer of '42, everyone, it seemed, was involved in some way in the war effort. Fans were urged to return foul balls hit into the stands at a Tigers game. The balls were shipped overseas for soldiers' recreation, and the fans received a twenty-five cent war stamp for each ball. Baseball play-by-play broadcasters were forbidden to mention weather conditions, for fear of helping potential air attacks by the enemy. With the country at war and the fans in a patriotic mood, "The Star Spangled Banner" was played prior to every game.

Captain Ruben Iden survived the Japanese attack on Pearl Harbor. However, the three-year Marine Corps veteran dive bomber pilot was killed at Guadalcanal on September 20, 1942, while on a photo reconnaissance mission. The 24-year-old Iden was one of the first—if not the first—Jewish Detroiter killed in action during World War II.

The Young Israel-sponsored Adult School of Jewish Education, which met on Monday evenings at Central High School, moved to the Yeshiva Beth Yehudah building on Dexter. Temple Beth El instituted a monthly Sabbath morning service for children. A Sabbath Eve service for confirmands and their parents began preceding Confirmation. In August, Rabbi

Herschel Lymon was appointed minister of religious education for Beth El.

A new pulpit dedicated for the future building of Temple Israel was donated by Mr. and Mrs. Harry W. Gilberg. Temple Israel introduced more tradition in their prayer service at the Auditorium of the Detroit Institute of Arts. Rabbi Fram and the Cantor wore prayer shawls and the congregation—unlike Temple Beth El—was encouraged to sing along with the Cantor. Fram preached the use of more ritual in homes. The lighting of candles and the blessing over the wine on Sabbath Eve was encouraged. Impressive High Holy Day Services were held, featuring a mixed choir of 16 voices under the direction of Dan Frohman. Detroit's Emma Schaver, the nationally known concert artist, also sang.

In a New York Times page ten article on November 25, 1942, Dr. Stephen S. Wise, chairman of the World Jewish Congress, said, "The State Department finally made available the document which confirmed the stories and rumors of Jewish extermination in all Hitler-ruled Europe." Wise stated that sources confirmed about half of the estimated 4 million Jews in Nazi-occupied Europe had been slain in an extermination campaign.

A year and a day after Pearl Harbor, Albert Kahn died. The famed architect had designed Temple Beth El's first and second structures on Woodward and several other Detroit landmarks. Kahn, a member of Beth El, gave generously to the Allied Jewish Campaign but was far removed from any traditional observance in life and death. The body lay in state at the William R. Hamilton Co. chapel, and private services were held at the Kahn residence on Mack at John R. At the time of his death, Kahn, 73, had been married to Ernestine Krolik Kahn for 46 years.

Detroit rabbis gathered on Thursday, November 12, at the Shaarey Zedek to honor Rabbi A.M. Hershman prior to his departure for a half year's sabbatical leave. Seated, from left: Rabbi Joseph Thumin, president, Council of Orthodox Rabbis; Rabbi Joseph Eisenman, Congregation Beth Tefilo Emanuel; Rabbi Hershman; Dr. Leo M. Franklin, Rabbi Emeritus of Temple Beth El; Rabbi Moses Fischer, Congregation B'nai Moshe. Standing, from left: Rabbi Leizer Levin, Congregation of David W. Simons Branch of United Hebrew Schools; Rabbi B. W. Hendels, Yeshiva Chachmey Lublin; Dr. Naphtali Carlebach, Yeshiva Beth Yehudah; Rabbi Max Wohlgelernter, Congregation Beth Tefilo Emanuel; Rabbi Jacob Kurland, Yeshiva Beth Yehudah; Rabbi Joshua S. Sperka, Congregation B'nai David: Dr. Samson R. Weiss, Yeshiva Beth Yehudah,; Rabbi Morris Adler, Congregation Shaarey Zedek; Dr. B. Benedict Glazer, Temple Beth El; Rabbi Herschel Lymon, Temple Beth El; Rabbi Jacob Ungar, Yeshiva Beth Yehudah; Rabbi Meir Levi, director of Michigan Synagogue Conference; Rabbi Jacob Nathan, Congregation B'nai Moshe; Rabbi S. P. Wohlgelernter, Congregation Bicur Cholem, Seattle, Washington; Rabbi Jacob Hoberman. Congregation Beth Itzchack; Rabbi Leon Fram, Temple Israel; Rabbi Joseph Rabinowitz, Congregation Beth Shmuel.

(Courtesy of archives of Shaarey Zedek)

Albert Kahn was 73 when he died on December 8, 1942.

(Courtesy of Burton Historical Collection of the Detroit Public Library)

Rabbi Ernest Greenfield became the new spiritual leader of the First Hebrew Congregation of Delray. Rabbi Greenfield succeeded his brother, Rabbi Harry Greenfield, who had served the congregation for nine years and departed for Chicago to devote his efforts to defense work. When the new Rabbi Greenfield assumed the pulpit, the Delray congregation had 70 sons of members in the service and two WAACS. In December 1942, 67 doctors out of approximately 100 on the staff of the North End Clinic were serving in the armed forces.

Patriotic Americans were sending newspapers, books and even comic books to soldiers overseas. Thousands of copies of Batman and Robin, Captain

The first Temple Beth El confirmation class of Dr. B. Benedict Glazer in 1942.

(Courtesy of Rabbi Leo M. Franklin archives, Temple Beth El)

Marvel, Flash Gordon, Green Hornet, Lone Ranger, Spiderman, Superman, and Wonder Woman were passed around barracks. Hollywood stars and voices heard on juke boxes brought their talents and latest tunes from America: "All or Nothing at All," "As Time Goes By," "Oh What a Beautiful Mornin'," and "The Surrey With the Fringe on Top," were the latest hits of 1943 heard by the soldiers overseas.

Early in the year, the community heard about the death of Corporal Max Bernstein. A member of the Jewish Community Center before going off to war, Bernstein, 34, served in the United States and Ireland before being sent to North Africa after receiving honorary diplomas as a tank technician. Bernstein was killed in a tank he commanded. Lieutenant Jack Winokur was killed in a plane accident in the Southwest Pacific. The Central High graduate had enlisted a month after Pearl Harbor.

Detroiters Mr. and Mrs. A. Panush had three sons serving in the army. Pvt. Bernard Panush was stationed at Camp Butner, North Carolina; Pvt. Irving Panush was stationed at Camp Kern, Utah; and 1st Lt. Sol Panush was in Sicily. Alfred Epstein of the Pfeiffer Brewing Company hosted a dinner party for over 800 servicemen at the Book Cadillac Hotel on Washington Boulevard. Benno Levi volunteered on behalf of the Yeshiva Beth Yehudah to distribute bibles and prayer books to departing servicemen at the Michigan Central Depot. A few months later, after a goodbye party by the staff of the Jewish News for his 15 months of service, Levi was inducted into the army. Avern Cohn left his studies at the University of Michigan for army service. Marvin Eliot Schlossberg, known as "Sonny" to his family, was trained as a pilot and took part in several bombing missions from Northern England.

Point rationing of canned goods was in effect. Ration points were spent for butter, cheese and meat. Coffee, flour, oils, sugar, and other items also were purchased with stamps at the markets. At Dexter-Davison, most of the male employees were in the armed forces and many of the female members of the Cottler family filled in. Customers who had sons and husbands in the army or navy found a patient, sympathetic ear in owner Norman Cottler. Richard Law, Parliamentary Undersecretary for Foreign Affairs in Britain's House of Commons, reported that the total number of refugees who entered Palestine between April 1, 1939, and February 18, 1943, was 39,227.

Deportations from the Warsaw ghetto took place in the summer of 1942. When the Germans entered the ghetto to deport more Jews in the first month of 1943, they were attacked by several groups of unorganized Jews. Withdrawing after four days without deporting as many Jews as intended, the Nazis chose to wait before finishing their task.

The Nazis roared into the ghetto on the eve of Passover, April 19, 1943, to remove all the Jews. The Jews resisted, using homemade bombs and any ammunition and weapons they were able to smuggle or barter. The Nazis responded by setting buildings afire. By May 16, 1943 the Warsaw ghetto was in ruins and the resistance was crushed.

Artur Zygelboym, who escaped from Warsaw in 1939 and found refuge in London, took his own life on May 12, 1943, as the Jews in the Warsaw ghetto bravely fought off the Nazis. The 48-year-old Zygelboym left a letter of explanation.

Marvin Schlossberg was a pilot and took part in several bombing missions.
(Courtesy of Sonny Eliot)

I cannot be silent. I cannot live while the remnants of the Jewish population of Poland, of whom I am a representative, are perishing. My friends in the Warsaw ghetto died with weapons in their hands in the last heroic battle. It was not my destiny to die together with them but I belong to them and in their mass graves.

By my death I wish to make my final protest against the passivity with which the world is looking on and permitting the extermination of the Jewish people.

The *Detroit Jewish Chronicle* reprinted a letter that was posted on several synagogue bulletin boards in 1943. The letter, titled "A Letter to Two Million Souls in Heaven" by Samuel Duker, originally appeared in "Furrows," a publication of the "Habonim."

I am writing to you; two million souls of Jewish men, women and children, who have been murdered by Hitler in the three years since September, 1939.

I write to you in Heaven, for, however evil your lives before, your agonies since September 1939 have cleansed you of all guilt and sin.

Though written to you, my words are addressed to those four million of our brothers and sisters whom, too, Hitler has foresworn to wipe out. My words cannot reach them. I cannot tell them what is in my heart. Yet I must write. I know that in -every moment preceding their allotted destiny of death they want to hear from us, they want our help. In her death vision the mother sees her babies saved by us. Children share their last crust in the hope of extending their hold on life until the day of liberation. Their eyes are turned to us for help. And we?

"Hold fast," we say. "Humanity and Civilization will never forget you. We will liberate you. Hold. fast. We will avenge you. You are a shining light of human courage and sacrifice. Hold fast. Hold fast."

Thus three years have passed. And all this time Hitler has been hard at work liberating you. Freeing you forever from life, from false hopes, freeing eighty men, women and children every minute— day after day, night after night, weeks spinning into months, into years.

"Hold fast. You are not forgotten."

No, indeed. On the third anniversary of the beginning of the slaughter, you, the two million, were remembered. Not too prominently, lest some think that this war is being fought on your account. An editorial, a news-story, a stern warning to Hitler, You were not forgotten. Nor will the next two million be forgotten, or the two million after them.

I have thought, dear brothers and sisters, that it is a great pity that you were Jews. How much sweeter your lot had you been born dumb brutes, animals of the field and forest. Surely, a world of Humanity and Civilization would have decreed a limited hunting season on you. Surely had a dread huntsman like Hitler appeared and sworn to exterminate you, the world of Humanity and Civilization would not permit it.

See how proud is our record of care for animal lives. The buffalo is sheltered; the reindeer, the beaver, all have been given their little islands of safety, their seasons of life. In the dark continent of Africa there is the Kruger National Park, 8,000 square miles of land set aside to keep animal kind safe from hunters, to preserve their breed from extinction.

It was once thought that we, too, should have had our island of safety; not much bigger than. Kruger Park—we are Jews, not chimpanzees and zebras—but our island of safety nevertheless: Palestine. It was ours, Humanity and Civilization told us.

There are many of you who could be there now. Among the living you left behind, many could be rescued yet. Through Sweden, through Rumania, through Bulgaria, through Turkey.

Would Hitler let them go? Who knows? The nations who make up Humanity and Civilization have been afraid to ask him to let the Jews go. .They might be asked to let those Jews in. It is better, perhaps, that Hitler should liberate them in his own way.

I hear you souls in heaven say that I am unnecessarily bitter. Perhaps. Now, you souls in Heaven, look around for some 760 among you who were once passengers on a boat called "Struma." Hitler sought to liberate them from their earthly troubles. But they refused to die. They fled to Turkey, whence they sought entry into Palestine, their little island of safety. So 760 men, women and children were put out to sea in a leaky fifty-ton cockel-shell which went down to the bottom.

"But," the souls in Heaven whisper, "you cannot condemn England. The two survivors from that sinking were allowed to enter Palestine."

How can I, my four million brothers and sisters, speak of the powers constituting Humanity and Civilization when they have such defenders in Heaven? How can I mention the "St. Louis," the "Patra," the "Darien" or the "Atlantic," ships of our misfortune, when the practitioners of Humanity and Civilization have warm defenders?

I cannot. For I hear a voice say to me: "It is better for us Jews in Heaven: Long before the war,

Poland said a million of us were 'surplus.' Wherever we would turn to flee our oppressors we are told, 'There are enough Jews here. We want no Jewish problem created by your coming.' Even in Palestine, our little island of safety. Great Britain told us that we must never, never become more than a third of the population. But here in Heaven there is no limitation on Jews' admission. None at all."

Perhaps, brothers living under Hitler and destined to die under him, those souls in Heaven are right. Heavenly ways are inscrutable.

Edsel Ford, who had been ailing during the war years, was only 49 when he died on May 26, 1943. Henry's only child was a talented designer and a generous humanitarian. Edsel and his son, Henry II, had tried to undo the damage the elder Ford did with his anti-Semitic publications. Edsel's lawyers had threatened the Ku Klux Klan with a lawsuit unless the Ford name was dropped from publications it was distributing. Because of the war, cars weren't being sold, but Edsel earmarked almost $84,000 for advertising in Jewish publications.

The war created more job opportunities at higher wages, and thousands of black families moved to Detroit in the year and a half after war was declared. Southern whites also joined the influx and competed for many of the same positions open to blacks.

The fires that raged within both groups couldn't be extinguished easily and added to the prejudice already reigning in the city. June 20, 1943, was a hot Sunday afternoon. Rumor fueled small incidents between blacks and whites. Each side heard that a woman and her baby of their color was thrown off the Belle Isle Bridge during a racial melee.

Mobs seeking to defend their side roamed the streets looking for trouble. Blacks struck first when an unsuspecting white pedestrian was beaten unconscious and run over by a taxicab. White-owned stores were looted and motorists were pulled from their cars and severely beaten.

Mobs of blacks stoned streetcars going north on Hastings Street, figuring it was the direction in which whites traveled home. White passengers were beaten and chased as mobs also attacked streetcars going north on Oakland near Westminster.

Whites, however, did much of their damage on Woodward. The Detroit News reported that whites were "stopping streetcars by pulling trolleys off the wires, and removing and beating Negroes from Woodward Avenue toward John R and Brush streets."

There were few Jews left residing in the Oakland-Westminster area at the time of the riot. The Detroit News reported that homes that had "'This is a colored home. Do not break in' signs in the window were untouched, while others, which did not have signs, were wrecked and plundered. Police had barricaded the Negro residential areas and were barring white men from entering. Within the area, Negroes were smashing store windows and looting business buildings."

Mayor Jeffries ordered all bars in the city to close. Police ordered all pawnshops and hardware stores to remove from windows and shelves all guns, ammunition, and knives. Race tracks were ordered closed and Tigers games were canceled until Wednesday afternoon.

Blacks trying to escape the downtown mayhem by paying admission to movie theaters and hiding in the darkness weren't always successful. A black man was found dead in a theater seat with six bullet wounds, and another seeking refuge in the Federal Building was beaten to death on its Fort Street steps.

Many blacks were beaten in the presence of police officers. Many were beaten by police officers. Many were killed by police officers. Police killed a total of 17 people—all black.

On Monday night the first contingent of federal troops arrived. They made themselves visible and encamped on the vast lawn of the Public Library and various other public locations.

The violence produced 34 deaths and 676 injuries. Of the 1,838 arrested, 82 percent were black. It was time for Detroit's officials to take a hard look at the 3,400-man police force. The boys in blue were only slightly over one percent black.

On the Tuesday after the riot, the *Jewish News* reported that "Mayor Edward J. Jeffries, Jr., assured a group of merchants from the Hastings and Oakland-Westminster sections, at a meeting at the

Workmen's Circle Education Center on Linwood, that more and better police protection than before will be given these storekeepers. The assurance was made to encourage the merchants to open their stores."

More than 500 people jammed the Jericho Temple on Joy Road for an impressive rally sponsored by the Turover Aid Society. The organization honored its 89 sons and daughters serving in the U.S. armed forces by unveiling an impressive Roll of Honor. Mayor Jeffries, a popular speaker in the Jewish community as he attended many rallies on behalf of European Jews, praised the work of the Turover USO, as the organization regularly sent packages to those serving overseas.

Ed Meer grew up in a large home on Broadstreet. His parents were involved members of Congregation B'nai Moshe on Dexter. Ed starred on Central High's football team, and a few months after graduation, he was drafted and sent to Alabama for basic training. Ed would be in uniform for 30 months in diverse areas of combat.

Harry B. Keidan, a Recorder's Court Judge for eight years who had been appointed to the Wayne County Circuit Court in 1927, died at age 60. Rabbi A. M. Hershman, of Shaarey Zedek Synagogue, officiated at the simple funeral services held at Clover Hill Park Cemetery chapel. Hershman praised Keidan as an active, generous member of Shaarey Zedek and a supporter of Jewish education. If needed in court on the Sabbath, Keidan, an observant Jew, would walk to the downtown courthouse from his Chicago Boulevard residence.

Sam Osnos, who founded Sam's Cut Rate, Inc., in 1917, died at the age of 72. In 1943 Sam's sold more work clothes than any store in the world. It ranked among the country's largest retailers of cosmetics, drugs, and tobacco. It operated the largest prescription department in the state and had Detroit's largest grocery under one roof. Active in several charities, Osnos endowed a fellowship in the Yeshiva Beth Yehudah and was a member of the Chesed Shel Emes, Mishkan Israel, and Shaarey Zedek.

Shaarey Zedek and the community lost another important member in David Zemon. A former president of the Hebrew Free Loan Association, Zemon, 67, was long identified with civic and charitable causes. The community also lost another well-known personality in Peter Vass, 56, who served as president of Congregation B'nai Moshe from 1921 to 1924 and was active in several organizations.

The Detroit Board of Education took over the Jewish Children's Home on Petoskey for the duration of the war. Operated as a child center on a 24-hour, around the clock schedule for children of mothers employed in furthering the war effort, the home accommodated the needs of women involved in any of the three war plant shifts.

Philanthropist Irwin I. Cohn was named chairman of the Detroit committee of Vaad Hahatzala—the emergency campaign to raise funds for war-torn

Ed Meer was only 18 when he underwent basic training at Camp Rucker, Alabama, in 1943.

(Courtesy of Ed Meer)

yeshivoth, rabbis, and laymen. Jack A. Robinson, who lived on Sturtevant between Wildemere and Lawton, celebrated his Bar Mitzvah at the nearby Congregation B'nai Israel on Linwood. Fresh Air Camp increased its rates in 1943, and children of servicemen were given priority, even if families couldn't pay.

Rabbi Leon Fram and the membership of Temple Israel were excited over plans for their site on Manderson Road. "Our new Temple will be a structure of grace and dignity and will enhance the beauty of the entire Palmer Park section," Fram told the Jewish Chronicle. "We have over two acres of land in our site which nature has already adorned with numerous magnificent trees. Picture a stately building in the center of this large area, surrounded by well-planned landscaping and containing a large auditorium of worship, a chapel, school rooms, administrative offices and the usual social facilities. When this dream of our temple-to-be is realized, the entire Jewish community of Detroit will share the pride of our achievement."

Congregation Beth Tefilo Emanuel had a mortgage burning ceremony followed by a festive dinner at the 19-year-old synagogue on Taylor and Woodrow Wilson. Congregation Beth Shmuel on Blaine near Twelfth purchased a lot on Dexter and Buena Vista for a new synagogue. Founded in 1939, Congregation Gemiluth Chasodim claimed a membership of 160 families in 1943. Rabbi Herschel Lymon, minister of religious education for Temple Beth El, entered the U.S. Army chaplaincy. Shaarey Zedek's Rabbi Morris Adler also enlisted as an army chaplain. Congregation B'nai Zion on Humphrey had 75 sons serving in the armed forces, while Young Israel of Detroit had 55 members serving.

Yeshivath Chachmey Lublin announced that Rabbi Leizer Finkel would relocate from Chicago to become the school's instructor of Talmud and ethics. Rabbi Leizer Levin was appointed executive director and instructor of ethics. The joy of opening the new school was visible on the face of Samuel Bookstein, its major benefactor. Two junior high school classes and four elementary classes graduated from the United Hebrew Schools in 1943. The Farband Schools, sponsored by the Jewish National Workers' Alliance and the Pioneer Women's Organization, operated three branches. They were located at 1912 Taylor, 12244 Dexter, and the Thirkell School, Delaware and 14th. The curriculum included Bible, Hebrew, Yiddish, Jewish history, singing, and Jewish social problems.

The Ladies' Auxiliary of Yeshiva Beth Yehudah opened the Beth Jacob School for Girls in memory of Lena Holtzman. The girls' division paralleled the afternoon Hebrew instruction for boys. Evening classes for older girls age 13 to 17 were planned for the future. A kindergarten department began in honor of the 60th birthday of Mrs. Hyman Rottenberg. Mrs. Pearl Rottenberg, president of the ladies organization that sponsored the girls' division and kindergarten, said 65 children were enrolled in the two new divisions.

Rabbi Moses Fischer, chairman of the Vaad Ha-Chinuch of Yeshiva Beth Yehudah, sent the following report to the Jewish News and Jewish Chronicle. "At present [late 1943] 271 students attend the Yeshiva, 228 in the main building and 43 in the two branches. Nine instructors constitute the staff of the Yeshiva and 15 classes are offering instruction to the students according to their level of knowledge. The elementary

Irwin I. Cohn served on the boards of many charitable organizations.
(Author's collection)

department of the Yeshiva contains two grades. The high school is formed by five classes while the Talmudic Academy consists of the five upper classes. The branches at present have elementary classes and one high school class."

While the Yeshiva Beth Yehudah was gaining students, Congregation Mogen Abraham, located in the front of the building on Dexter at Cortland, was gaining members and religious articles. Already using Torah scrolls and Bimah (reading desk) from Congregation Beth Jacob's Montcalm Building, Congregation Ahavath Zion left its Oakland neighborhood and turned over its assets to the Yeshiva and Mogen Abraham and went out of existence. Congregation Etz Chaim, organized in 1924, vacated its Englewood Street location and also dissolved, turning over its Torah scrolls, prayer books and other assets.

Will Rogers, Jr., the son of the great humorist, enlisted in the army shortly after Pearl Harbor and eventually gained an officer's commission. While serving in a Tank Destroyer Battalion at Camp Hood, Texas, Rogers was elected to Congress from California, representing the Hollywood area. A tireless fighter on behalf of the rescue of Jews from Nazi-occupied lands, Rogers went to England to confer with British officials to explore the possibilities of rescuing Jews. Rogers came to Detroit at a meeting sponsored jointly by the Jewish Welfare Federation and the Detroit Service Group for War Chest Campaign Workers and contributors, held in the Brown Memorial Chapel of Temple Beth El. The popular Rogers received a standing ovation from the audience, who were well acquainted with Rogers' humanitarian activities.

The constituent groups of the Greater Detroit B'nai B'rith Council celebrated B'nai B'rith's centennial on Sunday, December 12. Morris Schaver, the recognized leader of the labor Zionists in Detroit, celebrated his 50th birthday in December with a host of friends and admirers and his wife, Emma. Born in Poland, Schaver came to Detroit in 1913 and was well-known by the time he enlisted in the army in 1918. In the local elections for the American Jewish Conference, Schaver led the ticket in the selection of delegates.

Assistant Secretary of State Breckenridge Long, an evil, prejudiced man masquerading as a righteous one, wrote a memo in 1940 that sealed the fate of thousands upon thousands upon thousands of Jews.

"We can delay and effectively stop for a temporary period of indefinite length the number of immigrants into the United States," Long advised. "We could do this by simply advising our consuls to put every obstacle in the way and to require additional evidence and to report to various administrative devices which would postpone and postpone and postpone the granting of visas."

Within a year following Long's memo, immigration was cut in half and all immigration requests were bogged down in a State Department-controlled Washington office, subject to a system of reviews, and reviews of reviews.

While politicians and Jews were mostly unaware of Long's efforts to thwart the rescue of European Jews,

Pvt. Cohn Sent To Stanford U.

Pvt. Avern Cohn, son of Mr. and Mrs. Irwin I. Cohn of 18450 Fairfield Ave., is now attending pre-medical school at Leland Stanford University in Palo Alto, Calif., by special assignment made by the U. S. Army.

A graduate of Central High School, Pvt. Cohn studied at the University of Michigan for a year and a half before his enlistment.

Popular in many local activities, Pvt. Cohn is known among many former Tamakwa Campers as one of their most popular counselors.

His sister, Rita, will commence her studies at the University of Wisconsin this fall.

The *Jewish News* devoted a page in each issue to the activities of Detroit's Jewish soldiers and often featured an accompanying photograph, as in this 1944 article on Avern Cohn.
(Courtesy of Jewish News)

400 Orthodox rabbis marched to the capitol steps in Washington two days before Yom Kippur in 1943 to plead with President Franklin Delano Roosevelt on behalf of the incarcerated and about-to-be exterminated Jews.

On the advice of certain American Jewish leaders (non-Orthodox) who didn't feel it was proper to make the request so public, or perhaps, they were embarrassed by the manner of dress the Orthodox rabbis presented, FDR claimed he was too busy to meet the rabbis. (Time and the president's appointment book would reveal President Roosevelt's availability.) The rabbis, however, were received by Vice President Wallace and leaders of Congress. A message from the rabbinical delegation was given to the president's secretary.

Early in 1944, at the urging of Secretary of the Treasury Henry Morgenthau, a Jew, President Roosevelt established the War Refugee Board. Politics shaped the president's decision. Roosevelt didn't want a public debate on the Senate floor questioning the motives of the State Department for its lack of effort—which was becoming known among other government agencies and politicians—to admit Jews to the United States.

The War Refugee Board was able to bring Jews to America and to establish camps such as at Fort Ontario, New York. However, it was too late for tens of thousands that already had been blocked by Long and subsequently murdered by the Nazis.

Detroit's Jewish community felt the loss of the passing of Jacob Levin, less than two months after his family celebrated his 83rd birthday at a Thanksgiving dinner at the Jewish Home for the Aged on Petoskey. The Polish born Levin, who settled in Detroit in 1874 when he was 13, went on to establish a successful cleaners' supply company on Randolph Street. In addition to being the founder and president of the Old Folks Home, Levin was an active member of the boards of directors of Congregation Beth Tefilo Emanuel, Yeshiva Beth Yehudah, House of Shelter, Mizrachi, and the Michigan Synagogue Conference. At the age of 18, Harold Berry left his comfortable home on Glendale between Dexter and Wildemere in October 1943 and enlisted in the United States Army Air Force. Berry had delivered the valedictory address at the Shaarey Zedek commencement exercises, served as president of the synagogue's Junior Congregation, and was active in planning its religious activities.

In addition to his speaking and organizational abilities, Private Berry wrote an essay in 1944 titled, "Why I Fight." "I am fighting for a day when suffrage and education are universal, unemployment no problem, and intolerance and bigotry extinct," Berry stated. "I do not want to help win this war and then return to life that is filled with hypocritical contrasts between ideal and reality. I want a real Democracy, a real peace, and real good will among men."

While Private Berry was writing many more paragraphs, his father, Louis, well known for doing good deeds, devoted much of his time and resources to rescuing Jews from Europe and bringing them to Palestine.

Henry Keywell and Isadore Kowal, owners of the Barlum Hotel, hosted more than 200 servicemen for the year-end holidays. Meals and hotel rooms at the hotel in Cadillac Square were provided free of charge for the soldiers. Ann Millman served on the Red Feather Drive, the forerunner of the current Torch Drive, helping to raise the spirits of those serving in the armed forces overseas. Known as the "Gray Ladies" because of the manner and color of their dress, they were trained as nurses' aides, helped sell war bonds, and pitched in where needed to raise funds and spirits.

Newly-married Stanley Winkelman became Ensign Winkelman in 1944 while Lt. Monte Korn of the United States Marine Corps was recuperating at the Great Lakes Naval Hospital in Chicago. The well known Gershenson brothers, Charles and Samuel, of Ned's Auto Supply, were in their third year of military service. Mr. and Mrs. Adolf Smilo, who resided on Clements near Linwood, had four sons serving in the military. Herman was in the Navy before being honorably discharged, while Martin remained in the Navy and Sidney and Barney were in the Army. Mr. and Mrs. Hyman Dresner, of Santa Rosa south of Seven Mile

Road, had five sons serving in the military. The oldest of the brothers, Jack, 36, graduated from the University of Michigan and Cornell University and became an attorney. The others serving ranged in age from 18-year-old twins to 27 and 34.

In April 1944, the Air Force notified Mr. and Mrs. Jacob Schlossberg, residents of Calvert near Wildemere, that their son, Lt. Marvin Eliot "Sonny" Schlossberg, was missing in action. Lieutenant Schlossberg, a pilot, was shot down on his sixteenth mission in central Germany. When two of the engines on the plane failed, Schlossberg signaled the nine members of his crew to bail out. It took him longer to eject, as gunfire got him in the knee and back. He landed far from the others on a field near a farm. Captured and interrogated, he was then shipped to a German prisoner of war camp, where he would be reunited with his crew and interred for the next 14 months.

On the anniversary of the revolt in the Warsaw ghetto, Detroiters of all faiths joined Detroit Mayor Edward Jeffries, Jr.; Reverend Edward Mooney, Archbishop of Detroit; and leaders of the local Jewish community at the Cass Technical High School Auditorium. The capacity audience heard several speakers, including Rabbi Maurice N. Eisendrath, director of the Union of American Hebrew Congregations.

After seeing action as a Captain on B-29 bombers and helping to establish bases for B-29s in China, Hank Greenberg was transferred to New York and would be given the duty of visiting defense factories in New England for the duration of the war. Bill Davidson was in naval training school in Boston for a 16-week course. A Navy storekeeper, Davidson was responsible for maintaining and ordering supplies and payroll. Davidson, who would be transferred to the Pacific later in the year, also received training in accounting, purchasing, and inventory control.

Ed Meer spent much of his service time on ships sailing to and from Hawaii, Guadacanal, and in different areas of the Pacific theater. Meer experienced a typhoon while on a troop ship on the China seas on the way to Okinawa, where battles were common as it was only 300 miles from Japan. Looking for a missing watch saved Meer from being a casualty of war. He went to help a friend search for the watch while the others continued on in a different direction and ended up being killed or wounded. Meer witnessed Japanese Kamikaze (suicide) pilots aiming their planes into American ships docked nearby. "They must have lost several hundred planes," Meer recalled, "but they got eight or nine of our ships."

The community mourned the death of Lt. Robert S. Deutsch, in the United States Naval Hospital. The son of Mr. and Mrs. Adolph Deutsch, he was survived by his wife Diane and their children. Brothers Alfred

Left to right: Chaim Moldawsky, Rabbi Moldawsky, and Sol Moldawasky.

(Courtesy of Jewish News)

and Charles also were serving in the military. Services were held at the B'nai Moshe synagogue.

Congregation B'nai Moshe lost several of its sons in 1944. After 28 months of military service in which he participated in five major campaigns in the South Pacific, Lt. Eugene Freedman was killed in action on Leyte Island. Lt. Lester Katzen's plane went down after a successful bombing mission, again grieving the congregants of B'nai Moshe.

The community was shocked to learn that the youngest son of Rabbi Ben Zion Moldawsky, of Congregation Shaar Shomayim on Muirland, was killed in action in Italy. Another son, Chaim, was serving with the air corps when his plane crashed 17 months earlier. A third son, David, was serving in the army and stationed in Arizona.

Raoul Wallenberg left the safety of Sweden in July of 1944 and traveled to Budapest on a personal mission to save Jews. He helped many before disappearing to an uncertain fate.

Lieutenant Raymond Zussman, the only Michigan recipient of the Jewish faith in World War II to be awarded the Congressional Medal of Honor, earned the nation's highest honor for courage, heroism, and valor under fire when he gave his life in battle in the invasion of southern France. The military wrote its account of Zussman's battlefield exploits in an official citation.

On 12 September 1944, Lieutenant Zussman was in command of two tanks operating with an infantry company in the attack on enemy forces occupying the town of Noroy le Bourg, France. At 1900 hours his command tank bogged down. Throughout the ensuing action, armed only with a carbine, he reconnoitered alone on foot far in advance of his remaining tank and the infantry, returning only from time to time to designate targets, direct the action of the tank and turn over to the infantry the numerous German soldiers he had caused to surrender. He located a road block and directed his tank to destroy it. Fully exposed to fire from an enemy position only fifty yards distant, he stood by his tank directing its fire. Three Germans were killed and eight surrendered. Again he walked before his tank leading it against an enemy held group of houses, machine gun and small arms fire kicking up the dust at his feet. The tank fire broke the resistance and twenty enemy soldiers surrendered. Going forward again alone he rushed an enemy occupied house from which the Germans fired on him and threw grenades in his path. After a brief fire fight he signaled his tank to come up and fire on the house. Eleven German soldiers were killed and fifteen surrendered. Going on alone he disappeared around a street corner, the fire of his carbine could be heard and in a few minutes he reappeared driving thirty prisoners before him. Under Lieutenant Zussman's heroic and inspiring leadership eighteen enemy soldiers were killed and ninety two captured.

Lt. Raymond Zussman was 27 when he was killed in action in France. Michigan's biggest Jewish hero barely made the military's minimum height requirement.

(Author's collection)

Congregation B'nai Moshe lost one of its oldest and most devoted members and officers with the passing of Sigmund Gunsberg. He was a founder of the synagogue's religious school and an officer for several other activities. Gunsberg also was a member of the boards of many of Detroit's Jewish institutions and provided financial help to many boys attending Yeshiva Beth Yehudah.

The B'nai Moshe hosted a mass rally of the Women's League for Sabbath Observance. Mrs. Esther Etkin Mossman, a past president of Detroit's Junior Hadassah, was one of the speakers and a stirring, dramatic presentation entitled "Kindling the Sabbath Lights" was well received by the audience. Due to the efforts of the organization, within two months, 18 groceries had closed their stores on Saturdays. Women were urged not to shop on Saturdays and to patronize the shops that closed on the Sabbath.

In the summer of 1944, Rabbi Isaac Stollman told Detroit's two Jewish weeklies that the city's Orthodox rabbis would like to publicize the fact that many establishments claiming to be kosher were guilty of false advertising. Rabbi Stollman said that the merger of the Merkaz and Vaad Harabonim had resulted in improved supervision. The rabbis issued a notice stating, "At the present time no restaurants or delicatessen stores are under the hashgocho of the Vaad Harabondim and Merkaz, and that those restaurant or delicatessen stores that handle non-kosher products must remove immediately the Kosher sign from their windows because the Michigan Kosher laws prohibit them from having Kosher signs in the window if they sell non-Kosher products and that those who sell non-Kosher products are obligated to have a sign in the window informing the public that they are selling non-Kosher products."

Fresh Air Camp raised its rates for campers to $18 per week in 1944. As before, because of the war, children of servicemen were taken in despite their financial status. The Mt. Sinai Hospital Association, founded in 1937, had 4,000 members in 1944 who were interested in pursuing construction of a Jewish hospital in Detroit. At the time, Detroit was the only city in America's ten largest without a Jewish hospital. As the year progressed, the Jewish Hospital Association of Detroit was incorporated toward construction of a 200-bed, $2 million facility.

Following the appointment of Dr. Hugo Mandelbaum as principal of the elementary department, Rabbi Simcha Wasserman was named dean of

Rabbi Avrohom Abba Freedman (top) and Rabbi Sholom Goldstein were rabbinical students under the tutelage of Rabbi Simcha Wasserman in New York before joining the teaching staff of the Yeshiva Beth Yehudah.

(Author's collection)

In addition to the educational programs of Chachmey Lublin, Yeshiva Beth Yehudah and the United Hebrew Schools, parents had the choice of Arbeiter Ring, Farband Folk, and Sholem Aleichem schools in 1944.

ARBEITER RING SCHOOLS	FARBAND FOLK SCHOOLS	SHOLEM ALEICHEM SCHOOLS
School 1 Arbeiter Ring Center 11529 Linwood	School 1 1912 Taylor Avenue cor. 12th Street	School 1 3754 Monterey
School 2 Custer Public School 15531 Linwood Ave. Room 303	School 2 Thirkell Public School 7724 14th Ave.	School 2 Brady Public School 2920 Joy Rd., 115, 121
	School 3 12244 Dexter Blvd. cor. Cortland	School 3 MacCulloch Public School 13120 Wildemere rooms 110, 210

the Yeshiva Beth Yehudah, replacing Dr. Samson R. Weiss, who left for New York to become educational director of the national religious educational movement Torah Umesorah. At a festive dinner held in August at the Yeshiva building on Dexter and Cortland, the burning of the mortgage was celebrated. The following month, the fall term began for the three departments conducted in the main building and at the two branches at Congregation Beth Tefilo Emanuel, located at Taylor and Woodrow Wilson, and at Hampton School, 18460 Warrington Drive.

With the new day school program, the Beth Jacob School for Girls, and the existing afternoon school, the budget was placed at $85,000. The enrollment of 440 included the 112 pupils in the day classes. Rabbi Avrohom Abba Freedman., who would have a huge impact on the student body and many people in the community, joined the teaching staff after the day school was planned and operational in the fall term.

Reb Hersch Cohen (see page 59), did not live to see his dream of children attending a yeshiva day school in Detroit, as he passed away only a few weeks before the school opened for the fall semester. Rabbi M. J. Wohlgelernter was so moved by Cohen's passing that he took time out from his busy schedule as president of the Yeshiva to write a lengthy article for a Midwestern Jewish publication:

"The departure of Hersch Cohen caused little stir in the Detroit Jewish community," wrote Rabbi Wohlgelernter. "Not a single notice was published by the express wish of the family, no hespedim [eulogies] were delivered, and only a small group of people attended the funeral. As quietly as the man lived, so unostentatiously did he pass away.

"One is moved to the observation that very little notice is frequently given to events of great significance. Were the influence of a personality such as that of the deceased to be judged by mass reaction, it would be considered negligible. Yet Reb Hersch was a man of true greatness, veritably a 'Zadik' [righteous man], and measured by actual achievement, his life belongs to history."

Many paragraphs later, Rabbi Wohlgelernter concluded: "In the course of years his labors bore fruit and he raised in his own household two generations of loyal Jews who developed a distinct religious climate around themselves. The influence of these homes is radiated into the community and, apart from the direct participation in communal affairs by the members of the family, has helped to create Torah environment in Detroit out of which grew support of Orthodox institutions throughout the world, observance of the Sabbath and family purity. Both directly and through hidden channels the power of Reb Hersch has thus made itself felt beyond the limited sphere of his habitat."

Jewish Detroiters were talking about a small article which appeared in the Jewish News in late 1944. Harry Rubenstein, chairman of the business industry division of the National Labor Committee for Palestine, told the annual convention about a young German Jewish woman's underground activities for Histadrut, the Jewish Labor Federation in Palestine. Rubenstein called the heroine, a "modern Esther." The young lady, who easily passed for a Nazi, traveled to and from Germany several times on forged passports. Each time she would steal into Germany and marry a Jew, leave, and accompany the man to Palestine. She did this 18 times. "The nineteenth time, however, she did not return," Rubenstein sadly told the audience.

In September 1944, Benno Levi's outfit was ordered to capture a strategic mountain on Guam. American planes mistook Levi and his fellow soldiers on the ground as the enemy. As the planes strafed and bombed the American troops lying flat on the ground seeking cover, Levi jumped up, seized the signal panels, and waved them until the pilots realized they were firing at Americans. Levi was awarded the Silver Star for gallantry in action.

While the medals recognizing Levi's bravery under fire meant a lot to him, so did a developing friendship with another Jewish Detroiter. Benno Levi and Frank Faudem didn't know each other until they met after Rosh Hashonah services on Guam. Both were graduates of Central High, where Faudem, a couple of years older than Levi, starred on the baseball team, leading to a contract with the Detroit Tigers. Faudem was in the minor leagues when he was drafted and

PFC Frank Faudem
(Courtesy Benno Levi)

was looking forward to resuming his career and his dream of playing with the hometown Tigers.

Levi and Faudem became more than army buddies. Their love of Judaism (Faudem and its wife, the former Lydia Ruth Kepes, were from families affiliated with Congregation B'nai Moshe), love of baseball, and love of Detroit created a tight bond.

Levi and Faudem shipped out together from Guam to the Philippine island of Leyte, where the mission of the American forces was to clean the island of enemy troops. Levi was in "A" Company and Faudem marched with "B" Company.

An infected foot and a fever sent Levi to the Battalion Aid Station. In passing he encountered Faudem, who told him the good news—Faudem's wife had given birth to a healthy baby girl. "We talked for a while and then parted," Levi recalled, "I to the hospital and he to join the last attack up in the hills. It was the second week of January, 1945.

"Two days later the wounded came in and when I met someone from "B" company I asked the usual question, "How's Faudem?"

The reply was devastating: "He's dead."

"The following day I hobbled on my crutches up a little hill in the hospital area to the tent where they brought the bodies before burial at the Division cemetery in Valencia. I found the stretcher with Frank's name on it. It was covered with a poncho. I stood alone and silently said a prayer.

"I remembered our last meeting at the aid station. There was sadness in his eyes mixed with the pride and joy of fatherhood. Did he have a premonition of what was ahead or was he aware that with so much more to live for, the dangers faced on every patrol were so much harder to accept?"

Had the 24-year-old Faudem lived, resumed his baseball career, and become a major leaguer with the Tigers, he would have been the only Detroit born Jew to ever play for the Detroit Tigers.

As the Americans advanced and Japanese fought on, Ernie Pyle visited the area where Levi was stationed. The famed war correspondent was only 50 yards from Levi's foxhole when machinegun fire killed him.

Sergeant Myron Rosenthal, 19, the youngest son of Mr. and Mrs. Isaac Rosenthal of Blaine Avenue, was reported missing in Action early in 1945. Myron., a gunner., and the rest of the nine-man crew disappeared over Germany while on a bombing mission. He was a graduate of Central High School and a member of its baseball, football, and debate teams. A graduate of the United Hebrew Schools, a member of the

Sgt. Myron Rosenthal was only 19 when he disappeared on his eighth bombing mission.
(Courtesy Zelda Selmar)

choir of Congregation Beth Tefilo Emanuel, and an officer and cantor of Shaarey Zedek's Junior Congregation, he also assisted chaplains and served as cantor for services as a member of the Air Force based in England,

Habonim labor Zionist youth groups around the country mourned the death of Lt. Daniel Ginsburg, a Detroit marine killed in battle on Iwo Jima. The 22-year-old from the small Mack Avenue Jewish enclave was a graduate of Wayne State University and a talented writer and artist.

His fame, however, came as the head of the Habonim movement, and he was credited with the establishment and building of Camp Kineret at Chelsea, Michigan. Two days before the battle that took his life. Ginsburg wrote a lengthy letter to friends in Detroit. At the end of the letter, he instructed his friends on what to say to his parents if he didn't survive.

"We're all only little cogs in a machine, and if some of us have to fall by the way-side in order that the machine should continue to run smoothly, it's worthwhile. After all, it's the machine that counts, not the little cogs;" Ginsburg wrote.

"And if I don't come back, will you try to make my folks understand that it isn't such a tragedy—that their son isn't any better than anyone else's son—and unfortunately, he happened to be just as vulnerable."

Marvin Eliot (Sonny) Schlossberg knew the end was near. He just hoped to survive. Word was that the Russians were advancing toward the prisoner of war camp he and almost 9,700 other American airmen were shuttered in.

"The Germans decided to move all the Jewish airmen out." Sonny recalled. "But the Russians broke through from the east. The Germans planned to move the Jews by train but couldn't because the Russians were getting too close. While the Germans were collecting all of the Jewish airmen, a Catholic chaplain ordered me to go back to my barracks and keep my mouth shut. So I wasn't put with the other Jewish airmen in one barrack. The Russians liberated us before the Germans could do anything to the Jews. When they liberated us, we all ran wild. We went into the German camp offices to find our files. Written across my picture was a great big 'Jude' [Jew]. So they knew all along I was Jewish."

On April 30, 1945, the day Sonny was liberated, the nutsie who became chief Nazi, Adolf Hitler, hiding in a Berlin bunker, put the front end of a pistol in his mouth and pulled the trigger.

Eighteen days before Hitler killed himself, President Franklin Delano Roosevelt died at the age of 63. Vice-President Harry S. Truman was inaugurated as president. At the time of Roosevelt's burial in Hyde Park, New York, at 11 a.m. on Sunday, April 15, Detroit's synagogues held special services to pay their last respects to the man many Jewish papers referred to as "Israel's best friend." Time and information, however, would prove the facts otherwise.

Thousands attended the funeral of Hyman Altman at the Chesed Shel Emes on Joy Road. The overflow crowd spilled onto the sidewalk to honor the founder and director of the 16-year-old weekly Jewish Radio Hour.

The Jewish world mourned the passing of Henrietta Szold at the age of 85. Mrs. Dora Ehrlich,

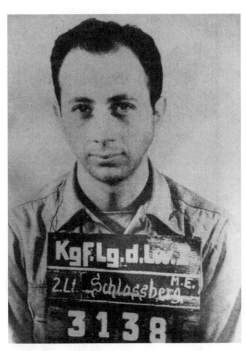

Lt. Marvin Schlossberg as a prisoner of war. He staged mock talent shows to keep up the spirits of prisoners, which helped hone his skills after the war when he became Sonny Eliot.
(Courtesy Sonny Eliot)

active in Hadassah the organization Miss Szold founded, told Detroit's Jewish weeklies, "Her name will go down in history. She had the mind of a man and the soul of a woman," Mrs. Ehrlich continued. "She had a very charming personality and was simple and unaffected in manner. She was a mother to all. She loved and understood children and young people. Her last few years were devoted to the Youth Aliyah movement, which she mothered."

A front page article in the Friday, May 4, 1945, edition of the *Jewish Chronicle*, caused concern about the future. "Only 2,000 Jewish boys and girls are attending week-day Hebrew or Yiddish afternoon or day classes, and only 3,000 children are getting instruction in Jewish Sunday schools," the article stated. "This was revealed by the Citizens Committee which met last Sunday afternoon at the Jewish Center to study the recommendations of the Detroit Self-Study.

"The survey of Detroit's Jewish educational, recreational and cultural activities was conducted by Elias Picheny and Israel B. Rappaport. Detroit has a Jewish population of about 85,000 with at least 25,000 Jewish children of school age."

"This means that from 75 to 80 percent of the Jewish children receive no Jewish schooling," Phillip Slomovitz wrote in the *Jewish News*. "What hold will Judaism have on children who know practically nothing of the great and exciting history of their people?

"What hold will religion have on the youth if they are ignorant of the Bible, of the teachings of the Prophets and the great Rabbis?"

Cramped for space, as over 500 students attended the Yeshiva Beth Yehudah day and afternoon school and the Beth Jacob School for Girls, a two-story building on the east side of Dexter across from the main building was purchased. Until the building could be converted to school use, some classes continued to meet at Congregation Beth David, Elmhurst and 14th; Congregation Beth Tefilo Emanuel, Taylor and Woodrow Wilson and the Hampton Public School, 18460 Warrington Drive.

Several months later, Abe Kasle, president of the United Hebrew Schools, called attention to the educational needs of the growing Jewish presence in the northwest area of Detroit.

According to Kasle, "the section from Linwood west to Wyoming and from Puritan north to 8-Mile Road now numbers approximately 6,000 families. It is believed that more than 2,000 Jewish children in this section are in the main left today without any sort of Jewish training.

"A small portion of these children, numbering not more than 200, now are attending Hebrew school classes—130 of them being enlisted in the United Hebrew Schools' branch of the Bagley School. Another 1,000 attend classes only once a week in the various Sunday schools of the community.

"A study of the northwest section," Kasle contin-

Mr. and Mrs. Sam Cohen and daughter, Dena, were reunited after the war. All of their children and grandchildren are observant Jews, many involved in Jewish education and day schools.

ued, "reveals that in one public school alone, the Bagley, at Curtis and Roselawn, 10 blocks west of Livernois, there are 704 Jewish children.

"In another school, at the Hampton, one block east of Livernois, near Curtis, there are more than 480 Jewish pupils. We have established quarters in the Bagley School where we use five classrooms, and have filled them to capacity with our 130 pupils. It is the maximum we can accommodate in that school.

"The longer we wait, the more children will be lost to us and the greater the indifference that will arise in Jewish ranks."

Allen A. Warsen became director of the Adas Shalom Religious School after its first semester of operation. The school had opened the previous February with 75 students at the Bagley School at Roselawn and Curtis.

Temple Beth El had 1,182 members in 1945, a gain of 169 in five years. Jerusalem-born Cantor Hyman Adler, 34, moved to Detroit from Cleveland to become cantor of Congregation B'nai David. Mrs. Sam Cohen was elected president of the Detroit Women's League, and her sister-in-law, Mrs. Lillian Cohen, became treasurer. The latter also served as treasurer of the PTA of the Yeshiva Beth Yehudah. The Women's League sent packages to servicemen, sponsored Young Israel youth groups, and helped elevate community awareness regarding Taharas Hamishpocho (family purity) toward construction of a ritularium.

Solomon N. (Sam) Cohen, who was married on December 7, 1941, returned home after being discharged from an army hospital. Cohen was wounded while storming enemy lines in Italy and was awarded the Bronze Star, Combat Badge, and Purple Heart for his heroics. The son of the late Reb Hersch Cohen became the regular Baal Kore (Torah reader) for Young Israel and was active in the Yeshiva Beth Yehudah.

Young Israel of Detroit, working out of rented quarters in an office on Dexter and Cortland, had hired Rabbi Israel Turner as its spiritual leader the previous Chanukah. Renting the Jericho Temple at 2691 Joy Road and the Yeshiva Beth Yehudah-Mogen, Abraham at Dexter and Cortland for religious services, architectural plans were drawn for a large Young Israel synagogue and youth center on Dexter near Glendale.

Each of the 55 soldiers belonging to Young Israel serving in the military were sent a copy of "Machne Israel," a book written by the late Chofetz Chaim. The book, translated in English and published by the National Council of Young Israel, contained special instruction for Jews in the military.

Bob Torgow, who celebrated his Bar Mitzvah at Congregation Mogen Abraham around the corner from his home around the time the Yeshiva Beth Yehudah Day School started in the building, ushered at Briggs Stadium in 1945 at the age of 13.

Florence Abels Ashin and several of her girlfriends worked for the New York Central Railroad in the Michigan Central Depot. They would meet on the 14th Street bus and gab on the way down. They often saw the Tigers, and Florence's hero, Hank Greenberg, at the terminal.

Florence bought tickets for her family for Greenberg's first game back from the service. Greenberg joined the Tigers for the game on July 1. He hit a home run in his first major league game in more than four years as 47,729 paying fans including Florence and a 13-year-old usher cheered.

Seymour "Cy" Block was an infielder for the Chicago Cubs before he became a member of the armed forces. Block was aboard a ship on its way to Japan when an American crew flying a B-29 five miles high over Hiroshima on August 6 released an atomic bomb. Almost 80,000 people were killed and four square miles were leveled.

The Commander of Block's ship was informed of the bombing and ordered to turn back to the States, as it was clear the war would soon be over. The Chicago Cubs wired Block to report to the team as soon as possible.

Block marched to the Commander and saluted, requesting permission for discharge to help his team win the pennant. The Commander agreed on the condition that he get four World Series tickets.

On August 9, the Americans dropped another bomb on Nagasaki. The casualties and damage were less than the previous bombing as the population wasn't as dense. Five days after the bomb fell on Nagasaki, the government of Japan surrendered through a document transmitted to neutral embassies.

Lise Meitner, a Jewish physicist, gave birth to the atomic bomb. She was dismissed from her position at a German university by the Nazis in 1933 but continued on her research in Berlin. She was finalizing her discovery when she was exiled from Germany for being a Jewess. In 1939 her calculations led to the splitting of the atom. The 69-year-old Meitner published her findings and the United States won the nuclear race.

In several areas of Detroit's Jewish neighborhoods, after President Truman announced the end of the war on radio on Tuesday night, August 14, men, women, and children took to the streets. A band played along Dexter, with a surging crowd adding to the celebration. On Linwood and Twelfth streets, people congratulated each other and small, out-of-step parades formed. A Purim-like mood prevailed as noisemakers added to the din. Joyous Jews took the Dexter bus downtown to join the already large crowd in celebration.

All synagogues and temples in Detroit also held well-attended V-J services of rejoicing and thanksgiving.

The joy on Dexter turned to fear a few weeks later as police guarded synagogues. Incidents occurred on a Tuesday and Wednesday night in which non-Jewish gangs targeted Jewish youths, but were finally driven off by Jewish young men hearing the commotion.

On Thursday night, September 6, almost 500 Jewish boys gathered on Dexter from Elmhurst to Richton, ready to defend their turf. Arriving police dispatched to head off any trouble assured the crowd they would offer protection, and things returned to normal.

The surviving Jews in Europe weren't as lucky as the Jews in Detroit. The war may have ended but the anti-Semitism didn't. Reports of beatings and killings of the few remnants of Polish Jewry were being made public. In Lodz, 128 Jews were killed in one month. In Radom, Polish gangs posted signs warning Jews to leave or they would be killed. Poles wanted to keep what they stole from the Jews when they were shipped to the camps.

Emma Lazaroff Schaver traveled to Germany as a member of the first cultural mission sponsored by the World Jewish Congress and spent six months performing for survivors in displaced persons camps. On behalf of the United Jewish Appeal, Louis Berry and Joseph Holtzman visited DP camps and Palestine on a fact-finding mission. When the pair returned to Detroit, they informed the community that the suffering and horror was, if anything, understated. Rabbi Morris Adler, who took a leave from Shaarey Zedek in 1943 to enlist as an army chaplain, became the first Jewish chaplain to serve in Japan and see Hiroshima after its destruction by the atomic bomb.

Detroit relatives were cabled the news that Pfc. Lester Tenenberg had survived the "Death March of Bataan" and a Japanese prisoner of war camp. Celia Shetzer, daughter of Mr. and Mrs. Isaac Shetzer of Chicago Boulevard, returned to Detroit after serving 22 months overseas with the Red Cross. While watching uncut films of Nazi death camp atrocities in the

Emma Lazaroff Schaver

Rouge plant auditorium, Henry Ford suffered a stroke. From that day on, according to his secretary, his mind and physical abilities were never the same.

Returning soldiers found six radio stations in Detroit: CKLW, WJBK, WJLB, WJR, WWJ, and WXYZ. As they dreidled around the dial they heard the latest tunes of 1945. "April Showers," "June is Bustin' Out All Over," "I Love You for Sentimental Reasons," "Let it Snow," "Sentimental Journey," and the lingering hits of the previous year, "Don't Fence Me In," and "I'll Walk Alone."

There were some changes in the community, too. Even though most Jewish owned stores were still functioning on Twelfth Street, business was down as more families relocated closer to Dexter and even north of McNichols between Livernois and Wyoming. Congregation Beth Yehudah (the Pingree Shule) was planning on relocating northwest and had sold its Pingree synagogue the year before. A branch of the JCC—operated by the Detroit branch of the National Council of Jewish Women—had opened at the Twelfth Street Council Center at Dexter and Davison the previous December.

Detroit's Jews were following Hank Greenberg closely. Greenberg batted .311 and hit 13 home runs in only three months, leading the Tigers to the World Series. Greenberg also starred in the World Series by hitting two home runs and batting .304 in seven games, bringing the Tigers to a championship. Cy Block, however, only got into one game as a pinch-runner and spent more money than his World Series share. Block paid for four tickets for his former Coast Guard commander and had to shell out for the commander and his wife to come to Chicago to watch the games.

On Monday, October 8, a one-hour protest was held in front of the City Hall. From 4 to 5 p.m. thousands of Zionists, outraged by the British white paper restricting immigration of Jews into Palestine, also demanded a Jewish national home in the land of Zion.

During the protest downtown, stores along Dexter, Linwood and Twelfth were closed. On the other side of Woodward—opposite City Hall—hundreds marched along Woodward and Cadillac Square in front of the building that housed the office of the British consulate. Detroit's Jewish leaders at the demonstration included heads of Zionist organizations and schools, as well as several Christian leaders, including Rev. Henry Hitt Crane, pastor of the Central Methodist Church.

Rabbi Leon Fram introduced Dr. Crane to the crowd. Crane proceeded to give his reasons for supporting President Truman's plea to the British government to allow Jews into their ancestral homeland.

"I endorse the President's appeal because I am a Christian," Crane said, "and as such I feel so vastly indebted to my spiritual forebears, the Jews. You are in very truth the fathers of our faith. The human race owes more to the Jewish people than to any other three races. You gave us the idea of monotheism. Every inch of land the Jews possess in Palestine they paid for."

Hank Greenberg was back in the swing of things after the war.
(Courtesy of Ernie Harwell Collection, Burton Historical Collection of the Detroit Public Library)

Years of planning by groups supporting the ideal of a Jewish hospital in Detroit—the old Hebrew Hospital Association, the Mt. Sinai Hospital Association, and the North End Clinic Workers—seemed to come to fruition in April 1945 as the Detroit City Planning Commission approved a 36-acre site. Bounded by McNichols, Outer Drive, and Whitcomb and Lauder avenues, construction was expected to start as soon as materials were available. Even though over $2.5 million was raised for construction with a target opening of January 1948, it became apparent more funds were needed. A $1 million bank loan was secured, and the firm of Albert Kahn Associated Architects and Engineers was engaged for design work.

Formed in 1943, the Northwest Congregation held services in the home of its president and founder, Alex Margulies, on Ohio north of Curtis. The following year, a split occurred over where to build a synagogue. One faction wanted to locate on Wyoming and the other closer to Livernois.

To honor its president, the group loyal to Margulies, Orthodox in tradition, renamed itself Beth Aaron, after Margulies' Hebrew name, and chose a lot on Wyoming and Thatcher on which to construct its synagogue. On Sunday, July 22, 1945, Dr. Max Abramson, of 18247 Santa Barbara, and the Feldman Family Club were given the honor of laying the cornerstone. Construction was rushed in time to use part of the structure for high Holy Day services.

The group wanting to build closer to Livernois, the Northwest Hebrew Congregation and Center, had been holding services at the Bagley School at Curtis and Roselawn since November 11, 1944. After new elections, with Ira G. Kaufman as president and Irwin I. Cohn on the 16-man board of directors, ground was broken on November 25, 1945, on the south side of Curtis two blocks west of Livernois.

Max Nusbaum was unanimously elected chairman of the Detroit Federation of Polish Jews. "It will not be a drive for money in the ordinary sense of the word," Nusbaum told the Jewish News. "Nor will it be merely an attempt to appeal to Detroit Jewish individuals for the sake of the local Federation for Polish Jews.

"It will be a call to mobilize our powers to become foster fathers of at least 200 Jewish orphans throughout Europe and to give a helping hand to the Jews surviving in Poland. Any individual or organization can select a child for adoption."

The cost to become a foster parent was $300 per year. Nusbaum's organization supplied foster parents with names, addresses, photographs, and family backgrounds to encourage correspondence. The Detroit Federation of Polish Jews also conducted a clothing drive.

Celebrating its 50th anniversary, the Hebrew Free Loan Association recalled its humble beginnings at the rear of Selig Koploy's Shoe Store on Gratiot. In 1915 the maximum loan was $25; in 1945 it was $500. As it had for the past 22 years, operating funds for its office and staff on Linwood and Joy Road came from the Detroit Community Fund, and since 1926 the Jewish Welfare Federation, through Allied Jewish Campaigns had supplied more than half of its working capital.

North End Clinic's medical staff welcomed returning members from the armed forces on December 11, 1945. The Jewish News reported, "A total of 76 members of the Clinic's prewar medical and dental staff of 125 served with the Armed Forces, some having entered the army and navy prior to Pearl Harbor, and three members were casualties."

Four weeks before the end of the war, Lt. Henry Bodzin, a navigator on a bombing mission, was lost over Germany, and the family notified. Six months later, the family received a sealed casket for burial. The Bodzin family never knew if any remains were inside as the casket was lowered into the ground.

More than 600,000 American Jews, including more than 10,000 Jews from Michigan, served during the war. According to the National Jewish Welfare Board (JWB), "Forty Jewish families throughout the United States have lost two sons each in the service and one is known to have lost three sons. There were 22,042 Jewish men and women who were combat casualties." Two hundred twenty-five were from Detroit.

The deaths of young men killed in war took its

toll on many Jewish Detroiters, including Rabbi Ben Zion Moldawsky, who lost two sons. In June the Jewish National Fund Council of Detroit presented Rabbi Moldawsky with a certificate commemorating a garden of trees planted in Palestine in memory of the two servicemen.

The *Jewish News* covered the presentation. "Rabbi Moldawsky's response moved the gathering to tears," the paper reported. "It was a brief but brilliant dissertation on the value of man's life and on the worth of vegetation and trees. Since his sons lives can not be restored, he expressed hope that the trees planted in their honor in Palestine will fulfill an important mission in behalf of our people's redemption."

Less than four months later, Rabbi Moldawsky suffered a fatal stroke while chanting Sukkoth services at Congregation Shaar Hashomayim on Muirland. Besides being one of the community's great cantors, other cantors claimed that more than one hundred of his liturgical works are chanted in synagogues throughout the world.

In the early 1920s, Rabbi Moldawsky's long legal fight in Russian courts over the right to practice his religion in Russia attracted worldwide notice. After he won the case in 1925, Rabbi Moldawsky moved to Detroit.

13
1946-1953
THE POSTWAR YEARS

Housing in the Dexter and northwest neighborhoods was hard to come by in 1946. Families were leaving the Twelfth Street area, and soldiers were getting married and needed a place to live. One family of four resorted to placing an ad in the *Jewish News* willing to pay $100 a month in rent and offering a $250 reward "for information leading to rental of a 6-room flat or single home, in the vicinity of Dexter or 6 Mile Road." It wasn't unusual for Jewish couples to walk up to people they didn't know strolling along Dexter, begging for any leads on available housing.

Even with streetcar fares raised to ten cents, more people were heading downtown to shop and mingle with the pedestrians. With wages and prices inching up, a 1946 Pontiac with all the trimmings went for $1,646. A strike against General Motors lasting nearly four months was settled, and within two weeks afterward, Walter Reuther was elected president of the UAW-CIO. The old Willow Run Bomber plant became the new Kaiser-Frazer automobile plant, with more potential union members. There were enough households in Detroit to publish a two-volume phone directory for the first time.

Three studies were conducted—one each by the state, county, and city—on where to place a new metropolitan airport. The studies agreed that the airport should be at Eight Mile Road and Schaefer. However, city councilman Billy Rogell, who was a teammate of

In 1946 a busy Woodward had a lane for those entering and exiting streetcars. Hudson's and Kern's department stores can be seen on the right.

(Courtesy of Burton Historical Collection of the Detroit Public Library)

ECHOES OF DETROIT'S JEWISH COMMUNITIES

Hank Greenberg as a shortstop for the Tigers the previous decade, thought it should be within the confines of Wayne County and fought for its Romulus location.

In 1946 the British created the Arab country of Jordan on land in Palestine east of the Jordan River. All Jews living on that land were forced out. After almost three years in the Navy, Walter Zukin returned to his home on Philadelphia near Twelfth and took over operations of Zukin's on Twelfth Street. After serving more than four years in the Navy, Walter E. Klein was named research director of the Jewish Community Council. Former Navy officer Irwin Shaw was appointed as administrative assistant on the executive staff of the Jewish Welfare Federation.

High school football star Abe Eliowitz also starred in college on the baseball diamond and won the heavyweight boxing championship at Michigan State University. He went on to earn a degree in education and started his teaching career in Detroit in 1940. After teaching at Denby, Eliowitz moved to Cooley High and coached the football team to the Detroit prep championship in 1946. Sherwin Wine, a 17-year-old Central High senior, was the winner of the Hearst $2,000 award in Victory Bonds. Wine edged 41 finalists throughout the country in the annual Hearst Newspapers American History Awards. A brilliant student who posted perfect scores, Wine also was a noted speaker and actor while at Central.

Two Detroit Jews working as civilian employees of the war crimes trials at Dachau, Irving J. Hayett and Sally Rose, were married in Dachau. The main ballroom of the War Crimes Officers Club was gaily decorated with an American flag made of roses and carnations for the traditional Jewish wedding. William Weinstein enlisted in the Marine Corps in 1941, a year after he graduated from Wayne State University Law School. He finished officer Candidate School as a second lieutenant and saw action in the Pacific Theater, where he earned a Bronze Star Medal and Purple Heart. Married in 1944, Weinstein returned to Detroit and continued to serve as a marine reserve while operating a law practice on the 24th floor of the National Bank Building.

A year after he was reported missing, Mr. and Mrs. Isaac Rosenthal were notified by the War Department that their son was presumed dead. Sgt. Myron Rosenthal was part of a nine-man crew lost on a bombing mission over Achen, Germany. Avern Cohn, who was assigned by the Army to a pre-medical program at Stanford University in 1944, left the army and Stanford to enter law school at the University of Michigan in 1946. President Harry Truman appointed Theodore Levin as United States Federal District Judge.

The Joint Distribution Committee and twelve leading National Jewish Women's organizations,

Strollers along McNichols past Pennington found several large stores, including Cunningham's, Atlantic & Pacific Food Market, Sanders, Kroger, and Neisner Brothers. Colorful awnings provided protection in hot or wet weather.

(Courtesy of Dr. Chuck Taylor)

through the league of Jewish women's organizations of Detroit, called on the women of Detroit to donate items for the needy Jews of Europe. Through a collection depot at Temple Beth El, foodstuffs, children's items, household supplies, and other necessities were collected. Radomer Aid Society celebrated its 25th anniversary at a gala banquet. The organization announced it adopted three orphans from Europe. Besides providing for their maintenance, it also donated $4,000 to charitable causes, with most going to Gewerkashaften. In 1946, loans by the Hebrew Free Loan Association to 290 individuals totaled $52,525. Under the chairmanship of Nate S. Shapero, head of Cunningham Drug Stores, Inc., the Allied Jewish Campaign topped the $2 million mark for the first time.

Many survivors of the concentration camps moved to Detroit to be reunited with relatives. They had lost parents, grandparents, siblings, aunts, uncles, and cousins. They had been reduced to walking skeletons when liberated. They experienced the whole vortex of violence. They arrived at their hell on earth in sealed boxcars amidst the stench of urine, vomit, and the dead.

Now—many months later in a new country and city—they had to contend with learning a language, and learn to trust and contend with their grief. They would have to watch others lucky enough to have parents, grandparents, brothers, and sisters. They would not be like others. The numbers on their arms would always remind them of that.

The Jewish Welfare Federation's Resettlement Service appealed for housing for the war-shattered remnants. According to Harold Silver, executive director of the Jewish Service Bureau, most of the arrivals "were between 20 and 40 years of age. A few are elderly. Of the orphaned children who have arrived to date, all are at least 16 years old. Many still feel frightened and insecure. A man of 25, who came with his 16-year-old sister, would not let her out of his sight for fear that she, like their parents, might be taken away to her death."

Alex Kuhn, a native of Hungary, spent his early teenage years experiencing the horror of concentration camps. Out of seven children, only a brother survived. Their father was killed a month before the war ended. Alex, born into an observant Jewish home, abandoned Judaism, and for a year and a half lived with a non-Jewish family in Austria without practicing any faith. Helped by Jewish agencies to come to the United States, Alex was in New York when asked if he wanted to live with an observant or non-observant Jewish family.

"I told them I wanted an observant family," Kuhn related. "They put me on a train and I arrived in Detroit the next morning. The other choice was to stay in New York and go to the West Coast. I didn't know

The area of McNichols (Six Mile) and Prairie had many shops catering to men and women.

(Courtesy of Dr. Chuck Taylor)

the West Coast from the East Coast. But I made up my mind that I wanted to be observant again as soon as possible.

"Social workers met me at the train station and drove me to Cortland and Dexter, to Moshe Kaner and his family. Mr. Kaner was a teacher in Central High and he told me that he took part in bombing missions in Vienna. It turned out he bombed the very factory I worked under the Nazis in.

"I was 15 years old when I arrived in Detroit," Kuhn continued. "At that time I didn't speak any English. They enrolled me in Hutchins Intermediate to learn English. In the afternoon they sent me to Chachmey Lublin on Linwood for Jewish studies. I spoke Hungarian, German, and understood a little bit of the Slavic languages. I learned Yiddish from the camps.

"The second day in Detroit, Mr. Kaner introduced me to a man who spoke Hungarian, Mr. Grossman, who was walking home from shule [synagogue]. He came to this country when he was ten. I didn't know it then, but I would become his son-in-law."

On July 4, 1946, 42 Jewish survivors who returned home to Kielce, Poland, were murdered by their former fellow citizens. Poles, frothing with hate passed down through generations,. dug out thousands of corpses in Jewish cemeteries throughout Poland, searching for gold teeth. Two Jews returning to Miskoic, 80 miles from Budapest, were lynched. Authorities arrested 16 people responsible; however, an anti-Semitic mob went on a rampage, freed the prisoners, and murdered any Jews they found.

Emma Lazaroff Schaver returned from a six-month trip to the previous German area of occupation. Mrs. Schaver performed in 50 concerts, raising the morale of 100,000 displaced persons. Besides singing in Hebrew and Yiddish, Mrs. Schaver sang in several languages, bringing back memories of happier times in Europe. Morris Schaver, Poale Zion representative to the World Zionist Congress in Zurich in 1946, joined his wife for the latter part of her concert tour.

In 1939, the Nazis had celebrated the destruction of the Jewish soul of Lublin, Poland. A Nazi newspaper printed the following: "Finally, we succeeded in destroying the greatest Jewish strategic position of international value, the Rabbinical College of Lublin." Eventually, the contents of the big Jewish library were taken to the town square and set afire in the presence of Nazi officials and cheering Polish citizens. The former Rabbinical College was transformed into the Gestapo headquarters.

Faculty and students were hunted down, beaten, tortured and killed. Some managed to escape and reached Vilna, Lithuania, where they temporarily reopened a much smaller version of the rabbinical school. As the Nazis approached, the Jews traveled to Kobe, Japan, and on to Shanghai, China, where the school was reopened again. One of the remnants of the yeshiva was the young scholar, Rabbi Moshe Rothenberg, who made it to America and Detroit and reopened the famous yeshiva on Linwood and Elmhurst.

By 1946, after four years of operation, Yeshivath Chachmey Lublin had 12 grades, and students were receiving Hebrew and English instruction. At the same time, Rabbi Rothenberg worked tirelessly to obtain visas for surviving students from Europe. In 1946, eight young rabbis arrived in Detroit, including many members of the Gardin family, as well as Rabbi Yitzchok Kuperman.

Polish Murder Bands Looting, Killing Jews

WARSAW (JPS).—While mass graves containing the corpses of tens of thousands of Jews slaughtered by the Nazis are still being uncovered everywhere in Poland, anti-Semitic Polish murder bands are ranging through Polish villages, killing Jews and looting their possessions.

Armed Polish anti-Semites raided the home of Pinchas Goldstein, President of the Jewish Community of Gniewaszow, and warned all Jews to leave the town within six hours or be killed. When the ultimatum expired, the gang returned and murdered Goldstein and his wife, Elijah Kirshbaum and two Jewish women, Chafa Miechaber and Eva Beinheil.

Readers of the *Jewish News* anguished over articles describing postwar horror in 1946.
(Courtesy of Jewish News)

Around the same time, Rabbi Eliezer Finkel, Rosh Yeshiva (head of Hebrew studies), returned from Palestine after eight months and brought his wife and four children to Detroit. A son of the famous Rosh Yeshivah of Hebron, Rabbi Abraham Shmuel Finkel, and a grandson of the founder of the Slobodka Yeshivah, Rabbi Nosson Zvi Finkel, he followed the family tradition and became famous for learning and instructing.

Rabbi Finkel's brother operated Finkel's Kosher Restaurant, Detroit's only restaurant under the rabbinical supervision of the Council of Orthodox Rabbis, on Linwood at Taylor. Finkel's was open from Sunday through Thursday from 6 a.m. to 1 a.m.

The Stoliner Rebbe, Rabbi Yaakov Perlow, came to Detroit on an annual visit to stay at the Wainer family home on Elmhurst, a few doors down from the Stoliner Shule. He passed away on May 7, 1946, and was buried by his followers through Chesed Shel Emes (Hebrew Benevolent Society) in Mt. Clemens.

The Yeshiva Beth Yehuda had two new additions in the summer of 1946. Rabbi Solomon H. Gruskin, a 28-year-old native of Avoca, Pennsylvania, who had previously served as executive director of a yeshiva in New York, was named executive director. The Ladies of the Yeshiva purchased the school's first bus, which was parked in front of the building on Dexter at Cortland for display on Sunday, August 11, at the annual picnic.

A few hours after the picnic, many returned to the Yeshiva Beth Yehudah building for a memorial service for the 93 Beth Jacob students and teachers in Warsaw who gave up their lives rather than to submit to the Nazis on August 11, 1942.

Part of the letter sent to Rabbi Leo Jung of New York, and published in the *New York Times* on January 8, 1943, was read, amidst loud sobbing and cries of anguish.

I do not know whether this letter will reach you. Do you still remember who I am? We met in Warsaw…When this letter will come into your hands, I shall not live any more…

Yesterday and the day before we were given hot baths and we were told that German soldiers would come tonight to visit us. We yesterday swore to ourselves that we shall die together. The Germans do not know that our last bath is our purification before death. Today everything was taken away from us…All of us have poison. When the soldiers will come we shall drink it. Today we are together and all day we are saying our last confession. We have no fear.

We thank you, good friend, for everything. We have one request: Say Kaddish for us, your 93 children…

To the memory of the young martyrs, the Ladies of the Yeshiva Beth Yehudah dedicated a living memorial with the founding of the Beth Jacob School in May 1943. In three years the school grew to over 60 students, ranging in age from six to 18.

Congregation Beth Aaron dedicated its new synagogue on Wyoming in 1946.

(Photo by author)

Congregation Beth Aaron dedicated its new synagogue on Wyoming and Thatcher on Sunday, June 23. Reverend Marshall Goldman, a student studying for the rabbinate at Chicago's Hebrew Theological Seminary who lived with his parents above their fruit store on Twelfth Street, was engaged as cantor for the High Holy Days. A short time later, Rabbi Chaim Weinstein was elected the first full-time spiritual leader. Rabbi Weinstein completed his rabbinical courses at Detroit's Yeshivath Chachmey Lublin.

Congregation Beth Aaron Israel sold its building on Oakland and announced its cessation as a synagogue. Organized in 1905 as Tifereth Israel, part of the congregation seceded in 1922 and is also known as the Stoliner Shule on Elmhurst and Linwood. Funds from the sale of the Oakland building were distributed to Detroit's Jewish day schools and other worthy causes.

Rabbi Herschel Lymon, former educational director of Temple Beth El, became director of the University of Michigan Hillel Foundation. Rabbi Milton Rosenbaum assumed the pulpit of Temple Israel in Pontiac. Rabbi Alvin Poplack, who was executive director of the Yeshiva Beth Yehudah, assumed the same title and also became spiritual leader of Young Israel, succeeding Rabbi Turner. Because of Rabbi Hershman's ill health, Congregation Shaarey Zedek hired a temporary rabbi until Rabbi Morris Adler returned from the army. In 1946, Rabbi Hershman was elected rabbi emeritus and given a pension, while Rabbi Adler became the full-time spiritual leader.

(Courtesy of Jewish News)

Rabbi Dr. Leopold Neuhas, the only surviving rabbi of the former Frankfort Jewish community, became spiritual leader of Congregation Gemiluth Chassodim on Joy Road. The rabbi and his wife were among 400 survivors of the 300,000 Jews of Frankfort. After his liberation from three years in a concentration camp and a reunion with his wife, they helped reorganize Jewish life in the American-controlled zones of Germany.

Dedication ceremonies for the Northwest Hebrew Congregation and Center, Curtis and Santa Rosa, were held on Sunday afternoon, September 8. Recently hired spiritual leader Rabbi Jacob Segal, a graduate of the College of the City of New York and the Jewish Theological Seminary, and who had completed a period of Army chaplaincy, was the principal speaker. As the doors opened for the dedication, a solemn procession took place, led by president Ira G. Kaufman and board members carrying six Sifrei Torah which were placed in the Ark. The Eternal Lamp was kindled, and Reverend Jacob Sonenklar recited the blessing.

Hank Greenberg showed power in 1946 by hitting 44 home runs, and his 127 RBIs led the league, but the 35-year-old slugger only batted .277, the first time he was under .300 for a full season. After a year and a half without a professional Yiddish theatrical performance in Detroit, Abraham Littman, who had managed the Yiddish Theater in Detroit for a generation, brought in a troupe for two one-day Sunday October performances at the Masonic Temple.

Irving Nusbaum celebrated his Bar Mitzvah at Congregation Beth Abraham on Linwood in a unique manner. The Bar Mitzvah boy's parents, Mr. and Mrs. Abraham Nusbaum, covered the expenses of bringing in the well-known Cantor Labele Waldman and choral leader Oscar Julius and his choir from New York for Sabbath services. Worshippers bought tickets in advance, and all gifts to Irving, along with the proceeds of the tickets, were turned over to a committee for distribution to charitable causes. Max and Julian Nusbaum opened Central Floor Covering in 1946. The small, 20-by-40-foot store handled remnants and short rolls and got its name from its location on Vernor and Central, and from Julian's Alma

Mater, Central High School.

The Jewish Radio Hour began its eighteenth year on WJLB in the last month of 1946. Mrs. Hyman Altman oversaw the program since the death of her husband over a year earlier. Actually longer than an hour, it aired from 8:30 to 10 p.m. on Saturday nights and on Sundays. Many families ate lunch as they listened from 11:45 a.m. to 1 p.m. to Harry Weinberg's "The Yiddish Hour," which started on WJBK in 1932. In 1946 the program featured fewer public service announcements and more talk with guests.

After seeking fame and fortune in New York and finding neither, the former Marvin Eliot Schlossberg legally changed his name to Sonny Eliot in 1946, returned to Detroit, and enrolled in Wayne University to bone up on writing. Fran Striker, head writer of the Detroit-based national Lone Ranger radio program, was Sonny's instructor at Wayne. Striker was writing three half-hour programs a week and bought one of Sonny's scripts. Sonny even got to play a bad guy on the WXYZ program, based in the Macabees Building on Woodward.

Hank Greenberg turned 36 on the first day of 1947. Tigers owner Walter O. Briggs thought his skills were eroding and wanted to trade him while he would bring some value. Briggs didn't want Greenberg in the American League where he might haunt the Tigers, so he sold him to the lowly Pittsburgh Pirates of the National League. The Jewish community was shocked. Greenberg was shocked. Except for the war years, a whole generation grew up following Greenberg's career with the Tigers.

Sonny Eliot was shocked over Greenberg's departure. Like most young Jewish men he grew up following the exploits of the Tigers' star player. Sonny even earned some extra change in the summer wiping off seats at the ballpark and got to see the games for free. Greenberg spotted Sonny one sunny morning and asked the Central High student if he'd like to shag fly balls as the slugger wanted to take some extra batting practice. That morning turned into several as Greenberg and Sonny would arrive early.

Sonny's mom, who was much more comfortable speaking in Yiddish than English, didn't know the difference between first base and second base, but she listened to the ballgames on radio to find out how Greenberg was doing. "One afternoon," Sonny recalled, "the announcer said the pitcher went for the resin bag (a bag of chalky substance used to wipe off sweat on fingers).

"Rosinbeg, Rosinbeg!" Sonny's mother exclaimed. "Noch a Yid offen Tigers? [Is there another Jew on the Tigers?]"

Life went on without Greenberg for Sonny and the Jewish community. A professor at Wayne told Sonny about a new phenomenon that would debut

Former first lady Eleanor Roosevelt chats with Emma Lazaroff Schaver on a visit to Detroit in 1947.

(Courtesy of Mrs. Schaver)

in Detroit. They called it television. Sonny was very excited and went down to the WWJ studios (Detroit's first television station and the sixth in the country), auditioned, and was hired.

There were about 2,000 households in Detroit with televisions when WWJ-TV, Channel 4, made its debut on June 3, 1947. Sonny was the voice of "Willy-Do-It," the starring puppet on a program aimed to kids, and he played an average golfer in need of lessons on a program for adults interested in golfing. Sonny also played inside animal suits and gave voice to several animals in a circus show. When station operators realized it could sell a weather segment on newscasts to advertisers, Sonny's personality and experience won that audition as well.

Mrs. Franklin D. Roosevelt preached at Temple Beth El's Saturday morning services in March under the auspices of the Jewish Welfare Federation. Later in the year, Rabbi Sidney Akselrad became assistant rabbi of Beth El. Arthur Goulson, a fourth generation member of Temple Beth El who served as president of the Beth El Young Peoples Society, was elected president of the Men's Club. Ira Sonnenblick, with a background in education and Jewish causes, became executive director of the Jewish Home for the Aged. Jerry Bielfield, grandson of the longtime president of the House of Shelter, became its president in 1947.

Stores along Livernois celebrated the 75th anniversary of the founding of the street. In 1872, a road was cut through the old ribbon farmland owned by Joseph Livernois, Sr., and Joseph Livernois, Jr. Danny Raskin bought his first automobile in 1947. Raskin shelled out eleven hundred dollars for the 1946 Oldsmobile 98 model, the first with automatic transmission. Henry Ford died of a cerebral hemorrhage shortly before midnight on Monday, April 7, at the age of 83. Governor Kim Sigler ordered flags on state buildings to fly at half staff until the funeral on April 10.

In 1947 Yeshiva Beth Yehudah had an average enrollment of 600, about two-thirds of whom were in the afternoon school program. Sixty-one children were registered in the two kindergartens. Rabbi Moses Fischer, spiritual leader of Congregation B'nai Moshe since 1923, announced his retirement as he realized most of the younger members were moving further from orthodox tradition. The community mourned the passing of Abraham Rogvoy at 46. Rogvoy, the head of the department of social studies at Pershing High School, had been with the Detroit Public Schools since 1923. For 24 years, Rogvoy taught at the Shaarey Zedek Sunday school and was supervisor from 1943 to 1946.

Back in civilian life, Ed Meer was working in his father's dental supply business. The company consisted of the two Meers and a secretary. In 1947, the

Stores such as these along Livernois near Fenkell celebrated the 75th anniversary of Livernois in 1947.

(Courtesy of Dr. Chuck Taylor)

estimated population of Oak Park was 1,700 people. The area had more oaks than people. At the same time, the Jewish Parents Institute (JPI) began. Mervin Pregulman, former All-American tackle at the University of Michigan in 1943, played with the Green Bay Packers in 1946 and was with the Detroit Lions in 1947. *Gentlemen's Agreement* won several awards including best movie of the year. Gregory Peck starred as a gentile posing as a Jew to expose anti-Semitism in America. Laura G. Hobson, the Jewish woman who wrote the book, earned $75,000 for the screen rights. Hands that slaved under the Nazis hit baseballs for the first time as 250 survivors, new residents of Detroit, enjoyed a picnic sponsored by Tom Borman. The owner of Tom's Quality Markets arranged for transportation and for a refrigerated truck filled with kosher food for two picnic meals for the group.

Abe Pasternak, who survived Auschwitz, Buchenwald, the loss of his parents and two brothers, death marches, and slave labor camps, arrived in Detroit in 1947. After his liberation in 1945, Pasternak returned to Budapest where he had relatives and found Hungarians living in the homes previously owned by Jews. Hungarians claimed more Jews survived the death camps than were sent away and refused to give up any of the homes they occupied. Jews were threatened and five were killed while Abe was there. He decided it was not safe to remain in Europe.

By the time Abe arrived in Detroit, he was 23 and his uncle was president of Congregation B'nai Moshe. With seven dollars in his pocket, he was given a room in his uncle's Chicago Boulevard home and got a job in Grunt's Market on Linwood for twenty-five dollars a week. After getting a job for forty-five dollars a week as a stock clerk at Federal's Department Store, he was able to pay his uncle rent and pay back a twenty-five dollar loan from Hebrew Free Loan.

There were Saturday night Federation-sponsored dances at the Jewish Community Center for survivors, where the latest in American music could also be learned. Bands played the big hit song of 1947, "I'm Looking Over a Four Leaf Clover," and the hits of the previous year: "Dancing in the Dark," "Tenderly," and "They Say That Falling in Love Is Wonderful."

The happy music couldn't shake the memories. Abe's mind often brought him back to Auschwitz. As his parents and their four sons were ordered off the train, his parents were sent to a line on the left and Abe, his two older brothers, and a younger one, were sent to the right.

Thinking as a good brother would, Abe told his younger brother, Solly, to go with his parents. Solly listened and followed his parents. Abe didn't know the line would lead to the gas chambers. Abe never stopped agonizing over his advice to his younger brother.

The Dexter Theatre was owned by Harry Slatkin. His son, Joseph, owned Dexter Chevrolet. *Gentlemen's Agreement* and *The Al Jolson Story* were popular movies in the Jewish community in 1947.

(Courtesy of Manning Brothers Historic Photographic Collection)

In July 1947, the 4,500 refugees of Hitler's hell aboard the ship *Exodus* were not allowed to dock in Palestine. The ship returned to France. The refugees refused to disembark and the ship was towed to Germany, where they were forced off. The stressful voyage gained national attention and sympathy for Jews seeking a homeland in Palestine.

On November 29, the United Nations voted to partition Palestine—which was reduced when Transjordan was created—into Jewish and Arab states. The Jews accepted the plan but the Arabs attacked.

An Arab mob torched Jewish stores outside the old city of Jerusalem, and Arab snipers shot at Jewish children walking to school in Jaffa. As Israel's War of Independence began, Arab soldiers from neighboring countries poured in to help wipe out the Jews. Arabs living on land that was the Biblical Jewish homeland were told by Arab authorities to "temporarily" evacuate their areas until the Jews were driven out.

The British rule of Palestine ended on May 14, 1948, as a result of the vote taken the previous November, and Jews around the world celebrated as the State of Israel was proclaimed.

The *Detroit News* headline read: "Jews Proclaim Nation of 'Israel.'"

The *Detroit Times* headline in large red block print read: "REPUBLIC OF ISRAEL SET UP." A subheadline underneath read: "Arab Nations Declare War."

The first five paragraphs of the *Free Press* editorial entitled, "Israel is Born," read:

After two thousand years Israel is a nation and the Jews again have their own state in the world family of nations.

Few events of our time have had a deeper historical significance. The world over, the drama of the moment finds a warm response in the hearts of Jews and gentiles alike.

The Jewish nation steps into independence with a full-fledged fight for survival on its hands. To what extent it will be aided materially by other powers, and how effective the influence of the United Nations will be in bringing about a peace that will protect the security of Jews and Arabs, time alone can tell.

The amazing development was the startlingly precipitate action with which President Truman, apparently going it alone and without reference to or consultation with his State Department, extended United States recognition to Israel.

That it was an unusual procedure, typical of the impetuosity of the President in matters of foreign policy, goes, without saying. The question, of course, is whether, from the standpoint of United States relations with the world, he was right or wrong.

Two days later, on May 16, an estimated crowd of 22,000 came to the athletic field of Central High School on Linwood on a sunny Sunday to soak up the events surrounding the celebration.

Sky-writing aircraft spelled out "Israel" and out-

(Courtesy of *Jewish News*)

lined the Star of David in white against the blue sky. Hundreds upon hundreds of blue and white flags with the Star of David in the center fluttered gently.

Cantor Hyman Adler, of Congregation B'nai David, blew the Shofar, stirring the emotions and creating a silence. Tears of emotion, pride, and joy fell upon the cheeks of many in the hushed crowd as Emma Lazaroff Schaver, Detroit's famous soprano, sang the Hatikva—the Jewish national anthem.

Children representing Detroit's Jewish schools, as well as adults from every Temple, Synagogue, and Jewish organization were in attendance. Rabbi Isaac Stollman, head of the Council of Orthodox Rabbis, had the honor of reciting the Shehecheyanu (the blessing of thanks to the Almighty "for having caused us to live to see this day"). A loud "Amen" echoed among the thousands assembled.

As many returned home from the afternoon of prayer, song, and speeches, the talented *Detroit News* Foreign Service writer Wallace R. Deull's front page story was a sobering reminder of what was ahead.

After almost 2,000 years of aspiration and striving, the new state was being prematurely born. It was not ready for life. Its contours were not yet complete as they had been hoped for and designed. Its organs were not yet fully functioning. Yet it must spring to arms in the very moment of its birth, for the millions of surrounding Arabs were implacable, and would destroy it if they could.

The new Israel was a cartographer's—and a defending general staff's—nightmare. It was three almost entirely separate territories, rather than one, each touching only one of the others and only at one small point: a narrow coastal strip; a wedge inland in the north at the Sea of Galilee; and a rough, triangular shard of a piece of desert in the south pointing to Akaba.

Top: The cover of the May 21, 1948, edition of the *Jewish News.*

(Courtesy of Jewish News)

Right: An estimated crowd of 22,000 gathered on the athletic field of Central High School on Linwood to celebrate the return of Jews to their Biblical homeland.

(Photo by Shlomo Sperka)

Immediately at hand were the more than 30 million Arabs of seven adjacent states.

There were demographic disabilities within, as well as without, the new state. The Jews were less than three-fifths of the population; the Arabs, more than two-fifths. The figures were: Jews, 538,000; Arabs, 397,000. This was high co-efficient indeed of antipathy and disaffection.

The following day, in Monday's *Free Press*, staff writer Sam Petok opened his article with the following:

A mournful bray of resolution from Detroit's Jewry was sounded Sunday afternoon and hurled across the seas to the bloodstained soil of a newborn state.

The Shofar, the ram's horn blown only at sacred holidays, sent its sonorous notes floating into the cloud-flecked skies.

In a hushed moment, 2,000 years of wanderings through the world, of being pilloried, of turning the cheek and of national ignominy flashed through the minds of the throng.

Israel, the Jewish state, had been proclaimed.

Only four days after Sunday's celebration, Detroit mourned the loss of Fred Butzel, one of America's most admired and distinguished Jewish leaders. A follower of Reform Judaism, Butzel endeared himself to all through his acts of kindness and to the observant community through his long-time Zionist activities.

An estimated crowd of 1,500 persons from all segments of the Jewish and non-Jewish communities attended Butzel's funeral services at Temple Beth El. Detroit's newspapers of May 22, 1948, carried glowing tributes to Butzel. From the editorial page of the *Detroit Times*:

It is rare that a civic leader's death can leave such a real sense of loss in so many places as did the death of Fred M. Butzel.

If any one in the history of Detroit had the right to be called "beloved" in the true sense of the word, it was he. For none in a lifetime of 70 years could do more for so many in a selfless benevolence that knew nothing of race, creed, color or station in life.

Fred Butzel loved his fellow man so well that he gave all who came to him of his time, money and his heart. It mattered not to him that occasionally his trust was betrayed. He expected the vagaries of human nature to mock his efforts now and then but it never made him bitter or less understanding.

His philanthropies were many. His interests were as broad and as deep as his fine mind.

Fred Butzel never gave of himself or his money because he expected anything in return except the personal gratification of relieving humanity in whatever way he could. He headed Jewish charities and participated in the affairs of his people but he was too much of a humanitarian to be confined into even such a mold.

He founded the Boy Scouts in Detroit and the

Looking south from around Davison and Lawton, the large Central High School's athletic field (center left) on Linwood was where the largest celebration ever by Detroit's Jewish groups took place.

(Courtesy of Burton Historical Collection of the Detroit Public Library)

Boy's Republic and the city's playground system. But more than his public benefactions were those of which none knew except the recipients who came to his office and his modest home.

Fred M. Butzel won many high honors during his lifetime. But his memorial is in the hearts of those in high places and low who found in his wisdom and kindness and human understanding, as well as in his boundless charity, the way to a renewed hope and a better form of life.

Part of the *Detroit News* editorial stated:

Professionally, a lawyer must interest himself in the troubles of others, but with Fred M. Butzel a life long preoccupation with people in difficulty was a part of his nature.

The law, in which he made a splendid name, was but an instrument among several to carry out the impulses of a great and generous heart.

He was to a supreme degree outgoing, for his giving was not only of his substance, but of himself, of his time and his good counsel and of his skill at bringing to practical fruition the countless humanitarian undertakings which enlisted his dynamic sympathy.

As with an occasional great soul who is without wife and children, Mr. Butzel made the community his family and his charge, and the marks of his compassion and concern are found in countless places upon it, in its organized agencies of welfare to which he contributed so much in the way of wise and inspiring direction, and also in the lives of people who, one by one, were beneficiaries of his endless devotion.

Fred Butzel was loved, admired, and respected and held numerous offices in Jewish and humanitarian causes.
(Courtesy of Archives of Jewish Welfare Federation)

As Detroit synagogues said daily prayers for the safety of Israel, the events of May 22 cast a pall on the community. Arab armies killed 1,490 Jews, men, women and children, and took control of Jerusalem's Old City, seizing Jewish owned land and possessions. Jewish religious books were burned and fifty-eight synagogues would be destroyed.

Rudy Newman, who claimed he was 17 when he was 16 so he could join the Navy in 1943, was in law school in 1948 when a professor suggested his services were needed in Israel. Newman, an experienced flier, arrived in Israel and helped organize a flight school and shape Israel's Air Force. Detroiter David Fink, 20, also went to Israel to serve and became a gunner-bombardier on one of Israel's three B-29s.

The last burial in Beth Olam Cemetery in Hamtramck took place in 1948. Beth Olam—Yiddish for "House of the People"—opened in 1862 when the one-year-old Congregation Shaarey Zedek purchased a parcel in what then was farmland.

Detroit's first self-serve drugstore, Wrigley Drugs, was opened by Julius Spielberg next to Wrigley's Supermarket and Darby's Restaurant on Seven Mile Road. Milton Marwil, a former public school teacher, founded Marwil's Bookstore on West Warren in 1948. Sam Bishop, a native of Benton Harbor in whose parents' home the town's first Jewish services were held, became athletic director at Detroit's Northwestern High. Sy Wasserman relocated from New York and purchased Henry the Hatter, Detroit's famous hat store on Broadway near Gratiot.

Emma Lazaroff Schaver's experiences in DP camps in Europe were published in a 176-page Yiddish volume, titled: "Mir Zeinen Do [We Are Here]." Mrs. Schaver told about the activities of Detroiter Ann Liepah, who supervised the Hachsharah training camp for pioneers in Palestine, and of Detroiter Sheldon Lutz, who aided resettlement efforts in Munich. Mrs. Schaver, backed by 27 members of the NBC Orchestra and a 16-voice choir, also released an album of songs she recorded while on tour. Approximately a thousand people crowded into the Shaarey Zedek Synagogue to honor Mrs. Schaver after the release of the album.

Moshe Dombey, the well-known personality in the intellectual Yiddish community, passed away at 55. Dombey was a favorite on radio and at personal appearances, where he performed under the name of "Mr. Chizik" and read selections of stories in Yiddish. Dombey, who made his living selling insurance, was a connoisseur of books and owned a large library of Yiddish volumes. Mrs. Fanny Rodin, who founded and helped organize several Jewish institutions, died at the age of 87. She was one of the last links to the Division Street Talmud Torah, the Old Folks Home, the Hebrew Orphans Home, and the Hebrew Baby Day Nursery, and she was active in Congregation Shaarey Zion and Ladies of the Yeshiva Beth Yehudah.

The number of contributors to the Allied Jewish Campaign of the Jewish Welfare Federation passed 30,000 for the first time in 1948. The 30,734 contributors donated $5,756,133, $1,787,561 more than in 1947. The United Hebrew Schools began its Midrasha College of Jewish Studies for advanced studies, and Albert Elazar became associate superintendent of UHS. Bill Davidson, who earned a business degree at the University of Michigan in 1947, was attending law school at Wayne University and working evenings as assistant manager of the family owned Avalon Theatre on Linwood.

Rabbi Leo Goldman, former chief rabbi of Oslo, Norway, assumed the spiritual leadership of Congregations Shaarey Zion at Linwood and Cortland, and of Adas Yeshurin at Linwood and Tyler. Schooled in the famous rabbinical seminaries in Europe, Rabbi Goldman also graduated from the Wilno University law school. The community honored Rabbi Joseph Eisenman at a dinner at Lachar's as the rabbi and his wife were leaving the city to take up residence in Israel. Rabbi Eisenman previously served Congregation Beth Tefilo Emanuel on Taylor at Woodrow Wilson, until his retirement in 1937 at age 65. Dan Frohman directed eleven Detroit Cantors at a concert in B'nai David for the benefit of refugee European cantors.

Above: Rabbi Joseph Eisenman, who came to Detroit in 1910, left in 1948 to take up residence in Israel.
(Courtesy of Dr. & Mrs. Arnold Eisenman)

Left: Bill Davidson was attending law school at Wayne University and working evenings at the Avalon Theatre on Linwood.
(Courtesy of Manning Brothers Historic Photographic Collection)

Abe Nusbaum, of the New York Linoleum Company, who was head of the Yeshiva Beth Yehudah's financial and budget committee and a member of the administration board, assumed the extra duties of membership chairman of the school.

With the mounting duties the position of president of the yeshiva presented, it became necessary to hire an assistant for Rabbi Wohlgelernter. Hillel Abrams, a young man who had returned after three years of military service, was hired as secretary of the yeshiva. The title did little justice to Abrams, who at the time, was vice president of Young Israel, president of the Young Israel Young Adult Group, and treasurer of the Midwest Council of Young Israel. Abrams was also division chairman of the Young Israel division in the Allied Jewish Campaign's Junior Service Group, forerunner of today's Young Adult Division.

Some of Abrams' duties in his yeshiva role included directing the work of five people in the office, handling business correspondence, overseeing the efforts of volunteers, and accompanying Rabbi Wohlgelernter on important missions.

While history was being made at Michigan and Trumbull in June 1948, as the Detroit Tigers played their first ever home night game, history was also being made that June night at Dexter and Cortland as the Yeshiva Day School produced its first high school graduates.

The Parent-Teacher Association also was formed in 1948, and the school provided six elementary grades for girls.

Lt. Raymond Zussman, who was awarded the Congressional Medal of Honor posthumously, fell in battle in September 1944. His body was returned for reburial and services were held from the Shaarey Zedek Synagogue with numerous civic and military dignitaries in attendance.

Jews and non-Jews mourned the passing of Dr. Leo M. Franklin on August 8, 1948. Franklin, who was 78, become spiritual leader of Temple Beth El in 1899. In his almost half a century in Detroit, the Jewish population rose almost tenfold—from 10,000 in 1899. Detroit's papers devoted editorials to Franklin.

The *Free Press*:

The long list of civic bodies in which he labored reveals the serious side of this man of many parts. A rare sense of humor won him honorary membership in the international Mark Twain Society.

A cultured gentleman, a fine citizen in every respect, Dr. Leo M. Franklin served his fellow man as few Detroiters have since Father Gabriel Richard. His mission fulfilled, he has left us, rich in years and in esteem.

The *Detroit News*:

Dr. Leo M. Franklin was that occasional figure of distinction, the spiritual leader who becomes a civic possession. He was interested in people as people, as a family. The whole community was the beneficiary of his good works, which ran far beyond the secular. Few were the sides of the common life which failed to enlist his active interest and wise and stimulating counsel.

It was the catholicity of this interest which moved the University of Detroit in 1923 to award a rabbi an honorary doctorate of law.

In his years in Detroit the flock at Temple Beth

More than three years after he was killed in battle without realizing his dream of seeing his newborn daughter and playing for the Detroit Tigers, Frank Faudem was buried in the Chesed Shel Emes Cemetery in Mt. Clemens.

(Photo by author)

El outgrew two synagogues and became the largest and influential Reform Jewish congregation in the country. In the role of leader there, he stood for democracy in the church, for a vigorous program of religious education which did not overlook the adult, and for an intimate pastoral relationship built up in countless hours of visiting the sick, the lonely and bereaved.

In September the sports sections of Detroit's newspapers carried a small item regarding the return of the body of Frank Faudem for burial. The former Tiger farmhand was a 24-year-old outfielder when he entered military service in 1942. He was killed on Leyte in early 1945. Had he lived to realize his dream of playing for the Tigers, Faudem would have been the only Detroit-born Jewish ballplayer to ever play for the Tigers.

Around the time Faudem was laid to rest with military honors, the Tigers brought up 21-year-old catcher Myron Joe Ginsberg from the minor leagues. Ginsberg was born in New York and moved with his family to Detroit. Unlike Faudem, whose family and wife's family attended Congregation B'nai Moshe, Ginsberg was not raised in a Jewish neighborhood, never had a Bar Mitzvah, and married out of the faith. Ginsberg's father operated the Triangle Cafe on Michigan Avenue, a few blocks from the ballpark.

The Tigers didn't have a Jewish player in 1947 as Hank Greenberg played the final season of his career with the Pittsburgh Pirates. In 1948 Greenberg took an executive position with the Cleveland Indians.

Congregation Beth Shmuel sold the house on Blaine east of Twelfth Street, which it had used for services since 1932, to Congregation Dovid Ben Nuchim. The first floor of the home was used as the synagogue, while Rabbi Joseph Rabinowitz and his family lived upstairs. The formal dedication of Beth Shmuel's new synagogue on Dexter and Buena Vista was held on Sunday, September 19. A procession of marchers and automobiles marked the transferring of the Sifrei Torah from the old location at 1736 Blaine. The new building's auditorium had a seating capacity of 700, while the social hall held 400. There were two modern kitchens to handle functions in accordance with Jewish law, and a library for study.

Rabbi Moses Lehrman, who served a congregation in Buffalo, New York, and was a descendant of ten generations of rabbis, assumed the pulpit of Congregation B'nai Moshe in September. Under Rabbi Lehrman's leadership, the synagogue became affiliated with the United Synagogue of America, the Conservative movement. Polish-born Shalom Ralph, who lived in Palestine and Philadelphia before coming to Detroit, became sexton of Congregation B'nai Moshe in 1948. Cantor Samuel Glantz, assisted by his son, Leo, conducted High Holiday services for B'nai Moshe.

Rabbi Pinchas Katz became spiritual leader of Congregation Beth Aaron in September. Rabbi Katz, who studied at the Hebrew Theological College in Chicago and received his rabbinical ordination in Winnipeg, also served as cantor for Beth Aaron's High Holiday services. The Downtown Synagogue held High Holiday services under the direction of Rabbi Herman Rosenwasser at the G.A.R. Recreation Building Auditorium on Grand River and Cass.

In October 1948, WXYZ, Channel 7, became Detroit's second television station. The cameras and crew occupied the top two floors of the Maccabees

A graduate of Cooley High School, Myron Joe Ginsberg became a Detroit Tiger in 1948.

(Courtesy of Ernie Harwell Collection, Burton Historical Collection of the Detroit Public Library)

Building. Detroit's third station, WJBK, Channel 2, debuted later in the month. At the time there were an estimated 9,000 television sets in the Detroit area.

Several new programs went on the air, including the Milton Berle Show, Perry Como's Chesterfield Supper Club, Arthur Godfrey's Talent Scouts, and Ed Sullivan's Toast of the Town. Singers on the programs often performed the latest hits of 1948: "Baby, It's Cold Outside," and "Buttons and Bows."

While more Jewish Detroiters were buying television sets, many wealthy Iraqi Jews were arrested. Some were hanged, and Zionism was declared a crime. The events would lead to the confiscation of property and bank accounts by Iraq, and to 126,000 Jews going to Israel

Besides his duties as president of the Yeshiva Beth Yehudah and his involvement in many facets of the community, Rabbi Max J. Wohlgelernter assumed the pulpit of Congregation Mogen Abraham in 1949. B'nai David became the first congregation in the country to use the newly published Hebrew-English Nusach Sfard daily prayer book. For Torah readings, a uniform Hebrew-English chumash was purchased by an officer as a gift to the congregation, for use by each worshipper. Rabbi Israel Halpern became assistant rabbi under Rabbi Joseph Thumin at the Beth Abraham Synagogue on Linwood.

The Northwest Hebrew Congregation and Center—which would become Congregation Adas Shalom—celebrated the completion of its small chapel section and schoolrooms on Curtis and Santa Rosa. The religious school, which began in 1945 at the Bagley School a few blocks west on Curtis, grew to 800 students in 1949 and began sessions in its own building, and it affiliated with the United Hebrew Schools. 1949 was the last year UHS used the Philadelphia-Byron location as a branch, as the building was sold to the Boys Club of Detroit.

Rabbi Samuel Stollman, son of Rabbi Isaac Stollman of Detroit's Mishkan Israel Synagogue on Blaine, became spiritual leader of Congregation Shaar Hashomayim in Windsor. A graduate of the Rabbi Isaac Elchonen Theological Seminary of New York and Columbia University, Rabbi Stollman previously served a congregation in Scranton, Pennsylvania. Walter Godfrey starred on the Cass Technical High School basketball team and in the city championship game in 1949. As he passed a newsstand on Linwood near Blaine on his way to Sabbath services at Congregation Mishkan Israel, he stopped and looked at the headline. "His name was in the front page story," his brother, Rabbi Jerry Godfrey, recalled. "He didn't say anything. He just continued on walking to services."

Louis Milgrom, who joined Mercury Paint Company after the war, revolutionized house painting in 1949 by developing a "custom flat" wall paint, which was washable and gave an excellent appearance the day after application. Morton Feigenson, general manager of the Faygo Beverage Company, was elected treasurer of the largest independent soft drink organization in the country, the National Carbonated Beverage Institute. Alfred Epstein, president of Detroit's Pfeiffer Brewing Company, announced that Pfeiffer was the top beer seller in Detroit. Avern Cohn graduated from the University of Michigan Law School and practiced law with his father, Irwin I. Cohn.

The first neighborhood branch of the Jewish Com-

Rabbi Joshua Sperka, of Congregation B'nai David, greets Rabbi Isaac Herzog, chief rabbi of Israel, in 1949.

(Courtesy of Shlomo Sperka)

munity Center was dedicated at Davison and Holmur in January. Included in the large, two-story building was a memorial room in honor of Jews who lost their lives while in military service. Adjacent to the building was a playground measuring 210 feet by 170 feet. B'nai B'rith took over the Abington Theatre—formerly Littman's People's Theatre—on Twelfth Street and Seward for six days of showing of the movie, *The Illegals*, based on the Haganah's exploits in bringing Jewish refugees to Israel. *Sword in the Desert*, the first full-length feature film on Israel to come out of Hollywood, starred Dana Andrews and Jeff Chandler as members of the Jewish underground fighting for the establishment of a Jewish state. The movie played downtown at the Adams and in several neighborhood theaters.

Danny Raskin found many places of nourishment while strolling along Dexter, as there were eight delicatessens within ten blocks: Hy Horenstein's off Boston, Bill Boesky's at Collingwood, Plate's at Burlingame, Lefkofsky's at Tuxedo, Wilson's at Richton, Liberman's between Cortland and Sturtevant, Leinoff's near Waverly, and Ben & George's between Tyler and Buena Vista. Hockey fan Dave Sandler, who lived on Fullerton near Dexter, would walk south along Dexter with his brother all the way to Olympia Stadium in good weather. In bad weather, they took the Dexter bus, exited at Grand Boulevard, and took a short walk to the home of the Red Wings.

Seymour Simons, brother of distinguished jurist Charles C. Simons and son of David W. Simons, died at the age of 53. Like his father, Seymour was active in Jewish causes and in Congregation Shaarey Zedek. Best known for his musical talents, he co-wrote "Breezin' Along with the Breeze," in 1926, and "All of Me," in 1931. Blanche Hart, founder of Fresh Air Camp, died in 1949. Around the same time, Executive Director Irwin Shaw was eyeing a tamarack tree farm in Ortonville as a camp site. Rabbi Stephen Wise, a founder of the American Jewish Congress, the National Association for the Advancement of Colored People, and the American Civil Liberties Union, died at the age of 75. Henry Butzel, brother of the late Fred Butzel, was reelected to the Michigan Supreme Court.

Israel's first Knesset (parliament) was elected. David Ben-Gurion became prime minister, and Chaim Weizmann president. On May 11, 1949, Israel became a member of the United Nations. As Jews from Arab countries ran for their lives, leaving behind property and bank accounts, the 1949 population of Israel was estimated at a million, around 350,000 higher than the year before.

Every seat in the State Fair Coliseum was filled as the community marked the first anniversary of Israel's independence. Thousands stood and the crowd estimated at 15,000 applauded as Emma Lazaroff Schaver led the singing of the Star Spangled Banner and Hatikva. Detroit cantors and musicians performed, and addresses were delivered by Zionist and civic leaders, along with Rabbi Morris Adler of Congregation Shaarey Zedek.

Rabbi Isaac Herzog, chief rabbi of the state of Israel, visited Detroit in 1949. The Mizrachi Organization of Detroit held a special tribute for Rabbi Herzog at Congregation Beth Aaron on the occasion of his 60th birthday. Congregation Agudath Israel, 11331 Linwood, invited all former European refugees now living in Detroit to an Oneg Shabbat. The Saturday night program included dealing with problems facing new arrivals and seeking relatives, in addition to music and refreshments.

World War II veteran Jules Doneson risked his life by undertaking a secret mission in Palestine in 1946, and he returned in 1948 to help fight for Israel and command a company. In 1949, the Zionist Organization of America offered him a job in either Detroit or Los Angeles. After choosing Detroit, Doneson rented a room on Calvert and Linwood and went to Congregation Shaarey Zedek, where he met and fell in love with Ann Saulson. While working for the ZOA and pursuing Saulson, Doneson pursued the dream of opening his own travel agency Second Lieutenant Daniel Ginsburg, who was killed at Iwo Jima on March 8, 1945, was reburied in 1949. A community-wide Zionist tribute was paid to Ginsburg at the Lewis Brothers Funeral Home Chapel on Dexter and Puritan, as the fallen soldier was a leader in Habonim, the labor Zionist youth movement, before entering the military.

Known for his brilliance and scholarship, Rabbi Leib Bakst, who studied in the famous rabbinical schools of Europe and in Shanghai, accepted the post of Yeshiva Beth Yehudah's Dean of the Beth Hamedrash for advanced Rabbinical Studies. At the time, the Yeshiva's day school had 175 pupils. Rabbi Samuel Prero was hired as director of Young Israel activities. Rabbi Prero, who was engaged in fund-raising activities for the Yeshiva Beth Yehudah, oversaw the completion of the new Young Israel building on Dexter and Fullerton in addition to assuming the pulpit. When the building, budgeted at $120,000, was completed in 1949, Morris Karbal was given the honor of affixing the Mezuza on the doorpost at the dedication, and Henry Keywell cut the ribbon placed across the front doors.

Boris M. Joffe became executive director of the Jewish Community Council. Joffe was assistant to the executive vice chairman and assistant secretary for overseas operations of the Joint Distribution Committee. According to a population survey by the American Jewish Committee, the United States had 4,500,000 Jews in 1949 and Detroit's Jewish population was estimated at 90,000. It was estimated that 49 percent of Detroit's Jewish population resided in the Dexter area, and 27 percent in the northwest section.

The Downtown Synagogue, sponsored by the Isaac Agree Memorial Society, celebrated its tenth anniversary. The synagogue, located at 1205 Griswold, was under the direction of Rabbi Herman Rosenwasser. WJBK-TV, Channel 2, televised the High Holy Day service on September 29, from Temple Beth El. Temple Israel broke ground for its impressive first building, at 17400 Manderson in the Palmer Park area, on November 27, 1949.

As a 1949 Ford Tudor Sedan stickered for $1,456.27, the minimum wage was raised from forty cents to seventy-five cents per hour. Bill Davidson earned a law degree from Wayne University. Detroit's last streetcar was removed from service. The residents of Oak Park defeated a proposal for a race track. The weekly Sunday morning Jewish Chronicle Hour began its radio run on WKMH, 1310 on the dial.

Rabbi Leib Bakst taught advanced Hebrew studies at the Yeshiva Beth Yehuda. From left: Uri Mandelbaum, Freddy Rubin, Walter Rubenstein, Shlomo Sperka, and Rabbi Bakst.

(Courtesy of Yeshiva Beth Yehudah)

The Young Israel Youth Center on Dexter at Fullerton.

The Gelberman family arrived in Detroit in 1949. It was quite a journey.

David Gelberman, like many Europeans of the time, had seven gold-capped teeth. A guard in a Hungarian work camp noticed the teeth. Gelberman was held down while a guard with a pair of pliers extracted the seven teeth.

During heavy bombing by the allies, Gelberman ran for it. A thin, frail man with red hair, Gelberman could pass for a non-Jew. With bombs exploding all around and blood oozing from his ears, Gelberman ran and fainted. When he regained consciousness, he noticed his shirt was torn and the yellow star torn away. A German soldier was screaming at him.

The German thought he was a farmer running away from the bombing, placed him in a half-track, drove Gelberman into town, and dropped him off near a building that was used as an air raid shelter. Gelberman managed to hide until he was reunited with his wife. Together again they managed to outwit the Nazis and secure papers from Raoul Wallenberg's group, claiming the family were all citizens of Sweden.

Now Mr. and Mrs. Gelberman and their two children had to evade the Nazis while they made their way to a neutral site. David Gelberman tried a unique approach. He decided to wait until a honest looking German officer would pass by. When he thought he found one, he explained the situation. Gelberman offered the German officer the clothing factory he owned in exchange for transportation to the neutral site.

The transfer was made. However, shortly after arrival, Gelberman went looking for food and was recognized by the very guard he had escaped from during the bombing. Gelberman was arrested and sentenced to hang, but his wife was able to bribe officials, and with a hood over his head while on the gallows, her husband was released.

However, Gelberman was put on a cattle car with other Jews, tools, and equipment heading to Auschwitz. The men dug a hole in the bottom of the speeding cattle car. They dropped down one at a time. Out of 75 men, fourteen survived the fall. Gelberman, who weighed under 80 pounds at the time, survived and hid in the forest for the duration of the war.

United again, the family escaped to Germany and ended up in a DP camp for over two years, awaiting visas to come to the United States under the sponsorship of David Gelberman's brother. They arrived in New York in the last week of 1948 and boarded a train for Lakeland, Florida, where Gelberman's brother was a rabbi of a large congregation.

Rabbi Gelberman found jobs for his brother and

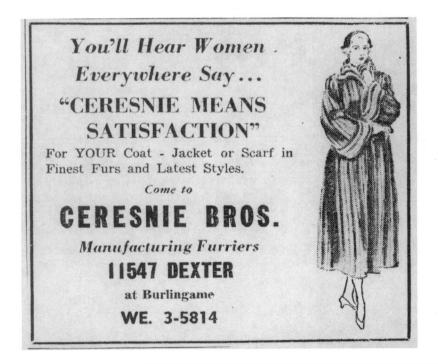

Ads appearing in the *Jewish News* in 1949.

sister-in-law as cooks in a restaurant. Their two children, George and Erica were dropped off by a movie theater with the proper food and spent the days watching cowboy films. The kids learned to speak English and their teachers were Gene Autry and Roy Rogers.

The family went to Sabbath services and were shocked by what they found. The men and women were seated together, and people drove cars to the synagogue. People were praying in English, and services were much shorter than they were used to. Rabbi Gelberman explained that this was America and that was how many enlightened Americans worshipped. David Gelberman packed up and the family went back to New York. He loved America's freedom, but he didn't want to compromise his religious beliefs. HIAS helped the family in New York, and Mrs. Gelberman placed an ad in a Yiddish newspaper looking for a lost cousin. The ad was answered by two old friends from Hungary who were then living in Detroit. They invited the Gelbermans to came to Detroit for a visit.

The Gelbermans came in the summer of '49.

And the Gelbermans stayed.

As the 1940s came to a close, the songs heard most often on radio were from the Broadway musical *South Pacific*: "Bali Hai" and "Some Enchanted Evening" pushed aside previous hits, "Ghost Riders in the Sky," and "Mule Train."

History was made on December 30 when Mary V. Beck was sworn in as the first woman elected to the Detroit City Council. There was change at the top, too, as Albert E. Cobo, city treasurer for seven terms, was elected mayor.

According to the United States Bureau of Census, Detroit's 1950 population was 1,849,568, a gain of 246,116 over the previous decade. In those 10 years, the black population doubled and topped 16 percent of the city's 1950 total.

Detroit remembered former mayor John C. Lodge, who died in February at age 87, by naming the newly opened stretch of its north-south expressway in his honor. As Avern Cohn chaired the Junior Division of the Jewish Welfare Federation of Metropolitan Detroit, A. Alfred Taubman, 25, secured a $5,000 bank loan and began his real estate and shopping mall business. The Detroit Business Men's Group City of Hope brought Mickey Katz and his son, Joel Grey, to Detroit to perform their popular English-Yiddish revue, "Borscht Capades." The four days of performances at the Music Hall proved to be a good fund-raising tool.

April 30 was officially proclaimed as Israel Day throughout Michigan by Governor G. Mennen Williams. The State Fair Coliseum was adorned with blue and white banners and American flags. An estimated crowd of 12,000 poured into the building as heavy rain fell outside. With Jules Doneson shouting orders in Hebrew, American veterans of Israel's War of Inde-

Speaking more comfortably in Hungarian than English, George Gelberman quickly fit in with other youngsters on the Yeshiva Beth Yehudah playground.

(Courtesy of Yeshiva Beth Yehudah)

pendence marched to the center of the platform and were presented a flag by the Jewish Community Council. Governor Williams paid tribute to the 500,000 American Jewish soldiers of World War II and the 50,000 who became casualties. Following greetings by Mayor Albert E. Cobo, Rabbi Jacob Segal of the Northwest Hebrew Congregation gave the main address.

In May the United Auto Workers and General Motors announced a five-year contract calling for guaranteed annual wage increases, cost of living adjustments, and a $100 monthly pension at age 65 after 25 years of service. Auto workers were earning $73.25 weekly or $3,809 yearly, while the average major league ballplayer earned $13,228.

Dave and Fayga Dombey rented a flat on Monterey and Linwood for $55 a month. Dombey began teaching math in the Detroit Public School System for around $3,000 a year. To augment his income, Dombey embarked on a second career as a photographer. "The field of wedding photography was wide open in 1950," Dombey recalled. "The big problem, in those days, was in buying flash bulbs and film, which were in short supply after the war. I was forced to take trips into Canada to buy those items. I stopped at every small town and bought up all their stock. There was no duty to pay since the items were all manufactured in the United States."

Mayor Hazen Pingree had suggested back in 1890 that Detroit should build a civic center on the downtown waterfront. It took until June 11, 1950, for the city to open the first structure—the Veterans Memorial Building. It marked the beginning of the end of the numerous Jewish-owned wholesale clothing store establishments housed in old buildings close to the waterfront on land earmarked for the civic center.

Louis Berry headed the pre-campaign cabinet of the Allied Jewish Campaign. Berry was the chairman of last year's campaign and national campaign chairman of the United Jewish Appeal. Fresh Air Camp purchased its Ortonville camp site. Tamarack was named after the Tamarack Hills Farm occupying part of the area. A downtown office building at 163 Madison was purchased to serve as a headquarters for the Jewish Welfare Federation and its member agencies. The handsome building, located close to Grand Circus Park and across the street from the Detroit Athletic Club, was named after the late Fred M. Butzel.

After spending 1949 in the minor leagues, catcher Joe Ginsberg was brought up by the Detroit Tigers. The Tigers also had a Jewish pitcher in the 1950 season, New Yorker Saul Rogovin. Rabbi Israel Rockove,

Construction of the new freeway, named after former mayor John C. Lodge, would help ease the heavy traffic going north on Woodward near Grand Boulevard.

(Courtesy of Michigan Views)

who came to Detroit as a fund-raiser for the Yeshiva Beth Yehudah, assumed the position of executive director of the Hebrew Benevolent Society. The Committee on Taharas Hamishpochah (family purity) of the Detroit Council of Orthodox Rabbis were raising money to build a new Mikveh (ritualarium) on Davison and Holmur.

Temple Beth El celebrated its 100th anniversary in 1950 with a large banquet at the Book-Cadillac Hotel. United States Federal Judge Charles Simons was the toastmaster. In 1950, Beth El's religious school had 900 children attending classes. A hundred years earlier, Beth El's school met daily with German, Hebrew, and English instruction. As Detroit's public schools developed, the all-day school was discontinued in 1869 and the Sunday school was founded the following year. In 1950, Flint's Temple Beth El began construction of its building on a five and a half-acre plot on the city's outskirts.

Rabbi Benjamin Gorrelick, who was director of education of Congregation Shaarey Zedek, became spiritual leader of Congregation Beth Aaron. The synagogue, with a membership of 165 families, became affiliated with the conservative movement. Rabbi Max J. Wohgelernter, who organized the Sisterhood of Congregation Mogen Abraham in late 1949, organized the synagogue's Men's Club and Junior Congregation conducted by Rabbi David Zwick in 1950.

Rabbi Ernest Greenfield, who left the First Hebrew Congregation of Delray in 1944 to assume a pulpit in Los Angeles, returned to Detroit as spiritual leader of Congregation Beth Tefilo Emanuel (Taylor Shule) in 1950.

The Jewish Center on Davison officially opened early in the year, and Temple Israel finished its auditorium shortly before the Jewish New Year. Construction on new synagogues for Ahavas Achim on Schaefer north of Seven Mile, Beth Moses on Linwood and Oakman, and B'nai Israel on Linwood and Leslie was under way. Northwest Hebrew Congregation began construction on its main chapel.

Young Israel held its first services in the northwest section at the Bagley School on Curtis on Saturday morning, October 28. Rabbi Samuel Prero left his home on Elmhurst in the Dexter section for the Sabbath to stay in the northwest to speak at services.

Eddie Cantor, who was celebrating his third decade in radio in 1950 and beginning a Sunday night television comedy hour for NBC, performed a two-hour, one-man show for a capacity crowd of 5,000 at Masonic Auditorium. The evening of comedy and song pushed the B'nai B'rith women's fund raising and membership campaign over its $100,000 goal. Cantor received a standing ovation when he performed the hit tune of 1950, "If I Knew You Were Comin' I'd Bake a Cake."

The waterfront housed many Jewish-owned wholesale clothing establishments.

(Courtesy of Burton Historical Collection of the Detroit Public Library)

Rabbi Leon Fram, one of the most ardent supporters of Zionism in Detroit even when it wasn't popular among the Reform Jewish community, challenged Orthodox leaders to abolish Tisha b'Ab—the ninth day of the Hebrew month of Ab, a Jewish fast day commemorating the destruction of the Temple.

After all, the spiritual leader of Temple Israel reasoned, the Jews are back in their Biblical homeland. The debate and letters continued in the latter part of 1950 as both sides posted letters on congregational bulletin boards.

Detroiter Abraham Levin, a student in the Rabbinical College of Telshe Yeshiva in Cleveland, answered Rabbi Fram in a letter published by the *Jewish Chronicle*.

**Tisha b'Ab Not Outmoded,
Says Theology Student**
To the Editor:

In an editorial in your July 27 edition, Rabbi Leon Fram states:

"Once again (on Tisha b'Ab) Jewish people pray for the redemption of Judea, yet Judea has already been restored... Here is a challenge to Jewish Orthodoxy. Is it capable of adjusting itself to unmistakable facts?... Within a relatively short time there will be absolutely no basis left for the lamentations that are recited on Tisha b'Ab. Every verse, every phase of the Book of Lamentations and of the Kinnot will be contradicted by the facts."

It is difficult to believe that these words could have been written by one who knows and comprehends the reasons for the original establishment of Tisha b'Ab or by one who ever truly has lamented and mourned for that for which Tisha b'Ab stands.

It is not a coincidence that those who never fasted or wept are those who now voice their opinions for the abandonment of this age-old day of mourning, while those who have always grieved realize that not yet has the time come for the end of the lamentations.

Tisha b'Ab was not established only because of the destruction of the Jewish state, indeed, that was a secondary reason; it was established because of the destruction of the Beth Hamikdash, the center of Jewish religious life.

Our rabbis tell us, "The Jewish people were punished doubly and in the future shall be consoled doubly." The explanation of this saying is that the Jews were punished physically as humans and spiritually as Jews.

As humans, their homeland was destroyed; they were dispersed over the face of the earth; every generation experienced a Diaspora; they faced oppression wherever they were driven.

But they suffered more so as Jews. They lost their Beth Hamikdash; God's divine presence no longer rested among them; in many countries they were not allowed to observe their Judaism; they forgot and forsook many of the laws of the Torah; they lost the true beauty of their religion.

The Jewish nation has always found consolation in that we shall also be redeemed doubly.

We have witnessed our redemption as humans with the restoration of part of Eretz Israel as the

The Jewish Welfare Federation bought an office building at 163 Madison and named it after Fred M. Butzel.

(Photo by author)

homeland of the Jews, the beginning of our spiritual redemption is yet to come.

Jerusalem is still void and desolate if is not filled with the holiness of G-d. Our Holy Land is not yet redeemed if the spirit of Torah does not pervade throughout it and engulf it completely.

It is not time for the abandonment of Tisha b'Ab at a period when human society is not yet free from iniquitous corruption and oppression.

It is not time for the abandonment of Tisha b'Ab at a period when the Jews are yet forsaken by their G-d. Only with the coming of the Messiah will the prophetic aspiration of "Be consoled, be consoled my people" be fulfilled.

Only when shall we attain the true beauty of our Jewish Torah-state, of Jewish Torah-living, When our leaders become those who are examples of Torah-true Judaism; when our state becomes a total monarchy, with the Torah its constitution and G-d its monarch; when the Lord once again returns to Jerusalem and all the inhabitants of the globe shall perceive and know him; then, and only then shall world Jewry transform Tisha b'Ab into a day of joy and festivity.

In conclusion, I would like to note that Tisha b'Ab while being a day of mourning has in a certain sense also remained a holiday among Jews. Jewish law prescribes rites for Tisha b'Ab which are practiced only on holidays.

Every one of the Kinnot ends with a note of condolence, of hope, of triumph. Tisha b'Ab has always served as a reminder to the Jew of his glorious past and of the more glorious future which awaits him. He always remembered the Rabbinical adage, *"All who mourn for Jerusalem shall in the future share in her comfort."*

May the omnipotent Almighty once again shine the light of his countenance toward world Jewry and may we all live to see the time when Israel shall become a sound state politically, economically, and spiritually, when "From out of Zion shall come forth the Torah and the word of G-d from Jerusalem."
Abraham Levin
Student, Rabbinical College of Telshe
Cleveland, Ohio

The 96-piece Israel Philharmonic Orchestra performed before a sold-out audience of 5,000 at the Masonic Auditorium on a cold Sunday afternoon in February 1951. Despite angering the 13-member Arab League and its Boycott Office, which blacklisted firms doing business with Israel, Henry Ford II donated gifts to universities in Israel. Ford also gave generously to the United Jewish Appeal and extended liberal credit terms to Israel in its purchases of Ford products.

For the third consecutive year, the State Fair Coliseum was the site of the festive Israel Day celebration. Golda Myerson, Israel's minister of labor and its future prime minister, was the main speaker and urged the 9,500 in attendance to buy interest-bearing Israel bonds in addition to donating to the United Jewish Appeal.

Eight days later, on Monday, May 21, 1951, more than 2,000 people gathered around the Woodward

Governor G. Mennen Williams applauds as the prime minister of Israel steps to the podium. Henry Ford II, who donated Ford automobiles to Israeli leaders, provided eight limousines for Ben Gurion's motorcade.

(Courtesy of Leonard N. Simons Jewish Community Archives)

Avenue side of the City Hall to see and hear David Ben-Gurion, the Prime Minister of Israel. Ben-Gurion paid tribute to the city of Detroit and its 250th anniversary by stating that Israel was eager to learn from Detroit's know-how and achieve a standard of living equal to the United States.

"But," Ben-Gurion pointed out, "we are not behind you in devotion to liberty and democracy." Ben-Gurion also reminded the crowd that Israel was not born three years earlier, but rather, Israel was reborn.

Ben-Gurion had come to Detroit for the first time in 1916 to recruit volunteers for the newly-formed Jewish Legion, serving under General Allenby in Palestine to restore the country to the Jews as a national home.

Norman Cottler enlisted the following year and served in the same unit with Ben Gurion, sharing the same tent. Cottler, who had staked out the corner of Dexter and Davison for an open-air fruit stand in 1930 and nine years later moved across the street into his first store at 13301 Dexter, opened a branch of Dexter Davison at 18207 Wyoming (at Curtis) in 1951. The corner also featured Daring Drugs, Kaplan Brothers (butchers), and Mertz Bakery.

Jews lost a good friend as Michigan Senator Arthur H. Vandenberg died. For over 20 years, Vandenberg was in the forefront of speaking out on behalf of Jewish rights in Palestine. Vandenberg was the first senator to endorse President Harry S. Truman's recognition of Israel. Former Fresh Air camper Irwin Shaw became its executive director in 1936. In 1951, Shaw assumed a dual role and also became executive director of the Jewish Community Center. Shaw, who had a degree in education from Wayne University, founded the Book Fair in 1951 to increase Jewish content at the JCC.

In the two-day dedication ceremony of its new Temple, Temple Israel's sisterhood presented for hanging in the building an oil portrait of spiritual leader Rabbi Leon Fram in honor of his 25 years of ministry. Congregation Beth Moses hired Rabbi Isidor Schneebalg as its spiritual leader and dedicated its new synagogue on Linwood and Oakman. Congregation Ahavas Achim, at Schaefer north of Seven Mile Road, began using the Vernor Public School at Pembroke and Lesure for its Sunday school sessions. Congrega-

Left: Norman Cottler engages customers in conversation as he checks the cash register at his Dexter Davison Market.

Above: Cottler opened his second Dexter Davison Market in 1951 on Wyoming at Curtis.

(Courtesy of Sylvia Cohen)

tion B'nai Moshe added a school building to its synagogue on Dexter and Lawrence. The United Hebrew Schools used the new addition for daily classes, except on Sundays when the B'nai Moshe Sunday School used the facilities. The UHS also opened a new branch on Schaefer near Seven Mile Road. The Sholem Aleichem Folk-Institute (Jewish Peoples Schools) built its northwest building at 18495 Wyoming at Margareta, two blocks south of Seven Mile. Branch Two of the United Jewish Folk Schools moved from the Schulze Public School into the new facilities.

The *Jewish News* moved a few blocks north into the David Stott Building on Griswold and State, a half block from the last stop of the Dexter and Linwood bus lines. Danny Raskin, who had been on the *Jewish News* writing staff since its inception, loved the area.

"Lunchtime was always a look-forward-to event," Raskin recalled. "At Shep's Restaurant on Griswold, across from Kosins Clothes, waitress Shirley Kaufman always knew to bring me a lot of Jewish rye bread. It was more than enough slices to dunk into the delicious gravy from Harry Shepherd and Sol Pitt's wonderful beef brisket and stew. Across the street from there, at Kosins Clothes, if a customer asked Ben Kosins what size a particular garment was, he'd say, 'What size do you want it to be?'"

After 25 years and two months, the last issue of the *Detroit Jewish Chronicle* was published on July 13, 1951. In a front page "Goodby," publisher Seymour Tilchin explained, "The reasons for the sale of the *Chronicle* are purely of a personal nature, since I have decided to leave Detroit and settle in Florida. Obvi-

The formal dedication of the Beth Moses synagogue on Linwood and Oakman took place in 1951.

(Courtesy of Jewish News)

Temple Israel dedicated its new building in 1951.

(Photo by author)

ously, absentee ownership would have placed the paper in an awkward position and put it at a disadvantage. Therefore, sentiments had to give way to practical considerations."

Tilchin and *Jewish News* publisher Philip Slomovitz issued a joint statement under the headline, "DETROIT TO HAVE UNIFIED JEWISH PAPER JULY 20."

"In the best interests of our community, the *Detroit Jewish Chronicle* will be merged with the *Detroit Jewish News* beginning with next week.

"The *Jewish Chronicle* will suspend publication with its issue of July 13.

"The *Jewish News*, having purchased the *Jewish Chronicle*, assumes all right to its name, to its subscription and advertising lists and all its rights in the Jewish publication field. Unexpired paid subscriptions to the *Jewish Chronicle* will be fulfilled by the *Jewish News*."

Through the year, Detroit celebrated its 250th birthday with events, conventions, and parades. Decorative bunting adorned buildings, City Hall, and Briggs Stadium, site of the major league All-Star Game.

President Harry S. Truman spoke to a huge crowd on July 24, and four days later the biggest Detroit parade in 250 years took place. When the celebrations became a memory, Detroit had permanent exhibitions as the new Detroit Historical Museum was opened.

Near the museum, a billboard advertised a 1951 Dodge two-door sedan—including taxes and license plate—for $1,897.50. Newspapers advertised a seven-room colonial on Pasadena between Dexter and Holmur for $14,000. In the northwest area on Stoepel north of Curtis, the asking price for a large three-bedroom with a breakfast room and first floor lavatory was $17,500. For the affluent who could afford Huntington Woods, a three-bedroom on Borgman, three blocks south of Eleven Mile and a half block east of Coolidge, was priced at $18,950.

Congregation B'nai David instituted the custom for all male worshippers to wear yarmelkes (skull caps) at Sabbath and Holiday services. Some men with receding hairlines who liked to wear hats thought it was an imposition. Congregation Gemilus Chasodim moved from its rented quarters in the Jericho Temple on Joy Road to the D. W. Simons Building on Tuxedo and Holmur. Flint's Congregation Beth Israel hired Rabbi Philip Kieval as spiritual leader and officiating

Politicians, celebrities, and civic leaders were part of the largest parade in Detroit's history as it passed Campus Martius.

(Courtesy of Michigan Views)

cantor for the High Holidays. A native of Baltimore, Rabbi Kieval was ordained at the Jewish Theological Seminary in 1947 and previously served a Benton Harbor, Michigan, congregation.

Mrs. Fannie Saulson became president of the Metropolitan Detroit Chapter of Hadassah in 1951. The local chapter was established in the home of her parents, Mr. and Mrs. Joseph Wetsman, when the movement's founder, Henrietta Szold, was a house guest. The Greenfield brothers, Ernest, Eugene, and Harry, all rabbis who served the First Hebrew Congregation of Delray, founded the Greenfield Noodle and Specialty Company. In 1951, Nate Shapero's Cunningham's was the number-one television and radio advertiser in Michigan and Detroit's second largest newspaper advertiser. Charles Grosberg was a pioneer in the supermarket industry and had opened a warehouse-type food store in 1931. Evolving into Packers Super Markets, the chain merged with the Wrigley Super Markets in 1951. Grosberg retired from the food business and devoted more time to charitable causes.

Gertrude Berg was starring in *Molly* at the Adams downtown. On the other side of Grand Circus Park, Gregory Peck and Susan Hayward were featured in *David and Bathsheba* at the Madison. At this time, Sander Levin, who was attending the University of Chicago, was elected president of the student government.

Rabbi Joseph Elias assumed the post of principal of Yeshiva Beth Yehudah after Rabbi Simcha Wasserman left to establish the West Coast Talmudical Academy in Los Angeles. Enrollment passed 500, of which close to 200 were in the day school as the budget rose to $175,000. Byron Krieger, who began fencing at Northwestern High School in 1937, competed with 300 fencers in an eight-day national fencing tournament at the Grosse Pointe Neighborhood Club. Krieger was the only fencer to enter two finals, and he placed third in foil and fourth in saber ability.

The Detroit Jewish Community Council helped set a ceiling on Kosher beef prices with the Office of Price Stabilization. The 1951 price ceilings were: Choice grade seven-inch rib steaks—$1.11; good, $1.01. Choice and good boneless brisket, $1.06. Ten-inch rib steak, choice, $1.00; good, 92 cents. Chuck, 85 cents. Hamburger, 79 cents. Choice and good shank, bone in, 51 cents. Even though more homes were turning from radio to television in 1951, the radio version of "Your Hit Parade," on Thursday nights at ten on NBC, was where most dials were tuned. The most often sung songs were, "Be My Love," "C'mon 'a My House," "My Heart Cries for You," and "Tennessee Waltz."

Alex Kuhn, the young veteran of Nazi death camps who arrived in Detroit at the of 15 in 1946, was employed in the wholesale clothing industry near the Veterans Memorial Building. In September 1951, Kuhn married native Detroiter Dorothy Grossman and took up residence on Edison near Dexter. Dr. Charles D. Aaron, the first Jew born in Detroit to attend the Michigan College of Medicine, died at the age of 85. Aaron was considered the chief gastroenterologist in Detroit for several years and helped train many doctors. He was famous as a lecturer and author in the medical field. A member of Temple Beth El, Aaron was buried in Woodmere Cemetery.

When Rabbi Judah Levin and fellow marchers along Hastings Street raised awareness for the need of a Jewish hospital in 1912, they collected more than $7,000 in nickels and dimes while carrying signs with the slogan, "Buy a Brick to Save the Sick." The invest-

Five years after arriving in the new world of Detroit, Alex Kuhn married Dorothy Grossman.
(Courtesy of Alex and Dorothy Kuhn)

Pfc. Mandell Yuster
(Courtesy of Jewish News)

ment of collected funds grew to $52,500 in 1950 and was contributed for the construction of Sinai Hospital. Some of the marchers of 1912 and Isaac Rosenthal, one of the founders of the Jewish hospital movement and president of the Hebrew Hospital Association for 12 years, beamed with pride as Nate S. Shapero turned a spadeful of sod.

As the cornerstone, which contained a history of the hospital movement, letters and messages sent by individuals and organizations, was set in place on a clear, sunny October 14, Dr. Julian Priver contemplated the future. Priver, a native New Yorker who was associate director of Mount Sinai Hospital in New York, assumed the position of executive director of Detroit's Jewish hospital as construction was about to begin.

Mr. and Mrs. Sam Yuster were living in the four-story Dexter Lodge apartment building between Collingwood and Lawrence when they received the dreaded telegram. Their 21-year-old son, Mandell, was killed in the raging battle to recapture Seoul. He became the first Detroit Jewish casualty of the Korean War. Mandell had excelled as a member of the Shaarey Zedek Boy Scouts and as an athlete in Northern High School. Only weeks after Yuster's death, reports of more Detroit Jewish soldiers killed in battle became known.

As the war in Korea wore on in 1952, affecting several of Detroit's Jewish families, escapism was found in television. "Howdy Doody," Kate Smith, and Perry Como were the most popular television programs in the country. Number four came from Detroit's WXYZ studios in the Macabees Building on Woodward, and was called "Auntie Dee." Dee Parker's children's program was the only locally produced program in TV's top ten.

Winston Churchill visited Washington in 1952 and spoke to Congress about the world situation. About Israel, Churchill said: 'From the days of the Balfour Declaration I have desired that the Jews should have a national home, and I have worked for that end. I rejoice to pay my tribute here to the achievements of those who have founded the Israelite State, who have defended themselves with tenacity, and who offer asylum to great numbers of Jewish refugees. I hope that with their aid they may convert deserts into gardens; but if they are to enjoy peace and prosperity they must strive to renew and preserve their friendly relations with the Arab world without which widespread misery might follow for all."

Eleanor Roosevelt visited Israel in 1952. "Going from the Arab countries through the Mandelbaum Gate into Israel was, to me, like breathing the air of the United States again," the widow of Franklin Delano Roosevelt, would write in her book, *On My Own*.

Dr. Chaim Weizmann, the first president of Israel,

Isaac Nagel, 105, and his 103-year-old wife celebrated their 81st anniversary in 1952.
(Courtesy of Jewish Home for the Aged)

died at the age of 78. Albert Einstein, 76, who left Germany in 1933, moved to the United States, and became a Professor at Princeton, declined David Ben Gurion's request to assume the presidency of the State of Israel, and Izhak Ben-Zvi became second president of the Jewish state.

In 1948, the former Children's Home on Petoskey was linked to the Jewish Home for the Aged by a connecting corridor, creating one unit. In 1952, the home had 190 residents, 65 of whom were in the infirmary. The oldest resident was 105-year-old Isaac Nagel. His wife, Mary, was 103, and the couple had been married for 81 years. A branch of the Jewish Center opened in the D. W. Simons building at Tuxedo and Holmur. The United Hebrew Schools had used the building since 1928 but vacated the premises after agreeing to use the new school building of Congregation B'nai Moshe.

On May 13, 1952, the spiritual leader of Temple Beth El, Dr. Benedict Glazer, died at the age of 49 of a cerebral hemorrhage. Glazer had served Beth El for less than 11 years and was given life tenure in 1951 on his twenty-fifth year in the rabbinate. Leaders of Beth El thought of moving north, and conversations consummated in the purchase of 22.5 acres on Northwestern Highway between Nine and Ten Mile Roads.

According to Federation figures, about 3 percent of Detroit's Jewish community lived in Oak Park in 1952. About 35 Oak Park and Huntington Woods residents of the newly-formed Suburban Temple used the gymnasium of Burton Elementary School. It would evolve into Temple Emanu-El. At a meeting in the Oak Park Boulevard home of Max Nusbaum, the Oak Park Synagogue Center was formed. David Dombey was elected chairman of what would become Young Israel of Oak Woods.

Adas Shalom, formerly known as Northwest Hebrew Congregation and Center, built in stages on Curtis, dedicated its new synagogue in 1952. Two years after holding its first services in the Bagley School, Northwest Israel Synagogue opened its small build-

Top: Northwest Israel Synagogue, located at 17376 Wyoming, opened in 1952.

Above: Adas Shalom, formerly Northwest Hebrew Congregation and Center, was built in stages on Curtis.
(Courtesy Leonard N. Simons Community Archives)

Right: The imposing Adas Shalom from Santa Rosa.
(Photo by author)

ing at 17376 Wyoming, which would evolve into Young Israel of Northwest. Windsor, which had three orthodox synagogues, had an estimated Jewish population of 2,800 in 1952.

Neighbors on Gladstone and Lawton were used to hearing the thump of basketballs being dribbled on the sidewalk. Walter Godfrey, who helped lead the Cass Tech High School basketball team to two undefeated seasons and City Championships, put up hoops on telephone poles and spent most of the summer days playing. Word got around, and Godfrey's fame attracted more and more young men to the area. Finally, the city paved a corner and put up a basketball court because of the young basketball star, who would join the Michigan State University basketball and baseball teams. Godfrey was also being scouted by the Tigers as his 9-0 pitching record helped Trumbull Chevrolet to the American Baseball Congress title.

Byron Krieger was named to the United States Olympic fencing team in 1952. Krieger trained for three weeks in New York before leaving for the Olympics in Helsinki, Finland. Krieger had gained international fame the year before when he competed in the U.S. Pan American Games and won two gold medals in foil and sabre. Rabbi Joseph Eisenman, who served Congregation Beth Tefilo Emanuel (Taylor Shule) before moving to Jerusalem, returned to Detroit for the wedding of his grandson, Dr. Arnold Eisenman, to Miss Beatrice Greenfield. Rudy and Ann Newman, who served in Israel's War of Independence, left Israel and settled in Detroit.

Polish Holocaust survivor Henry Dorfman, 39, founded a small butcher shop with Alan Charlupski in the Eastern Market. The shop would grow to become Thorn Apple Valley. Another Polish Holocaust survivor, Fred Ferber, received his Bachelor of Arts in Electronics in 1952 and began his professional career with Mark & Ferber Television Service.

Borenstein's Book & Music Store kept their Twelfth and Blaine store as a branch and opened a new main store at 12066 Dexter, at Monterey. Joseph Spitzer, who operated Detroit Hebrew Bookshop on Dexter near Cortland, opened a second establishment at 18294 Wyoming, north of Curtis. Spitzer's brother-in-law, Hillel Abrams, took over operations of the Dexter store.

Isaac Rosenthal was among the small circle of founders of most of the important institutions in Jewish Detroit in the first half of the twentieth century. He helped bring about the Children's Home, Detroit Mizrachi, Hebrew Hospital Association, House of Shelter, Jewish Community Council, Old Folks'

Borenstein's Book and Music Store opened a new main store on Dexter in 1952.

(Courtesy Abraham Borenstein)

Isaac Rosenthal was at the birth of several of Jewish Detroit's important institutions.

(Courtesy of Zelda Selmar)

Home, Yeshiva Beth Yehudah, Yeshivath Chachmey Lublin, Young Israel, and several synagogues. Rosenthal (page 42), 71 at the time of his death, also was active in the Gold Star Parents of the Jewish War Veterans. Rosenthal helped others, like himself, whose sons were killed in World War II. Many leaders of Detroit's Jewish community attended Rosenthal's funeral from his brother-in-law, Ira Kaufman's, chapel on Dexter.

In the August 29, 1952, edition of the *Jewish News*, the Council of Orthodox Rabbis listed 72 kosher butchers under its supervision.

The Committee on Kashruth in the Detroit Sinai Hospital drafted a letter to the board of Sinai Hospital, hoping to bring about kosher facilities for observant patients, The *Jewish News* published the committee's open letter on the lower right of page 5 in its November 7, 1952, edition.

Our Weekly Message To the Jewish Housewife

Our attention has been called to the fact that there are butchers in Detroit who claim to sell Kosher meats, but who to the best of our knowledge are not recognized or under the supervision of the Vaad Harabbonim or the Merkaz. For your protection, the following list is that of all the Kosher butchers in Detroit.

J. Auster ....8736 Linwood
N. Baker and
I. Zaks ....12316 Dexter
Boxman Bros.,
O. and F. ....7624 W. McNichols
H. Boxman ....11716 Dexter
B. Boxman ....13575 W. 7 Mile
F. Band ....12303 Linwood
J. Braverman ....12228 Dexter
J. Burg ....10240 Dexter
B. Burg & Son 12735 Linwood
E. Burke ....12540 Dexter
B. Canvasser ....12110 Linwood
B. Cohen ....12030 Linwood
M. Cohen ....8704 Twelfth
L. Cohen & Son 8833 Twelfth
S. Cohen and
B. Zager ......12733 W. 7 Mile
D. Cohen ....12212 Dexter
L. Castelman .....12148 Dexter
I. Dubin ....3332 Joy Rd.
Dobrusin and
Schwartz ....3736 Joy Rd.
B. Eizelman .....11849 Linwood
S. Eisenstat .....12419 Linwood
H. Finkelstein ...10222 Dexter
H. Freedman 18279 Livernois
M. Krause ....13723 Linwood
N. Fradkin ....12100 Petoskey
N. Finegold 8540 W. McNichols
M. Finkel and
D. Hoskowitz 3353 W. Davison
A. Goldin ....929 Westminster
M. Goldin ....10214 Twelfth
J. Goldman ....12121 Linwood
S. Greenberg .....8830 Twelfth
H. Golsky ....13936 Dexter
A. Goldstein and B.
Eizelman ....11725 Dexter
O. Klaper ......3269 W. Davison
Kaplan Bros. ..18211 Wyoming
S. Lapinsky ......8653 Twelfth
J. Lansky ....11538 Holmur
M. Levy ....12170 Dexter
M. Lupkin ....13140 W. 7 Mile
H. Lopatin ....13704 Linwood
H. Markofsky ....4709 Kay St.
A. B. Margolis ...11738 Dexter
S. Mirvis and S.
Trabman 7641 W. McNichols
H. Pearlman &
Son ....11527 Dexter
A. Polukoff ......13133 Dexter
N. Reznick ....8440 Twelfth
H. Reznick ....11358 Dexter
L. Richter ....13430 W. 7 Mile
K. Rosen ....13418 W. 7 Mile
M. Roth ....4440 Elmhurst
N. Rubenstein ...13310 Dexter
J. Sandberg ......3136 Fenkell
B. Sweet ....13639 Linwood
S. Sherman ....12649 Linwood
Schechter Bros. ..12020 Dexter
H. Schechter .....8800 Twelfth
I. Schwartzberg 8825 Twelfth
A. Shear ....7718 W. McNichols
A. Skore ....13132 Linwood
B. Shapiro ....2615 Pasadena
J. Singer and P.
Swaren ....9831 Dexter
M. Swarinsky ...12123 Dexter
N. Samotnik ....12220 Dexter
Shaffer ....12017 Linwood
B. Smith ....7736 W. McNichols
B. Tomarin ......12500 Dexter
Vikser & Landau
.......................7336 W. 7 Mile
J. Weisman ......12050 Dexter
S. Weingarten ...8526 Twelfth
A. Weinstein ....8780 Linwood
D. Weisblatt ....8909 Linwood
S. Weisz ....10243 Linwood

THIS WEEK'S SPECIALS:

HAMBURGER 64¢ Lb.

CHUCK ROAST 79¢ Lb.

LISTEN TO THE VOICE OF THE KOSHER BUTCHER ON ALTMAN'S JEWISH HOUR AT 9:30 P.M. SATURDAY, AND AT 10:30 A.M. SUNDAY OVER RADIO STATION WJLB.

AN OPEN LETTER
To the President of Detroit's Sinai Hospital

Dear Mr. Osnos:

We take this means of presenting the question of Kashruth in the Jewish Hospital before the public, since our repeated presentations to the Board of Sinai Hospital have failed to meet with success.

We maintain that Sinai Hospital as an institution of the Jewish community must fully adhere to the tradition and discipline of the Jewish dietary laws. It is, of course, understood, that certain special diets dictated by purely medical considerations shall not be covered by the general policy of Kashruth.

A hospital known by Jews and non-Jews as a Jewish hospital must not violate traditions sacred to many Jews. We have no desire to exert coercion in the private conduct of an individual. An institution, however, is representative of the Jewish community and of Jewish life as a whole and has no right to flout practices which have been part of the Jewish way of life throughout the ages, practices which still claim the loyalty of large numbers of our people.

The refusal of your Board to reconsider its original decision to have kosher facilities for only a fraction of its patients, violates the basic principles expressed above and runs counter to the sentiments of the majority of Jews in our community.

In the face of failure in our negotiations with the Board we convened a meeting of Jewish organizational representatives on Monday, October 27th. The spontaneous response surprised even us who had always believed that we were expressing the will of Detroit Jewry. Men and women came in such large numbers that we had to take the meeting to the auditorium of the Jewish Center on Davison. Even there the space was insufficient. Landsmanshaften, lodges, fraternities, veterans' groups, synagogues—all spoke as with one voice through their representatives—expressing their indignation at the thought that our Jewish hospital should be anything but completely kosher. Observant and non-Observant Jews alike were unanimous in their demand that our hospital should honor the traditions by which our people has lived.

Their sentiment was deep and strong. It revealed an unwavering determination to resist any decision which, in the words of one of the speakers, would "build a ghetto for Jews who wish to keep Kashruth."

Prayerfully we ask you to reconsider this entire matter, to respect the will of multitudes of Jews and to make the Jewish hospital worthy of its sacred function as a Jewish institution.

It is no shame to admit error. It is a trait of greatness to review one's judgment and to accept the overwhelming wish of the community.

We look forward with eagerness to your early reply. The responsibility now rests with you and your colleagues on the board of Sinai Hospital.

—COMMITTEE ON KASHRUTH IN THE DETROIT SINAI HOSPITAL.

As the year wore on, Rabbi Jacob Chinitz was installed as spiritual leader of Congregation Ahavas Achim. Leonard Borman, a student at the Yeshiva Beth Yehudah, celebrated his Bar Mitzvah at Congregation Shaarey Zedek. To mark the occasion, Leonard's parents, Mr. and Mrs. Abraham Borman, contributed an amount equal to the week's payroll for the Yeshiva's teachers.

Nate S. Shapero cut the ribbon at the main entrance of the new Sinai Hospital in the first week of 1953. Approximately 10,000 well-wishers roamed the beautiful hospital under controlled guided tours over a four-hour span. The hospital doors officially opened for business on January 15, without a kosher kitchen.

For several months, the Council of Orthodox Rabbis, reinforced by support of conservative rabbis, used advertising, mailings, meetings, and posters to publicize that the Jewish hospital under construction should provide a kosher kitchen to serve observant patients. However, many on the hospital board thought the kosher facilities old-fashioned from a religious standpoint and too costly from a practical standpoint.

As the sun set on January 15, and the Sinai Hospital sign atop the building turned on, the last two letters of the hospital's name didn't light. The bright sign read SIN HOSPITAL. Some thought it was a message from above. Most of the hospital board felt it just had to send a message to the maintenance department

The debate wore on, and one day after the obstetrical department opened, the first baby was born on April 21. Finally, about six months after the first patients were admitted, agreement was reached in the first week of June between all parties resolving the kosher kitchen and kosher food issues. Rabbi David Bakst, who was spiritual leader of the Joseph Allan Synagogue in the Jewish Home for the Aged, became supervisor (mashgiach) of the kosher facilities of Sinai Hospital.

Soupy Sales (Milton Supman) came to Detroit in 1953 after television stints in Cincinnati and Cleveland. His salary was $13,300 a year, and the Sales family moved to northwest Detroit, where they shared a common back fence with Dr. Maier Belen and his family. "Lunch With Soupy" quickly became the most popular television program with kids and many adults. Soupy also began a nightly variety show on WXYZ-TV and was considered the most popular personality in Detroit.

More than 600 admirers of Morris Schaver gathered to honor him on his 60th birthday at the Sheraton-Cadillac Hotel. Schaver, president of the Histadrut Campaign for 16 years, pledged $60,000 toward a civic and cultural center in the Israeli town of Ramleh. Avern Cohn, who went to Israel in 1952

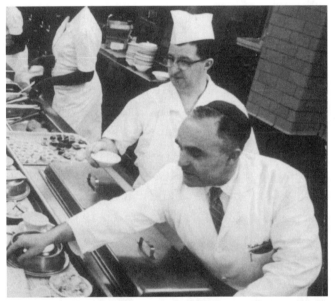

Left: Sinai Hospital was on a 34-acre site bounded by Outer Drive, Whitcomb, McNichols, and Lauder.

(Courtesy of Leonard N. Simons Jewish Community Archives)

Above: Rabbi David Bakst and Charlie Williams inspect kosher facilities at the Sinai Hospital Kitchen.

(Courtesy of the Bakst family)

Soupy Sales moved to Detroit for a $13,000 a year salary in local television.
(Courtesy of Burton Historical Collection of the Detroit Public Library)

to assess conditions, was named head of the Junior Division of the 1953 Allied Jewish Campaign. Industrialist Abe Shiffman contributed $25,000 to memorialize the late Henry Meyers through a fund to help construct a new Jewish Community Center in northwest Detroit.

Hank Greenberg, in his role of general manager of the Cleveland Indians, was responsible for all player moves within the organization. He engineered a multi-player trade with the Detroit Tigers, sending catcher Joe Ginsberg to Cleveland. Earlier the Tigers had swapped pitcher Saul Rogovin to the Chicago White Sox, leaving no Jewish players on the Tigers roster.

The *Jewish News* moved from the David Stott Building downtown to West Seven Mile Road between Southfield and Evergreen. The *Jewish News* lettering was proudly displayed as the building's sole tenant was Detroit's Jewish weekly. The building in the predominantly Jewish area became a frequent target for swastika painters. Alfred Bounin, who enlisted in the Jewish Legion for service in Palestine in 1917 under General Allenby, and who went on to operate an insurance agency, became president of the Metropolitan Detroit B'nai B'rith Council. Harry Weinsaft, who worked for the Haganah as a security officer on the ship *Exodous* trying to smuggle Holocaust survivors past the British into Palestine, moved to Detroit in 1953 and became well known in art gallery circles.

President Dwight D. Eisenhower, who had liberated Buchenwald as a general in 1943, kept his inauguration promise when he took office as the 34th President of the United States by ending the Korean War within six months. The Joseph L. Bale Memorial Playground was dedicated at Winthrop and Margareta in a colorful ceremony by members of the Jewish War Veterans, including Mayor Albert E. Cobo, Rabbi Morris Adler, and others. Bale earned the nation's highest honor, the Distinguished Service Cross in 1945 when he single-handedly knocked out a German tank in battle. The action cost the Central High graduate his life but saved the lives of many in his unit.

Miriam (Mary) Nagel passed away at the age of 104. Residents of the Jewish Home for the Aged said the Nagels were as devoted to each other as they were on their wedding day. Isaac Nagel, going on 106, still referred to his wife as "my bride." They had been married in Poland and came to the United States in 1906. Ira Sonnenblick, executive director of the Home, said the couple often sat for long stretches of time in silence, just holding hands. Barton's Chocolate opened its eighth store in Detroit in 1953. The new store on Livernois north of Seven Mile Road was part of a national chain of 56 stores. Barton's, which had two stores on Dexter, introduced ice cream prepared exclusively for Passover.

Alfred L. Deutsch, a founder of American Savings Association in 1947, became president of Congregation B'nai Moshe in 1953. One of the most popular stops on Dexter was the American Savings building on the corner of Cortland, as the window display featured large photographs pertaining to current events. In 1953 the bank window advertised it gave 2 percent interest on savings accounts and charged four and a quarter percent interest on FHA mortgages. Dr. Samuel Levin, who began his career in education as a teacher at Central High School (now Old Main on Cass) for $110 a month in 1913, retired as chairman of the Economics Department of Wayne State University in 1953. Widower Max Fisher married divorcee Marjorie

Switlow in New York. After a honeymoon in Hawaii, the couple and their children took up residence in Max's Parkside home.

Holocaust survivor Abe Pasternak came to Detroit in 1947 and served in the United States Army during the Korean conflict. He was working for the National Dry Goods Company in 1953 when he married Gerry Nagler on Flag Day, June 14, 1953, at Congregation B'nai Moshe. Gerry graduated from Central High School and the University of Michigan. "She corrected me almost every sentence as she majored in English in college," Abe recalled.

Yeshiva Beth Yehudah opened an afternoon school branch in the Northwest Israel Synagogue on Wyoming, bringing the enrollment to over 600. The Yeshiva also purchased a lot north of the school on Dexter for use as a playground. While Beth Aaron and the United Hebrew Schools entered into an agreement in 1952, the heating facilities in Beth Aaron's Wyoming building weren't usable until 1953. Shaarey Zedek built a branch building for school and youth activity use on Seven Mile Road and Lesure. Sonia Syme began teaching at Temple Israel's religious school in 1953.

Rabbi Joshua Sperka retired as spiritual leader of Congregation B'nai David and was replaced by Rabbi Hayim Donin of New York City. M. Robert Syme became assistant rabbi of Temple Israel under Rabbi Leon Fram. After ten years with Flint's Temple Beth El, Rabbi Morton Applebaum left to assume a pulpit in Akron Ohio. Leonard N. Simons became the thirty-third president of Detroit's Beth El, and Dr. Richard C. Hertz, associate rabbi of the Chicago Sinai Congregation and a graduate of the Hebrew Union College, became senior rabbi of Temple Beth El. Hertz reintroduced the bar mitzvah ceremony after an absence of almost half a century. Clarence Enggass, who owned one of Detroit's largest jewelry establishments, claimed he was the last to be bar mitzvahed at Beth El before confirmation replaced the ceremony. Congregation Ahavas Achim dedicated its facilities on Schaefer north of Seven Mile Road.

The Oak Park Synagogue Center, formed in 1952, became the Oak Woods Jewish Center in 1953 with Morris Novetsky as its president. The name change was the result of a split in the group's differing on the level of observance for the congregation. The less traditional would go on to form Congregation Beth Shalom, while Novetsky's group would eventually become Young Israel of Oak Woods.

Congregation Ahavas Achim had its own building for the first time since 1940 when it left the Oakland section.

(Photo by author)

Abe and Gerry Pasternak were married in 1953.

(Courtesy of the Pasternaks)

14

1954-1959
THE COMMUNITY SPREADS

Northland Center, called the largest regional shopping mall in the country, opened in 1954. At the time, the Detroit Board of Commerce estimated the city's population had reached 2 million.

Joe Falls, brought up in the Catholic faith, was a young sportswriter from New York who always felt comfortable in the company of Jews. When he accepted a position with the *Detroit Times* in 1953, Falls moved to the Dexter section. He took a room in the flat of a Jewish couple on Pasadena near Dexter and loved the area.

Falls saw movies at the Avalon and Dexter Theaters, shopped at Dexter-Davison and frequented the delis. The Esquire Grill on Dexter and Leslie, open 24 hours, seven days a week, featured complete dinners and take-out. They fit in well with the schedule of a sportswriter who had to pound out columns and stories after a night game.

Dexter had everything Falls needed. Especially the Dexter bus, which he relied on to get to Olympia Stadium to cover the Red Wings, Briggs Stadium for the Tigers and Lions, and to the *Times* office around the corner from the last bus stop. Falls, who couldn't afford a car, loved to scan the windows of Dexter

Between the Dexter and northwest Jewish areas, many blocks along Livernois were lined with used car lots.

(Courtesy of Manning Brothers Historic Photographic Collection)

ECHOES OF DETROIT'S JEWISH COMMUNITIES

Chevrolet as the bus passed by. He'd purposely walk past the closer showroom windows of Kotzen Motors, on Dexter at Buena Vista, to peer at the Studebakers. Falls would press his nose against the window of Wilshire Motor Sales two blocks down at Fullerton to see the Chryslers and Plymouths.

Falls couldn't scrape up the money or afford the payments for a new automobile costing around $2,000. In 1954, like many looking for a used car, he roamed the numerous used car lots along Livernois. Falls settled for a two-door used Plymouth for $600. It had a silver button on the far left of the dashboard. Falls pushed the starter in and was on his way.

Detroit would start going the wrong way in 1954 as more people would leave the city than move in. Detroit would begin to lose population each and every year into the next century. Northland Shopping Center would be the beginning of the end of downtown Detroit as a commercial shopping center. As more suburban shopping malls would open, more downtown stores would close.

There also was change in the Dexter section in 1954. For the first time, African Americans dominated the population of many streets. Several Orthodox families living in the southern and eastern end of the Dexter area were relocating farther north and west, closer to Cortland, Sturtevant, Fullerton, Leslie, and Glendale, within short walking distance of the Yeshiva Beth Yehudah where their children were enrolled. Others were moving farther northwest north of Six Mile Road, while some were pioneering new homes in Oak Park.

While the Sholem Aleichem School was located on Wyoming near Curtis, the other two yiddish schools were still on Linwood. The United Jewish Folk School of the Farband was on Linwood near Grand, and the Workmen's Circle School was close to Burlingame. In 1954 it was estimated that Jewish schools were giving over 4,000 children some type of Sunday school education.

The Annual Report of Oak Park reported that from April 1952 to July 1, 1954, Oak Park experienced a 312 percent population growth. The report also stated that 6,558 building permits were issued from 1951 to mid-1954. In 1932, Huntington Woods had 650 residents when it incorporated. In 1954 the city had a population of 7,500. In 1954, Congregation Shaarey Zedek purchased a 15-acre tract of land on Northwestern Highway and Ten Mile Road for its future synagogue site. Congregation B'nai David acquired a nine-acre tract on Southfield Road near Nine and a Half Mile for its new synagogue. Hadassah, operating from offices on Joy Road and Linwood, moved into their own building at 16240 West Seven Mile Road.

Sam and Sol Hammerstein opened Hammerstein Drugs on Nine Mile Road, one block west of Coolidge. The Borenstein Brothers, who operated Zeman's New York Bakeries on Dexter and on Twelfth Street, opened

The Esther Berman branch of the United Hebrew Schools was built in 1954 at Schaefer and Seven Mile Road.

(Courtesy Leonard N. Simons Jewish Community Archives)

another at 12945 West Seven Mile Road. The Labor Zionist Educational and Cultural Center on Schaefer near Seven Mile was under way. The Esther Berman Branch of the United Hebrew Schools at Schaefer and Seven Mile Road was built in 1954. Abe Kasle, president of UHS, was given the honor of laying the cornerstone. With $85,000 of the projected $135,600 cost of the project in hand, the Yeshiva Beth Yehudah started construction of its three-story annex. Congregation Aaron Moshe, 29th and Michigan, disbanded and donated $5,000 of its assets to the Yeshiva building fund. The Yeshiva also started a high school for girls. The annual Yeshiva dinner, held at the Latin Quarter on Grand Boulevard, attracted 700 people at $25 per plate.

As Congregation Shaar Hashomayim was building its synagogue on Ten Mile Road and Cloverlawn in Oak Park, Rabbi Leo Goldman, spiritual leader of Northwest Israel, received his master's degree in philosophy and psychology. Rabbi Goldman was ordained in his native Poland. When the Russians invaded Poland, he was jailed and sent to Siberia. After his release, Rabbi Goldman joined the Polish army and was wounded during combat with the Nazis. After the war, Rabbi Goldman was elected as chief rabbi of Norway and served in that post for two years before coming to the United States. Rabbi Goldman would become well-known in his many roles, including decades as spiritual leader of Congregation Shaar Hashomayim, mohel (ritual circumciser), and hospital chaplain.

Rabbi Leopold Neuhas, one of only two rabbis to survive the notorious Theresiensdadt concentration camp, and who went on to serve Congregation Gemiluth Chasodim from 1946 until early 1954, died at the age of 75. Rabbi Joel Litke, a native of Germany ordained by the Canadian Theological Seminary in 1947, was elected spiritual leader of Congregation Gemiluth Chasodim, which was using rented quarters in the D. W. Simons Building on Tuxedo and Holmur.

Rabbi Milton Arm came to Detroit for what he thought would be a nine-month stay at Congregation Shaarey Zedek to fill in for Rabbi Morris Adler, who would take a sabbatical leave. Rabbi Philip Rabinowitz, son of Rabbi Joseph Rabinowitz, became spiritual leader of Congregation Beth Moses. Known as the Oak Park Synagogue when it organized as a Conservative religious body in January 1953, it renamed itself Congregation Beth Shalom and engaged the services of Rabbi Herbert Eskin. In 1954 it held High Holiday Services at the Northland Auditorium. Oak Park Jewish Center built its building on Coolidge north of Oak Park Boulevard, hired Rabbi Yaacov Homnick, and affiliated with Young Israel, becoming Young Israel of Oak Woods. The Suburban Temple reinvented itself as Congregation Emanu-El.

Max Fisher made his first trip to Israel with the United Jewish Appeal's first study mission. Mrs. Morris (Emma Lazaroff) Schaver became the first woman Israel Bond Trustee by purchasing a $10,000 Israel Bond. The "Old Timers," who played, socialized, and were educated in the Hannah Schloss Memorial Building, held their first official reunion. The Hannah Schloss old-timers reunion drew 80 persons to the Dexter-Davison branch of the Jewish Community Center. Walter Godfrey pitched Michigan State University to the Big Ten title by winning all four of the games he started.

Rabbi Aaron Ashinsky, the oldest living rabbi in the country, died at the age of 87. In 1889, two years after he left his native Poland, Rabbi Ashinsky came to Detroit as joint rabbi of B'nai Israel, Beth Jacob, and Shaarey Zedek. In 1896 he assumed a pulpit in Montreal, then returned to Detroit in 1926 for six years as rabbi of Congregation Emanuel before moving on to Pittsburgh. An ardent Zionist, one of his five daughters was a national vice-president of Mizrachi Organization of America and another daughter's husband, Rabbi Irving Miller, was president of the Zionist Organization of America and chairman of the American Zionist Council.

In a survey carried out by the Joint Distribution Committee, there were only 790 Jews left in China in 1954. The 790, a remnant of the 24,000 when World War II broke out, included some 18,600 refugees from

Central Europe. Between 1945 and 1949, most were moved out by the JDC. Of the remaining 790, most lived in three cities: 350 in Harbin, 310 in Shanghai, and 120 in Tientsin. The 70-year-old Hebrew Immigrant Aid Society, founded to help Jews fleeing from Czarist Russia, merged with the United Service for New Americans and the Migration Department of the Joint Distribution Committee to form United Hias Service, Inc.

The number of donors to the Allied Jewish Campaign of the Jewish Welfare Federation dropped by 1,606 from 1953 to 26,795 in 1954. The amount raised dropped by $308,640 to $4,150,612. Temple Beth El had 1,663 members in 1954, an increase of 163 in five years. The Temple's president, Leonard Simons, had many interests besides his family and advertising agency with partner Lawrence Michelson. While cartooning, playing cards, and golf occupied some of his free time, his biggest hobby was collecting books. On his fiftieth birthday, Simons donated over 2,000 books on the history of Detroit and Michigan to Wayne State University. A. E. Barit, a member of Temple Beth El, began his auto industry career in 1910 with the Hudson Motor Car Company. Barit advanced to president in 1936 and remained in that post until 1954. George Romney became president after Barit.

Raised in the El Moshe Synagogue area of Michigan and 29th, Senator Charles S. Blondy, elected to the State Senate in 1940, served as Senate Democratic Floor Leader in 1953 and 1954. His brother, Allen H., served with him in 1953 and 1954. The two brothers in the Senate at the same time was a historic first in Michigan. B'nai B'rith Women's Council sponsored an all-star fund-raiser at the Masonic Temple. Ventriloquist Paul Winchell and his wooden partner, Jerry Mahoney, headlined the event, which also featured television personality Jan Murray and the up-and-coming Joel Gray and the Yiddish singing Barry sisters.

Nathan J. Kaufman, assistant prosecuting attorney for Wayne County, was sworn in as Judge of Common Pleas Court by Gov. G. Mennen Williams in 1954. Over 600 people—including Kaufman's spiritual leader, Rabbi Israel Halpern of Congregation Beth Abraham—witnessed the ceremony in the County Building downtown. A contingent of the Jewish War Veterans presented Judge Kaufman with an American flag, which became a fixture in his courtroom.

While Judge Kaufman was being sworn in, construction continued on the new City County Building on Woodward and Jefferson. In 1955 Mayor Cobo led a procession of city officials from the old City Hall down Woodward to their new governmental home, as the second building in the civic center was opened. Motorists were moving faster as the interchange linking the John C. Lodge and Edsel Ford Expressways opened.

Isaac Nagel turned 108 in 1955, helping to bring the average age of the 204 residents of the Jewish Home for the Aged to 82. Many younger people turned out for the dedication of the gym of the Davison Jewish Center. The workload of being executive director of both the Jewish Community Center and Fresh Air Camp required a full time director of each in 1955. Irwin Shaw, who had directed both agencies since

Community leader Leonard Simons donated over 2,000 books to Wayne State University on his 50th birthday in 1954.
(Courtesy of Rabbi Leo M. Franklin Archives, Temple Beth El)

1951, decided to remain with the JCC. Almost a third—9,000—of Oak Park's 28,000 residents were Jewish in 1955.

Mercury Records released songs by Emma Schaver. The long-playing record of 12 songs titled, "From the Heart of a People," was recorded in Jerusalem. The *Detroit Times* and *Detroit News* music critics reviewed and raved about the talent of Detroit's famed soprano. At the time, the Detroit music charts were topped by "Rock Around The Clock," by Bill Haley & the Comets. Ranked second through five were: "The Yellow Rose of Texas," "Love Is A Many-Splendored Thing," "Autumn Leaves," and Tennessee Ernie Ford's "Sixteen Tons."

Mrs. Bessie Wetsman, a Detroit resident for half a century, died at the age of 92. Associated with Hadassah, Congregation Shaarey Zedek, Jewish Home for the Aged, Mizrachi, and the United Hebrew Schools, her daughters, Mrs. Ralph Davidson and Mrs. Morse Saulson, were presidents of the Detroit Chapter of Hadassah. World-famous professor Albert Einstein, a strong and vocal supporter of Israel, died at the age of 76 at Princeton Hospital. While hospitalized, Einstein was working on a radio address on behalf of Israel.

In a candlelight Sephardic ceremony at the Elmwood Casino, Shirley Chicorel married Marcel Behar. The bride, secretary of the Sephardic Community of Detroit, attended Wayne State University. The groom, a mechanical and design engineer, was a graduate of Birmingham University, England. The couple would go on to be staunch leaders of the Sephardic Detroit community.

Tom Borman's supermarket chain, Lucky Stores, and Al Borman's chain, Food Fair, merged in 1955. The brothers kept the Food Fair name for all the stores. Eppie Friedman, who married Detroiter Jules Lederer in her native Sioux City, Iowa, in 1939, started writing the Ann Landers advice column for the *Chicago Sun Times* in 1955. Bernard Isaacs, who had been associated with the United Hebrew Schools since its inception in 1919, retired as superintendent in 1955. The new three-story Daniel Laven Building of the Yeshiva Beth Yehudah was dedicated. The school's enrollment topped 700, with over 400 in the Day School as the 1955 budget went over $250,000 for the first time.

M. Robert Syme, who became assistant rabbi to Rabbi Leon Fram of Temple Israel in 1953, began a daily prayer service in 1955. Around the same time, Syme founded the Temple Israel Hebrew School and was the only instructor of the school's 12 students, which included his son, Daniel. More congregants began following Rabbi Syme's optional introduction of traditional Judaism, such as wearing a prayer shawl and head covering during services.

In 1955, the Council of Orthodox Rabbis (Vaad Horabonim) recognized six kosher caterers. Four of

Congregation Beth Abraham relocated from Linwood to Seven Mile Road and Greenlawn in 1955.

(Courtesy Leonard N. Simons Jewish Community Archives)

the six were located on Dexter and one on Wyoming. Bel Aire was located on Woodward, within walking distance of the Jewish Community Center; Rainbow, on Wyoming south of Seven Mile Road; Moss on Dexter at Boston Boulevard; Horowitz on Dexter near Sturtevant; and Mayfair on Dexter near Waverly.

As 38 families subscribed $158,290 to raise funds for its new synagogue, Congregation B'nai David broke ground for the project on Southfield Road near Nine and a Half Mile. Congregation Beth Aaron enlarged its building on Wyoming south of Curtis. Congregation Beth Abraham relocated to its new building on Seven Mile Road and Greenlawn. The new synagogue, which offered three sections of seating at services, men, women, and mixed, didn't sit well with Rabbi Jacob Thumin, 81, who retired and remained in the Dexter section. Rabbi Israel Halpern, who came to Detroit in 1949, assumed spiritual leadership of the congregation in its new location. The former synagogue on Linwood was transferred to Young Israel ownership, which would use the facilities as a branch.

Rabbi Joseph Chinitz and the 250 families of Congregation Ahavas Achim were pleased that their synagogue on Schaefer was completed in time for the 1955 High Holidays. Congregation Emanuel-El held Sabbath services in the music room of Burt School in Huntington Woods, and when scheduling problems arose, in the Tyler School in Oak Park. Holiday services were held at the Methodist Church in Royal Oak.

Many of the temple's 375 families happily watched Rabbi Frank Rosenthal officiate at the cornerstone laying ceremony for the new building on Ten Mile Road in October. Congregation Beth Shalom, south Oakland County's only Conservative synagogue, held its 1955 High Holiday services at Carpenters Hall, on Twelve Mile Road south of Coolidge, under the direction of its new spiritual leader Rabbi Mordecai Halpern. When ground was broken for their new synagogue building on Lincoln in December, membership was close to 300 families.

Streetcars were history in 1956 as the Detroit Street Railway became completely motorized. Thousands turned out to witness Detroit's last streetcars screeching to a permanent halt on April 7, 1956. Mexico City offered more than a million dollars for 184 of Detroit's streetcars.

The 2,926-seat, newly-opened Henry and Edsel Ford Auditorium became the new home of the Detroit Symphony Orchestra, as the Ford Motor Company sold its common stock to the public for the first time. Wayne University became a state university in 1956 and dated its founding from 1868, when the School of Medicine opened.

The Labor Zionist Institute, on Schaefer North of Seven Mile Road, was dedicated. The three floors housed activities for Habonim Youth and offices for Farband, Histadrut, Pioneer Women, and United Jewish Folk Schools. Mayfair Kosher Caterers became ex-

With the new three-story annex in use, the Yeshiva Beth Yehudah playground was between its two buildings.

(Photo by author)

clusive caterers in the air-conditioned social hall, which had a seating capacity of 600. Sam Marcus, who was associated with Fresh Air Camp for the past three years, assumed the post of camp executive director in 1956.

Julian Krolik, past president of the Jewish Welfare Federation, was vice-president of the United Jewish Charities when he passed away a few month's shy of his 70th birthday in 1956. Krolik, who managed the wholesale Krolik Dry Goods company founded by his father, was a member of the boards of the Federation Detroit Service Group, Jewish Community Center, Jewish Community Council, North End Clinic, and Sinai Hospital at the time of his death. Also active in Zionist organizations, Krolik was a member of Temple Beth El. Gus Newman, active in many Jewish charities, owned a Ford dealership on Dexter but never learned to drive a car. In 1956, at the age of 65, Newman took up driving because his sister and brother-in-law moved to Oak Park. To help provide nursing staff for the 210-bed Sinai Hospital, the Shapero School of Nursing was officially dedicated in 1956.

Morton Plotnick, who had an outstanding scholastic and community service record, was awarded a scholarship to Wayne State University by the B'nai B'rith Young Adults. The WSU junior, who lived on Fullerton near Dexter, planned on using the scholarship to prepare for a career in teaching administration. The Detroit Lions signed Marvin Frankel to a 1956 football contract, pending a tryout when the team started workouts. Frankel, who starred for the Hillsdale College team from 1951 to 1954, was attending Wayne University Law School and working with his father in the Frankel Insurance Agency at the time of the signing. Walter Godfrey was invited to spring training with the Tigers and given a tryout. Godfrey's pitching abilities impressed team officials

Jews have proudly viewed Hank Greenberg's Baseball Hall of Fame plaque since 1956.

(Photo by author)

Cars were wider and longer in 1956, and prices were well under $3,000.

(Author's collection)

enough to offer him a minor league contract. However, an arm injury hindered his ability to throw at full speed, and Godfrey declined the contract. Byron Krieger, who was a fencer in the 1952 Helsinki Olympics, competed in the 1956 Games in Melbourne, becoming the only Jew from Michigan to participate in two Olympics. Hank Greenberg was inducted into the National Baseball Hall of Fame in Cooperstown, New York.

Adolph Deutsch's American Savings opened its newest branch, the sixth, at 13700 West Nine Mile Road, near Coolidge in Oak Park. Deutsch, active in Congregation B'nai Moshe for decades, celebrated his 75th birthday in 1956. Si Weingarden, a member of Temple Beth El and its Men's Club, celebrated his 75th birthday by operating his newsstands as always, in front of the Majestic Building at Woodward and Michigan. Bill Davidson, part of Guardian Industries, began full production of curved, laminated windshields. After receiving his undergraduate degree from Swarthmore College, Carl Levin went to Harvard to pursue a law degree.

When Rabbi S.P. Wohlgelernter arrived in 1956 to assume his brother's Yeshiva Beth Yehudah duties, Isidore Cohen already had served a three year term as president of the school, and his brother, Wolf Cohen, was the current president. Enrollment increased by a hundred over the previous year, to over 800 students. The United States Immigration Service recognized the Yeshiva, and students from Windsor began attending. After three years of planning, the United Jewish High School merged with the United Hebrew Schools. After conducting classes for a short time in the Rose Sittig Cohen branch of UHS, the combined high school relocated to the UHS Esther Berman Branch at 18977 Schaefer. Rabbi Sherwin Wine became assistant rabbi at Temple Beth El under Rabbi Richard Hertz. Rabbi Herbert Eskin, formerly with Mt. Sinai Congregation in Port Huron and Beth Shalom, became spiritual leader of the Evergreen Jewish Congregation.

The Ten Mile Branch of the Jewish Community Center was dedicated on October 21, 1956. Rabbis of the three synagogues in Oak Park—Rabbi Mordecai Halpern of Congregation Beth Shalom, Rabbi Yaakov Homnick of Young Israel of Oak Woods, and Rabbi Milton Rosenman of Temple Emanu-El—as well as John Marshall, Mayor of Oak Park, were some of the speakers. The Jewish National Fund of America announced a tree-planting effort concentrated in the Galilee hills region for each of Hadassah's 325,000 members. While the *Detroit News* referred to "Detroit's community of 85,000 Jews," in an article about the Suez crisis on Tuesday, October 30, 1956, a study by Albert J. Mayer of Detroit's Jewish population claimed it grew from around 75,000 in 1940 to 93,700 in 1956. Mayer also studied the community's branches of Judaism and concluded that 42 percent were Conservative, while those considering themselves Ortho-

The Ten Mile branch of the Jewish Community Center was dedicated in 1956.

(Courtesy Leonard N. Simons Jewish Community Archives)

dox and Reform accounted for 22 percent each.

As Egypt blocked the use of the Suez Canal to ships bound for Israeli ports, Jews fished for news. Leading up to the radio newscasts, the songs most often heard were Dean Martin's, "Memories Are Made of This," and Elvis Presley's "Love Me Tender."

In November, as Israel advanced into the Sinai peninsula and British and French troops landed at the northern end of the Suez Canal, retired British politician Winston Churchill, issued a statement that was picked up by many major newspapers:

In spite of all the efforts of Britain, France, and the United States, the frontiers of Israel have flickered with murder and armed raids. Egypt, the principal instigator of these incidents, rejected restraint. Israel, under the gravest provocation, erupted against Egypt. Our American friends will come to realize that, not for the first time, we have acted independently for the common good.

Earlier in the year, Churchill wrote to President Dwight D. Eisenhower and stated his feelings about Israel and the situation at the time:

I am, of course, a Zionist, and have been ever since the Balfour Declaration. I think it is a wonderful thing that this tiny colony of Jews should have become a refuge to their compatriots in all the lands where they were persecuted so cruelly, and at the same time established themselves as the most effective fighting force in the area. I am sure America would not stand by and see them overwhelmed by Russian weapons, especially if we had persuaded them to hold their hand while their chance remained.

In 1956 Detroit had a fourth major league franchise as the Fort Wayne Pistons basketball team became the Detroit Pistons and moved into Olympia Stadium. Detroit also gained Zollner Pistons, an automotive supply company, which produced 70 percent of all pistons used by America's truck manufacturers. Owner Fred Zollner thought Detroit would produce more revenue for both businesses.

Eastland Shopping Center opened in 1957, the same year Jimmy Hoffa became boss of the Teamsters Union. City Council president Louis C. Miriani was appointed mayor after the death of Albert E. Cobo, who died in office. The Max Fisher family moved from their Parkside home to the suburb of Franklin. Sidney Krandall and Sons, located on Second Avenue in Highland Park,, celebrated their 50th year in the jewelry business. "The Ten Commandments," starring Charlton Heston and Yul Brynner, was enjoying a run of several months on a reserved seat basis at the Madison Theater downtown. A year after the breakup of the team of crooner Dean Martin and comedian Jerry Lewis, the gangly comedian came to Detroit for a cocktail party at the home of Mr. and Mrs. Tom Borman on behalf of Israel Bonds.

In 1957, Jack A. Robinson, a 27-year-old pharmacist, founded his first in what would be a chain of Perry Drug Stores. The location was in the city of Pontiac at Perry Street and East Boulevard. The "Lou Gordon News," presented each midnight on WXYZ-TV, was making television history as Gordon became the first commentator to work without a prepared script. The 12-man Israeli Olympic basketball team visited Detroit to play an exhibition game against the "Michigan All Stars," at University of Detroit's fieldhouse. After Emma Schaver sang the national anthems of both countries, Walter Godfrey starred for the locals and the Israelis were defeated 82 to 58 before a crowd of 6,100.

Two years after he received special recognition for donating a half million dollars for the establishment of the Shapero School of Nursing, Nate S. Shapero celebrated his 65th birthday. Shapero and his wife, Ruth, were members of Temple Beth El and associated with numerous charitable causes. In 1957 Shapero's Cunningham's and its subsidiaries exceeded 195 stores. The Young Adult Department of the Jewish Community Center held a social dance at the Ten Mile Branch. Jack Levin and his orchestra played several of the hits of '57 suited to the event including, Pat Boone's "April Love," and "Love Letters in the Sand," Paul Anka's "Diana," and Sam Cooke's "You Send Me."

One of the most popular residents ever at the Jewish Home for the Aged, Isaac Nagel, died in his sleep at the age of 110. Born in Poland in 1847, Nagel came to the United States almost a half century later and made his living as a Hebrew teacher. Nagel and his wife, who lived to be 103, became residents of the

Cheerful Isaac Nagel at his 105th birthday in 1952. He passed away in 1957.

(Courtesy Leonard N. Simons Jewish Community Archives)

Rabbi Moses Fischer died at the age of 77 in 1957.

(Author's collection)

Home in 1937. Despite cataracts which had caused blindness five years earlier, Nagel was cheerful and alert and able to conduct religious services when called upon. He left a son, two daughters, 18 grandchildren, 22 great-grandchildren, and three great-great-grandchildren.

Henry Wineman, who operated People's Outfitting Company, one of Michigan's leading mercantile establishments, died at the age of 78. Wineman was active in many Jewish and civic causes. The flag on the Butzel Building of the Jewish Welfare Federation on Madison was at half mast in tribute to Wineman, who financed the study which led to the formation of the Jewish Welfare Federation in 1925. Mrs. Ernestine Krolik Kahn, widow of famed architect Albert Kahn who had died 15 years earlier, died at the age of 88. Mrs. Kahn graduated from the University of Michigan in 1892 and was married four years later.

Harry F. Sucher, co-founder and chairman of the board of the Speedway Petroleum Corporation, died. A native of Austria, he opened a hay and feed store that later became a coal yard. As the automobile age was ushered in, a gas station was opened adjacent to the coal yard. It marked the beginning of what would grow into the largest independent gasoline company in the world, with over 800 stations in 1957. Speedway "79" signs and billboards were in many Detroit locations. A member of Congregation Adas Shalom, Sucher was also involved in many community causes.

In 1947 the Jewish Welfare Federation allocated $118,850 to the United Hebrew Schools. Ten years later, one year after Albert Elazar became superintendent after the retirement of Bernard Isaacs, the allocation was $324,894. Almost 2,900 students were enrolled in the UHS in 1957, an increase of close to 300 over the previous year. The Federation also supported the afternoon school programs of the United Jewish Folk School and Yeshiva Beth Yehudah, with subsidies totaling $33,000.

The Yeshiva Beth Yehudah sponsored the opening of the Hebrew Academy, a day school serving the Northwest and suburban areas. Rabbi Hayim Donin, of Congregation B'nai David, was instrumental in launching the schools, which taught the modern Hebrew language. The operational budget of all departments of the Yeshiva was put at $280,000 as enrollment was close to 900. The Yeshiva and the community was saddened by the passing of Rabbi Moses Fischer, chairman of the Board of Education and former spiritual leader of Congregation B'nai Moshe.

As Israel evacuated the Sinai and United Nations observers were placed on the border with Egypt, Shaarey Zedek purchased a 40-acre site on Northwestern Highway and Eleven Mile Road. Congregation B'nai Moshe chose Ralph Fortney as architect for its new synagogue on Ten Mile Road at Kenosha. Fortney was the architect for both Adas Shalom on Curtis and Congregation Ahavas Achim on Schaefer. After changing its name from the Suburban Temple three years earlier, Temple Emanu-El grew at a rapid pace and dedicated its completed structure in 1957. Remarks were given by spiritual leaders of the areas Reform Temples, as well as rabbis of Oak Park's Congregation Beth Shalom and Young Israel of Oak Woods.

The Downtown Synagogue was forced to move to the seventh floor of the David Stott Building on Griswold and State as their former location was razed. Because of the death of Rabbi Herman Rosenwasser, Rabbi Leo Steinhauser, a graduate of the Hebrew Rabbinical College of Wurtzberg, Germany, was named spiritual leader. Rabbi Shraga Kahana, spiritual leader of Congregation Nusach Hari on Holmur and Duane, passed away in 1957. The Labor Zionist Institute Building on Schaefer and Seven Mile Road was officially named in memory of Hayim Greenberg. Congregation Shomrey Emunah, formed by Rabbi Sholom Flam, a teacher at Yeshiva Beth Yehudah a year earlier, was holding services in the auditorium. Rabbi Flam's brother Israel, also on staff of the Yeshiva Beth Yehudah, was spiritual leader of Congregation B'nai Israel, which relocated from Linwood to a farmhouse and garage on Ten Mile Road east of Greenfield in 1955.

Irwin Shaw, executive director of the Jewish Community Centers, presented a shovel to Samuel Frankel, chairman of the building committees, to turn the first shovelful of dirt for the $2,500,000 Jewish Community Center, on Curtis and Meyers, on December 1, 1957.

Hank Greenberg, an executive with the Cleveland Indians since 1948, became part owner of the Chicago White Sox in 1958. For the second year in a row, the six branches of American Savings were giving three percent interest on savings accounts while most Detroit area banks were holding at a half-percent less. Emma Schaver, the Jewish world's renowned concert soprano, participated in the celebration of the arrival in New York of the *S.S. Theodor Herzl's* maiden voyage. Festivities were held in the Zim liner's ballroom and included Israeli and New York civic leaders.

Joseph Adler, a 40-year veteran of the Detroit Fire Department who rose through the ranks to become Battalion Chief and Deputy Fire Chief, was appointed fire chief in 1958. Rabbi Joshua Sperka, former spiritual leader of Congregation B'nai David, retired from his 17-year post as Jewish chaplain to state prison inmates. Rabbi Morris Shapiro, of Jackson's Temple Beth Israel, assumed Sperka's duties. Stanley Winkelman's father, Leon W, died suddenly of a heart

(1957 advertisements courtesy of *Jewish News*)

attack at the age of 63. Relatives, friends, employees, and customers of the 30-year-old Winkelman chain were part of the more than 800 in attendance in Temple Beth El's Brown Chapel. Harry Weinberg oversaw "Weinberg's Yiddish Hour" until his retirement in 1955. His oldest son, Robert, continued the program until September 1958.

Dedication exercises of the Hebrew Academy of Oak Park, an affiliate of the Yeshiva Beth Yehudah, was attended by over 300 people. The building, at 13855 West Nine Mile Road west of Coolidge, was named in honor of Peter and Pauline Goldstein. The yeshiva also opened a branch in Livonia at the Botsford School, on Lathers Road, three blocks north of Seven Mile Road. With the branch at Young Israel of Northwest Detroit on Wyoming, and the day school operating from Dexter and Cortland, the yeshiva had over 900 pupils in 1958.

Avern L. Cohn, one of the community's active younger leaders was appointed chairman of the annual Jewish National Fund Conference. Much of the conference revolved around the role of youth in Jewish communal life and Israel. Seymour Greenstein, 17, a member of the Congregation B'nai David choir and a student at Wayne State University, was accepted into membership in the Michigan Opera Company of Detroit. Greenstein's father operated the Golden Valley Dairy Company. John E. Lurie, who opened his first self-service supermarket in 1937 and was executive vice-president of the ACF-Wrigley Stores, Inc., in 1958, was honored by Yeshiva University for donating a chemistry laboratory in memory of his mother. Lurie, affiliated with Congregations Adas Shalom, Shaarey Zedek, and Temple Beth El, helped develop Super-Sol Limited, the first supermarket in Tel Aviv, Israel. The Borman brothers, heads of Food Fair Supermarkets, announced a store expansion program expected to create nearly a thousand additional jobs.

Max Fisher, Allied Jewish Campaign chairman, and seven other Detroiters including Paul Zuckerman and Jack O. Lefton, were among members of the 1958 United Jewish Appeal Mission to Israel. Fisher celebrated his 50th birthday and the marriage of his daughter, Jane, to Larry Sherman in 1958. David Hermelin and Doreen Curtis were united in marriage by Rabbis Morris Adler and Moses Lehrman. In 1958, couples danced to "All I Have to Do is Dream," by the Everly Brothers, and "Volare (Nel Blu Diponto Di Blu)," by Domenico Modugno.

Guided spiritually for 35 years by Rabbi Isaac Stollman, Congregation Mishkan Israel began building its new synagogue in Oak Park on Nine Mile Road, between Parklawn and Cloverlawn. Services were still being held at the Blaine, just west of Linwood location. Rabbi Stollman was spending much of his time in New York in his role as president of Mizrachi-Hapoel Mizrachi Organization of America.

Abraham Nusbaum Dies at 57; Was Bar-Ilan Founder; JNF Forest in Israel Planted in His Honor

Abraham Nusbaum, of 4216 W. Outer Drive, one of the community's most distinguished orthodox and Mizrachi leaders, died Monday morning at the age of 57, after a long illness. Funeral services were held Tuesday morning at Congregation Beth Abraham.

The large sanctuary was filled to overflowing. Officiating at the service were Rabbis Israel I. Halpern and Joseph Thumim and Cantors Shabtai Ackerman and Leibele Waldman. The latter, for many years a close friend of the deceased, came here from New York to pay tribute to Mr. Nusbaum's memory.

Born in Poland, the departed leader came to Detroit in 1926 and established the New York Linoleum and Carpet Co. on Jos. Campau. The firm has since grown to five stores in Detroit and Lansing.

At the time of his death, Mr. Nusbaum was president of Congregation Beth Abraham. He was an officer in the local and national Mizrachi-Hapoel Hamizrachi Organization, was active in the Jewish National Fund, Young Israel, Pisgah Lodge of Bnai Brith and served on the boards of Chesed shel Emes, the Yeshivot Beth Yehudah and Chachmey Lubien and Congregation Ahavas Achim.

A forest was planted in his honor several years ago by the Jewish National Fund in Israel.

One of the founders of the Israel Bar-Ilan University, he was chairman of the Detroit Bar-Ilan Committee. He established a science lecture hall in this university in Israel, and was one of the most generous contributors to it and one of the most ardent workers in its behalf.

Active in many communal affairs, he was a former president of the Yiddish Folks Ferein.

Surviving him are his wife, Laura; son, Irving; daughter, Mrs. Joseph Fetter; two brothers, Max and Solomon, and three grandchildren.

ABRAHAM NUSBAUM

Abraham Nusbaum, who opened his first linoleum store in 1927, became a respected businessman and community leader.

(1958 article courtesy of *Jewish News*)

Rabbi Jacob Chinitz, who became spiritual leader of Congregation Ahavas Achim in 1952, resigned but announced he would stay with the congregation until another rabbi was chosen. Rabbi Hayim Donin and Cantor Hyman Adler officiated at the transfer of Torahs to the new synagogue of Congregation B'nai David on Southfield Road and Mt. Vernon. Three Torahs were kept in the ark of the 14th and Elmhurst location for the remaining residents still using the synagogue for daily and sabbath services.

As plans for a $3,500,000 synagogue on a 40-acre Southfield site were being finalized by leaders of Congregation Shaarey Zedek, Philip Hart, lieutenant governor of Michigan, and other local officials participated in the groundbreaking ceremonies of Congregation B'nai Moshe on Ten Mile Road at Kenosha. Young Israel of Greenfield, which owned land a few blocks west toward Greenfield, was holding weekly services in private homes.

Farther east on Ten Mile, between Kipling and Gardner, Congregation Shaarey Shomayim's building was finally under way after several false starts. The synagogue was an ambitious project for a membership small in number and high in age. Disbanded for a number of years, the congregation at its previous Muirland near Fenkell location was known for its scholarly members and Cantor Benjamin Moldawsky. Recently hired as spiritual leader after five years of serving Northwest Young Israel, Rabbi Leo Goldman undertook trying to rebuild membership and an educational program. The school portion of the building was completed in time for High Holiday services.

Founded in the home of its first president, Josef Horowitz, in 1951, the Evergreen Jewish Congregation grew to close to 200 families in 1958. Services were held in the Mettatal School and St. Matthew's Church. A few months after groundbreaking on its site on Evergreen, just north of Seven Mile Road, Rabbi Hyman Agress replaced Rabbi Herbert Eskin as spiritual leader. Israel celebrated its tenth birthday in 1958, and its Jewish population was put at 1,719,624. According to Dr. Albert J. Mayer, a professor of Wayne State who engaged in a long study, northwest Detroit accounted for 62 percent of the metropolitan area's Jews, and the Dexter neighborhood diminished to only nine percent. Dexter Chevrolet joined the exodus as the Chevy dealership relocated to Eight Mile Road.

In 1959, as the first grade and kindergarten classes of the new Hillel Day School were completing their first semester year, Kern's Department Store on Woodward south of Hudson's disbanded. Detroit police patrol car teams were racially integrated for the first time, and the Detroit Tigers baseball team had its first ever African-American player.

Alfred Epstein retired as president of the Pfeiffer Brewing Company in 1959 at the age of 64. His son, Herbert, assumed the presidency of the company. Drinkers quipped that the difference between Stroh's beer and Pfeiffer was that one was "fire-brewed and the other was heb-brewed." Fred Ferber founded House of Imports Corporation, which imported electronics from Japan for distribution in the United

Penny Bernstein became Penny Blumenstein and president of the Jewish Welfare Federation decades later.

(1958 article courtesy of *Jewish News*)

States. Brothers Emery and Eugene Klein founded Alaron, Inc., an international electronics company. Max Fisher negotiated a merger of the Aurora and Ohio oil companies, which became known as the Marathon Oil Company.

Judge Victor Baum was reelected to the Wayne County Circuit Court bench, Charles N. Kaufman was elected Common Pleas judge, and John M. Wise became Traffic Court referee. The 106-bed Shiffman Clinic wing of Sinai Hospital opened and the services formerly provided by the North End Clinic were transferred to the Shiffman Clinic. Ilka Chase, actress, author, and television personality, and film star Jeff Chandler participated in the France-Israel Fashion Festival Dinner Dance at the Knollwood Country Club. More than 300 Israel Bond Trustees, Builders of Israel, guardians, and sponsors attended. Admission was open only to those who purchased a minimum of a thousand dollars in Israel Bonds for 1959.

Bertha Robinson, who was principal of Central High School from 1952 through 1958, became principal of Henry Ford High School in 1959. Miss Robinson's sister, Mrs. Sarah Fagin, was on the English staff of the Yeshiva Beth Yehudah Day School.

(1959 advertisement courtesy of *Jewish News*)

The *Tamar* of the Zim American Lines became the first Israeli ship to arrive in the port of Detroit. The ship, with an all-Israeli crew of 35, only stayed a few hours on May 18, 1959, before sailing on to Toledo.

Because of its bathhouses, Mt. Clemens was a popular tourist destination in the summer and around the Passover holiday. Hotels such as the Arethusa, Colonial, Kraemer's Olympic Hotel, and Max and Sam Madorsky's Riverside Hotel catered to those who kept kosher dietary laws and those who desired kosher cuisine in addition to mineral baths.

A bitter dispute over mixed seating during religious services at Congregation Beth Tephilath Moses kept Mt. Clemens in the news in 1959. The four-year fight led to reduced membership and to a state Supreme Court ruling to resolve the issue. The Supreme Court opinion, written by Justice Thomas M. Kavanagh, recognized that a tenet of Orthodox Judaism was separate seating for men and women during services and that the congregation was defined as Orthodox. Baruch Litvin, who spent his own money fighting the seating battle in the courts, said of the victory: "No synagogue in Michigan, which is constitutionally designated as Orthodox, can now attempt to seat men and women together." A synagogue board member said of Litvin: "His victory has won him a congregation but lost him the congregants."

The death of Nathan W. Lurie was mourned by rabbis of Detroit's Orthodox, Conservative, and Reform community. Funeral services for the member of two Conservative synagogues were held at Temple Beth El and conducted by Dr. Richard C. Hertz. Lurie was a generous supporter of the Orthodox day school movement and active in Zionist causes and the Jewish Welfare Federation. Lurie helped develop the Supersol Supermarket in Tel Aviv, and in a tribute to his memory, the supermarket was closed during the hour of the funeral service. Solomon Chesluk, one of Detroit's Jewish bookstore pioneers, died two days after the passing of his longtime friend, Isaac Herzog, the Chief Rabbi of Israel. Rabbi Abraham Hershman, former spiritual leader of Congregation Shaarey Zedek, died at the age of 79 in New York, where he had been living for the past two years with his daugh-

Rabbi Leizer Levin, head of the Council of Orthodox Rabbis in 1959, was often called on to settle disputes.

(Author's collection)

ters. His body was brought back to Detroit, where it was estimated 1,200 people turned out for the funeral services and burial. Rabbi Hershman's wife, one of the first presidents of Detroit Chapter of Hadassah, had died five years earlier.

Congregation Dovid Ben Nuchim, which was renting a storefront on Dexter near Sturtevant, bought Congregation Beth Shmuel's synagogue across the street and less than two blocks north. The Livonia Jewish Congregation, holding services in the Clarenceville Central Elementary School since 1958, officially organized in 1959. High Holiday services were held in a tent on the grounds of the Botsford Inn. Beth Aaron enlarged its building and absorbed the 22 members of the defunct Congregation Shaarey Zion, which had abandoned its Linwood location a year earlier. While continuing to reside in the Dexter section, Rabbi Solomon Gruskin, spiritual leader of Congregation B'nai Zion on Humphrey and Holmur, opened a branch on Seven Mile Road near Mendota. Rabbi Milton Arm, who served under Rabbi Morris Adler at Congregation Shaarey Zedek since 1954, assumed the pulpit of Congregation Ahavas Achim in 1959. After seven years of meetings in basements, school auditoriums, and a church social hall, the first wing—the social hall—of the Evergreen Jewish Congregation building was completed in April 1959.

The Curtis and Meyers Jewish Community Center opened with 10,000 members, and board members voted to open the Center on Saturday afternoons. Many leading rabbis from Detroit's branches of Judaism appealed to the board to reverse its decision. Rabbi Leizer Levin, of Congregation Beth Tefilo Emanuel Tikvah, was part of a committee settling on a compromise with the board of the Center. The building would remain open Saturday afternoons to only cultural and religious programs permitted under religious law, but the parking lot would remain closed.

Congregation B'nai Moshe honored Adolph Deutsch by naming the synagogue chapel after him at dedication ceremonies of the new building. 1959 also marked the tenth year of Rabbi Moses Lehrman as spiritual leader of the congregation. The Lehrman family took up residence on Gardner in Oak Park, a not-too-distant walk from the synagogue's Ten Mile Road location. Young Israel of Greenfield, which was holding services at the Ten Mile Road Jewish Community Center, held groundbreaking ceremonies at its Ten Mile site west of the Center. Congregation Shaarey Shomayim dedicated its new sanctuary and classrooms in September. Spiritual leader Rabbi Leo Goldman, Rabbi Leizer Levin, Chairman of the Vaad Harabonim (Council of Orthodox Rabbis), and Mayor Alexander of Oak Park were among those addressing those assembled.

Three-year-old Congregation Shomrey Emunah

The Curtis and Meyers Jewish Community Center opened in 1959 with 10,000 members.

(Courtesy of Jewish Community Center)

ECHOES OF DETROIT'S JEWISH COMMUNITIES

Rabbi Sholem Flam's Congregation Shomrey Emunah built its synagogue on Schaefer in 1959.

(Photo by author)

completed its new synagogue on Schaefer south of Seven Mile Road. A mile west and a few blocks north, groundbreaking for the first synagogue building of Congregation Gemiluth Chassodim was held at the proposed site at Greenfield and Vassar Drive. Most of the 250 members of the congregation were born in Germany and neighboring countries. Services, which previously were held at the D. W. Simons Building on Tuxedo and Holmur, were moved about a mile north to the Davison Jewish Center pending completion of the new building.

Dr. Albert Mayer of Wayne State University released an updated survey in 1959 putting the area's Jewish population at 93,700, with 27,000 families. The associate professor of sociology's chart of age composition showed 28,700 persons (31 percent) under the age of 15; 8,400 (9 percent) between 15 and 24; 24,700 (26 per cent) between 25 and 44; 25,400 (27 percent) between 45 and 64; and 6,500 (7 percent) over the age of 65.

In November 1959, the large, long-awaited, newest link in the Dexter-Davison chain opened in Oak Park at Ten Mile Road and Coolidge. The 30,000-plus square foot supermarket was staffed by 110 employees.

Dexter-Davison's Oak Park store opened in November 1959.

(Courtesy of Sylvia Cohen)

15

1960-1969
THE SIXTIES

While Jews were relocating to northwest Detroit and further into the northern suburbs, black families were moving to Detroit. For the first time in the century, Detroit's population declined from the previous decade. The 9.6 percent decline left 1,670,144 Detroiters, including 482,229 black residents, who now made up 23 percent of Detroit's population.

Oak Park offered eight houses of Jewish worship in 1960: Young Israel of Oak Woods, Young Israel of Greenfield, Congregation B'nai Israel, Congregation Mishkan Israel and Congregation Shaarey Shomayim comprised the five Orthodox synagogues. Congregation Beth Shalom and Congregation B'nai Moshe were the two Conservative synagogues, and Temple Emanu-El was Reform.

Young Israel had four locations in 1960—Dexter, Northwest, Oak Woods, and Greenfield. With the dedication of the Greenfield building at 15150 West Ten Mile Road, each had its own building. Rabbi Samuel Prero, formerly of the Dexter branch, was installed as spiritual leader of Young Israel of Northwest Detroit on Wyoming north of McNichols. Under Rabbi Prero's direction, the synagogue embarked on a building program to provide more room for worshippers, meetings, and school rooms. Rabbi Prero also undertook the additional duties of director of the Young Israel Council of Metropolitan Detroit.

Oscar Kanat, president of Congregation Beth Shalom, named a planning commission to work with New York architect Percival Goodman to create a sanctuary for the synagogue, an addition to its present building on Lincoln in Oak Park. In 1960 Temple Beth

Congregation B'nai Israel was a short walk west of the new Young Israel of Greenfield.

(Courtesy of Leonard N. Simons Jewish Community Archives)

The Young Israel of Greenfield dedicated its building in 1960.

By 1960 the Mercury Theater on Schaefer near Six Mile Road became the favorite movie house for Jewish Detroiters.

(Courtesy of Manning Brothers Historic Photographic Collection)

The smaller Royal Theater on Seven Mile Road near Meyers was within walking distance for many Jewish families.

(Courtesy of Manning Brothers Historic Photographic Collection)

El claimed a membership of 1,305 families and was the fourth-largest Reform Jewish congregation in the United States. Almost 2,000 persons witnessed the colorful procession led by Rabbi Chaskel Grubner from Congregation Dovid Ben Nuchim's rented quarters, on Dexter and Cortland, north on Dexter to its new location. The congregation bought the former Beth Shmuel Synagogue on Dexter and Buena Vista. As the exodus from the Dexter neighborhood continued, many families concentrated in the blocks around Cortland to Buena Vista which housed the Young Israel and Yeshiva Beth Yehudah.

Baruch Litvin, the Mt. Clemens businessman who won a lengthy court battle against mixed seating of the sexes in Mt. Clemens' Congregation Beth Tefilas Moses, wrote a book describing his struggle. *The Sanctity of the Synagogue,* a 442-page English volume with Hebrew appendia, contained the contributions of many rabbinical authorities and Biblical passages.

Max and Julian Nusbaum, who opened a small, 20-by-20 foot store on Vernor and Central in 1946 handling remnants and short rolls, opened their fourth store. Central, named after the original location, mushroomed into Michigan's largest dealer of Bigelow Carpeting. Holocaust survivor Abe Pasternak, who came to the United States in 1947 with seven dollars in his pocket, started his own business—King Tire Center in Pontiac. In 1960 ACF-Wrigley became Allied Supermarkets, Inc., as it acquired more grocery businesses in other states. Borman Foods went public and purchased Detroit Pure Milk Company, Wesley Quaker Maid Ice Cream, and Arnold Drugstores.

Herman Radner, a former treasurer of the Allied Jewish Campaign, died of cancer in Ford Hospital at the age of 67. Active in community affairs in Detroit and Windsor, Radner provided free meals to hundreds of needy persons in the depression years of 1932 and 1933 when he was president of the Walkerville Brewery, Ltd. A member of Congregation Shaarey Zedek, civic, and Jewish groups, Radner operated a downtown hotel. The family sat shiva at their home on Wildemere north of Six Mile Road. Fifteen years later, Herman's daughter, Gilda, would make her debut on NBC's "Saturday Night Live."

Mrs. Gunia Pesis was married to Jacob Ringer in Lithuania when she gave birth to a daughter in a concentration camp in 1942. Her husband and other men in the village were shot, and the baby was smuggled out of the camp when it became known that all children were to be executed. The baby, named Feiga, was found and taken by an aunt to Russia. Feiga's mother was sent to Dachau where she eventually met her present husband. In 1960, after years of trying and numerous appeals from politicians and vice-president Nixon, the Russians finally granted Feiga an exit permit, and mother and daughter embraced for the first time outside of a Nazi concentration camp.

Adolph Eichmann was kidnapped to Israel to stand trial for war crimes. The Israel Philharmonic Orchestra toured several American cities, including Detroit. The orchestra was the featured attraction at the annual Balfour Concert of the Zionist Organization of Detroit at the Masonic Auditorium. An estimated crowd of fifteen hundred people jammed the

The multi-story American flag on the Woodward side of the Hudson's store was a familiar sight to downtown shoppers for decades. Even though Detroit was losing population to the suburbs in 1960, all major downtown stores were operating.

(Courtesy of Michigan Views)

In September 1960, 1,500 people attended the festive dedication ceremonies of Congregation B'nai Moshe at Ten Mile and Kenosha in Oak Park.

(Photo by author)

Seven convertibles, each holding one of the Sifre Torah from Congregation Gemiluth Chassodim, were part of a motorcade to the new synagogue at Greenfield and Vassar Drive.

(Courtesy of Benno Levi)

The Gemiluth Chassodim Synagogue at Greenfield north of Seven Mile.

(Photo by author)

Adas Shalom social hall to celebrate Israel's twelfth anniversary. Almost 600 were turned away and milled about on Curtis.

In 1960, Fresh Air Camp was renamed "Fair Acres Camp," and Marvin Berman became program director. Walter E. Klein, who joined the staff of the Jewish Community Council in 1945, was appointed executive director of the Council. Stanley J. Winkelman became president of the Council in 1960. The Book Fair moved from the Davison Jewish Community Center to the Curtis and Meyers building. 25,010 donors contributed $4,865,717 to the 1960 Allied Jewish Campaign of the Jewish Welfare Federation.

Robinson Furniture Company celebrated its 50th business anniversary by honoring its president, Louis Robinson, at a dinner at the Statler Hotel near the company's main building on Washington Boulevard. Originally known as the Robinson-Cohen Company at its founding on Hastings and High street, the company moved to the Washington Boulevard location thirteen years later. Cobo Hall, Detroit's large exhibition hall named after the late Mayor Albert E. Cobo, opened in August and hosted the National Auto Show.

An estimated 60,000 people crowded into the Campus Martius area on a sunny Labor Day to hear Democratic hopeful John F. Kennedy speak in front of old City Hall. The following month, thousands lined both sides of Woodward to catch a glimpse of President Dwight D. Eisenhower stand up and wave from a slow-moving open-top limousine. In November, the *Detroit Times* ceased publication and was bought by the *Detroit News,* which raised its price by a penny to eight cents. The generation of Detroiters who grew up with the Howdy Doody puppet program were saddened by NBC's decision to end the show's 13-year run. While Elvis Presley had several top tunes on the charts, including "It's Now or Never," and "Are You Lonesome Tonight?" Chubby Checker introduced the Twist.

The Evergreen Jewish Congregation dedicated its new social hall earlier in the year. In December it merged with Congregation Beth Moses, which was located on Linwood. The merged congregations would use the Evergreen facilities and be known as Congregation Beth Moses,

On the first day of 1961, Briggs Stadium was officially renamed Tiger Stadium. Singer Diana Ross of the Supremes bought a two-flat home for her family on Buena Vista, two houses off Dexter near the synagogue of Congregation Dovid Ben Nuchim. Irwin I. Cohn, 65, a counsel member of the law firm of Honigman, Miller, Schwartz, and Cohn, and active in Jewish and civic causes, received the Fred M. Butzel Award from the Jewish Welfare Federation. On that day, February 6, 1961, Irwin I. Cohn Day was proclaimed in Detroit, and he was named a Detroit Hon-

Congregation Beth Tefilah Emanuel Tikvah remodeled a building on Wyoming south of Seven Mile road into a synagogue in 1961.

(Courtesy of Joe Kramer)

orary Citizen.

Standard Federal was offering three and a half percent interest on savings accounts. A popular branch among the Jewish community was on Schaefer near the Mercury Theater. David T., James M., and Joseph Z. Nederlander, managers of the Shubert, Riviera, and other theaters around the country, oversaw the transformation of the Fisher Theater to a playhouse. Movie star Jeff Chandler, born as Ira Grosel in Brooklyn 42 years earlier, died of complications following surgeries of a ruptured spinal disc in a Hollywood hospital. Chandler often visited major cities, including Detroit, on behalf of Jewish causes. In lieu of flowers, the family requested that contributions be made to the United Jewish Appeal.

Detroiters celebrated the 13th (Bar Mitzvah) anniversary of Israel's independence in the Mumford High School Auditorium on Wyoming south of Curtis. Max Fisher, 53, was named chairman of the Torch Drive, the first time in the history of Detroit that a Jew was selected to head the philanthropic organization. Besides working on behalf of the Federation and on Israel's development through the Jewish Agency, Fisher was the biggest donor to the Shaarey Zedek building fund. Tom Borman, president of Food Fair of Michigan, accepted the post of general chairman of the Detroit Israel Bond Committee. Outgoing chairman David Safran was honored at the Bar Mitzvah of Israel banquet at the Sheraton Cadillac hotel. The Detroit Chapter of Hadassah honored Dora Ehrlich on her 80th birthday at the Sheraton Cadillac. Seven years earlier, Mrs. Ehrlich was saluted for her 50 years of distinguished service and leadership to Hadassah. In her honor, the Dora Ehrlich Operating Theater was established as part of Detroit's Chapter Orthopedic Surgical Wing in Jerusalem's new medical center.

The five-year-old Regal drug stores, founded by Sidney Dworkin, Isadore Berger, Arthur Kellman, and Bernie Shulman, acquired the 41-state Standard drug chain in Cleveland in 1961. The combined chain was renamed Revco (Registered Vitamin Company). According to Board of Education figures, Mumford High School, which opened in 1949, had 3,201 white students and 616 black students in 1961. The Yeshiva Beth Yehudah defeated Oak Park High School on Channel 4's Sunday TV program, "Quiz 'Em." The quiz contest on current events involved five high school students from each school. The most popular musical tunes among high school students in 1961 were "Big Bad John," by Jimmy Dean; "Hit The Road Jack," by Ray Charles; "Runaway," by Del Shannon; and "The Lion Sleeps Tonight," by the Tokens.

Michigan Senator Charles Blondy charged that a pending bill in the State Senate that provided for "humane slaughter" was inspired by manufacturers of "stun guns." Blondy told the Jewish News that the

Bulldozers started demolishing the old City Hall along Michigan Avenue in September 1961.

(Photo by Harry Wolf)

devices to render animals insensible before being killed were not being sold "fast enough." Blondy sponsored two amendments that assured protection for continued ritual Jewish slaughter.

As the parade of witnesses took the stand in the lengthy Eichmann trial in Jerusalem, the judge requested that each cover his head with a yarmulke while taking an oath over the Hebrew bible. As evidence of more atrocities were uncovered in Jerusalem, *My Story*, a book by Gemma LaGuardia Gluck, dominated conversation among many women's groups in Detroit. Mrs. Gluck, the sister of the former mayor of New York, was born in New York in 1881 to a Jewish mother and Italian father. Her father's position as U.S. Army bandmaster took the family to Europe, where she remained behind and married a Hungarian Jew. The couple had a daughter, who also married a Jew. The Nazis sent both couples to the notorious Ravensbruck concentration camp. Months after their liberation, the women—who survived only because the Nazis feared reprisals if they killed relatives of New York's mayor—learned that their husbands were murdered by the Nazis. Shortly before his death in 1946, Fiorello LaGuardia was able to bring his sister and niece to New York.

Fresh Air Camp, which was renamed "Fair Acres Camp," in 1960, was renamed Camp Tamarack at Brighton in 1961. After about two years of meetings with rabbis, laymen, and the board of the Curtis-Meyers branch of the Jewish Community Center regarding which Saturday activities could be allowed at the Center, the board voted 27 to 8 to open the Center on Saturday afternoons after 1 p.m. The Northwest Child Rescue Women began a program for people with special needs at the JCC.

Mandel L. Berman, president of the United Hebrew Schools, and Wolf Cohen, president of Yeshiva Beth Yehudah, announced the affiliation of the Afternoon Hebrew Schools they represented. The Yeshiva would continue to develop its own afternoon curriculum under the supervision of the UHS. The affiliation did not affect the Yeshiva Day School. Rabbi Moses Rothenberg, dean of Yeshivath Chachmey Lublin, announced plans to move from the school's Linwood and Elmhurst location to a projected new campus in Southfield at Greenfield and Lincoln. Morris Lachover, a member of the faculty of the United Hebrew Schools for almost 40 years, died at the age of 59. Lachover helped organize the B'nai Moshe branch of the school and served as its principal.

Prominent attorney Leo I. Franklin, son of the late spiritual leader of Temple Beth El, was elected president of the temple at its 111th annual meeting of the congregation. Beth El lost two of its well-known members in the same week with the passing of Leo M. Butzel and Miles Finsterwald. The latter, who was 63 at the time of his death, was president of the Fintex Corporation founded by his father. In 1961, the company had 20 men's stores in Detroit and Pittsburgh. Butzel, one of the area's best known lawyers and financiers, was 86 years old.

Temple Israel dedicated two additions to its Manderson Road facilities. The Harry Sucher School and Sarah Schmier Memorial Chapel were part of the third phase of the temple's building program. The Livonia Jewish Congregation purchased land, a structure, and a farmhouse on Seven Mile Road and Osmus and hired Rabbi Nathaniel Steinberg as spiritual leader. Congregation Beth Tefilah Emanuel Tikvah, led by Rabbi Leizer Levin, moved from its Petoskey location in the Dexter section to Wyoming at Margareta, two blocks south of Seven Mile Road.

The process of planning the new Shaarey Zedek facility on Northwestern Highway began in April 1958. More than three years later, construction on the huge complex began. The congregation also celebrated its one hundredth anniversary in 1961. Celebrating their fiftieth anniversaries were Congregation B'nai Moshe and Congregation Mogen Abraham.

Morris Schaver, founder of the Central Factory and Overall Supply Company and first president of the Labor Zionist Organization of Detroit, died at the age of 67 on Saturday, October 28, 1961. Schaver and his wife of 37 years, Emma, the talented opera singer, were active in numerous causes on behalf of Israel and local organizations. More than a thousand people packed the Morris L. Schaver Auditorium of the Hayim Greenberg Labor Zionist Institute on Schaefer to hear

Rabbi Morris Adler and others deliver eulogies.

Jack Faxon, 25, took a leave of absence from teaching civics and history at Southwestern High School to become the youngest delegate ever to the Michigan Constitutional Convention. Mel Ravitz, professor of sociology at Wayne State University, was elected to the Detroit Common Council. Dr. Ravitz became the first Jew to serve on the council since David W. Simons in 1920.

Jerome P. Cavanaugh, a 33-year-old attorney, scored a stunning upset over Mayor Louis Miriani to win a four-year term as Detroit's chief executive. Cavanaugh, who lived on Wisconsin near Thatcher in the Six Mile-Wyoming area next door to Rabbi Ernest Greenfield, put his house up for sale, as he now could afford a more impressive residence, while earning $25,000 a year as the mayor of Detroit.

In 1962, Astronaut John Glenn became the first American to orbit the earth. Down below, Adolf Eichmann, who administered the systematic Nazi extermination of the Jews, became a resident of hell after he was hanged in Jerusalem. In response, local Nazi sympathizers painted a red swastika on the Ahavas Achim synagogue on Schaefer. Entertainer Frank Sinatra gave seven concerts in Israel to help fund a Nazareth youth center.

Danny Raskin was doing the town and recalled a mostly unheard of young singer from Brooklyn. As Raskin tells it, "Harold Levine, of Ewald Steel, asked Boris Greisdorf if he would let a young girlfriend of his daughter sing at Boris' Menjo's on Woodward. Harold felt sorry for the young lady and told Boris he'd pay half her salary, which was about $125 a week. However she only lasted a couple of days since the band leader said he couldn't play with her singing. Her name was Barbra Streisand."

Max Pincus, former president of Hughes and Hatcher men's stores and executive vice president of United Department Stores, purchased the London Chop House from Lester Gruber. The latter, who also owned the Caucus Club, booked Barbra Streisand in that establishment in 1962. After five years of being America's number one television program, "Gunsmoke" slipped to number three behind two other westerns, "Wagon Train" and "Bonanza."

Isidore Sobeloff, executive director of the Jewish Welfare Federation, was honored for 25 years of service to Detroit. In that 25-year span, the number of contributors to the Allied Jewish Campaign rose from 6,000 to more than 23,000. Campaign income was $250,000 in 1937 and $4,860,000 in 1962. The Livonia Jewish Congregation, which had been conducting services in a renovated farmhouse, announced plans for construction of a synagogue on the site at 32070 West Seven Mile Road, Livonia. To serve the estimated 1,500 Jewish families in the area, the United Hebrew Schools dedicated the Maly and Samuel Cohn Branch at 31840 West Seven Mile Road.

Young Israel of Northwest completed its addition in 1962.

(Courtesy of Leonard N. Simons Jewish Community Archives)

Joseph Haggai, one of the founders of the Labor Zionist movement in Detroit and a Hebrew teacher for 55 years, died. Haggai was associated with the United Hebrew Schools for 30 years. Rabbi Joseph Thumin, former spiritual leader of Congregation Beth Abraham, died at the age of 89. Dean of area rabbis in years of service and age, Rabbi Thumin organized Detroit's Vaad Harabonim (Council of Orthodox Rabbis) and served as its president for many years.

Young Israel of Northwest Detroit dedicated its enlarged structure at 17376 Wyoming. The Agree family bought a building on Griswold and Grand River for the downtown synagogue, to be officially called the Isaac Agree Downtown Synagogue. Rabbi A. Irving Schnipper was elected spiritual leader of Congregation Beth Moses. Rabbi Schnipper previously served a congregation in Pittsburgh. At Friday evening services in September, Cantor Harold Orbach was installed by Dr. Leon Fram and Rabbi M. Robert Syme, rabbis of Temple Israel.

Congregation B'nai Jacob and the Eight Mile Synagogue merged and became known as Congregation B'nai Jacob. From 1942 until mid 1962, Congregation B'nai Jacob held services in its small building at Linwood and Richton. As their structure was being built at 20470 Hubbel south of Eight Mile Road, the merged congregation arranged for the use of space in the Artillery Armory, on the north side of Eight Mile at Hubbel.

The four-year-old Hillel Day School began its fifth year of operation in September in new quarters in the Ten Mile Jewish Community Center. Hillel Day School grew from an original 29 students to more than 110 in 1962. Anxiety reigned in schools as reconaissance photographs showed Russian missile sites in Cuba capable of housing missiles with a 2,000 mile range. President John F. Kennedy ordered a blockade of Soviet ships approaching Cuba. Because of the firm U.S. stance in what became known as the Cuban Missile Crisis, Russian premier Nikita Kruschev agreed to remove the missiles if the United States agreed not to invade Cuba.

Around 500 people attended ground-breaking ceremonies for Hebrew Memorial Chapel, being built by the Hebrew Benevolent Society, on Greenfield south of 11 Mile Road in Oak Park. Abba Eban, a member of Israel's Knesset, spoke at the Israel Bond Dinner in Detroit's Cobo Hall. Israel lost one of its long-time friends as Eleanor Roosevelt, widow of FDR, died in New York at the age of 78. Abraham Levine, a regular Sabbath and holiday attendant at Congregation Shaarey Zedek, was re-elected mayor of Mt. Clemens. Also re-elected were Common Pleas Court judges George Kent and Joseph Pernick. Mayor Jerome Cavanaugh pushed for a 1 percent Detroit city income tax. The tax was approved. Louis Berry, who owned the David Stott Building where he maintained his headquarters, formed the Fisher New Center (FNC) with Max Fisher and George Seyburn and purchased the Fisher Building and other nearby properties.

(Courtesy of Jewish News)

On Thursday December 20, 1962, the Torah scrolls were removed from Shaarey Zedek's Chicago Boulevard location and transferred to the new synagogue in Southfield. Two days later, as more than 3,900 people attended the Sabbath service marking the dedication of the new sanctuary, leaders of the congregation formed a procession, carried the Torahs removed two days earlier, and placed them in the new synagogue Ark.

Camelot reigned in 1963. America loved the attractive residents of the White House. JFK, as president Kennedy was often referred to, first lady, Jacqueline, and their two young children captivated many around the world. America had unique tastes in television entertainment as the "Beverly Hillbillies" became the country's most-watched regular television

At its cornerstone laying ceremony on June 17, 1962, Louis Berry, chairman of the development fund; David M. Miro, synagogue president; Rabbi Morris Adler; and Mandell L. Berman hold the contents of the cornerstone from the Shaarey Zedek synagogue on Chicago Boulevard. Items from 1962, including Israeli coins and newspaper articles, were added inside the new stone.

(Courtesy of Congregation Shaarey Zedek)

Left: After 101 years in Detroit, the Shaarey Zedek Synagogue opened in the Northwestern Highway, Bell Road, and Eleven Mile area in December 1962.

Above left: On Saturday, December 22, 1962, leaders of Congregation Shaarey Zedek placed the Torahs removed from the synagogue's old location into the Ark of the new sanctuary.

(Courtesy of Congregation Shaarey Zedek)

ECHOES OF DETROIT'S JEWISH COMMUNITIES

program.

As cars sped along the newly-opened Chrysler Freeway on what used to be Hastings Street, less than a mile west on Woodward on Sunday, June 23, 1963, an estimated 125,000 people including many Jews, participated in a civil rights march led by Dr. Martin Luther King. Many linked arms as they marched down Woodward from Adelaide Street to Cobo Hall.

Jacob Chicorel, the religious leader, cantor, and president of the local Sephardic Spanish Jewish community, died at the age of 69. A native of Turkey, Chicorel operated a cafeteria in the *Detroit Times* newspaper building before establishing the Kenwood Lounge at Fenkell and Telegraph. His accomplishments included speaking seven languages: English, French, Greek, Italian, Latin, Spanish, and Turkish.

Justice Henry M. Butzel, an older brother of the late Fred M. Butzel, died a the age of 92. Butzel was admitted to the Michigan Bar in 1892 and headed the law firm of Butzel, Levin and Winston from 1915 to 1929, when he was appointed to the Michigan State Supreme Court. A past president of Temple Beth El, Butzel was active in the Allied Jewish Campaign and the American Jewish Committee. David T. Nederlander, well-known on the local theatrical scene since 1914 and operator of the Fisher Theater, died at the age of 81.

United Hebrew Schools marked the 40th anniversary of its first graduating class in June 1923 by inviting members of that class to participate in the 1963 graduating exercises. Temple Israel opened a branch of its religious school in Oak Park's Clinton School. Rabbi Joseph Elias, who became principal of the Yeshiva Beth Yehudah in 1951, left to assume a similar post in a larger school in New York. He was replaced by Rabbi Chaim Hollander, a graduate of Telshe Yeshiva in Cleveland. The Yeshiva also announced the purchase of land previously owned by Yeshivath Chachmey Lublin, on Lincoln in Southfield, to house its growing student population. In 1963, enrollment at the Day School and the Oak Park Hebrew Academy numbered 550. Around 300 students attended the afternoon program.

Detroiter Muriel Greenspon, awarded a Grinnell scholarship in 1960 to study voice in New York, signed a contract with the New York City Opera in 1963. Former Tigers catcher Joe Ginsberg, who went on to play for five other teams, closed out his 13-year career with the New York Mets in 1962 and returned to Detroit. Ginsberg and his father operated a bar in Hamtramck in 1963 behind Dodge Main. The Hiller family opened the Shopping Center Market at Greenfield and Ten Mile Road in Southfield. Kitty Wagner opened a European facial salon on James Couzens in Detroit. Sol Nusbaum's Carpet Center's "Carpet City" opened at 21170 West Eight Mile Road. One of America's largest retail carpet stores, virtually every style, color, and texture of carpet was displayed

The new Chrysler Freeway took away traffic from Woodward in 1963.

in the huge, 40,000-square-foot retail selling area. The structure also housed the headquarters of the chain.

Governor George Romney appointed Benjamin Burdick to the Wayne County Circuit Court bench. Mark Schlussel married Rose Lynn Meckler in a ceremony performed by Rabbi Morris Adler and Rabbi Israel Halpern at Congregation Shaarey Zedek. Norman Allan was elected president of Congregation Adas Shalom, and Robert A. Steinberg became the youngest president ever at Congregation Shaarey Zedek. Rabbi Noah Gamze came to Detroit from Chicago to assume the pulpit of the Isaac Agree Downtown Synagogue. Sherwin Wine founded the Humanistic movement and the Birmingham Temple, rejecting Torah and G-d.

Groundbreaking ceremonies for Congregation Beth Isaac and the Downriver Jewish Community Center took place in July. Ralph Aronson, spiritual leader of the congregations, gave the invocation. At the time, an estimated 150 to 200 Jewish families resided in the downriver communities of Wayne County. Congregation B'nai Jacob occupied its new synagogue on Hubbel in July and immediately became known as the "Hubbel Shul."

A second Home for the Aged, to be known as Borman Hall, was scheduled to be built on Seven Mile Road and Sunderland. The new facility, to house 188 residents, would bring the total of those receiving residential care to 488. The Borman brothers donated $250,000 toward the estimated $2,500,600 construction cost. Isidore Sobeloff, executive vice president of the Jewish Welfare Federation, announced he accepted the position of executive director of the Jewish Federation, Council of Greater Los Angeles, and would leave next summer. William Avrunin, associate director of the Federation since 1948, would assume Sobeloff's duties in mid 1964.

President John F. Kennedy was assassinated in Dallas, Texas, on November 22, 1963. When the official announcement of his death came Friday afternoon, Detroit's city and county governments began sending employees home, readying for a complete shutdown to mourn with the nation. Saddened Detroiters walked slowly to their cars, and motorists left the downtown area driving slowly, eyes on the road and ears tuned to the sad radio reports from Dallas.

The news affected scheduled and group activities. The Saturday college football games in Ann Arbor and Lansing were canceled. The Red Wings Sunday game at Boston was called off, as was the Pistons home game at Cobo Arena. The National Football League announced its Sunday games, including the Lions at Minnesota, would go on as scheduled, but all radio and television coverage would be canceled.

Local and national radio and television stations canceled all entertainment programs and carried only special news and memorials without commercial ad-

Tom Borman (left), Abe Borman, and Gus D. Newman, longtime president of the Jewish Home for the Aged, go over plans for the Borman Hall facility.

(Courtesy of Jewish Home for the Aged)

> Vol. XLIV—No. 14   17100 W. 7 Mile Rd., Detroit 35   November 29, 1963
>
> ## JFK's Memory Blessed in Tributes by World Jewry
>
> Detroit Jewry joined with all elements in the population and with other faiths here and throughout the nation in paying tribute to the memory of John Fitzgerald Kennedy, assassinated President of the United States.
>
> Religious services in tribute to the deceased President were held in nearly all of Detroit's synagogues. Adas Shalom, Ahavas Achim, Beth Moses, Temple Israel, Beth Abraham and Shaarey Zedek conducted special services on Monday.
>
> The numerous special services commenced with the memorial service that was conducted in Shaarey Zedek on Saturday morning, and the tribute to President Kennedy at the services at Temple Beth El and the other Reform congregations on Sabbath Eve.
>
> Dr. Richard Hertz has arranged for a special memorial service at Temple Beth El tonight. Rabbi Leon Fram addressed the city-wide memorial service on the old City Hall site Monday morning. There were 1,800 at the Adas Shalom service and more than 1,100 at the Shaarey Zedek that night.
>
> Beth Moses and the other synagogues were filled to capacity. The rabbis of the respective synagogues delivered eulogies and appropriate prayers were chanted. The kaddish was recited and the El Molei Rachamim was chanted in several of the synagogues.

(Courtesy of Jewish News)

vertising until after the Monday funeral.

The Fisher Theater canceled *Hello Dolly!* starring Carol Charming, through Monday evening. The United Artists lost a lot of revenue as it canceled its showing of *Cleopatra*, starring Elizabeth Taylor, and the Cinerama Music Hall canceled *How the West Was Won*.

All of the downtown movie houses soon followed with closing announcements until after the Monday funeral.

The day after the funeral, Mayor Cavanaugh proposed naming the old City Hall site for the late President.

In only three years, the white student population at Mumford High School on Wyoming plummeted from 3,201 to 1,513. The black students numbered 1,190, almost doubling in the same span. At the record stores, high schoolers were buying "A Hard Day's Night," by the Beatles and "Pretty Woman," by Roy Orbison. Married couples preferred Dean Martin's "Everybody Loves Somebody."

HIAS—Hebrew Immigrant Aid Society—celebrated its 80th year of existence in 1964. After World War II, a new organization called Service for New Americans assisted refugees from war-torn Europe. The organization merged with HIAS, forming United Hias Service. In April, *Look* magazine published an article titled, "The Vanishing American Jew." Sociologist Erich Rosenthal's study indicated that "about 70 percent of the children of mixed marriages were not being raised as Jews." Other indicators pointed to the fact that the American Jewish community would drop from 2.9 per cent of the population to 1.6 per cent by the year 2000.

Oak Parkers Larry Loewenthal and his mother, Renee, graduated together from Wayne State University. Larry received a bachelor of science degree in preparation for the Wayne State College of Medicine, while his mother received a bachelor of science in education. To celebrate the event, the Loewenthals went to Israel for a month.

Clarence Enggass, past president of the Jewish Welfare Federation who was scheduled to be honored by the Zionist Organization of Detroit, died at the age of 80. Born in Detroit in 1883, Enggass headed the family jewelry business for 56 years, retiring in 1958 when the three stores were purchased by the Meyer Jewelry Company. Judge Charles C. Simons, the youngest man to be elected to the Michigan State Senate in 1903, died at the age of 87. At his retirement in 1959, he was the chief judge of the Sixth U.S. Court of Appeals in Cincinnati. His father, David W. Simons, was elected to the first nine-man Detroit City Council in 1918.

Israel Davidson, who developed the family business into the 33-store chain making up Federal Department Stores, died at the age of 76. Active in Congregation Shaarey Zedek and Zionist organizations. Davidson helped establish the Hadassah House on Murray Hill and Seven Mile Road. Well-known restaurateur William Boesky died at the age of 63. At the time of his death, Boesky was president of the Brass Rail Chop House on Adams fronting on Grand Circus Park. Entertainer Eddie Cantor, a tireless worker on behalf of many Jewish causes, died at 72. Cantor came to Detroit several times for B'nai B'rith, Israel Bonds, and the United Jewish Appeal. As many mourned the passing of comedian Harpo Marx, veteran comedian Phil Silvers of Sergeant Bilko fame was performing at Windsor's Elmwood Casino.

The PLO—Palestine Liberation Organization—was established in 1964. Its aim, according to their covenant, was the destruction of the state of Israel. In 1964, Judea-Samaria, referred to as the "West Bank," by many media outlets, and eastern Jerusalem were Arab-occupied. This negates the claim of future years that the PLO violence is a response to Israeli occupation.

Rabbi Milton Arm, spiritual leader of Congregation Ahavas Achim, accepted the post of assistant to the president of the Jewish National Fund in New York. The Livonia Jewish Congregation purchased a church on Six Mile Road in Livonia and renovated it into a synagogue.

Congregation Mishkan Israel, built on Nine Mile Road in Oak Park in 1958, merged with the Lubavitch Center and was renamed Congregation Mishkan Israel Nusach H'Ari Lubavitcher Center. Congregation Ahavas Achim dedicated its new auditorium and expanded quarters, marking the culmination of the three-stage program of construction. Rabbi Benjamin Gorrelick, who had served Congregation Beth Aaron for the past 15 years, was granted life tenure. Congregation Beth Isaac was dedicated at 2730 Edsel Drive in Trenton. The name of the 51-family member synagogue was selected to honor the memory of the late Isaac Ellias, whose son donated the site.

The Yeshiva Beth Yehudah acquired the Shaarey Zedek school building on Seven Mile Road near Lesure. The building, vacated in 1962 when Congregation Shaarey Zedek moved to Southfield, would now house the kindergarten and the 215 students of the Beth Jacob Girls Division. The afternoon school program, which was using facilities in Northwest Young Israel, also moved to the Seven Mile building.

Later in the year, an estimated 400 people attended the cornerstone laying ceremonies of the new Yeshiva building on Lincoln Road in Southfield. Edward

The Yeshiva Beth Yehudah was the only day school offering Jewish studies for all 12 grades in 1964. Fund-raising efforts to help keep YBY operating were undertaken by Rabbi Shmuel Adler, Rabbi S. P. Wohlgelernter, and Rabbi Norman Kahn.

(Courtesy of Yeshiva Beth Yehudah)

Fleishman, founder of Checker Cab Company, a leader in the oil refining business, and president of the Jewish Home for the Aged in 1964, was given the honor of placing the cornerstone. With the funds of the sale of the property previously used by Yeshivath Chachmey Lublin, the latter planned on relocating to a suburb of Haifa, Israel.

Akiva Hebrew Day School opened at 19161 Schaefer in the Labor Zionist Building in September. Serving 90 students in kindergarten through the fifth grade,, Rabbi Manfred Pick, previously principal of the Hillel Academy in Denver, was principal of the new school. United Hebrew School opened a branch at the Glenn Schoenhals Elementary School on Lincoln Road at Southwood in Southfield.

Sander Levin, a partner in the law firm of Schwartz, O'Hare, and Levin, was elected to the State Senate in Oakland County's 15th District. The Hebrew Memorial Chapel of the Hebrew Benevolent Society was dedicated on Greenfield south of Eleven Mile Road. "The Hebrew Benevolent Society provides the entire funeral and burial, from beginning to end, without regard to whether it will be amply reimbursed to cover the costs," Rabbi Israel Rockove, director of the organization, stated. Three years earlier, the Society paid for 52 monuments and placed them on unmarked graves. In Hebrew, the society of benevolence is known as Chesed Shel Emes (true kindness).

A chartered plane from Detroit carried a hundred local Jews to New York for a formal dinner honoring Max Fisher as he assumed the general chairmanship of the United Jewish Appeal. Fisher, who was president of Detroit's Jewish Welfare Federation from 1959 to 1964, had served as adviser to the Israeli government for its petrochemical and refining industry. A pioneer in developing Michigan's oil industry, Fisher was a director of Pax Oil Company, Israel's largest petroleum distributor. The United Jewish Appeal was the major agency providing humanitarian aid to immigrants to Israel, refugees, and Jews in need overseas. Hyman Safran, president of Safran Printing Company who had served as vice president of the Jewish Welfare Federation for the past five years, became president of the organization.

With the 1965 Jewish population of the Detroit area pegged at around 85,000, 46 percent lived within the confines of Oak Park and at least 50 percent were

Akiva Hebrew Day School students.

(Courtesy of Dave Dombey)

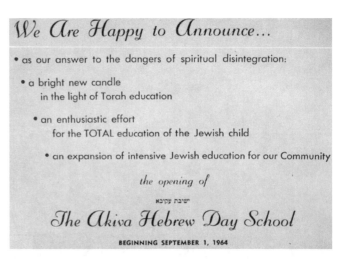

Advertisement used by Akiva Hebrew Day School in 1964.

(Author's collection)

Manuel Merzon was one of Detroit's best known attorneys.

spread around northwest Detroit. Most of the northwest's observant Jews lived within walking distance of Wyoming. Within a half-mile on Wyoming, there were several synagogues to choose from. Facing Rainbow Kosher Catering on the opposite side of the street, Congregation Beth Joseph Anshei Ruzhin was at 18450 Wyoming. Congregation Beth Tefilo Emanuel Tikvah, led by Rabbi Leizer Levin, was at the corner of Margareta. South of Curtis was Congregation Beth Aaron (Conservative), Across Thatcher at 17556 Wyoming was Congregation Beth Yehudah. Formerly the Camel Hebrew School and Congregation a decade and a half earlier, the building and number of worshippers with a Polish background grew to become the Beth Yehudah Synagogue, led by Rabbi Joshua Spero. Across Santa Clara, Rabbi Samuel Prero was spiritual leader of Northwest Young Israel.

The second office door on the north side of Santa Clara, between Congregation Beth Yehudah and Northwest Young Israel, housed the law office of Manuel Merzon, perhaps Detroit's most recognizable attorney. A short man with a quick gait, Merzon—who didn't drive—was easily spotted around town wearing a large black yarmulke. Besides being respected for his knowledge of Jewish and law books, Merzon was held somewhat in awe during World War II when he wore the yellow star of David on his sleeve in solidarity with the Jews of Europe.

Across Wyoming from Merzon's office, Mumford High School had more black students than white for the first time in its history. The 1965 student population consisted of 1,606 black students and only 965 white. Northwest residents realized that within a few years, the area around Wyoming and Curtis would for the most part be populated by blacks and observant Jews.

Dr. Irving Panush, a department head in the Detroit school system and a longtime Hebrew school

Beth Aaron was the largest synagogue on Wyoming.

(Courtesy of Leonard N. Simons Jewish Community Archives)

administrator, became assistant superintendent of United Hebrew Schools. Rabbi Simon Murciano became headmaster of Hillel Day School. The 1965 high school graduating class of Temple Beth El consisted of 43 students who had attended religious school for 14 years. Akiva Hebrew Day School offered a complete elementary program—kindergarten through sixth grade—and had an enrollment of 120 students in rented quarters at the Labor Zionist Building on Schaefer. The Zionist Organization of Detroit dedicated its new cultural center at Ten Mile Road west of Southfield Road. Temple Israel opened a branch of its religious school at Lederle School, Nine Mile Road and James Couzens in Southfield.

Actress Judy Holliday, who had been ill for several years, died in New York's Mt. Sinai Hospital at the age of 41. She was the opposite of the "dumb blonde" roles she had played in many stage and screen roles. An avid reader with an IQ of 172, Holliday devoted much of her time to causes aiding Israel. Her father, the late Abraham Tuvim, worked for the Jewish National Fund and visited Detroit several times to meet with Federation leaders. Judy derived her stage name from her last name, implying "good holiday" in Hebrew.

As Yasser Arafat recruited members for his newly-founded Movement for the National Liberation of Palestine, another Arab group whose aim was the destruction of Israel, Israel lost one it its best friends. Winston Churchill died at the age of 90. A lifelong supporter of a homeland for the Jews, Churchill often was Israel's lone defender among political leaders. "Anti-Semitism is when you hate the Jews more than necessary," Churchill chided those who didn't share his views on Zionism or who harbored prejudice against Jews.

Max Fisher, national chairman of the United Jewish Appeal, served as toastmaster for the Israel Freedom Award dinner at Cobo Hall honoring Tom Borman. Noted actor Edward G. Robinson, who often aided Israel and humanitarian causes, was guest speaker.

"Israel is part of the twentieth century emerging from the gloom of centuries," Robinson said. "The fulfillment of the Kingdom of G-d and the brotherhood of man can't wait and must be fashioned today."

Irving W. Schlussel died at the age of 58. A graduate of the University of Detroit Law School, Schlussel

David Hermelin was gaining fame in the Jewish community in 1965.

(Courtesy of *Jewish News*)

These Services Included in Budgetary Authorization

Beth Yehudah Afternoon School	$ 38,230
Combined Jewish Schools	31,110
Community Workshop	29,302
Fresh Air Society	27,251
Hayim Greenberg Hebrew-Yiddish School	8,770
Hebrew Free Loan Association	4,138
Jewish Community Center	166,923
Jewish Community Council	103,782
Jewish Family and Children's Service	71,141
Jewish Home for Aged	126,700
Jewish House of Shelter	5,801
Jewish Vocational Service	103,094
Jewish Welfare Federation (Administration and Central Services)	122,282
Midrasha	27,200
Resettlement Service	67,245
Sinai Hospital	133,900
Tamarack Hills Authority	7,944
United Hebrew Schools	396,662

Jewish Welfare Federation allocations in 1965.

(Courtesy of *Jewish News*)

was active in numerous Jewish causes, the Jewish Welfare Federation, Young Israel, and Congregation Beth Abraham. Following in the footsteps of his father, Mark Schlussel graduated from law school and would become well known for his work on behalf of the Jewish community.

Isek Abraham, a black Jew, died at the age of 77. Abraham was born in Abyssinia (Ethiopia) and orphaned as a young child. Brought to America and reared by his grandfather in New York's Felasha (Jewish Negro) community, Abraham came to Detroit as the city grew rapidly due to the automobile industry and worked as a repairer of watches. An Orthodox Jew who attended services regularly at Congregation Adas Yeshurin on Tyler at Linwood, Abraham impressed all with his gentle, polite demeanor and devotion to prayer. A tall, handsome man with a small beard, Abraham was given many honors during services including opening the Ark, Aliyahs, and chanting the Haftorah. When Rabbi Leo Goldman assumed the pulpit of the synagogue in the late 1940s, he formed a close relationship with Abraham, who often ate Sabbath and Holiday meals with the Goldman family. Abraham, who kept a kosher home, lived alone and carried a card stating that he was Jewish. He owned a plot through the Hebrew Benevolent Society (Chesed Shel Emes) and was given a proper religious burial.

Manny Rosenthal, president of Mohawk Liquor Corporation, died at his office desk. The sprightly 70-year-old lived with his wife at the Sheraton Cadillac Hotel on Washington Boulevard and was an active member of the Isaac Agree Downtown Synagogue. The Rosenthal family had operated Mohawk since 1868 and Manny was the third generation of his family to be president. In 1965 Mohawk was one of the largest independent companies of its kind, producing 52 liqueurs and alcoholic beverages.

Baruch Litvin, who spearheaded the famous Mount Clemens court case regarding separation of the sexes during prayer services, died at the age of 85. Born in Russia, Litvin came to Detroit in 1918 at the age of 15 and worked as a carpenter. In 1935 he entered the lumber business, which was operated by his sons in later years.

B'nai B'rith opened its new building at 19951 Livernois. Avram B. Charlip, manager of the Covenant Credit Union serving B'nai B'rith members and their families, was given the honor of affixing the mezuzah. The new facilities of the Jewish Home for the Aged opened on Seven Mile Road and Sunderland, providing for 200 residents. The home on Petoskey in the Dexter section was still operating and housed 300 residents.

Louis Rosenberg, Canadian Jewish Congress research director, issued a study claiming that the inter-

Borman Hall of the Jewish Home for the Aged on Seven Mile Road and Sunderland.

(Author's collection)

marriage ratio among Canadian Jews rose from 3.8 percent in 1931 to 16.5 percent in 1962, to 18.5 percent in 1963. Canadian Jewish leaders were alarmed that the rate would top 20 percent in 1965. Wilbert Simkovitz, who already had degrees in mechanical engineering and electrical engineering, received a law degree from the Detroit College of Law and was admitted to the Bar on the same day his wife was admitted to the hospital to deliver her fifth child. Simkovitz, a founder of Young Israel of Oak Woods, was chief of the test and analysis branch in the research and engineering directorate of the U.S. Army Tank-Automotive Command.

1965 was a good year for the music industry. Some of the several memorable hit tunes included "Downtown," (Petula Clark); "I Got You Babe," (Sonny & Cher); "My Girl," (The Temptations); "Help Me Rhonda," (Beach Boys); "Stop In The Name Of Love," (The Supremes); and "Yesterday," (The Beatles). *Fiddler on the Roof*, starring Zero Mostel, was enjoying a successful run at the Fisher Theatre. Tickets ranged from $2.65 to seven dollars. In recognition to her service to humanity, actress Gertrude Berg (Molly Goldberg) received a Myrtle Wreath Award at the Hadassah fashion show at Temple Israel.

Founded in 1926 in an abandoned carpet factory on Collingwood, Congregation B'nai Zion purchased a site at Humphrey and Holmur. Because of the Depression, it took almost four years to raise the funds to complete the building. In 1965 the building used for Sabbath services was for sale. A year earlier, the new synagogue for Congregation B'nai Zion opened on Nine Mile Road in Oak Park. The B'nai Zion in northwest Detroit opened in a converted building on Seven Mile Road between Birwood and Mendota in 1959. Spiritual leader Rabbi Solomon Gruskin served all three in 1964 and 1965. Gruskin resided in the Dexter section and was at the Humphrey location on Friday nights. Saturday morning he walked to Seven Mile, and for afternoon services he walked to Nine Mile Road. In 1965 he moved to Oak Park, and the congregation continued to maintain its northwest branch.

Rabbi Isaac Stollman, spiritual leader of Congregation Mishkan Israel and affiliated with numerous Orthodox organizations, moved to Israel to become dean of the new Yeshiva of Radin, located in Netanya. Stollman, 69, helped organize the new yeshiva named after the first school he attended in Radin, Russia. Congregation Beth Shalom dedicated its new sanctuary addition, marking the formal opening of the building. Also in 1965, construction of the sanctuary and school additions to B'nai David Synagogue in Southfield began.

As banks were giving 4 percent interest on savings accounts, Richard Strichart became city control-

Congregation B'nai Zion, on Nine Mile Road in Oak Park, is the smallest synagogue building in the suburbs.

(Photo by author)

ler for his former neighbor, Jerome P. Cavanaugh. A law professor at New York University before coming to Wayne State University in 1956, Strichartz became an active member of Temple Beth El. Due to his implementation of affirmative action and urban renewal programs, and for lowering property taxes, Cavanaugh was reelected mayor of Detroit.

The last commercial airlines left Willow Run Airport in 1966, and all airlines were operating from Metropolitan Airport. The Kern store—out of business for seven years—became a memory as the store and surrounding block at Woodward and Campus Martius were razed.

Nonwhite family income was only 60 percent of whites' in 1966. The Jewish Labor Committee worked alongside other organizations dedicated to ending discrimination in the work place. Bertha Robinson retired as principal of Ford High School and was succeeded by Samuel Milan. Milan was a counselor at Central High School in the 1950s when Robinson was principal there. Also in 1966, Bertrand J. Sandweiss became principal at Mumford High. Moishe Haar, educational director of Sholem Aleichem Institute for 35 years, died at the age of 68. Haar organized and directed the Yiddish Children's Theater at the Institute and immersed students in Yiddish culture, history, and literature.

Jacob Citrin, founder and president of Citrin Oil Company, died at the age of 61. From a one-pump service station in Detroit in 1920, Citrin Oil grew into Michigan's largest Standard Oil distributor. A past president of Temple Israel, Citrin served as treasurer of the Jewish Welfare Federation and was active in community affairs. Harry Mondry, president and founder of Highland Appliance, died at 67. A leader in the Labor Zionist Movement and active in Jewish causes, Mondry was a member of Congregation Shaarey Zedek.

Abe Boesky, owner of Boesky Restaurant on Twelfth Street until 1958 and manager of the Boesky Restaurant at James Couzens and Eight Mile, died at 70. Jacob Spolansky, former Federal Bureau of Investigation agent and author of a 1951 best-seller, *The Communist Trail in America*, died at the age of 76. Spolansky, who joined the FBI after serving in World War I, also was a security consultant for the National Association of Manufacturers and an investigator for a New York City law firm. He moved to Oak Park after his retirement and resided on Coolidge. Nathan Siegel, radio announcer on the Jewish Radio Hour for 12 years, died at 65. Siegel continued the radio program after the death of founder Hyman Altman until 1964. Siegel was sought after as a guest by many groups and presented humorous readings.

The Sinai Guild Staff Residence opened on the grounds of Sinai Hospital, providing apartments for

Rabbi Leizer Levin of Congregation Beth Tefilah Emanuel Tikvah (left), Rabbi Isaac Stollman (center), and Rabbi Chaskel Grubner of Congregation Dovid Ben Nuchim. In 1965, Stollman, former spiritual leader of Congregation Mishkan Israel, moved to Netanya, Israel.

(Courtesy of Yeshiva Beth Yehudah)

medical personnel. The Jewish National Fund honored Leonard N. Simons at a dinner in the Sheraton Cadillac and announced that a forest in Simons' honor would be planted in Israel. The United Jewish Foundation, the Federation's financial arm, acquired acreage in the Maple-Drake area for a future Jewish Community Center. Bernard Panush, head accountant for the City of Detroit Department of Public Works and director of the Beth Aaron Religious School, was elected president of Detroit B'nai B'rith Council. In a study conducted by Dr. Albert J. Mayer of Wayne State University, it was predicted that by 1975, 88 percent of Detroit Jewry would live in the suburbs.

In 1966, interest on savings accounts at banks edged up to four and a quarter percent, and a one-bedroom apartment at the Northgate Apartment complex on Greenfield north of Ten Mile Road rented for a $135 per month. The Northland Theater on J. L. Hudson Drive opened. Many Jews were first-nighters to see Paul Newman and Julie Andrews in Alfred Hitchcock's *The Torn Curtain*. Movie theaters faced stiff competition from drive-ins. In 1966, metro Detroit had 31 drive-in theaters. The West Side drive-in on Eight Mile and Schaefer was closest to most of the Jewish community

As the Hebrew Benevolent Society (Chesed Shel Emes), organized in 1916, celebrated its 50th anniversary, the Condors, the teen club at the Jewish Community Center on Curtis and Meyers, danced to the top tunes of 1966. "I'm a Believer," (The Monkees); "Monday, Monday," (The Mamas & the Papas); "Strangers In the Night," (Frank Sinatra), and "These Boots Are Made For Walkin'," (Nancy Sinatra) took turns topping the charts. S/Sgt. Barry Sadler recorded the popular "The Ballad of the Green Berets," as America was continuing to send more troops to Vietnam. The Palestine Liberation Army announced it would send troops to assist the Vietcong in their fight against America. At the same time, the Arabs said their forces would learn guerrilla warfare in preparation for waging war on Israel.

A double tragedy occurred before 900 congregants at Sabbath morning services at Shaarey Zedek Synagogue on February 12, 1966. After Rabbi Morris Adler's sermon, a 23-year-old, gun-waving, mentally disturbed man grabbed the microphone. The tape recorder preserved his words.

"This congregation is a travesty. It has made a mockery by its phoniness and hypocrisy of the beauty and the spirit of Judaism," he said as his parents, sister and grandmother and others in the pews recoiled in shock. After continuing to rebuke the congregation, he stated:

"With this act I protest the humanly horrifying

The Campus Martius block south of the Hudson's store was demolished in 1966.

(Photo by Harry Wolf)

Rabbi Morris Adler died three weeks before his 60th birthday.

(Courtesy of Congregation Shaarey Zedek)

and hence unacceptable situation." After saying, "Rabbi...," he turned to Rabbi Adler and shot him in the left arm. He then fired twice more, hitting Rabbi Adler once behind the left ear.

The assailant turned the gun around and shot himself through his temple. Medical treatment was administered almost immediately by three physicians attending services, and Rabbi Adler and his assailant were rushed to the hospital. The assailant died early Wednesday morning and was buried that afternoon at services officiated by Rabbi Irwin Groner and Cantor Reuven Frankel.

After being in a coma for 27 days, Rabbi Adler died on Friday morning, March 11, three weeks before his 60th birthday. Shaarey Zedek's synagogue was filled to capacity over an hour before the 2:00 p.m. Sunday funeral. Loudspeakers carried the messages and prayers from inside to those who packed rooms, lobbies, and the area outside the building.

In 1966, Yeshiva Beth Yehudah celebrated the 50th anniversary of its opening in the school building of the Mogen Abraham Synagogue on Farnsworth. Founded by Rabbi Judah Leib Levin and others in 1916 to provide Sunday and afternoon hours to post Bar Mitzvah boys, the school opened with eight students.

The Day School, which began in 1944, occupied its new Southfield Daniel A. Laven Building and Julius and Alice Rotenberg High School on Lincoln in February. While the new building was under construction, Rabbi Bakst's Beth Hamidrash Division took up temporary residence in the Young Israel of Northwest on Wyoming.

Becoming Detroit's second Reform temple in 1941 at its founding, Temple Israel's membership grew to over 1,600 25 years later in 1966. The 25th anniversary was celebrated with several events, including a Saturday night dinner dance at the Sheraton-Cadillac Hotel. Rabbi Milton Arm, who left the pulpit of Congregation Ahavs Achim in 1964 for a position with the Jewish National Fund office in New York, returned as spiritual leader of the same synagogue due to popular demand. In its 25th year of existence, the membership of Congregation Gemiluth Chassodim voted to institute mixed seating and change its name to Congregation Beth Hillel.

	Number of Households		Percent		Percent Change
	1963	1965	1963	1965	1963-1965
Northwest					
Seven Mile East of Meyers (1)	7,400	6,200	28	24	—16
Seven Mile West of Meyers (1)	7,100	6,700	27	26	— 6
Dexter	500	200	2	—(2)	—60
Oak Park	5,000	5,800	19	22	+16
Huntington Woods	1,400	1,600	5	6	+14
Southfield	2,700	3,400	10	13	+26
New Suburbs (3)	1,000	1,300	4	5	+33
All other areas (4)	1,300	900	5	4	—31
Total	26,400	26,100(5)	100	100	— 1

(1) Geographic boundaries of these areas are as follows: Seven Mile East of Meyers includes Woodward to Eight Mile, to Meyers, to Six Mile to Woodward. Seven Mile West of Meyers includes Meyers to Eight Mile, to Telegraph Road to Six Mile to Meyers.
(2) Less than one per cent.
(3) Includes parts of Livonia, Birmingham, Bloomfield and West Bloomfield Townships, Franklin and Farmington Township.
(4) Includes parts of Detroit outside the Northwest and Dexter areas as well as all other suburban areas other than those distinguished in the table.
(5) About 300 households left the city during the two-year period. However, an unknown number of new households have come to Detroit.

The April 8, 1966, edition of the *Jewish News* contained a table showing the trend of Jewish population to the suburbs.

(Courtesy of *Jewish News*)

Wearing his yellow "hard hat" given him by the contractor of the new Cong. Bnai David, Rabbi Hayim Donin compares building plans with the nearly completed home of the congregation on Southfield Rd. near Nine Mile, in Southfield. The synagogue, located on a 10-acre site, will be dedicated Dec. 11.

Congregation Beth Jacob-Mogen Abraham relocated in the new Yeshiva Beth Yehudah building and began holding regular morning and evening daily services in September. Rabbi Shaiall Zachariash, a native of Los Angeles who received his rabbinical ordination from Ner Israel Rabbinical College, Baltimore, became spiritual leader of Congregation Shomrey Emunah. Rabbi Zachariash had recently received a master's degree in education from the University of Detroit while on the teaching staff of Yeshiva Beth Yehudah. Rabbi A. Irving Schnipper introduced the triennial system of reading one-third of the weekly Scripture portion at services. For a deeper insight and understanding, Rabbi Schnipper began a half-hour Bible study session on the weekly portion at Congregation Beth Moses.

As the Jewish population continued to shrink in the Dexter area, leaving the famous street without a synagogue, Congregation B'nai Zion on Humphrey at Holmur continued to function on Saturday mornings and holidays, while hoping to find a buyer for its building. After a year and a half of construction, Congregation B'nai David completed the last phase of its complex on Southfield Road in time for the High Holidays.

Hillel Day School, in existence for nine years and operating out of rented classrooms at the Ten Mile Jewish Community Center and the B'nai Moshe Syna-

The first page of the *Jewish News* after the Six-Day War.

(Courtesy of *Jewish News*

"S.O.S.—Save Our Shabbos" and "For a Perfect Summer Vacation—Try a Kosher Camp Location" were among the signs carried by the young participants in the Detroit areas' first Lag b'Omer Children's Parade and Outing Sunday. Organized and sponsored by Camp Gan Israel and Cong. Mishkan Israel, the Oak Park parade drew more than 500 children. Mayor Joseph Forbes addressed the children, who also heard a message from the head of the Lubavitch movement, Rabbi Menachem M. Schneerson of New York. The parade proceeded along Nine Mile and Coolidge Roads and down Oak Park Blvd. to Oak Park's Municipal Park, where there were games, races and contests with prizes.

(Courtesy of *Jewish News*)

gogue, embarked on a $1 million school building campaign. Over $200,000 was pledged at an October meeting presided over by school president Abe Kasle. Hillel had 265 students at the time, 50 more than the previous year. Opera star Jan Peerce came to Detroit from New York to perform with Emma Schaver on behalf of the school's fund-raising dinner.

Veteran entertainer Sophie Tucker, who had performed at Windsor's Elmwood Casino two years earlier, died at 79. A tireless worker on behalf of numerous Jewish causes, Tucker, born Sophie Kalish, did not work on Jewish holidays. She was one of the few performers to be successful in vaudeville, night clubs, and television,

In 1967 as Detroit's *Jewish News* celebrated its 25th anniversary, Detroit area banks offered six-month depositors of $5,000 or more 5 percent interest on their savings. Adolph Deutsch, founder and chairman of the board of the American Savings and Loan Association and former president of Congregation B'nai Moshe, died at the age of 86. Max Fisher, president of the United Jewish Appeal, became finance chairman of Michigan governor George Romney's presidential campaign.

Arson destroyed the sanctuary of Trenton's Congregation Beth Isaac. "Jeuden" and a large swastika were scrawled in large letters on a blackboard. The hate crime received national publicity and donations were received from around the country. Insurance paid for 80 percent of the damage, and within months the sanctuary was rebuilt and the congregation donated excess funds not needed for repairs to other charities.

A trial merger of twelve months between the Conservative Livonia Jewish Congregation and the Reform Temple Beth Am lasted two months. Livonia's cantor Henry Blank and the temple's Rabbi David Jessel said the differences in worship were too great to overcome. To help build its membership, the Livonia Jewish Congregation hired Rabbi Martin D. Gordon as spiritual leader.

On Sunday, June 4, 1967, thousands turned out for a rally for Israel at the Jewish Community Center at Curtis and Meyers. Days later the world was caught up in the events of the Six-Day War.

Doc Greene, the hard-drinking back-page columnist of the *Detroit News*, gave his take on Israel's speedy victory. "Despite the mutterings of Russia about Israeli aggressions, the initial aggressive act was the

Twelfth Street near Pingree prior to the July 1967 riot. Few Jewish owned stores remained of what was a generation earlier the center of Jewish commerce.

(Courtesy of Walter Reuther Library of Wayne State University)

blockading of Aqaba by Gamal Abdel Nasser," Greene wrote.

"Israel held still as Nasser demanded and got the withdrawal of UN troops by U Thant. The troops had been a neutralizer over one frontier.

"The young nation waited for the diplomacy of the major maritime powers while the surrounding countries piled troops around its borders.

"Reportedly, the Arabic group held superiority in both numbers and hardware, with Russia making much louder backup noises than were being offered on Israel's behalf by the United States.

"Then it erupted and for the third time in 18 years the tiny country prevailed."

In 1967—according to the Israel Central Bureau of Statistics, the population of Jerusalem was 263,626. Jews accounted for 195,700 of the aforementioned figure, Moslems 54,963 and Christians almost 13,000. The Berkley Theater on Twelve Mile Road provided escapism from the events in the Middle East with a good double-bill. Zero Mostel and Phil Silvers starred in *A Funny Thing Happened on the Way to the Forum*, and Robert Morse starred in the other entertaining musical, *How to Succeed in Business Without Really Trying*.

On Sunday, July 23, 1967, at 3:50 a.m., police raided an after-hours drinking spot and arrested 73. About an hour later when police were leaving with the last of those arrested, bottles and rocks began flying from a crowd gathered across the street.

The crowd surged down Twelfth Street in what a generation earlier was the heart of the Jewish community. By 6:30 a.m. the first fire destroyed a sacked shoe store as rioters didn't allow arriving firemen to put out the blaze. An all-black firefighting force was quickly put together in the hope they wouldn't be harassed and would be allowed to put out fires. It didn't work as they were also pelted with bottles, bricks, rocks, and cans.

Bullhorn pleas by John Conyers, Rev. Nicholas Hood, and other community leaders weren't accepted, and they were also forced into retreat.

Newspapers and radio and television stations honored a request by Damon Keith, at the time co-chairman of the Michigan Civil Rights Commission, for a blackout of the events unfolding on Twelfth Street. Businesses shut down on Monday and instructed their employees to stay home, and most streets were empty except for army vehicles. Governor Romney ordered 1,500 National Guardsmen into the city, and President Johnson sent 4,700 Army paratroopers.

Three thousand arrests were made on Wednesday, July 26. By the time the disturbance ended, 7,331 had

The July 1967 riots destroyed much of the commercial area along Twelfth Street. When the smoke from 1,300 fires had cleared, 2,700 businesses in Detroit had been looted.

(Courtesy of Walter Reuther Library of Wayne State University)

been arrested. The incarcerated were kept in local, county, and state jails, city buses, police garages, and gymnasiums, and in the Belle isle public bathhouse. The riot resulted in over 1,300 fires, 2,700 looted businesses, 347 injuries, and 43 killed. Thirty-three of the dead were black, and blacks accounted for most of the homeless. Many of the families whose homes were burned were housed in Fort Wayne.

In the waning days of the riot, in the Wyoming-Curtis area, a lone policeman pointing a rifle downward could be seen patrolling in front of stores. As some workers took the Woodward bus to their downtown offices, tanks and buses shared the same lanes.

By the end of July, the new Detroit Committee was formed by the mayor and governor. Henry Ford II became an active participant and announced that 5,000 workers would be hired from the black neighborhoods without written job tests. Ford also would provide bus transportation to take workers to and from the plants.

While blacks made up close to 40 percent of the city's population and 55 percent of the public school enrollment in 1967, only five percent of Detroit's police force was black.

B'nai David's new school building was dedicated in memory of Samuel Lieberman. The afternoon Hebrew School began in September 1954, led by Rabbi Donin with 29 students using space at Oak Park's Francis Scott Key School. Two years later, Rabbi Aaron Brander was hired as full-time educational director. In 1967 the B'nai David School had more than 600 pupils in 28 classes, staffed by 22 teachers.

Daniel Tickton, a well-known member of Congregation Adas Shalom, died at the age of 85. Despite losing his sight 43 years earlier, Tickton became a certified public accountant and wrote numerous articles for the *Jewish News*. Only a day before his passing, the Jewish News received an article by Tickton recalling the bygone years of Jewish Detroit. The article, printed in the September 29, 1967, issue of the *Jewish News*, ended thusly:

> There are not many of the people left. Some may be trying to outlive me but I'm not sure they'll succeed. I wish them good luck and a long life. Mere length of life is meaningless. A full life is better than a long one. It is the depth and creativity of a life that should be measured and not as mere temporal span.

George D. Keil, president of the Jewish Community Center, appointed Mrs. Arthur I. Gould and Julian Tobias as co-chairs of the Center's 16th annual Jewish Book Fair. One of the most popular speakers was Harry Kemmelman, author of *Saturday the Rabbi Went Hungry*. Golda Meir, Israel's foreign minister, came to Detroit in November to honor Emma Schaver, chair of the Women's Division of the Detroit Israel Bond Organization, at the Israel Miracle Year Dinner at Cobo Hall. Mrs. Meir presented her longtime friend with the Eleanor Roosevelt Humanities Award. Mrs. Schaver, 70, a noted concert singer, had given her last official performance on Mt. Scopus in Israel five months earlier.

Myron Milgrom, vice president in charge of sales for the Mercury Paint Company, was involved in two building plans. Mercury planned a huge new plant, and Milgrom was chairman of the Hillel Day School Building Fund Concert at the Ford Auditorium. The concert, featuring operatic tenor Richard Tucker, launched the school's drive to raise funds to construct its own building. Half of the $1.5 million needed to complete the building was raised by the time of the ceremonial groundbreaking on November 26 at the eleven-acre site on Middlebelt north of Northwestern.

For the very first time, the Jewish Welfare Federation allocated funds to the Yeshiva Beth Yehudah Day School. The Yeshiva High School received $9,500 from the Federation, 2 percent of the entire school's total budget. Brothers Wolf and Isadore Cohen, among the founders of the Yeshiva Day School and who served as school presidents, received the Golden Tora Award at the Yeshiva's annual dinner.

For the second time in as many years, tragedy struck Shaarey Zedek. Aice Green, a maintenance employee for 17 years, was hit on the head with a heavy object and died later in the day at Beaumont Hospital. The night maintenance crew found Green at 4 a.m. The safe near him had been broken into, and $150 was missing.

Rabbi Joseph Rabinowitz, known as the Brezner Rebbe after his hometown of Berezno and founder of Congregation Beth Shmuel, took up residence in Israel. Congregation Beth Shmuel sold its synagogue on Dexter to Congregation Dovid Ben Nuchim under the leadership of Rabbi Chaskel Grubner in 1959. In 1965, Congregation Dovid Ben Nuchim, the last remaining synagogue on Dexter, relocated in the basement of Rabbi Grubner's Oak Park home.

Even though Beth Shmuel ceased to exist as an active congregation after it sold its building on Dexter, it came alive again in 1966 for High Holy Day Services held in a storefront at 15215 West Seven Mile Road and ceased operations afterward.

Rabbi Rabinowitz received permission to use the Beth Shmuel name and funds to purchase two apartments in the Tel Aviv suburb of Givatyim. The rabbi's family used one apartment for a residence and the other for a synagogue. Rabbi Rabinowitz and his wife traveled to Israel by boat, but were reached in Athens when the Six-Day War broke out and urged to return to America. Instead they continued on to Israel, where he plunged into establishing the synagogue. In mid-December, at the age of 70, Rabbi Rabinowitz died.

As packages to 55 servicemen in Vietnam were mailed out by Mrs. Louis Winkle, servicemen's service chairman of Sholom Auxiliary, Jewish War Veterans, the community lost one of its sons. Pfc. Dennis Greenwald, a member of the airborne brigade, was killed in a fierce battle in Vietnam. Only three days short of his 19th birthday, the young Southfield resident was honored by the Southfield City Council with a minute of silent prayer for him and all the men in Vietnam. Greenwald's parents, longtime supporters of the Southfield Public Library, arranged for a plaque on the grounds and a picture of their son to hang in the library's study.

In 1968, the musical team of Simon and Garfunkel made "Mrs. Robinson" (Anne Bancroft's role in the movie, *The Graduate*) a household name. Detroit increased the pay of its police officers to $10,000 per year, the highest in the country. Lou Gordon quit his WXYZ commentary programs, deciding instead to host his popular, hard-hitting interview program on Channel 50.

Borenstein's Hebrew Book Store relocated to Greenfield Road north of Ten Mile Road in Oak Park. Billy Berris, who captained the Mumford High School basketball team for two years, was the leading scorer in 1968. Four years after she moved to Detroit, Mira Linder, who survived a Siberian labor camp during World War II, opened a spa that would make the owner and establishment famous. Sam Bishop, athletic director of Northwestern High School for 44 years, retired. Tigers left fielder Willie Horton was one of thousands who benefited from Bishop's coaching.

Lawrence Gubow, United States attorney for the Eastern District of Michigan, was elected president of the Jewish Community Council. Also in 1968, Gubow was nominated by President Lyndon B. Johnson and unanimously endorsed for the federal judgeship. Alan S. Schwartz, former president of Shaarey Zedek's junior congregation, graduated from Harvard Law School. He would join the famous Detroit law firm of Honigman, Miller, Schwartz, and Cohn, and would rise all the way to the top and become president of Congregation Shaarey Zedek along the way. Darby's

Rabbi Joseph Ben-Zion Rabinowitz

Mrs. Joseph (Dora) Ehrlich was a pioneer in many fields.
(Courtesy of Leonard N. Simons Jewish Community Archives)

Restaurant on Seven Mile Road and Wyoming was destroyed and gutted by fire. Managed by Sam Boesky, a member of Detroit's famous eatery family, Darby's had the reputation as the community gathering place to see and be seen.

The community mourned the loss of Mrs. Joseph H. (Dora Buchhalter) Ehrlich at 87. The funeral service was held in the sanctuary of Shaarey Zedek, the first time ever for a woman. The daughter of the late scholar and Hebrew teacher Hyman Buchhalter, she graduated from Central High School and received a bachelor's degree from the University of Michigan. She taught trigonometry, algebra, Latin, German, and ancient history at Western High School, besides Sunday school classes for Shaarey Zedek. A pioneer in many Jewish organizations, Mrs. Ehrlich was president of the Women's Division of the Jewish Welfare Federation, treasurer of the United Jewish Charities, served on many boards, and was the only woman ever to serve as vice president of Federation. Active in Hadassah for over a half-century, she was honored in 1966 as friends contributed funds in honor of her 85th birthday as the Dora Ehrlich wing at Hadassah Medical Center was dedicated.

Former State Senator Allen H. Blondy died at age 65. He was a legislator from 1954 to 1955, maintained a law office in the First National Building, and was a member of Congregation Adas Shalom. Bert Ruby, former junior heavyweight wrestling champion of the world turned promoter, died at the age of 57. The Oak Park resident was a member of Congregation B'nai Moshe.

Abe Bernstein, thought to be the brains behind the prohibition-era Purple Gang, died at the age of 76 in his Sheraton-Cadillac Hotel suite. Bernstein was arrested often but never served a long sentence. Bernstein wasn't targeted by rival gangs, as he was considered a peacemaker, which led to his survival while others were "bumped off" as the opportunity arose.

Supermarket pioneer Charles Grosberg, whose Packers Super Market chain merged with Wrigley Super Markets of Detroit in 1951, died at the age of 83. Grosberg was a major contributor to the Jewish Welfare Federation and involved in synagogue activities of several of Detroit's Conservative congregations. The community also lost John Lurie, 67, co-founder and former president of Wrigley Super Markets, and Nathan Epstein, 80, co-founder and vice-president of the former Keystone Oil Refining Company.

Orthodox scholar Rabbi Isaac Paneth died at 67. A well-known teacher, he served as spiritual leader of the B'nai Israel and Beth Moses congregations on Linwood and conducted High Holy Day Services at the Jewish Community Center. While interned at

SUMMARY OF RETAIL STORES IN SURVEY				
Street	Total Number of Stores Before Riot	Jewish Owned Before Riot	Total Number of Stores After Riot	Jewish Owned After Riot
Dexter	154	33	103	20
Linwood	203	22	188	12
Twelfth	176	23	122	7
TOTAL	533	78	413	39
PERCENTAGE DECLINE OF JEWISH MERCHANTS IN SURVEY AREA FOLLOWING RIOT				
	Number Jewish Owned Stores Before Riot	Number Jewish Owned Stores After Riot		% Decline
Dexter	33	20		39
Linwood	22	12		45
Twelfth	23	7		70
TOTAL	78	39		50
Percentage of Stores Owned By Jews Before Riot		Percentage of Stores Owned By Jews After Riot		
Total number	533	Total Number		413
Jewish Owned	78	Jewish Owned		39
Percentage	15	Percentage		9.5

(Courtesy of *Jewish News*)

Bergen-Belsen in World War II, Dutch Jews selected Paneth as their spiritual leader after their rabbi was killed. Paneth was presented with the rabbi's talis (prayer shawl) and it remained with him throughout his life. As per his wishes Paneth was buried with it.

A "Midnight Memorial Vigil," was held on Saturday night, April 27, at the Jewish Community Center. The vigil honored the memory of the victims of the Holocaust and recalled the heroic efforts of the Warsaw Ghetto Uprising 25 year earlier. The following night at the JCC, the 20th anniversary of the re-establishment of the State of Israel was celebrated.

Leonard Milstone, of the Jewish Community Council, evaluated the status of the formerly heavily populated Jewish areas that were affected by the riot of the previous year. Part of Milstone's study was published in an April edition of the *Jewish News*.

While campaigning for the Democratic Party presidential primary, Robert F. Kennedy was assassinated after making a speech in Los Angeles. The assassin, Sirhan Bishara Sirhan, 24, a Jordanian known to have a deep hatred for Israel, was angered by Kennedy's firm support for Israel. Only days earlier on national television, Kennedy supported the sale of Phantom Jets to Israel and felt that commitments to Israel should be kept, but that the United States should scale down many of its commitments elsewhere in the world.

Mr. and Mrs. Sigmund Rohlik contributed $100,000 for construction of a United Hebrew School building to be built on a five-acre site on West Twelve Mile Road and Murray Crescent in Southfield. The United Hebrew Schools honored Albert Elazar for completing 20 years of service as superintendent of

Additonal construction transformed Young Israel of Oak Woods on Coolidge in the late 1960s.

(Photos by author)

UHS. Elazar addressed the 1968 UHS joint commencement exercises for 362 graduates at Ford Auditorium in June. Joshua Joyrich, 68, received a bachelor of Hebrew Letters from the Midrasha College of Jewish Studies. Midrasha's oldest graduate ever, Joyrich operated an auto supply business, retired in 1966, and enrolled at the Midrasha.

Rabbi Joseph Zeitin was hired as the first full-time rabbi of Congregation Beth Isaac in Trenton. The son and grandson of rabbis, Rabbi Zeitin was born in Mainz, Germany. In 1939 he left Germany and made his way to Shanghai. Rabbi Zeitin came to America in 1947 and held pulpits in California, West Virginia, and Ohio. Congregation Beth Moses dedicated its new sanctuary on Evergreen in northwest Detroit. Adas Shalom launched upon a $3.3 million drive to build new facilities on Middlebelt Road in Farmington.

Congregation Beth Joseph Anshei Rizhin on Wyoming sponsored the construction of the youth center adjoining Congregation Mishkan Israel Nusach Hari-Lubavitche Center on Nine Mile Road in Oak Park. A dedication dinner climaxed a year of events at the enlarged building of Young Israel of Oak Woods on Coolidge. Congregation B'nai Israel of Pontiac hired Dr. Meyer Minkowich as rabbi to fill the vacancy left by the death of Rabbi Israel Goodman. Pontiac's Temple Beth Jacob was under the direction of Rabbi Philip Berkowitz in 1968.

On October 10, 1968, in St. Louis, the Tigers won the last game of the World Series and a tremendous celebration began in Detroit. Confetti rained from skyscrapers, horns blared, and people poured from buildings in the late afternoon ready to party. Blacks embraced whites and whites embraced blacks as the Tigers helped bring to unity the area's citizens. As the celebration became a memory, whites still were moving to the suburbs in increasing numbers.

As the exodus from Detroit into Oak Park was increasing, the Beth Jacob School for Girls building on Seven Mile Road was sold and the higher grades relocated in Congregation B'nai Israel on Ten Mile Road. Rabbi David Lieberman, who previously served as principal of a Chicago girls' school and synagogue, assumed the duties of Dean of the Yeshiva Beth Yehudah Schools. Rabbi Lieberman also became the spiritual leader of Congregation B'nai Israel.

Also in 1968, Ernest Citrin, president of Congregation B'nai Israel, and Meyer Levin, president of Congregation Beth Yehudah on Wyoming in northwest Detroit, announced the merger of the two synagogues.

The Emanuel Citrin Memorial Chapel was completed at 15400 West Ten Mile in September 1967 and would house the merged synagogues, to be called B'nai Israel-Beth Yehudah. B'nai Israel, organized in 1871 in downtown Detroit, was the oldest Orthodox

The Metropolitan Detroit Federation of Reform Synagogues advertised their Yom Kippur services in the *Jewish News* in 1968.

Jewish congregation outside of New York. Beth Yehudah, known as the "Polishe Shul," was organized downtown in 1909 and in the Twelfth Street area was called the "Pingree Shul" after its street location.

Itzhak Rabin, Chief of Staff of Israel's Defense Forces and the Ambassador of Israel to the United States in 1968, came to Detroit for the first time and attended the "Bond With Israel" dinner. George Jessel headlined the evening's entertainment at Shaarey Zedek.

The annual Jewish National Fund Dinner honored Paul Zuckerman. At the time, some of his community activities included vice president and executive board member, Jewish Welfare Federation; vice president, United Jewish Charities of Detroit; national chairman, United Jewish Appeal; and as a director of United Foundation of Detroit, Sinai Hospital, National American ORT, and several other organizations.

Zuckerman started his successful business career in 1937 with borrowed money. Operating out of a small rented building on Twelfth Street near the Detroit River, Zuckerman went into the peanut butter business and his acumen led to several ventures. In 1968, Zuckerman was chairman of the board and president of Velvet Food Products, Inc.; chairman of the board of Atlantic Utilities Corp.; chairman of the board of Dynatone Electronics Corp.; director of Southern Golf Utilities Corp.; director of Gibralter Growth Fund; and director of Gibralter Management Corp.

The former president of Krun-Chee Potato Chip Company and the Margate Utilities Corporation, Zuckerman was involved with other companies as a member of the board and also was involved in real estate.

Ahavas Achim and Beth Aaron merged into what would become Congregation Beth Achim. Rabbi Milton Arm and office staff operated out of its new Southfield location, where Congregation Ahavas Achim purchased the facilities of Northbrook Presbyterian Church on Twelve Mile Road in Southfield. Beth Aaron sold its building on Wyoming, and Rabbi Benjamin Gorrelick conducted services on Schaefer where Congregation Ahavas Achim was located.

Mr. and Mrs. Abe Kasle, who contributed $70,000 to the Hillel Day School building fund, donated $250,000 to the school for the creation of a special endowment fund, with the stipulation that the money was not to be used for construction of the school's new building. An outdoor candle-lighting pre-Chanuka ceremony marked the beginning of construction on the school's new facilities.

Early in 1969 the Jewish world reacted with feelings of anguish, pain, and revulsion when it was learned of the public hanging of 14 Iraquis, nine of them Jews, for alleged espionage. To make charges of a Zionist conspiracy seem credible, the Jewish community of 3,000 in Iraq was under house arrest with no telephone service and was denied access to their bank accounts.

Israeli Prime Minister Levi Eshkol shook with anger before the Knesset, describing the pre-dawn hanging as "genocide." Eshkol issued a statement that was carried in many papers worldwide. "The land of Iraq has become one great prison for its Jewish remnants; a gallows for its Jewish citizens."

The *New York Times* urged the United Nations to investigate long-standing Israeli claims of mistreatment of Jews in Arab countries. "Only when the world organization deals even-handedly with injustice and violence on both sides can it hope to play an effective role in promoting peace between the Arabs and Israelis," the *Times* editorialized.

Metro Detroit Jews reacted by showing solidarity with protests around the world. Thousands came to the Jewish Center and filled Shiffman Hall, the gymnasium and hallways. A demonstration by Jewish students in Kennedy Square led to a Sunday vigil in the same site. Local politicians mixed with demonstrators, and a telegram from Michigan Governor William Milliken was read, admidst other short addresses.

Mr. and Mrs. David Heisler and their three children were hidden in Nazi occupied Poland by Franciszek Siwek, a poor farmer. Siwek was given the family possessions and sold items when needed to buy food and newspapers for the Heislers.

After a few months of being hidden in an attic of the Siwek home, which was part of a barn, the Heislers moved to a hole in the barn floor for safety reasons. About three to four feet deep, the hole wasn't much wider than a large table and was lit by a small lamp and lined and covered with straw.

Through the years, the Heislers sent goods and money to the family that cared for them until their liberation in early 1945. In 1969, Mr. and Mr. Heisler brought Siwek to Detroit to spend two months with them. Heisler's son-in-law, Dr. Albert Kaner, provided dental care for Siwek during his stay.

After Heisler, a furrier, passed away, his wife continued to send funds to Poland out of gratitude to he family. The practice was continued by Mrs. Aline (Heisler) Schuraytz, her twin brother, and her younger sister.

David Kay dedicated a memorial to the 800 of his townspeople of Wtoszcowa, Poland, who perished in the crematoria of Treblinka on Yom Kippur 1942. Kay, who lost almost 200 relatives including parents, six brothers and two sisters, unveiled the memorial in Chesed Shel Emes Cemetery in Mt. Clemens in the presence of survivors of his hometown who came from Chicago and New York. Kay was a charter member of Congregation Beth Shalom and an active member of Sharrit Haplaytah, survivors of 1945.

Lt. Larry S. Weill, 21, was killed in action in Vietnam. Married a few months earlier when he was home on leave, Weill, a graduate of Bloomfield Hills High School, attended Michigan State University for two years before enlisting. At the time of his death, Weil was an infantry rifle platoon leader.

Capt. Paul M. Gold was awarded the silver star for gallantry in action while serving as squadron surgeon in the Medical Corps in Vietnam. Gold planned to return to Detroit and resume general practice in the field of osteopathic surgery.

In 1969, Bill Davidson's growing Guardian Industries moved from the Over the Counter market to the American Stock Exchange. The Soberman and Milgrom families of the Mercury Paint Company celebrated its 50th anniversary and dedicated the large new plant on a three and a half acre site on Schaefer near Lyndon in Detroit.

Southfield Mayor Norman Feder made public his opposition to a proposed domed stadium complex to house the Detroit Tigers and Detroit Lions near Northwestern Highway. "Whatever tax income might be generated would be more than offset by requirements for added city services and capital outlays," Feder said. "Besides," he added, "the disruptions to the lives of Southfield residents on game dates and other event dates have to be weighed."

At a meeting at the home of Dr. and Mrs. John Mames, a group of Detroit physicians and dentists

B'nai David on Southfield Road.

(Courtesy of Congregation B'nai David)

Mrs. Joseph Maltzer
(Courtesy of Jewish News)

helped form a group to sponsor the work of Red Mogen Dovid. Members of Shaarit Haplayta donated an ambulance to Magen David Adom and pledged continuous support.

Mrs. Joseph (Lillian) Maltzer became the first woman in the Midwest to hold the office of congregation president when she was elected president of Oak Park's Temple Emanu-El. A native of New York and mother of three, Mrs. Maltzer had a professional background as a nurse and had lived in the area since 1943.

The new Temple Beth El board of governors recommended that the congregation proceed with the building of new facilities on Telegraph and 14 Mile Roads. Temple Israel launched its fund-raising phase of a new building program for a 27-acre site on Middlebelt and 14 Mile Road in Farmington, which the temple had owned since 1965. Jack Caminker, vice president of the Fisher New Center Company and general manager of the Fisher and New Center Buildings, was elected president of Temple Israel.

Year-long talks of a merger between Congregations Beth Abraham and Beth Hillel ended with a negative vote by the membership of Beth Hillel. At the time in 1969, Beth Hillel had 202 members and Beth Abraham, 425. Rabbi Joel Litke of Beth Hillel also opposed the merger, which would have installed Rabbi Israel Halpern of Beth Abraham as rabbi of the merged congregations and Litke as associate rabbi and educator on a two year contract.

Congregation Beth Achim announced that its new building on Twelve Mile Road in Southfield would include the first ritualarium (mikva) under Conservative auspices. With close to 800 members, a permanent sanctuary seating 760 would be adjacent to a larger social hall.

With more than 18 months of planning behind it, Congregation Adas Shalom broke ground in September for its new facilities on a 25-acre site at Middlebelt south of Northwestern Highway, Farmington Township. The main sanctuary would provide permanent seating for a thousand and could be enlarged to 1,400. The 51-year-old Lansing Shaarey Zedek dedicated its new 270-seat sanctuary and large building in East Lansing.

At the annual meeting of the Jewish Welfare Federation, Paul Zuckerman received the Fred M. Butzel Memorial Award for distinguished community service. The Zuckermans endowed a public park in Jerusalem called the Detroit Park and in 1968, the Jewish National Fund named a forest for Mr. Zuckerman. The Detroit community benefited as the Paul and Helen Zuckerman Auditorium and Conference Center at Sinai Hospital was dedicated in 1968 and the couple donated the library site in West Bloomfield Township.

As U.S. astronauts walked on the moon, the 1969 population of Israel was estimated at 2,750,000. Jews

(Courtesy of Jewish News)

Paul Zuckerman with Israeli General Moshe Dayan.
(Courtesy of Leonard N. Simons Jewish Community Archives)

accounted for 2,380,000; Moslems, 275,000; Christians, 70,000; and Druzes, 30,000.

Because of the '67 riots and the exodus to the suburbs, businesses were forced to move north of Eight Mile Road in order to thrive and survive. Ceresnie Brothers and Offen, the furrier concern operated by Harry and Sol Ceresnie and Sam Offen, moved their establishment from Livernois and Outer Drive to Birmingham.

In only nine years, the percentage of white students at Mumford High School dropped from 84 percent to five percent. Only 152 white students out of 2,930 attended the big school with the light blue facade on Wyoming south of Curtis in 1969.

Joe Magidsohn, the first Jewish football star to earn an "M" at the University of Michigan, died at 80. A star halfback in 1909 and 1910, Magidsohn went on to be chief referee at U. of M. football games for 30 years and took an active role in Temple Beth El and Allied Jewish Campaigns.

The community mourned the loss of Abe Kasle, the founder of the Kasle Steel and Aluminum Corporation. Married for 54 years, the Kasles were well known nationally for their Zionist and Federation activities. Locally, Kasle served as president of United Hebrew Schools for 15 years and was an active member of Congregation Adas Shalom and a member of the board of trustees of Sinai Hospital. Kasle was the impetus behind the movement to construct the Hillel Day School Building scheduled to open in September, less than two months after his passing.

The 1969 Yeshiva Beth Yehudah budget was a record $475,000 and the accumulated deficit was $185,000. Despite the deficit, the Yeshiva opened a Mesifta program for 35 ninth and tenth grade boys to receive intensive study of Gemara (Talmud) under the direction of Rabbi E. C. Finkelstein.

Benjamin Friedman was elected to the position of Oak Park associate municipal judge. Mrs. Joseph H. Jackier was renominated for a second term as president to the Women's Division of the Jewish Welfare Federation. Four years after his brother Sander became a United States Senator, Carl Levin was elected to the Detroit City Council.

On the first November Sunday in 1969, ground was broken for the 15-story, 169-unit, Federation-sponsored senior citizen residence on West Ten Mile Road in Oak Park. Leonard Simons, who chaired the Federation Apartments steering committee for five years, was applauded for his efforts by the 200 people attending the ceremonies. Paul Zuckerman, President of United Jewish Charities, gave a brief address before leaving on a United Jewish Appeal study mission to Israel. "The UJC contributed the site for the apartments," Zuckerman said, "but it was through the energy and thousands of hours of work of Federation president Joseph Jackier that this project came to be."

In December, the *Jewish News* moved to the Honeywell Building at 17515 West Nine Mile Road in Southfield. Columnist Danny Raskin remembers cramped quarters in the rented offices of the high-rise building. "The advertising and circulation departments were together in the crowded, unorganized stock room, and the composing room, which many never saw, was in the building's basement," Raskin recalled.

16
1970-1979
DETROIT BECOMES A MEMORY

The Detroit of 1970 had 1,514,063 residents, according to the highest figure published by the United States Census Bureau. This figure was smaller than the city's 1930 population, and represented an estimated loss of nearly half a million since its peak of about 2 million in 1954. Over 660,000 African-Americans lived in Detroit in 1970 and accounted for close to 44 percent of the city's population..

Henry Ford II donated $100,000 to the 1970 Detroit Allied Jewish Campaign. Ford didn't yield to the Arab boycott of Israel, which impacted his automobile sales in the Middle East. The boycott of firms doing business with Israel meant that the Ford plant in Cairo was confiscated by Egypt, and many Arabs shunned Ford products. Ford, however, had a deep sense of fairness which helped bond a strong friendship with Max Fisher.

Meyer L. Prentis, who retired after 40 years with General Motors in 1951, died on his 84th birthday. The longtime treasurer of GM was active in several Jewish causes, in addition to Temple Beth El and the Jewish Welfare Federation. A gift from the Prentis family helped fund a facility in Southfield for Jewish aged persons, which would become known as Prentis Manor.

Rabbi David Bakst, former executive director of

Downtown Detroit also declined by 1970. The Kern's block south of Hudson's (lower right) was empty, and fewer shoppers were frequenting the stores along Woodward.

(Photo by Harry Wolf)

Detroit's Council of Orthodox Rabbis, and who served as spiritual leader of the synagogue in the Jewish Home for the Aged on Petoskey, died at 56. Best known as the supervisor of operations of Sinai Hospital's kosher kitchen, Rabbi Bakst also paid frequent visits to patients and served as unofficial chaplain.

Wolf and Isadore Cohen, founders of the Yeshiva Beth Yehudah Day School who went on to serve terms as president of the school, died in 1970. The brothers, who were engaged in real estate management, also owned some of downtown Detroit's outdoor newsstands.

Developer Louis Schostak, a founding member and past president of Temple Israel, died at 72. Schostak, who at one time studied for the rabbinate at Hebrew Union College, was active in B'nai B'rith and the Allied Jewish Campaign.

In June, a few months after the United Hebrew Schools complex on 12 Mile Road in Southfield was dedicated, the UHS held joint commencement exercises for 292 elementary and high school graduates at Detroit's riverfront Ford Auditorium.

Steve Greenberg, a first baseman like his father, Hank, was named captain of the 1970 Yale University baseball team. Camp Tamarack was swarming with 2,961 campers in 1970, and the Butzel Conference Center was added to the Tamarack skyline.

Vivian Smargon, who taught political science at the University of Detroit, and Terri Faxstein, an art teacher at Mott High School in Warren, were passengers on a bus ambushed by three Arabs on the road from Masada to Jerusalem. While a 48-year-old man from Brooklyn was shot and later died in an army hospital, the two Detroit area women, who were part of a tour group of 35, planned on visiting Israel again as soon as possible.

Barbara Walters, of NBC's Today Show, discussed "The World's Most Fascinating People" during Shaarey Zedek Sisterhood's Woman's World. The two-day conference at Shaarey Zedek also featured an appearance by comedian Henny Youngman. As the Shaarey Zedek Men's Club installed Myron L. Milgrom as its president, the B'nai David Men's Club brought in comedian actor Red Buttons and the singing Barry sisters to headline their night of stars at Ford Auditorium.

Jerry Liebman (also known as Specs Howard) converted a tiny saddlery on Schoolcraft Road in Redford Township into a school to teach the skills needed for careers in radio and television.

The Americana Theater on Greenfield catered to a predominantly Jewish audience during the long run of the movie, *Hello, Dolly!* starring Barbra Streisand. At the time, some of the tunes most popular with Jewish couples were "Aquarius/Let the Sunshine In," (Fifth Dimension); "Leaving On A Jet Plane," (Peter, Paul & Mary); "Raindrops Keep Fallin' On My Head," (B.J. Thomas); and "Bridge Over Troubled Water," (Simon & Garfunkel).

Temple Israel's Rabbi Leon Fram celebrated his 75th birthday, and Rabbi M. Robert Syme celebrated his 50th birthday and 25th year with Temple Israel. A new building to house the Labor Zionist Institute and Sholem Aleichem Institute, was scheduled to be built in Farmington Township on Middlebelt Road between 12 and 13 Mile Roads.

In September 1970, Akiva Hebrew Day School had an enrollment of 160 students in the first through ninth grades and a new principal, Rabbi Gerald Werner. Yeshiva Beth Yehudah opened a dormitory for 12 boys in a house adjacent to the school, on Fairfax just south of Lincoln. The tenth and eleventh graders in the advanced Hebrew studies Mesifta program dormed during the week and went home on weekends.

Temple Beth El, located on Woodward at Gladstone since 1922, undertook a $7 million dollar campaign to build a new synagogue complex at Telegraph and 14 Mile Roads in Bloomfield Township. Plans called far actual construction on the 28.7 acre site, purchased in 1966, to begin in the summer 1971, with completion scheduled for July 1973.

In 1952, at the recommendation of Leonard Simons, Temple Beth El had purchased 22.5 aces on Northwestern Highway between 9 and 10 Mile Roads for its future site. By the 1960s, though, many Beth Elers who originally thought the site too far out of town, thought it wasn't far enough, and the land, which cost around $145,000 was sold for approximately $1 million.

The Conservative movement in Detroit was on the move to the suburbs in 1970. Construction on the Adas Shalom complex to serve the congregation's more than a thousand members began in July. Plans called for completion of the project, on Middlebelt south of Northwestern, prior to the High Holy Days of 1972. Ground breaking for the new Congregation Beth Abraham on Maple Road, between Inkster and Middlebelt Roads, in West Bloomfield Township, was held in September.

Congregation Beth Achim sold its building on Schaefer north of 7 Mile Road and in October joined those already holding services in the former Northbrook Presbyterian Church, on 12 Mile Road in Southfield, since September 1969. As the interior was being refurbished, ground was broken to enlarge the building with additional units.

The Birmingham Temple, founded by eight families seven years earlier, broke ground for its new home on 12 Mile Road in Farmington in November. Ann Arbor's Temple Beth Emeth, founded four years earlier, moved to larger rented quarters in an Episcopal church.

Walter Reuther, who headed the UAW for 24 years and improved the lot of auto workers, was killed an a plane crash along with his wife, the former May Wolf. Reuther was a strong supporter of Histadrut, the Israel Federation of Labor, and other Jewish causes. Mrs. Reuther's father was a resident of Borman Hall at the time of the accident.

A month after Sander Levin ran unsuccessfully for Michigan governor on the Democratic ticket, his uncle, Theodore Levin, died at the age of 73. The elder Levin was appointed United States Federal District Judge by President Harry Truman in 1946,

The Detroit police force, which was only 5 percent black when the '67 riots broke out, was 15 percent black by 1971. One of Detroit's most colorful

Left: Architect's rendering of the Adas Shalom synagogue built in the early 1970s.

Below: Model of the Beth Abraham synagogue.

(Courtesy of Jewish News)

characters died in 1971. James F. (Prophet) Jones, who lived in a 54-room graystone chateau at 75 Arden Park in the Chicago Boulevard-Woodward area, died at the age of 63. The African-American preacher's church on Linwood at Philadelphia was the former large, elegant Oriole Theater, well known to a previous generation of Jewish Detroiters. Followers of the self-ordained prophet lavished expensive gifts on him. Jones had 12 servants, five Cadillacs, 400 suits, and a long white mink coat at his disposal.

The *Free Press* raised its price by a nickel, from ten to fifteen, cents in 1971, and Gordie Howe played his final game as a Red Wing. Dr. Norman Drachler, who began a teaching career in the Detroit Public Schools in 1937 and became superintendent of the Detroit schools in 1966, announced his retirement in 1971. The Hiller family opened a new Shopping Center Market on Orchard Lake and Maple.

Morris Garvett, senior partner of the law firm of Levin, Levin, Garvett, and Dillip died at 77. President of Sinai Hospital at the time of his death, Garvett also served terms as president of the Jewish Community Council and Temple Beth El. Besides a deep interest in Jewish causes, Garvett was considered an authority on music, the arts, American history, and the Civil War period.

With most of the Jewish population in the suburbs, the Petoskey building of the Jewish Home for the Aged was closed. Many residents moved to the recently purchased existing nursing home on Lahser in Southfield, which was renamed Prentis Manor in recognition of a financial gift from the Prentis family.

An impromptu gathering of cars and young people bearing flags at McNichols and Meyers turned into a parade up Meyers to the Jewish Community Center on Curtis to celebrate the 23rd anniversary of Israel's statehood. A Detroit police car—appropriately colored with blue lettering over its white body—joined the line of marchers, and the walkers merged with the crowd of over 2,000 already at the JCC.

Hillel Day School, with 265 students and a staff of 40, had been using its new facilities on Middlebelt Road since September 1970. On May 12, 1971, the building was officially completed with the laying of the cornerstone followed by a breakfast honoring plaque donors. Eleven days later, the dedication ceremony took place, with a cantoral procession and dedication of a Sefer Torah. In September, Akiva Hebrew Day School announced the establishment of a high school program starting with a tenth grade.

The Jewish Welfare Federation presented Jane Sherman with the Sylvia Simon Greenberg Award for outstanding young leadership. The Metropolitan Detroit Federation of Reform Synagogues hosted a reception at the Great Lakes Club. One of the speakers was Mrs. Moshe Dayan, wife of Israel's defense minister.

The same shovel used to break ground for the first and second Temple Beth El structures was used again as sod was turned for the new Beth El at Telegraph and 14 Mile Roads in April. The Birmingham Temple on West 12 Mile was dedicated in June, and the Livonia Jewish Congregation moved to Seven Mile Road.

On Sunday morning, August 29, police escorted a motorcade of open convertibles bearing Torahs from Beth Abraham's Seven Mile location to the new syna-

Max Fisher beams as his daughter, Jane Sherman, receives an award for community service.

(Courtesy of Jewish News)

gogue at 5075 Maple Road in West Bloomfield. Two days later, at 6 p.m., the first regular services were held in the new synagogue.

On Monday October 18, the merger agreement of Congregation Beth Abraham and Congregation Beth Hillel was formally signed. The merged congregation of 580 member families—400 of whom were from Beth Abraham—became Beth Abraham Hillel. Services were scheduled to continue at Beth Hillel's Greenfield synagogue in Detroit for the rest of the year while the building was for sale. Rabbi Israel Halpern, spiritual leader of Beth Abraham, stayed on as rabbi of the merged congregations, while Rabbi Joel Litke of Beth Hillel reached agreement on the settlement of his contract to end his relationship with the congregation.

It was the second merger for Beth Abraham. In 1956 the synagogue had merged with Congregation Beth Yitzchok, which was located on Detroit's east side, on Fischer Street north of Mack Avenue near Indian Village.

For the fourth consecutive year, Sam Karpel, a resident of Detroit's Blackstone Manor complex on Schaefer near Eight Mile, oversaw High Holiday Services in the complex's clubroom to serve the area's remaining elderly.

With several members of the Borman family at his side on the Mount Scopus campus of Hebrew University, Abraham Borman dedicated the Molly Borman House as a tribute to the memory of his wife.

The new Labor Zionist Institute, Hayim Greenberg Center, opened in October at 28555 Middlebelt. In addition to an auditorium, catering facilities, and classrooms for a Lubavitch school, the building housed offices for the Detroit Council of Pioneer Women, Habonim Labor Zionist Youth, Israel Histadrut Campaign, and United Labor Zionist Organization of America.

According to the American Jewish Yearbook, the world Jewish population in 1972 was estimated at 14,236,000. Detroit's estimated Jewish population of 80,000 was the twelfth largest in the United States.

Irving Bernstein, former executive vice chairman of the United Jewish Appeal, accompanied Henry Ford II and Max Fisher on a trip to Israel in 1972. Bernstein wrote a book, *Living UJA History*, describing the visit. Ford met with several Israeli officials, including Prime Minister Golda Meir. Ford advised the Israelis to focus on building trucks and buses, rather than automobiles. Finance Minister Pinhas Sapir agreed and asked if Ford would send engineering consultants. Within two weeks of the meeting, despite the Arab boycott of companies helping the Jewish State, Ford engineers were on Israeli soil.

Bernstein told how the helicopter bearing Ford and Fisher was forced to land because of mechanical

In 1972, trains transporting suburbanites working downtown rumbled through the area that would become the Renaissance Center.

(Photo by Harry Wolf)

problems. Another copter arrived to pick up the stranded Detroit area businessmen, but Ford requested that the yarmulke-wearing pilot of the damaged chopper fly them back and not the pilot who brought the fresh helicopter. "I am not flying with the new pilot, only with the one who saved our lives, as it just might be that he has a straighter line to God," Ford related to Bernstein.

In May, Henry Ford II announced at the Economic Club of Detroit that the riverfront development that would later evolve into Renaissance Center would begin soon.

Detroit had been tossing around a riverfront stadium idea as the city bid on the 1968 and 1972 Olympics. When the Olympics went elsewhere, Detroit proposed a domed stadium on the riverfront west of Cobo Hall that would seat 70,000 for football and 55,000 for baseball. Detroit Lions owner William Clay Ford, Henry's brother, wasn't happy with the traffic patterns of a riverfront stadium, decided a Pontiac location would better serve the interests of football fans, and the domed stadium plan was doomed.

Julius Berman, who was the oldest living member of Congregation Shaarey Zedek, died at the age of 93. Berman, a real estate developer and financier, built and donated the Esther Berman United Hebrew School building on Seven Mile and Schaefer, in memory of his wife.

Berman built several buildings around the Detroit area, including the Lafayette Building downtown. Prior to entering business, he led a colorful military career, serving in the Mexican border campaign tracking legendary bandit Pancho Villa. In World War I, Berman held the rank of captain and for decades participated in colorful uniformed Decoration Day parades.

Shaarey Zedek lost two more of its well-known veteran members: Joseph Holtzman and Philip Eisenshtadt. Holtzman, 77, went into the building business in 1919. In the 1930s, when his brother-in-law joined as a partner, the firm became Holtzman and Silverman. Many subdivisions were established by Holtzman and Silverman. The busy corner area of Maple and Orchard Lake Roads containing the Old Orchard shopping center was developed by the company. Eisenshtadt, who founded the Phillips Shoe Company in 1925 and built the company into a chain of 10 retail stores, died at the age of 80.

Established in 1896 on the corner of Gratiot and Hastings, Lefkofsky's moved to the new Broadway Market in 1912. In 1971, while it was located at the corner of Broadway and Witherell next to the Madison Theater Building, Lefkofsky's opened another sandwich shop on Second Avenue across from the General Motors Building. In 1972, another Lefkofsky's location opened at the Oak Park Lanes on Coolidge.

An estimated 1,500 persons attended funeral services for Rabbi Mordechai Halpern. The spiritual leader of Congregation Beth Shalom for 17 years, Halpern was 44 at the time of his death. Rabbi Joseph Eisenman died at the age of 98. After serving congregations in Russia, Rabbi Eisenman came to Detroit and became spiritual leader of Congregations Beth Jacob and Beth Tefilo Emanuel, as well as president of the Council of Orthodox Rabbis, before moving to Israel in 1949.

The Council of Orthodox Rabbis of Greater Detroit moved from Seven Mile Road to 17071 West Ten Mile in Southfield. Because of the generosity of Julius Rothenberg, who was active in many Jewish causes and a member of the board of Congregation B'nai David, the one-story building was dedicated as the Julius Rothenberg Building.

Merger talks between Temple Beth El and Temple Israel were discontinued. In April 1972, Beth El had a membership of 1,500 families and Temple Israel had 1,600 families. The merger of 3,100 families would have made the largest membership of any Jewish synagogue in the world. When merger talks ended, the new Temple Beth El structure was rising on Telegraph and 14 Mile Roads. Temple Israel had architectural plans for a new facility on 14 Mile and Middlebelt in Farmington Township.

Congregation Shomrey Emunah held ground breaking ceremonies for its new synagogue on Southfield Road and Filmore. Rabbi Shaiall Zachariash was overseeing construction with the help of an active core group, including Marvin Berlin and membership chairman Mark Schlussel.

Congregation Beth Achim dedicated the first phase of the 700-family-member congregation's building program. Phase two, including construction of a 750-seat sanctuary, started several weeks later.

Abraham Selesny was elected president of the newly-founded Young Israel of Southfield. The new congregation met for Sabbath services in the Stevenson School at Lahser and Eleven and a Half Mile (Winchester) Roads.

Even though the 202 residents of the high rise Federation Apartments on Ten Mile Road in Oak Park had moved in the previous August, the building was dedicated in May 1972. Because there were 1,100 applicants, Joseph Jackier, president of Federation Apartments, trumpeted the need for a second building nearby to serve the community's seniors.

The B'nai Moshe Cemetery in Royal Oak was desecrated. Twenty tombstones were damaged and anti-Semitic literature was strewn around. The National Guard helped transport 75,000 donated books for the Brandeis Book Sale from a Royal Oak sorting location to the Detroit Artillery Armory. The following day, the men moved the books to the sale site, a big tent in Northland's Lot D.

The Detroit Chapter of the American Jewish Committee celebrated its 25th anniversary year with a dinner honoring Avern Cohn at the Sheraton Cadillac Hotel. Cohn, who received the Isaiah Award for Human Relations for dedicated community service, was active in several Jewish and humanitarian roles. Recently appointed by Governor Milliken to the Michigan Civil Rights Commission, Cohn was well known for being active in civil rights for the Detroit Bar Association and the State Bar of Michigan.

After 3,342 Broadway performances, *Fiddler on the Roof* closed. However, the movie version starring Israeli actor Topol, was playing around the country. Senior Bernie Gonik, sophomore Marc Plonskier, and freshman Bob Cohen established a kosher fraternity house on the University of Michigan campus.

Sandy Koufax, who retired at the peak of his pitching career with the Dodgers in 1966 at the age of 30 because of the risk of permanent damage to his arthritic arm, was enshrined in baseball's Hall of Fame in Cooperstown, New York. As Koufax was an American celebrity, Mark Spitz became an international one by winning seven Gold Medals for swimming in the Olympic Games held in Munich. However, Jews around the world soon drowned in sorrow as Palestinian terrorist killers massacred members of the Israeli Olympic team.

Congregation Bais Chabad, 28555 Middlebelt near 13 Mile Road, Farmington, opened in time for the High Holidays under the spiritual leadership of

Congregation Beth Tefilo Emanuel Tikvah opened its synagogue in Southfield in 1972.

Rabbi Yitzchak M. Kagan. Congregation Beth Tefilo Emanuel Tikvah, led by Rabbi Leizer Levin, moved from its Wyoming location to Greenfield Road in Southfield. Young Israel of Northwest, the only remaining synagogue on Wyoming in northwest Detroit, sold its building, but the sale agreement allowed for continuance of daily services for another year.

William (Bill) Davidson turned 50 in December. The most popular tunes of 1972 at parties were "Candy Man," (Sammy Davis, Jr.) and "Song Sung Blue," (Neil Diamond).

In 1973, Standard Federal Savings paid 5.25 percent on all regular passbook accounts. A minimum deposit of $1,000 in a one-year certificate yielded 6.66 percent. A minimum deposit of $5,000 for four years yielded 7.19 annually.

Bill Davidson's Guardian Industries, which moved from the OTC market in 1969 to the American Stock Exchange, was listed on the New York Stock Exchange in 1973.

Israel Himelhoch, who helped develop the Himelhoch Brothers and Company into one of Michigan's major business firms, died at 87. After a successful law career, Himelhoch joined his brothers in the women's clothing business in 1910. He held leadership positions in the Jewish Welfare Federation and Allied Jewish campaign, and served five terms as president of Temple Beth El.

Edward G. Robinson, who appeared in more than 40 Broadway plays and 100 films, died at the age of 79. Robinson was generous and active in Jewish causes often lending his name and time and contributing large sums to several Jewish agencies.

Gustie Lederer, mother-in-law of advice columnist Ann Landers and her sister Abigail Van Buren, the syndicated "Dear Abby" columnist, died at the age of 79 in Borman Hall. Mrs. Lederer's sons, Jules and Saul, married the twin sisters in their hometown of Sioux City, Iowa, in 1939 (see page 151).

Yale graduate Steve Greenberg, a first baseman as his father Hank was, went to spring training with the Texas Rangers, but was sent back to the minor leagues without ever playing in a regular season major league game. Ironically, the Rangers already had another Jewish first baseman, Mike Epstein, who made the club

General Ariel Sharon retired after more than 28 years of military service in Israel and eyed a career in politics. Israel's Foreign Minister Abba Eban came to Detroit in May for the Israel Bond dinner honoring Louis Berry. Eban presented Berry with the Sword of Hagana in recognition of his many years of service to his community and to Israel.

Detroiters who served in Israel's War of Independence participated in the Israel Independence Parade in Oak Park. Avern Cohn was the grand marshal of the colorful parade featuring 14 floats marking Israel's 25th anniversary.

Walter E. Klein, who joined the staff of the Jewish Community Council in 1945 and became executive director in 1960, retired in 1973. Mrs. Joseph Jackier, former chair of the women's division of the Allied Jewish Campaign, was elected president of the board of directors of the Jewish Family and Children's Service. Max Fisher took time out from his busy schedule to celebrate his 65th birthday on July 15.

The Women's Orthodox League marked the 25th year in support of the Mikva, the observance of "taharat mishpacha" (family purity). A .spokesman for the group said that in 1973, 150 women were using the ritualarium each month.

Congregation B'nai David said farewell to their spiritual leader, Rabbi Hayim Donin, and his family, who were moving to Israel. Akiva Hebrew Day School also honored Donin, who was one of the founders of the school.

Shaarey Zedek's board of trustees approved an abbreviated Torah reading at Sabbath morning services. Instead of reading the entire Torah over a one-year period, Shaarey Zedek planned to take two years. Congregations Beth Moses and Beth Shalom were already applying abbreviated readings.

In 1973, the official rabbinical organization of the Conservative movement—the commission on law and standards of the Rabbinical Assembly—adopted a new regulation admitting women into the traditional minyan (10 males over the age of 13 needed for community prayer service).

The *Detroit Jewish News* polled several local Conservative rabbis on their views. Rabbi David Nelson of Beth Shalom and Rabbi Moses Lehrman of B'nai Moshe were strong supporters of the new regulation. Rabbi Jacob Segal of Adas Shalom "subjectively" approved, but felt further study of religious law was needed.

Rabbi Milton Arm of Beth Achim and Rabbi A. Irving Schnipper of Beth Moses were firmly opposed. Shaarey Zedek's Rabbi Irwin Groner expressed "a lack of enthusiasm," and gave a statement on the subject to the *Detroit Jewish News*.

> *The primary institution of Jewish life is the home, which has ever served as the source for the transmission of the Jewish heritage. Women were relieved of the religious responsibility of worship so that they could devote themselves to the nurture of children and the needs of the family. At a time when the Jewish home and family are under great stress, and exhibit grave weaknesses, this ruling will tend to further disintegrate the Jewish home. By implying that equality of Jewish men and women is to be understood as similarity of religious roles and duties, this decision accelerates the attack on the Jewish home. However, the Conservative movement is not monolithic and provides freedom for divergent viewpoints. The consequences of this decision will, therefore, be disclosed with the passage of time by those congregations that choose to follow it.*

As Israel was still recovering from the Yom Kippur War, its first Prime Minister died. After a moving religious ceremony in Jerusalem, attended by Israel's leading politicians and brought to the Jewish state live by radio and television, the coffin bearing David Ben Gurion was flown to Sde Boker in the Negev for burial.

Even though most Jews were no longer eligible to vote in Detroit elections, they followed events closely as State Senator Coleman A. Young became the first black mayor of Detroit when he defeated former Police Commissioner John F. Nichols.

Top vote-getter Carl Levin became president of the Detroit Common Council. In the suburban Jewish communities, David Shepherd was elected mayor of Oak Park. Charlotte Rothstein and Sidney Shayne were elected to the Oak Park city council, and Nelson Chase and Stephen Cooper became Southfield councilmen. Marvin Frankel and Benjamin Friedman kept their seats on the bench in Oak Park courts, and Sidney Alexander was elected commissioner in Huntington Woods. Jews around the country followed New York's election as Abraham Beame became the city's first Jewish mayor.

Tainted by the Watergate scandal, Richard M. Nixon resigned the presidency in 1974. Another leader who didn't exude trust, Yassir Arafat, addressed the United Nations General Assembly. Golda Meir resigned as Israel's Prime Minister, and Jews around the world agonized over reports that Jewish women in Damascus were raped and murdered.

Charles Lindbergh, who became an international hero in 1927 by flying solo across the Atlantic Ocean, died at 72 in Hawaii. The Detroit born Lindbergh was

Model of the new Temple Beth El, designed by the world-famous architect Minoru Yamasaki.

(Courtesy of Detroit Jewish News)

remembered by Jews as a sympathizer of the Hitler regime in the 1930s and for his criticism of Jewish influence in the United States. Lindbergh vehemently denied any anti-Semitism when the question arose during interviews.

Righteous gentile Oskar Schindler, who saved more than 1,200 Jews from the Nazis by employing and caring for them in his munitions factory, died at the age of 66. Schindler was arrested twice by the Gestapo and outwitted them in his numerous efforts to save Jews. Two years prior to this death, Schindler visited New York and was honored by over a hundred Jews he saved. Many recalled Schindler's courageous efforts to get Jews out of concentration camps.

The first Delray reunion drew more than 450 people, including many non-Jews. Former residents of the Hungarian-descended Delray Downriver community a couple of decades earlier danced to several Hungarian bands and swapped memories.

Mr. and Mrs. Nathan Silverman celebrated their 50th wedding anniversary in the presence of nearly 200 well-wishers. That same August Sunday saw the dedication of the Silverman Village for emotionally impaired children at Camp Tamarack in Ortonville. Over 1,800 children experienced Camp Tamarack in 1974.

Young Israel of Southfield's Byron Krieger, a two-time Olympian fencer in 1952 and 1956, was elected to the Michigan Amateur Sports Hall of Fame. Avern Cohn was elected national vice president of the American Jewish Committee and celebrated his 50th birthday in 1974.

Prominent jeweler Maurice Enggass died at 84. Along with his brother, Clarence, he operated the Enggass Jewelry Company until its sale in 1958. Enggass was an active member of Temple Beth El, the Jewish Welfare Federation, and other causes.

Bertha Robinson, who was principal of Central High from 1952 to 1959 and of Ford High School from 1959 to 1966, died at the age of 77. Listed in the "Who's Who of Women in Law," Miss Robinson held degrees from Detroit College of Law and served on many boards of Jewish organizations.

Louis Panush, principal of Detroit's Western High School, retired after a 40-year educational career. Panush was well known in Jewish circles, taught in area religious schools, and served as president of Zionist Organization of Detroit and Zionist Federation of Detroit.

The Akiva Hebrew Day School 10th anniversary dinner honored one of the school founders, Rabbi James Gordon of Young Israel of Oak Woods. Honorary dinner chairman Max Fisher introduced the guest speaker, Israeli diplomat Abba Eban. Akiva graduated its first class in 1974. Gary Torgow was among the ten seniors who spent the school year in Israel.

Rabbi Moses Lehrman, of Congregation B'nai Moshe, who often gave the opening prayer at Detroit City Council meetings, received a surprise gift. Council president Carl Levin asked Lehrman to wait as Councilman (Rev.) Nicholas Hood informed the rabbi that the old B'nai Moshe structure on Garfield and Beaubien was about to be demolished for the Medical Center. However, the wooden Mogen David (star of David) was saved and presented to Rabbi Lehrman. Appropriately, Barbra Streisand's "The Way We Were" topped the music charts at the time.

Former intern and resident of Sinai Hospital Dr. Steven Widlansky returned to Detroit after an association with the Indiana University Medical Center and joined the section of cardiovascular diseases in Sinai Hospital's department of medicine.

Congregation B'nai David installed former chief rabbi of Mexico City Rabbi Solomon Poupka as spiritual leader, replacing the departed Rabbi Hayim Donin. Beth Abraham-Hillel celebrated Rabbi Israel Halpern's 25 years with a silver anniversary testimonial dinner. Over 1,500 persons were at the Friday evening dedication services of Temple Beth El's three-day weekend ceremonies in September. Robert H. Naftaly, active in B'nai B'rith and the Jewish Welfare Federation, was elected president of Congregation Beth Moses. Robert A. Steinberg was reelected president of Congregation Shaarey Zedek, and Harold Berry and William Davidson were vice presidents.

Bill Davidson's Guardian Industries topped $100 million in sales for the first time in 1974. Davidson bought the Detroit Pistons basketball franchise for

$8.12 million, and the Lions played their last football game in Tiger Stadium. Sander Levin, who ran for governor on the Democratic ticket in 1970, tried again in 1974 and lost to Governor William Milliken.

In 1975, Detroit's population was 1,335,000, a drop of 28 percent in 25 years. The nonwhite population rose to over 700,000. According to the Jerusalem Municipality, the Jewish population of Jerusalem in 1975 was 250,000. Moslems numbered 85,000 and Christians 15,000.

For the fifth straight year, "All in the Family," was the number-one television program in the country. As Archie Bunker was the favorite bigot of couch potatoes, singer Glen Campbell turned up most often on variety programs singing "Rhinestone Cowboy." "Baretta," starring Robert Blake, hit the airwaves in 1975 and quickly became one of the most popular programs in the Detroit area. Many in the Jewish community tuned in to the new "Saturday Night Live" and enjoyed Detroiter Gilda Radner's characters.

In 1975 Congregation Shaarey Zedek accounted for 733 legible names of graves in its Beth Olem Cemetery in Hamtramck, now on property owned by General Motors. The early records of locations of graves were no longer available; however, it was believed that from the first burial in 1868 until the last in 1948, Beth Olem contained around 1,100 plots.

The official dedication of the Beth Achim Synagogue took place in February. The memorable weekend of festivities featured a Friday Evening Service of Prayer and Tribute honoring all of the past presidents of Beth Aaron and Ahavas Achim, which became Congregation Beth Achim.

Samuel Cohen and Sol Drachler, assistant directors of the Jewish Welfare Federation for the past decade, became associate directors of the Federation in 1975. Martin E. Citrin was elected president of the Jewish Welfare Federation of Detroit, succeeding Mandell L. Berman. Frieda Stollman became the first woman vice president.

Attorney George M. Stutz received the Fred M. Butzel Memorial Award in 1975 for service to the greater Detroit Jewish community. Southfield attorney Mark E. Schlussel, 34, was elected president of the Jewish National Fund Council of Greater Detroit. Popular and entertaining Leonard Simons, president of the Detroit Historical Society, was guest speaker at Temple Beth El's 125th anniversary dinner.

For activities in numerous Jewish causes, the father and son team of Louis and Harold Berry was honored by the American Jewish Committee at a dinner at Shaarey Zedek. Harold Berry, a board member of Congregation Shaarey Zedek from 1965 to 1970, secretary from 1971 to 1972, and first vice president from 1973 to 1974, was elected president of the synagogue in 1975. His father served two terms as Shaarey Zedek president.

The city of Detroit bought the Meyers/Curtis Jewish Community Center, and the cornerstone was laid for the new JCC at Maple and Drake Roads in West

Far left: Robert A. Steinberg was reelected president of Congregation Shaarey Zedek in 1975.
(Courtesy of Congregation Shaarey Zedek)

Left: Robert H. Naftaly was elected president of Congregation Beth Moses.
(Courtesy of Detroit Jewish News)

Harold Berry became president of Congregation Shaarey Zedek in 1975.
(Courtesy of Congregation Shaarey Zedek)

Bloomfield. Construction at the 120-acre site began in 1973 with the target date for completion in early 1976.

Isaac Litwak, an active supporter of Israel and the Jewish Welfare Federation, and a labor leader in the laundry industry, died at 83. Litwak was a close friend of Teamster leader Jimmy Hoffa, who disappeared outside the Machus Red Fox restaurant on Telegraph Road near Maple Road on July 30, 1975, a few weeks before Litwak's death.

Abraham Levine, mayor of Mt. Clemens from 1961 to 1973, died at 71. An active Zionist and a trustee of Congregation Shaarey Zedek, Levine resided in Mt. Clemens and had business interests there.

Bernard Isaacs, scholar and founder of United Hebrew Schools, died at the age of 93. Isaacs, who was associated with UHS for 36 years before retiring in 1955, was a member of Congregation Beth Achim and wrote two books and several short stories about Jewish life in America.

Professor Samuel Levin, who began his 45-year career in education as a teacher at Central High School in 1913 and went on to head the economics department of Wayne State University, died at the age of 87. A son of Rabbi Judah L. Levin, he was active in several Jewish agencies and was well known in the community as a lecturer and writer.

Abraham Borman, who joined his brother Tom in the food market business and helped build the grocery empire that became Farmer Jack Supermarkets, died at 77. Active in the community on behalf of the aged, youth education, Zionism, and other causes, Borman was a longtime member of Congregation Shaarey Zedek.

After serving as a local Young Israel rabbi for 27 years, Rabbi Samuel Prero retired from the active rabbinate at Young Israel of Greenfield. Rabbi Prero planned to spend part of each year in Israel overseeing a Young Israel housing development near Bet

Rabbi Samuel Prero (left) retired from the active rabbinate in 1975. Prero, along with Philip Stollman, David Berris, and Morris Berris, also was active in Akiva Hebrew Day School.

(Courtesy of Akiva Hebrew Day

David and Harry Rott
(Courtesy of Detroit Jewish News)

Shemesh, Israel. Young Israel of Greenfield donated an ambulance for Israel's Magen David Adom in the Young Israel community of Bet Shemesh.

Rabbi Robert Abramson became headmaster of Hillel Day School. A graduate of Brandeis University and the Boston Hebrew College, he attended the Jewish Theological Seminary and was ordained as a rabbi in 1968. Before taking the position with Hillel Day School, Abramson served as educational director of a school in the graduate program in Jewish education of Brandeis University.

Rabbi Jacob Segal, spiritual leader of Congregation Adat Shalom, died on the eve of Yom Kippur at 62 after battling leukemia. Affiliated with the synagogue since 1946, Rabbi Segal was a founder of Hillel Day School and its honorary president.

The Kollel Institute of Greater Detroit began operating in 1975. Rabbi Shmuel Irons, Rabbi Moshe Schwab, and several young rabbis moved to Oak Park to devote their time to Jewish studies and to teach in the Jewish community. A house was purchased on Lincoln east of Greenfield in Oak Park for a residence for the Irons family, while the basement was converted into use as a synagogue and study hall.

Congregation Dovid Ben Nuchim completed its building at 14800 Lincoln in Oak Park, a few blocks east of the Kollel. The synagogue was founded in 1947 by David Rott and his son, Harry, in the Twelfth Street section. The congregation, led by Rabbi Chaskel Grubner, then rented quarters on Dexter before purchasing the former Congregation Beth Shmuel. In 1970, the congregation used the basement of a home on Sherwood in Oak Park. A Torah procession from the home on Sherwood wound its way onto Lincoln to the new building, where Harry Rott placed a Torah in the Ark.

While the Kollel and Congregation Dovid Ben Nuchim opened its doors on Lincoln in Oak Park, Rabbi Elimelech Silberberg assumed the pulpit of Congregation Bais Chabad in West Bloomfield.

In 1976, the first two office towers of Renaissance Center opened, and William L. Hart became Detroit's first black police chief. William Avrunin, who became

Congregation Dovid Ben Nuchim opened its building in 1975.

Far left: Irving Nusbaum

Left: David Hermelin

(Courtesy of Detroit Jewish News)

chief executive officer of the Jewish Welfare Federation of Metropolitan Detroit in 1964, retired from the post at age 65. Lawrence S. Jackier received the 1976 Jewish Welfare Federation Young Leadership Award for outstanding community service. Jack O. Lefton, who held leadership positions in several Jewish organizations, was the recipient of the 1976 Fred M. Butzel Award.

1976 marked several milestones for Temple Israel. In its 35th year of existence, founding rabbi Dr. Leon Fram celebrated his 80th birthday, his 55th year in the rabbinate, and his 50th year as a Detroit rabbi. Thirty-five years after holding its first religious service at the Detroit Institute of Arts, Temple Israel boasted a membership of over 1,500 families, making it the largest Reform congregation in Michigan.

Maurice Aronsson, founder of Aronsson Printing Company, died at age 83. A well known philanthropist who held leadership roles in several Jewish organizations, Aronsson lent money without interest and often without expecting payment in return. Aronsson also was known for providing scholarships to many college students.

Judith Chicorel, who with her husband founded the Sephardic Community of Greater Detroit, died at age 79. Her husband, Jacob, served as the community's

Rabbi Irwin Groner (left), Walter L. Field, and Mandell L. Berman at the 115th anniversary celebration of Congregation Shaarey Zedek, December 12, 1976.

(Courtesy of Congregation Shaarey Zedek)

spiritual leader until his death in 1963.

David Hermelin and Irving Nusbaum co-chaired the Bar Ilan University dinner at Congregation Shaarey Zedek. Well known in the community for their service to several causes, Hermelin was elected president of the Detroit Men's ORT chapter.. Nusbaum's father, Abraham, was the first chairman of the Detroit Friends of Bar Ilan University committee, and the Nusbaums were instrumental in getting the first campus buildings established.

Congregation Beth Achim opened its Mikva (used for ritual immersion). Major donor was Mrs. Hannah Karbal and her late husband, Morris. In 1976 Young Israel of Southfield used a small home on Lahser Road for religious services. In October, the congregation held groundbreaking ceremonies on the adjacent lot south of the home for its new synagogue building.

As the Akiva Hebrew Day School seniors were engaged in their 12th grade studies in Israel, Rabbi Zev Schostak, a native Detroiter who headed a Hebrew day school in Brooklyn, returned home as the new principal of Akiva.

More than 350 people participated in Fresh Air Society's 75th anniversary celebration at the new D. Dan and Betty Kahn Jewish Community Center Building in West Bloomfield. Over a hundred people couldn't get reservations due to lack of space. Many of the Fresh Air celebrants returned to the JCC the following week as the 25th annual Book Fair was held in West Bloomfield for the first time.

A few weeks later, a testimonial dinner for retiring JCC executive vice president Irwin Shaw was held at the Center. Shaw, part of Detroit's Jewish history for several decades, was a teacher in the Detroit Public Schools and local synagogue religious schools. He became assistant director of the Federation in 1948 and executive director in 1951.

As 1976 drew to a close, more Jewish families bought themselves a Chanukah present: a large machine that attached to a television, needed for Sony's new Betamax videocassettes, to record television programs.

With the retirement of Irwin Shaw, effective January 1977, Dr. Morton Plotnick became executive director of the Jewish Community Center. Plotnick, who attended the first Jewish Youth Conference in Jerusalem in 1958, earned degrees from Wayne State University and Michigan State University and taught in the Oak Park school system. Plotnick joined the JCC staff in 1965 and had served as associate executive director for the past four years.

Following in the footsteps of his late father, Irving, who also was an attorney and president of the Jewish National Fund, Mark Schlussel was reelected to a third term as JNF president.

As Mrs. Anatoly Sharansky was traveling to major cities publicizing the plight of her imprisoned activist husband in Russia, the Jewish world lost two of its favorite entertainers. Groucho Marx died at the age of 86, and Zero Mostel at 62. Marx enjoyed decades of fame as he starred with his brothers in vaudeville and movies before hosting the radio and television versions of the quiz program, "You Bet Your Life." Mostel gained fame a decade earlier by starring as Tevye in the long-running Broadway production of *Fiddler on the Roof*.

The local Jewish community lost two of its great ladies of philanthropy. Gertrude Wineman was 87, and Helen L. DeRoy, 95. Mrs. Wineman, whose late husband, Henry, also was active in the community, received the Fred M. Butzel Award in 1962, headed the Women's Division of the Jewish Welfare Federation and the Allied Jewish Campaign, and took part in early UJA Missions to Israel.

Mrs. DeRoy, widow of prominent auto dealer Aaron DeRoy, was involved in many Jewish causes and Temple Beth El, where funeral services were held in Beth El's Helen L. DeRoy Sanctuary.

Local television talk show host Lou Gordon died at 60. The son of a former president of Congregation Shaarey Zedek, Gordon became a fiery radio commentator in 1957 and eventually switched to television. He joined WKBD-TV, Channel 50, in 1965, and in 1971 his Saturday and Sunday evening programs were syndicated in seven other large markets. More than 600 people attended funeral services at Temple Israel, where Gordon was a member.

Real estate developer William Gershenson died

at age 73. The Gershenson brothers brought about several malls, including Tel-Twelve, along with the Pontchartrain Hotel. Gershenson was active in Temple Beth El, the Allied Jewish Campaign Israel Emergency Fund, and civic affairs.

Legendary sports Detroit public school sports coach Sam Bishop died at 78, four days before he was elected to the Michigan Sports Hall of Fame. One of the founding members of Congregation Adat Shalom on Curtis, Bishop did volunteer work in retirement for the Downtown Synagogue Sisterhood when his daughter, Madelyn, became president.

The Pinsker Society of Greater Detroit marked their 50th anniversary with a communal dinner. With roots in the town of Pinsk in what was then Russia in 1927, the group living in Detroit banded together to help each other and perform acts of charity. In 1977, weekly meetings of the members were held at Congregation B'nai David.

The Metropolitan Detroit Chapter of Hadassah's oldest living president, Mrs. Ralph (Sally) Davidson (Bill's mother) was part of the huge crowd celebrating the 60th birthday of the organization at Congregation Shaarey Zedek. Hadassah, operating out of their own building on Seven Mile Road since 1954, made public that they were actively looking for a new suburban site and hoped that an announcement would be made early in 1978.

Norman Cottler, founder of Dexter-Davison Markets whose 10 Mile and Coolidge store in Oak Park had undergone remodeling as Farmer Jack Dexter Davison, served with the Jewish Legion of then Palestine and went to Israel to be part of the 60th anniversary celebration of the Jewish military unit.

In 1977, the well known advertising agency, Simons-Michelson Company, became Simons Michelson Zieve, Inc., when Lawrence Michelson's son, James, and Leonard Simons' son-in-law Morton Zieve took over for the semi-retired owners.

While Camp Tamarack counselors were earning from $400 to $700 for the 1977 season, Tapper's Diamonds and Fine Jewelry opened at 12 Mile and Northwestern. Operated by brothers Howard and Steven Tapper and their sister, Barbara, they would remain

Rabbi Morton Yolkut became spiritual leader of Congregation B'nai David in 1977.

(Courtesy of Detroit Jewish News)

in that location for another 18 years.

Alex Roberg and his wife, Ilse, retired after long careers with United Hebrew Schools. Mr. Roberg served as principal of several branches of UHS in his 37 years of service, while Mrs. Roberg taught in different branches for 28 years and was well known in the school system for her artistic talents.

To honor their daughter's memory, Norman Allan, president of Congregation Adat Shalom and his wife, Esther, endowed a new girl's school for Yeshiva Beth Yehudah. The former Valley Woods Elementary School at 14 Mile and Lahser was purchased by the Allans from the Birmingham School District, and the new home of the Beth Jacob School was renamed the Sally Allan Alexander School for Girls.

With the mayors of Oak Park and Southfield in attendance at the Bar Mitzvah, of Aryeh Posner at the Young Israel of Oak Woods on Coolidge, it was only fitting that Jan Dirk Moss and his wife be there, too. The Bar Mitzvah might never have taken place without the heroism of the non-Jewish Dutch couple. Aryeh's mother, Mrs. Erwin (Esther) Posner, was a little girl in 1943 and part of a family of six that was hidden for almost three years by Mr. and Mrs. Moss.

After Holland was liberated, the family migrated to the United States, Esther married Erwin Posner from Rochester, New York, and a job opportunity brought them to Detroit. Mrs. Posner never forgot the courage and kindness of the righteous gentiles who saved and sheltered her family. She brought them to America for a vacation and to be properly honored and thanked at the Bar Mitzvah.

Young Israel of Southfield held cornerstone laying ceremonies at its Lahser Road site, coinciding with the 55th anniversary of the Young Israel movement in Detroit. Rabbi Morton Yolkut, who headed a Chicago congregation, assumed the spiritual leadership of Southfield's Congregation B'nai David. Ann Arbor's Beth Israel Congregation, founded in 1916, held groundbreaking ceremonies for a new synagogue on Washtenaw Avenue at Austin.

Congregation Beth Moses merged with Congregation Beth Abraham Hillel and became Congregation Beth Abraham Hillel Moses. Rabbi A. Irving Schnipper, who was the spiritual leader of Congregation Beth Moses, joined the spiritual staff to help serve the larger congregation under senior rabbi Israel Halpern.

The new Beth Tephilath Moses building of Mt. Clemens opened in 1977, a few blocks from the original synagogue built in 1921. The old building was bought by the city and razed to make way for a senior citizens high-rise. While the community mourned the passing of Rabbi Moses Lehrman, who had served Congregation B'nai Moshe since 1948, Guardian Industries and Pistons owner Bill Davidson was elected president of Congregation Shaarey Zedek.

Sunday, October 23, marked the groundbreaking of the new Temple Israel complex in West Bloomfield on Walnut Lake Road between Farmington and Drake Roads. Rabbi Leon Fram, founding rabbi of Temple Israel in 1941, turned the first shovel of earth. Temple Israel's membership numbered 1,600 families in 1977.

Singer Pat Boone was known for his strong Christian beliefs and as a staunch defender of Israel. In 1977, his daughter, Debby, became famous with her rendition of "You Light Up My Life." While it was one of the most popular tunes of the year during dinners, the theme from the movie *Rocky*, "Gonna Fly Now" and the theme from *Star Wars* were most often heard from the dance floors.

Mercury Paints, operating out of its main office and plant at 14300 Schaefer in Detroit, had another branch in Detroit and others in Highland Park and Bloomfield Hills, and in 1978 opened another branch on Van Dyke in Sterling Heights.

David Hermelin became general chairman of the Greater Metropolitan Detroit 1978 Campaign for State of Israel Bonds. Irving Nusbaum was elected president of the Detroit Men's Organization for Rehabilitation Through Training (ORT), succeeding David Hermelin.

Because of a gift totaling a million dollars over a period of years, the thousand-plus acreage of Camp Tamarack in Ortonville, was designated the Benard L. and Roslyn J. Maas Recreation Area. Winkelman's, the well known women's wear store, opened in the Renaissance Center and celebrated the 50th anniversary of the chain, which had 86 stores in three states in 1978.

While "You Don't Bring Me Flowers," sung by Barbra Streisand and Neil Diamond, was America's most popular tune, feminist leader Gloria Steinem made national news when she charged that Saudi Arabia was a "Nazi Germany for women," and charged that the Carter Administration was silent regarding Saudi subjugation of women.

Capital Savings and Loan on Southfield Road

William M. (Bill) Davidson, owner of Guardian Industries and the Detroit Pistons, was elected president of Congregation Shaarey Zedek in 1977.

(Courtesy of Congregation Shaarey Zedek)

north of 11 Mile offered 8.24 percent interest on 26-week money market accounts with deposits of $10,000 or more. American Federal Savings also offered 8.24 percent on eight-year accounts with a minimum $1,000 deposit. Both savings institutions had five-and-a-quarter regular passbook accounts, as did Standard Federal Savings. However, the latter only offered 7.98 percent on deposits of $10,000 for 72 months.

Congregation Beth Shalom celebrated its 25th anniversary with a dinner at the synagogue. The 25th anniversary of Rabbi Richard C. Hertz as senior rabbi of Temple Beth El was observed at a testimonial dinner in Handelman Hall of the temple. Temple Israel celebrated their 25-year association of Rabbi and Mrs. M. Robert Syme. Rabbi Daniel B. Syme, director of education for the Union of American Hebrew Congregations, honored his parents at the weekend of events by delivering the Shabbat sermon. The 5,000-member Sinai Hospital Guild held a luncheon at Congregation Shaarey Zedek to commemorate their 25th year of service to the hospital.

On his 90th birthday, Henry J. Blank retired after a 70-year career as a cantor. Blank remained in the role of cantor emeritus of the Livonia Jewish Congregation. Rabbi Chaim M. Bergstein was named spiritual leader of Congregation Bais Chabad of Farmington Hills, which held Sabbath services at 32276 Tareyton. Rabbi Efry Spectre, who led a Philadelphia congregation, assumed the pulpit of Congregation Adat Shalom. Ann Arbor's Beth Israel Congregation, which used the facilities of the B'nai B'rith Hillel Foundation for services, moved to its new synagogue building at 2000 Washtenaw.

Lawrence Gubow, who was appointed to the federal bench by President Lyndon B. Johnson in 1968, died at the age of 59. Gubow, a decorated veteran of World War II action, was active in several Jewish charities and Congregation Shaarey Zedek. Rabbi Harry Greenfield, who led the Delray Hebrew Congregation from 1934 to 1942, died in Israel at the age of 70.

The local community embraced Joan Comay's newest book, *The World's Greatest Story*. Mrs. Comay tackled the history of the Jews and Israel and explained how Palestine is revisionist history.

The name of Palestine was derived from Philistia (in Hebrew, Peleshet), the territory of the Philistines, who had settled in the coastal plain in 17th Century BCE. After the emperor Hadrian crushed the revolt of his Jewish subjects under Bar-Kokhba, in 132-135 CE, he officially called the country Palestina in order to eradicate the name of Judea— in the same way as he gave Jerusalem the Latin name of Aelia Capitolina.

The word Palestine remained in use in the West as a name for the Holy Land. But after Roman times there was no political or territorial entity officially called by that name, until it was revived under the British Mandate at the end of World War I. The name disappeared again from the map at the end of the Mandate in 1948, when the state of Israel was established.

Jewish Welfare Federation President Martin R. Citrin announced an increase to local schools for the 1978-1979 year. United Hebrew School-Midrasha was slated to receive $827,500; Hillel Day School, $77,640; Yeshiva Beth Yehudah, $64,800; and Akiva Hebrew Day School, $40,440.

The annual Adat Shalom Israel Bond Dinner honored Norman and Esther Allan. The former president of E. L. Rice & Company and chairman of the board of Norman Allan Naco Jewelry Company, Allan was a founding member of Congregation Adat Shalom and president of the synagogue in 1978. The Allans were active in numerous charitable causes, and Mrs. Allan was a noted concert pianist and composer. She received her musical education at the London Royal Academy of Music and the Scottish National Academy of Music, and was listed in the international "Who's Who in Women," and the "International Who's Who in Women Composers." In 1975, Congregation Adat Shalom couldn't meet its mortgage obligation. Mr. Allan was instrumental in working out a payment proposal over a 10-year period, which was accepted by the Federal Bankruptcy Court.

In November, a groundbreaking ceremony was held for a 100-unit addition to the Jewish Federation Apartments on 10 Mile Road in Oak Park. Federation Apartments President Mark E. Schlussel said the six-story addition would be called the Anna and Meyer L. Prentis Towers.

With more than 600 people in attendance, Rabbi Meir Kahane, founder of the Jewish Defense League, and Rabbi Sherwin Wine, founder of Humanistic Judaism, squared off in a much-publicized debate at the Birmingham Temple.

Kahane and Wine gave passionate arguments on their views of Judaism, and it was doubtful that any of the minds belonging to those who witnessed the event were changed. "Wine's Judaism is like playing baseball without a bat and ball," one spectator said. "How can you call it Judaism when you deny G-d and the Torah?"

Even months before the November debate, Wine's views evoked reaction from readers of the *Detroit Jewish News*. Dr. Lawrence M. Loewenthal's letter was printed in the Readers Forum of the June 9, 1978, edition.

> Editor, The Jewish News:
>
> I think it's time that the Jewish community as a whole takes some stand concerning Sherwin Wine.
>
> I personally am willing to accept the fact that as a Jew, one can practice his religion as he sees fit, however, I cannot condone nor do I feel one has any right to call oneself rabbi and at the same time preach a philosophy that boasts disbelief in God.
>
> The basic tenet of Judaism is the belief in One Supreme Being and although an individual Jew may personally not believe in a deity, to call oneself a rabbi and hold this belief is unacceptable, a sham, hypocritical.
>
> True, rabbi means teacher, but it means more than that; it means a teacher of the Jewish religion and when used as a title in and of itself must acknowledge the existence of God.
>
> I think the Jewish community should make itself known and not accept Mr. Wine using the title rabbi and if he persists to flaunt and ridicule our religion in this way, I would even go so far as to suggest excommunication.
>
> I only hope we Jews do not stray so far from our religion that we succeed in doing to ourselves what Hitler and the Germans attempted to do to us during the Holocaust.
>
> Dr. Lawrence M. Loewenthal

Carl Levin, 44, who was a Detroit city councilman from 1969 to 1977, was elected to the U.S. Senate. Attorney Hilda Gage, vice president of the Sisterhood of Congregation Shaarey Zedek and active in community causes, won an Oakland County Circuit Court seat, as did Bernard Kaufman.

Peace talks resulted in a shared Nobel Prize for Egypt's President Anwar Sadat and Israel's Prime Minister Menachem Begin in December. However, the death of former Israeli prime Minister Golda Meir dominated the news. Mrs. Meir, who had been under treatment for lymphomia cancer, died at the age of 80 in Jerusalem's Hadassah Hospital.

The Jewish Community Council of Metropolitan Detroit and its rabbinical commission sponsored a memorial program on Sunday, December 12, 1978, at Congregation Shaarey Zedek, which more than 600 people attended.

Mrs. Meir made her stance on a Palestinian state perfectly clear during her tenure as prime minister from 1969 to 1974. On a trip to New York, she told the Jewish Telegraphic Agency:

> Is it necessary to have a 15th Arab country? There are 14, you know. Is that the problem of the tens of millions of Arabs in the world—that they only have 14 countries?
>
> There is an Israeli Arab, a member of Mapam, Zouabi, who made a statement some time ago that there is no such thing as Palestine—Jordan is Palestine. And he is right. When was there Palestine? Before the First World War it was called Southern Syria.
>
> When Britain got the mandate over Palestine, Palestine was then on both sides of the Jordan, the western bank and the eastern bank. And then Churchill divided it in 1922—I hope he will forgive me—because Abdullah was the only emir walking around the Middle East who didn't have something to rule. This is historical. So that this Palestine was divided into Palestine west of the Jordan and Transjordan. And in 1947, Palestine was again divided.
>
> Where are Palestinians? There are more Palestinians in Jordan than Jordanians. It's the same language, it's the same religion, it's the same people, it's the same way of life. Jordan cannot exist without that population. So why should we be interested in creating a 15th state?

In 1979 the Jerusalem municipality estimated that Jerusalem's Jewish population was 275,000. The number of Moslems were estimated at 95,000, and Christians at 15,000.

The Jewish National Fund honored Edith and Joseph Jackier at their annual dinner. Mrs. Jackier was president of the Jewish Welfare Federation Women's Division, Jewish Family Service, Sherwood and University Groups of Hadassah, and active in several other Jewish causes. Mr. Jackier was president of the United Jewish Charities, Jewish Federation Apartments, and served on boards of other Jewish organizations.

Herbert A. Aronsson was elected to a third term as president of the Jewish Home for the Aged. Vice presidents Marvin A. Fleischman and Robert A. Steinberg also were re-elected.

Leon Halpern, chairman of the Holocaust Memorial Center, which was founded by Shaarit Haplaytah, Survivors of the Holocaust, and Rabbi Charles Rosenzveig, HMC executive director, publicized the need for a building to house and serve as a memorial. Planned as a wing of the Jewish Community Center in West Bloomfield, a parlor meeting to raise funds was held at the home of campaign chairman Henry S. Dorfman.

Father Coughlin, the famous radio priest who preached numerous anti-Semitic sermons, died at 88. The Jewish community lost several of its pioneers. Max Weinberg, president and co-founder of Frank's Nursery Sales, died at the age of 63. A member of Temple Israel, Weinberg was active in several causes, including the Allied Jewish Campaigns and B'nai B'rith, and served on the boards of Faygo Beverages and American Federal Savings.

Isadore Winkelman, who along with his brother, Leon founded Winkelman Stores, Inc., the women's clothing chain, died at 77. Philanthropist Daniel Laven, who was active in the Federation and a major supporter of the Yeshiva Beth Yehudah, died at 79. Hersz G. (Tzvi) Tomkiewicz, the administrator of the local Mizrachi-Hapoel Hamizrachi office, died at the age of 84. Active in Orthodox causes and Akiva Hebrew Day Schools, his funeral caused the school's classes to be cancelled on the morning of the funeral to allow students from higher grades to attend the service at the Hebrew Memorial Chapel.

Dooley Cohan, who joined the Detroit Police Department in 1934 and became the first Jewish uni-

The Isaiah window was one of the six windows moved from Temple Israel's Manderson building to the new sanctuary.

(Courtesy of Temple Israel)

Edythe and Joseph Jackier were honored at the 1979 Jewish National Fund dinner.

(Courtesy of Jewish News)

formed sergeant in his 23-year career, died at 73. His son, Michael, a Detroit policeman, wore his father's badge.

As Congregation Shaar Hashomayim of Windsor celebrated its 50th anniversary, the 1,600 family member Temple Israel began construction of its complex on a 22.5-acre site on Walnut Lake Road near Drake. Plans called for the transfer of six stained-glass windows from the Manderson Building in the Palmer Park area to the new temple sanctuary in the summer of 1980.

Congregation Mishkan Israel Nusach H'Ari-Lubavitcher Center acquired the Labor Zionist Institute. The building on Middlebelt north of 12 Mile Road housing the Detroit Labor Zionist Alliance and the Chabad school would provide more space for the Lubavitch school as the Zionist offices relocated. Cantor Chaim Najman, previously in Omaha, Nebraska, was hired by Congregation Shaarey Zedek as cantor and music director.

President Jimmy Carter appointed Avern Cohn, a respected attorney with the firm of Honigman, Miller, Schwartz, and Cohn, to the federal bench as U.S. district judge for the Eastern District of Michigan. As Judge Cohn was moving from his Woodward and Cadillac Square law office to the Federal Building, the Detroit Red Wings relocated from cozy Olympia Stadium on Grand River to the new Joe Louis Arena on the riverfront.

The Detroit Red Wings played their last hockey game in Olympia Stadium in 1979. Years before, many Jewish kids took the Dexter and Linwood buses to the famed arena.

(Courtesy of Michigan Views)

17

1980-1989 THE SHIFT TO THE SUBURBS

Detroit's population declined by 35 percent in the three decades from 1950 to 1980. Detroit had 1,203,339 inhabitants in 1980, and figures showed the city had a black majority of 63 percent. While the city had lost over 300,000 residents in the previous decade, the black population increased to 758,939. The 1980 edition of the *American Jewish Yearbook*, published jointly by the American Jewish Committee and the Jewish Publication Society of America, estimated the Detroit area's Jewish population at 75,000. As CNN, the first 24-hour cable television network began operations, many local Jews and those around the country wondered, "who shot J.R.?" on the top-rated "Dallas" program, which resulted in nearly 80 percent of all viewers in the country tuning in. Theodore Bikel sent a scathing cable to actress Vanessa Redgrave, a notorious PLO supporter. Bikel, president of Actors' Equity and chairman of the national governing council of the American Jewish Congress, sent Redgrave the following cable after a terrorist attack on a kibbutz nursery in Israel that killed three Israelis, including a two and a half year old child. "Your friends have surely struck at the very heart of Zionist imperialism by attacking the Israeli nursery. Bravo."

The Kern's and Crowley's blocks around Hudson's were empty, and Detroit had a huge hole in the heart of downtown.

(Courtesy of Burton Historical Collection of the Detroit Public Library)

Bikel also took on Redgrave's role in attempting to have British Actors' Equity stop its members from working in Israel. Bikel charged that she was helping "the international campaign by PLO terrorists and their supporters to liquidate the Jewish state."

Esther Prussian, who helped structure the Detroit Jewish Welfare Federation, died at 86. Miss Prussian founded the Detroit Service Group in 1926, became its secretary, and helped develop the Women's and Junior Divisions. Her varied interests included avidly following the Detroit Tigers.

Nate S. Shapero, who became a pharmacist and philanthropist, died at 87. The past president of Temple Beth El, Sinai Hospital, and Franklin Hills Country Club was active in civic groups and the Jewish Welfare Federation for decades and was honorary chairman of the board of Cunningham Drug Stores, Inc. Shapero's Economical Drug Store chain merged with Cunningham in 1930.

The second phase of the Jewish Federation Apartments, on the north side of 10 Mile Road in Oak Park, was dedicated. The new Anna and Meyer L. Prentis Towers contained 100 one-bedroom apartments and connected to the original building. The senior citizen complex was a short walk from the Jewish Community Center, Young Israel of Greenfield, and Temple Emanuel.

Days after the May dedication, the 10 Mile JCC was renamed in honor of the late Jimmy Prentis Morris. A generous gift from Mr. and Mrs. Lester J. Morris and the Meyer and Anna Prentis Family Foundation honored the memory of the Morris' son, Jimmy, who died in October 1965.

George M. Zeltzer, president of the Jewish Welfare Federation, appointed Southfield attorney Mark E. Schlussel chairman of the Federation's culture and education budget and planning division. Schlussel, past president of Jewish Federation Apartments and Jewish National Fund of Detroit, continued serving on their boards.

The Organization for Rehabilitation through Training (ORT) began 100 years earlier in Russia to help Jews escape poverty. David Hermelin and Detroit Men's ORT president Irving Nusbaum co-chaired a successful dinner at which more than 500 persons attended. Later in 1980, Nusbaum was honored by the American ORT Federation at an award dinner in New York as the ORT Man of the Year.

The Jewish Welfare Federation upped its allocations to Jewish education for the 1980-81 year. United Hebrew School-Midrasha received a $30,000 increase to $885,570. Hillel Day School received a $6,000 increase to $86,500; Yeshiva Beth Yehudah's allocation of $71,500 was $4,000 higher than the year before; and Akiva Hebrew Day School's $10,000 increase gave them $52,000.

Akiva Hebrew Day School leased the former Annie Lathrup School at 27700 Southfield Road and started the September semester there. Rabbi Henoch Millen, principal; David Tanzman, president; and Dennis Eisenberg, administrative director, beamed proudly at the first day of school as 282 students filed in.

Rabbis Fram, Syme, and Loss officiated at the formal dedication of Temple Israel's new complex at 5725 Walnut Lake Road in October. The first service in the new sanctuary had taken place weeks earlier on September 5, 1980, when the Bar Mitzvah of David Comisar was observed. The six large, colorful windows, installed in Temple Israel's Manderson Road sanctuary in 1966 at the 25th.anniversary of the congregation, were moved to the new location.

Bill Davidson's Guardian Industries became global in 1981. A new plant in Luxembourg helped to dent the Western European glass market. The Detroit area auto industry was hurting as the Dodge Main Assembly plant in Hamtramck was closed. Ford also felt the financial pinch as its stock went down to $15.75, from a high point of $51.87 per share three years earlier.

Mischa Mischakoff, who moved to Detroit in 1952 after serving as concertmaster in New York, Philadelphia, and Chicago, and in the same role for the Detroit Symphony Orchestra until 1968, died at age 85. Mischakoff gave private lessons and taught at Wayne State University, and he often was part of various orchestras. A collector of rare violins, he owned three Stradivarius violins.

Long-time resident of Borman Hall, Simon

Weingarden, who operated the newsstand at the corner of Michigan and Woodward from 1910 to 1960, died at the age of 99. Isadore Levin, who participated in the Versailles Peace Conference in 1918 (page 65) and went on to become a distinguished Detroit attorney, died at 88.

Nathaniel Goldstick, who had a long career in Detroit legal circles as an attorney and law professor, died at 87. A past president of Temple Israel and the Old Newsboys Goodfellow Fund, he ran for Congress in 1936 but lost to incumbent John D. Dingell. David H. Shepherd, Oak Park's mayor since 1971, died at age 53. Shepherd operated an advertising agency and was the former publisher of the weekly *Oak Park News*.

Considered by many as the Grand Old Lady of the Jewish community, Rose Zuckerman died at 93. She was known by national and Israeli leaders through her decades of activities and her son, Paul's, efforts on behalf of Jewish causes. Her late husband, Joseph, was a linguist who could speak 12 languages and was a translator in Michigan courts, while Mrs. Zuckerman knew eight languages.

Nathan Silverman, a partner in the law firm of Holtzman & Silverman and active in numerous civic activities and Jewish causes, died at age 79. Silverman was well known for his decades of activities on behalf of the Fresh Air Society,

Sam Marcus, who succeeded Irwin Shaw as executive director of Fresh Air Camp in 1956 and oversaw the development of Camp Tamarack into Michigan's largest outdoor education program and America's largest year-round Jewish camp, retired.

For the past three years, the acreage around the camp was known as the Benard L. and Roslyn J. Maas Recreation Area. In 1981, 86-year-old philanthropist Benard Maas pledged $1.5 million to the camp, resulting in the Fresh Air Society renaming Camp Tamarack at Ortonville in honor of Maas and his wife.

Rabbi E. B. Freedman, who had been executive director of the Kollel Institute of Greater Detroit since 1977, was appointed administrative director of the Yeshiva Beth Yehudah. Rabbi Freedman also represented the Orthodox community in the planning of the I-696 decks over the freeway running through Oak Park and Southfield.

The 52nd anniversary banquet of the Council of Orthodox Rabbis of Greater Detroit honored the memories of Abe, Max, and Sol Nusbaum. The three brothers were active supporters of many organizations, schools, and synagogues in the Jewish community.

Former Detroiter Rabbi Joel Roth, associate dean of the rabbinical school at the Jewish Theological Seminary of America and a member of the Committee on Law and Standards of the Rabbinical Assembly, was the visiting scholar-in-residence at Congregation B'nai Moshe in March.

Rabbi Roth told the assembled that Conservative Judaism "is in trouble," according to Alan Hitsky's article in the *Detroit Jewish News*.

> Rabbi Roth said many Conservative congregations would be horrified if their rabbis were not observant Jews, although the members themselves are not observant.
>
> Rabbi Roth was adamant in his proposal that Conservative congregations should be more observant. He said non-observant members should not be allowed to sit on the boards of Conservative synagogues.
>
> He said this would be a divisive proposal that would lead to shrinkage and probably the end of some Conservative congregations: This would not necessarily be bad if it led to a stronger Conservative Judaism, he asserted.

An Arab ethnic guide produced by the Detroit Public Schools caught the eye of a Jewish teacher, Doris Yehiel of Grayling School. The guide contained a map of the Arab world showing Israel as "Arab land occupied by Israel." Mrs. Yehiel also objected to Jerusalem's listing as a city on the west bank of Jordan. Islamic and Christian holidays were listed but Jewish holidays were not. Mrs. Yehiel's objections led to Detroit Public School Region 6 superintendent Seymour Gretchko having the guide withdrawn and corrected.

While Michigan Congressmen James Blanchard, William Broomfield, Carl Levin, and Donald Riegle took an active role against the Reagan administration's proposed sale of enhanced equipment to Saudi Arabia for use on its U.S.-made F-15 jet fighters, Israel's 33rd birthday was celebrated with a parade at Southfield's

Civic Center on May 10. Planners claimed it was the biggest Israel Independence Day Celebration to date in the Detroit area.

Less than a month later, pilots of the Israeli Air Force destroyed an Iraqi nuclear facility under construction. Israel's premier Menachem Begin told the JTA that he acted because "it was virtually now or never to knock out Iraq's nuclear capability." Begin called Iraq's ruler, Saddam Hussein, "cruel and that he would not hesitate to drop nuclear bombs on Israel." Begin also expressed disappointment with the U.S. State Department for issuing a condemnation of Israel's action without ever hearing Israel's explanation for the raid.

Groundbreaking ceremonies for the Bais Chabad Torah Center in West Bloomfield were held on Sunday, September 13. Construction on the building, on the south side of Maple Road one-fifth of a mile east of Orchard Lake Road, was under the direction of member Ronald Rogers' building company.

Congregation Beth Abraham Hillel Moses announced the retirement of Rabbi Israel Halpern and Cantors Shabtai Ackerman and Israel Fuchs. After 35 years of service as cantor of Congregation B'nai David, Hyman Adler retired.

For the first time in Congregation Shaarey Zedek's history, women were given the honor of opening the Ark during High Holy Days. Women and men who served on the board opened the Ark for selected prayers.

With many of the audience of 600 in the Jewish Community Center's Shiffman Hall standing, the official groundbreaking ceremonies of the long-planned Holocaust Memorial Center took place on Sunday, December 6, 1981. Rabbi Charles Rosenzveig, executive director of the HMC, and chairman Leon Halpern led the assembled to the site in front of the JCC's main entrance.

Detroit Bank became Comerica in 1982, and pizza baron Mike Ilitch purchased the Detroit Red Wings. The 1982 Super Bowl was played in the Pontiac Silverdome, and Detroit hosted its first International Grand Prix Formula One auto race.

The J.L. Hudson Company, a Detroit landmark that had done business in the heart of downtown for 101 years, announced it would be closing early the next year The news shocked and saddened Detroiters and seemed to drive another nail in the city's coffin.

Sonny Eliot, a television weathercaster in Detroit since 1947, was terminated by WJBK-TV (Channel 2).

The *Free Press* headline told the story of the continuing abandonment of Detroit.

(Author's collection)

Clothier Max Pincus purchased one of Detroit's famed restaurant's, the London Chop House.

Edward Rosenthal, a former director of the Chicago Jewish National Fund, succeeded Percy Kaplan as the executive director of the JNF in Michigan. Jack Zwick, who served as president, vice-president, and treasurer of the Young Israel of Southfield and past president of the Association of Hebrew Day Schools of Greater Detroit, was elected president of the Jewish National Fund Council of Greater Detroit.

Mr. and Mrs. David B. Hermelin purchased a 10,000 tree forest in Israel through the JNF. It was the second forest to be established by the Hermelins. Doreen Hermelin, a member of the Detroit Women's Division Executive Board and numerous Jewish organizations, accepted the role of chairman of Metro Detroit Israel Bonds Women's Division.

Academy Award winner Henry Fonda starred in the movie, *On Golden Pond*, which played at the Berkley Theater. His daughter, Jane, who had spoken passionately in defense of Israel in recent years, criticized the media's double standard applied to Israel after its invasion of Lebanon.

"It's easy to sit over here, Jew and non-Jew, and criticize," the actress told the JTA. "However, we haven't lived on the border of Lebanon, and we were not shelled for 12 years by Palestinian terrorists.

" 'Israel can't make mistakes,' many people, including Jews, scream and yell. But who criticizes Yassir Arafat and what he represents?"

Yassir Arafat had learned to play to the U.S. media, according to syndicated columnist George Will. "The PLO is hiding behind the babies that Arafat is kissing for U.S. television cameras," Will wrote.

Another syndicated columnist, James Kilpatrick, said of the PLO:

> *The PLO is not a state. It is a cancer. Like other cancerous lesions, it must be cut out, roots and all, before the malignancy spreads. Left alone, whether through fear of surgery or hope of remission, cancer only gets worse.*
>
> *Who is to blame for the suffering in Beirut? Who prolongs the agony? The PLO moved into this beautiful and inoffensive city like a gangster mob, terrorizing the inhabitants.*

As several thousand members of the local community milled about the Southfield Civic Center on May 2 to celebrate Israel's 34th birthday, Congressman William Brodhead (D-17th District) gave the brief keynote address.

"It is not Israel's 34 years that count, but the Jewish People's 5,742 years of tradition and history that count," Brodhead said. "The United States must make it clear that it is totally committed to Israel. We must stop the insane policy of selling arms here and there and everywhere in the Middle East."

Congregation Shaarey Zedek lost some prominent members in 1982. Architect Charles Agree, who was among the founders and early presidents of Shaarey Zedek's Men's Club, and who served in an advisory capacity in construction of the synagogue buildings, died at age 84. Edward Fleischman, 84, an oil company executive and chairman of the board of Peerless Distribution Company, was a past president of the Jewish Home for the Aged and served on boards of several Jewish organizations. Hyman Safran, a former president of Shaarey Zedek and the Jewish Welfare Federation, was 69.

Jack O. Lefton, the retired president of Red Sea Oil Company and the Jewish Home for the Aged, and who served on numerous Federation committees, died at the age of 80. Charles Gershenson, a former lawyer who became president of Ned's Auto Supply and a shopping center developer, died at 81. Gershenson chaired the Allied Jewish Campaign and was president of the Jewish Community Council and the Franklin Hills Country Club, and he served on the board of Sinai Hospital.

Rabbi Joshua Sperka, former spiritual leader of Congregation B'nai David and affiliated with the Young Israel of Greenfield for the past 24 years, died at 76. Rabbi Sperka was president of the Detroit Friends of Shaarey Zedek Hospital in Jerusalem and official chaplain of the Council of Orthodox Rabbis to Jewish patients in local nursing homes. A noted scholar, Rabbi Sperka authored four books.

Rabbi Hayim Donin, spiritual leader of Congregation B'nai David before moving to Israel in 1973, died in Jerusalem at age 54. Harry Weinberg, active in

Yiddish Theater and director of Weinberg's Jewish Hour that was heard on WJBK and WJLB radio from 1932 to 1954, died at 92. For the previous 30 years, Weinberg directed the Yiddish performance at the Book Fair in the Jewish Community Center.

Rabbi Richard C. Hertz, who served Temple Beth El from 1953 until 1982, stepped down from the pulpit to become Rabbi Emeritus. Hertz also became Distinguished Professor of Jewish Studies at the University of Detroit, where an endowed chair was established in his name. Rabbi Daniel Schwartz, Beth El's assistant rabbi for the previous eight years, was promoted to senior rabbi.

Rabbi Yoel Sperka was appointed spiritual leader of Congregation B'nai Israel-Beth Yehudah. Rabbi Sperka, a son of Rabbi Joshua Sperka, held a master's degree from the University of Michigan and headed yeshivas (day schools) in Denver and Los Angeles.

Jewish Welfare Federation President Avern Cohn announced that Wayne L. Feinstein, director of long-range planning for the Council of Jewish Federations in New York, would assume the post of executive director of the Jewish Welfare Federation of Detroit.

As *Raiders of the Lost Ark* was held over at suburban movie theaters, the Ark at the Bais Chabad Torah Center at 5595 West Maple Road in West Bloomfield was opened for its first Sabbath service. However, the official dedication of the $150,000 facility containing the main sanctuary and offices would take place four months later in June. Future plans called for a library, kitchen, study hall, kiddush room, and ritualarium. Cantor Ben Zion Laxner, a native of Israel who served congregations in Brussels and Dallas, was hired as cantor of Beth Abraham Hillel Moses.

Groundbreaking ceremonies on the 160-acre senior citizen complex west of the Jewish Community Center in West Bloomfield, took place on Sunday, September 12. The Jewish Home for the Aged—celebrating its 75th anniversary in 1982—would operate the Edward I. and Freda Fleischman Residences and the Louis C. and Edith B. Blumberg Plaza. The Lillian and Samuel Hechtman Apartments would be the third phase of the Jewish Federation Apartments.

January 17, 1983, was a sad day as Hudson's closed its downtown store forever. Detroit lost another landmark as Olympia Stadium, closed three years earlier, was torn down. Comerica acquired Bank of the Commonwealth, and Domino's Pizza owner Tom Monaghan bought the Detroit Tigers.

On the same day Hudson's closed, fire consumed five Torahs, the sanctuary, social hall, lobbies, and front section of Congregation Beth Abraham Hillel Moses. The school wing of the structure suffered light damage but continued to serve as the school, and space was found for a temporary sanctuary and offices. The mortgage on the 12-year-old building had been paid off and the congregation opted to raise funds to be added to the insurance settlement for rebuilding. Investigators believed the cause of the devastating fire was a match or cigarette carelessly tossed in a trash can near the lobby entrance.

Through its 14-month Operation Ner Tamid fund-raising efforts, Congregation Adat Shalom paid off its $1.915 million mortgage. Rabbi Reuven Drucker, who

In 1982, Congregation Shaarey Zedek celebrated its 120th year. Officers were: (seated, left to right) David B. Hermelin, first vice president; Harvey L. Weisberg, president; Myron L. Milgrom, second vice president; (standing) Marvin Fleischman, treasurer; Irving Laker, secretary.

(Courtesy of Congregation Shaarey Zedek)

headed the Etz Chaim Center in Baltimore, was hired by Young Israel of Greenfield to replace Rabbi Feivel Wagner, who became spiritual leader of a Young Israel congregation in his native New York.

Gary Torgow, a 23-year-old attorney and third-generation member of Young Israel of Oak Woods, became the youngest congregation president in the 60-year history of the local Young Israel movement.

Kadima, the Jewish mental health agency, began in 1983 to provide psychological, residential, employment, and social services. David Hermelin, active in numerous charitable organizations and recently elected president of Congregation Shaarey Zedek, took on the additional role of national chairman of the U.S. Israel Bond Organization. Southfield accountant Robert Naftaly, a member of the Jewish Welfare Federation executive committee and serving on several boards of Jewish organizations, was nominated by Michigan governor James Blanchard to be state budget director.

As the Jewish world agonized over the arrest of hundreds of Iranian Jews and the disappearance of numerous Jews in Argentina, the main celebration of Israel's 35th Independence Day took place at the West Bloomfield Jewish Community Center on May 1. Thirty groups, led by the Jewish War Veterans, participated in the parade.

Judge Avern Cohn, serving his second term as president of the Jewish Welfare Federation, appointed Federation vice president Dr. Conrad Giles to head the study on helping the elderly to maintain independent living as long as possible.

Perry Drug Stores, founded in 1957 by 27-year-old pharmacist Jack A. Robinson was listed on the New York Stock Exchange for the first time in 1983. Shopping center magnate A. Alfred Taubman, along with industrialists Max Fisher and Henry Ford II, was part of a group of investors acquiring the well-known auction house Sotheby's. Several showings of Barbra Streisand's movie, *Yentl*, were booked by local Jewish organizations for fund-raisers.

The community lost some familiar names and faces in 1983. Michael Zaks, who became executive director of Fresh Air Society in 1981 after working in several facets of the camp since 1968, died at the age of 37. Former executive director of the Jewish Home for the Aged Ira Sonnenblick died at 75, and Joseph Sandweiss a member of the Jewish Legion in World War I, died at age 87.

Gus Newman, Detroit's first Jewish scoutmaster in 1906 who became a co-owner of Henry the Hatter and a Ford agency on Dexter, died a few weeks shy of 92. Newman was active in Jewish charities before the Federation was formed in 1926 and served several terms as president of the Jewish Home for the Aged.

Jacob Nosanchuk, who had celebrated his 75th wedding anniversary the previous year, died at 94. The Nosanchuks were major supporters of the Jewish National Fund and Jewish day school education.

The Detroit Tigers drew 34,124 fans to a Sunday doubleheader on June 12 against the Cleveland Indi-

Federation leaders Avern Cohn (left) and Max Fisher. In 1983, Judge Cohn was serving his second term as president of the Jewish Welfare Federation, and Max Fisher was celebrating his 75th birthday.

(Courtesy of Leonard N. Simons Jewish Community Archive)

ans. Jewish fans turned out in great numbers to see the between-games ceremonies retiring Hank Greenberg's uniform number. It was the former Tiger slugger's first trip to Detroit in almost 25 years.

A few weeks later, Greenberg joined former stars at Chicago's Comiskey Park for ceremonies surrounding the All-Star Game and the first star match-up held 50 years earlier at the same location.

As Detroit fans readied to join the national television audience, the last local commercial featured Irving Nusbaum extolling the virtues of the $4.88-a-yard sale at New York Carpet World. Nusbaum, already well known in the Jewish community for his charitable work, also was becoming a celebrity by doing television commercials for his own business firm.

Mrs. Sharon Hart, a board member of Hillel Day School and active in numerous Jewish organizations,

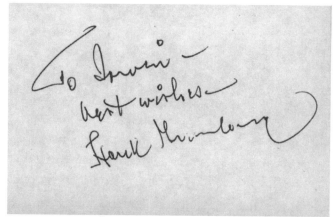

Above: Ernie Harwell (left) listens intently as Hank Greenberg addresses the crowd regarding his playing days in Detroit.

Left: The author took this photo of Hank Greenberg and his son, Steve, prior to the retirement of the former Tiger's uniform number between games of a doubleheader. In return for the photo requested by the Greenbergs, Cohen was given a personalized autograph.

(Author's collection)

Rabbi Sholom Goldstein, one of the Yeshiva Beth Yehudah's top educational leaders since 1947, died in 1984.

(Courtesy of Yeshiva Beth Yehudah)

was the chair of the school's 25th annual fund-raising dinner held at Congregation Shaarey Zedek. Five months later, in October, Hillel Day School celebrated its 25th anniversary by honoring the founders, graduates, and teachers at the school building.

As Ethiopian Jews were being brought to Israel in 1984, Detroit welcomed Jewish athletes from all over the world to compete in the Jewish Community Center Maccabi Games. Aaron Krickstein of Grosse Pointe became the youngest man to be ranked in the world's top ten tennis players. Counselors at Camp Tamarack were earning between $850 to $1,250 for the summer.

Charles A. Buerger, who published the *Baltimore Jewish News*, purchased Detroit's *Jewish News* from Philip Slomovitz and installed Gary Rosenblatt as editor. Operations were transferred to rented quarters in the Control Data Building on Civic Center Drive near the Prudential Town Center.

Akiva Hebrew Day School celebrated its 20th anniversary with a dinner at Congregation Shaarey Zedek. Avital Shcharansky, wife of jailed Soviet prisoner of conscience Anatoly Shcharansky, was the guest speaker. Rabbi Gerald Teller, superintendent of United Hebrew Schools, estimated that 60 to 70 percent of local Jewish children up to age 13 received some type of Jewish education. Many not in day schools, however, only received two hours of weekly instruction.

After the fire in the third week of 1983 which destroyed much of Beth Abraham Hillel Moses, the newly reconstructed sanctuary, lobbies, and front portion of the building were open for the High Holy Days of 1984. A few weeks later, some members of the synagogue were among the capacity crowd at Tiger Stadium at game five of the World Series as the Tigers defeated San Diego to become World Champions.

Almost three years after its groundbreaking ceremonies, the 12,000-square-foot Holocaust Memorial Center opened adjacent to the West Bloomfield

The Holocaust Memorial Center opened in October 1984.

Jewish Community Center. Nearby, on the Jewish Community Campus, the Edward I. and Fred Fleischman Residence of the Jewish Home for the Aged was dedicated.

Judge Avern Cohn was reelected chairman of the Jewish Welfare Federation's Executive Committee. Judge Cohn's father, Irwin I. Cohn, died a short time later at the age of 88. The elder Cohn had his own practice, which merged into the law firm of Honigman, Miller, Schwartz, and Cohn, and was active in numerous Jewish causes. Mandell Berman, Federation president from 1972 to 1975, was the first recipient of the American Jewish Committee's Cyrus Adler Distinguished Jewish Community Service Award.

In 1985, as buildings opened in the suburbs, buildings continued to close in Detroit. The Stroh Brewery announced its closing, as did the large downtown Woolworth store on Woodward. The huge Uniroyal plant near the Belle Isle Bridge met the wrecking ball, leaving acres of emptiness where the throng of workers used to create tires and traffic jams. Faygo Beverages, which had started back in 1907 when Ben and Perry Feigenson operated from the back of their horse-drawn wagon, celebrated its 50th year in its large plant on Gratiot, a mile east of the Eastern Market.

As M. Jacob & Sons celebrated the 100th year of the bottle business founded by Max Jacob, Carla Schwartz, a freelance writer, wrote an article on fashion for the *Jewish News'* first issue of a new glossy magazine, *Style*. Schwartz would eventually become editor of the stylish publication. Charlotte "Tavy" Stone, the fashion writer of the *Detroit News*, died at 57. Besides writing about fashion and features, Stone created "Contact 10," a front-page column answering readers who submitted a problem, and created Cleo, a nationally known astrologist.

The majority of local Conservative rabbis approved the ordination of women rabbis by their governing body. Some local rabbis maintained silence on the subject. However, Rabbi Milton Arm, of Southfield's Congregation Beth Achim, gave his opinion to the *Jewish News*.

The Conservative moment has veered far from its original principle of maintaining an identity with historical Judaism. It's getting to the point where it isn't really a movement anymore. The institutions are there, but there are very few Conservative Jews practicing on a daily basis.

The *Jewish News* article in its February 22 edition concluded:

While the Reform and Reconstructionist movements have been ordaining women rabbis for more than a decade, the issue has prompted a hot debate among Conservative Jews. Spiritual leaders like Rabbi Arm see last week's vote as a sign that Conservative Judaism is slowly drifting toward the Reform end of the spectrum.

The Muslim Students Association (MSA), a major anti-Semitic group found on campus, was selling copies of *The Protocols of the Learned Elders of Zion*. Muslims on the Wayne State University campus defended their right to sell the book cloaked in falsehoods. "Let the public buy it," a leader of MSA told the *Jewish News*, "and they will decide if its false or not."

Jane Sherman took on the role of national chair for Project Renewal to head a special task force for Project Renewal fundraising. A member of the Jewish Agency Board of Governors, past chair of the United Israel Appeal Project Renewal Committee, and co-chair of the United Jewish Appeal Project Renewal Committee since 1979, Mrs. Sherman served on several boards besides being a UJA national vice chair.

Jordan's Queen Noor al Hussein brought her revisionist history to Princeton University. "Israel must face the ineradicable human presence of millions of Palestinians resolved to regain their rights in their ancestral homeland," King Hussein's wife told the 1985 graduating class. The queen, born Lisa Najeeb Halaby in Washington 33 years earlier, was a member of Princeton's first coeducational class and graduated with a degree in architecture and urban planning.

Ethiopian Jews were being brought to Israel in "Operation Moses" in 1985, and 122 Detroit Jews spent 10 days in Israel with the United Jewish Appeal's Koach Mission. Led by Stanley D. Frankel and Michael W. Maddin, the largest such group ever to come from

Detroit met many new arrivals from Ethiopia.

The community lost two well-known women. Golda Krolik, who died at 92, taught Sunday school at Temple Beth El and English to new immigrants. She held office in numerous Jewish organizations and earned the highest community recognition as a Fred M. Butzel Award recipient. Esther (Mrs. Norman) Allan died five weeks after celebrating her 50th wedding anniversary. The daughter of the late Cantor Boyarsky of Congregation Beth Tefilo Emanuel, Mrs. Allan attended the London and Scottish academies of music and recorded two albums of her compositions. She was an involved member of 21 Jewish groups and musical organizations in the Detroit area.

Allen Warsen, who taught history in the Detroit public schools for 33 years and directed Adat Shalom's religious school for 18 years, died at 81. Warsen founded the Jewish Historical Society of Michigan in 1959 and wrote numerous articles, including 350 book reviews for the *Jewish News*.

Phillip Applebaum was named executive director of Akiva Hebrew Day School. President of Young Israel of Oak Woods and past president of the Jewish Historical Society of Michigan, Applebaum served on the board of the Midrasha College of Jewish Studies. After 29 years with Shaarey Zedek's Beth Hayeled nursery and kindergarten, Rosaline Gilson retired. Janet Pont, a professional singer and musician, became the new director of Beth Hayeled.

With the acquisition of all outstanding shares of common stock by Bill Davidson, Guardian Industries returned to private ownership. Davidson's mother and aunt attended the dedication of the Hadassah building on Orchard Lake Road in West Bloomfield. The wheelchair-bound sisters were the oldest living Hadassah presidents and original founders. The building, which formerly housed the West Bloomfield Township Public Library, was named the Sarah and Ralph Davidson Hadassah House.

Traverse City's Congregation Beth El celebrated its 100th anniversary. Arnold Sleutelberg, a Hudson, Michigan, native who attended Hebrew Union College in Cincinnati, was the congregation's student rabbi during the previous two summers.

The *Jewish News* reported that "the Yeshiva Beth Yehudah, composed of the boys' elementary school, the Sally Allan Alexander Beth Jacob School for Girls, and the boys' high school and college, voted to sever its relationship with the boys' high school and college and to allow that school to function as a separate entity under the name Yeshiva Gedolah." A state-recognized school, the Yeshiva Gedolah High School located in Congregation Dovid Ben Nuchim on Lincoln in Oak Park under the direction of Rabbi Leib

Sarah and Ralph Davidson Hadassah House in West Bloomfield was dedicated in 1985.

Bakst.

Rabbi James Gordon, of Young Israel of Oak Woods, completed 22 years of service as the congregation's spiritual leader. The Gordons revealed plans to make Aliyah to Israel. Young Israel engaged Rabbi Eliezer Cohen and Rabbi Reuven Drucker as spiritual leaders. Rabbi Drucker also led Young Israel of Greenfield.

Jack A. Robinson, chairman of the board and chief executive officer of the 300-plus Perry Drug Stores, received the Jewish National Fund's Tree of Life Award at a dinner in New York. The national award was given in recognition of exemplary professional leadership and humanitarian service. Later in the year, Robinson chaired the first anniversary dinner of the Holocaust Memorial Center Mrs. Jack (Aviva) Robinson, who was the first art teacher at Oak Park High School, went on to greater fame in the art world through her artistic talents.

The Jewish community's highest award for community service, the Fred M. Butzel Memorial Award, was presented to Edythe and Joseph H. Jackier. Both served on Federation's executive committee and headed different organizations. The Jackiers were the first husband-and-wife team to receive the honor.

Sports commentator Howard Cossell, author of *I Never Played the Game*, opened the 34th annual Jewish Book Fair at the West Bloomfield Jewish Community Center. One of the following day's speakers was Wolf Blitzer, Washington correspondent for the *Jerusalem Post*. The community paid tribute to Emma Lazaroff Schaver at a dinner and concert at Masonic Temple on Wednesday, November 20, on the occasion of her 80th birthday. The guest artist was Mrs. Schaver's longtime friend, violinist Isaac Stern.

The inaugural induction dinner of the Michigan Jewish Sports Hall of Fame took place on Wednesday, December 4, at Congregation Shaarey Zedek. The first inductees were Hank Greenberg, college football stars Benny Friedman and Harry Newman, and Pistons owner Bill Davidson.

The closing of Detroit landmarks continued in 1986 as the imposing 28-story Book-Cadillac Hotel on Washington Boulevard and Michigan Avenue shut its doors. Neighboring Highland Park suffered a tremendous blow as the Chrysler Corporation revealed plans to move half of its work force to Auburn Hills. In 1986, the Neighborhood Project began with interest-free loans to Jewish home buyers within designated Oak Park and Southfield boundaries. Also within the same designated boundaries, the community Eruv was used after 17 years of planning. The *Jewish News* defined it this way: "An eruv is a halakhically-approved boundary marking off a private domain, within which some actions normally prohibited by the laws of Shabbat are permitted."

After nine years in a Soviet labor camp, Anatoly Shcharansky was a free man in Israel. While enduring brutal conditions, Shcharansky repeatedly rejected offers of freedom. All he had to do was sign a confession that he was a spy for the C.I.A.

The huge Book-Cadillac Hotel on Washington Boulevard closed in 1986. It was the site of many major dinners of Jewish organizations through the decades. Several members of the Downtown Synagogue also resided there.

At his staged trial in Moscow in 1978, Shcharansky was allowed to make a statement. His closing words were: "For more than 2,000 years, the Jewish people, my people, have been dispersed. But wherever they are, wherever Jews are found, every year they have repeated, 'Next year in Jerusalem.' Now, when I am further than ever from my people, from Avital, facing many arduous years of imprisonment, I say, turning to my people, my Avital: 'Next year in Jerusalem.' "

After nine "next years" the heroic Shcharansky was reunited with his wife, Avital, his people in his homeland.

For the 25th consecutive year, bargain hunters and supporters flocked to the Brandeis Used Book Sale. Eight years earlier the sale moved to the Tel-Twelve Mall. Young Israel of Southfield continued its second year program, started by Erwin Posner, of twice-monthly Sabbath services for the elderly at Prentis Manor. Rabbi Chaim Bergstein, who came to Detroit in 1977 to implement a Lubavitch presence in the suburbs, opened Congregation Bais Chabad of Farmington Hills on Middlebelt Road. Rabbi Paul Yedwab was installed at Temple Israel by his father, Rabbi Stanley Yedwab.

Wayne L. Feinstein, executive vice president of the Jewish Welfare Federation of Detroit, was hired as chief executive officer of the Los Angeles Federation. Dr. Conrad Giles was elected 17th president of Detroit's Jewish Welfare Federation at its 60th annual meeting. Allen Gelfond, who served the Federation for seven years, was named director of the Allied Jewish Campaign.

The community lost three well-known charitable men who made their fortune in the food business. Paul Zuckerman died at 73; Norman Cottler died on the eve of his 90th birthday; and Tom Borman was 90.

Arthur Horwitz, only 32, but with an extensive background in several facets of the newspaper business, was brought to Detroit from the daily *Baltimore Sun* by *Jewish News* publisher Charles Buerger to become associate publisher. Hillel Day School's William, Ethan, and Marla Davidson Wing opened, creating 40 percent more space. Enrollment for the 1986-1987 school year hit a record high of 500 students.

Richard Golden became president and CEO of D.O.C, the optical empire his father, Dr. Donald Golden, began in 1946. Byron Krieger, a fencer with the 1952 Helsinki Olympics and in the 1956 Games in Melbourne, Australia, was inducted into the Michigan Jewish Sports Hall of Fame.

Hank Greenberg, the greatest Jewish baseball player of all time, succumbed to cancer at age 75 on September 4, 1986. Greenberg played for the Tigers for all or parts of 12 seasons with time out for four and a half years of military service. After spending his last season with the Pittsburgh Pirates in 1947, Greenberg became an executive with the Cleveland Indians and Chicago White Sox.

The financially independent Greenberg opted for the investment world after the 1963 season and spent his last years in Beverly Hills, California. Greenberg's last trip to Detroit was in 1983 when the Tigers retired his uniform number in ceremonies between games of a June doubleheader. Greenberg's physical condition left him unable to attend his induction to the Michigan Jewish Sports Hall of Fame the previous December.

Synagogue president Myron L. Milgrom presided over Congregation Shaarey Zedek's 125th anniversary. Festivities for Congregation B'nai Moshe's 75th anniversary began in September. Fred Ferber, a Holocaust survivor who founded House of Imports and became an active supporter of many Jewish institutions, became president of Congregation B'nai David.

Ferber's daughter, Shari, and Alon Kaufman were married at Congregation Shaarey Zedek by Rabbi Groner and Rabbi Yolkut of Congregation B'nai David. The bride attended the University of Michigan and University of Detroit Law School while the groom, employed by El Al Airlines Security, pursued studies at the New York Institute of Technology. The couple took up residence in London to continue their studies in law and business. The decades ahead would see them become one of Detroit's marquee couples known for business acumen and acts of charity.

Founders and officers of the Greater Detroit Chapter of Hadassah, Mrs. Sarah (known as Sal) Davidson

(Bill's mother), and her sister, Fannie Saulson, died in 1987. Mrs. Davidson was 96, and Mrs. Saulson was 95 when she died six months after her older sister. Longtime communal leader and attorney Joseph Jackier died at age 75.

Peter Weisberg, founder of Chatham Supermarkets, died at 96. His son, Harvey, a former president of Congregation Shaarey Zedek, began sponsorship of the annual Peter and Clara Weisberg Concerts after his charitable parents. Max Pincus, who owned the Hughes and Hatcher clothing chain with his brother, Bernard, until 1980 and went on to own the London Chop House and the Caucus Club, died at 63. Rabbi Leon Fram, founding rabbi of Temple Israel, died at 92.

Tillie Brandwine, active in several organizations, including Hadassah and Federation, was honored at a testimonial dinner by the Jewish National fund at Congregation Shaarey Zedek. Mrs. Brandwine also celebrated her 50th wedding anniversary in 1987.

The Greater Detroit Chapter of Hadassah celebrated the 75th anniversary of the national Zionist organization with a gala Saturday night reception at the Henry Ford Museum. Bobbie Levine, a past president of the B'nai B'rith Women's Council of Metropolitan Detroit, was appointed regional director of B'nai B'rith Metropolitan Detroit Council and Mid-Michigan Council. Sam Fisher replaced Steve Mankoff as executive director of Fresh Air Society Camps. WJBK-TV newswoman Sherry Margolis married Jeffrey Zaslow, a staff writer for the *Wall Street Journal*. Hancock, Michigan, 560 miles from Detroit, celebrated the 75th anniversary of Temple Jacob.

Because of declining numbers in admissions and insurance, Sinai Hospital was forced to eliminate 105 permanent and 20 temporary positions. Sinai's first-ever cuts of employees also prompted the change of 25 full-time jobs to part-time.

The Conservative movement was moving further from tradition with the ordination of women cantors. Rabbi Ronald D. Price, executive director of the Union for Traditional Conservative Judaism, explained his position in the March 6, 1987, edition of the *Jewish News*.

When the Jewish Theological Seminary announced that it would certify women as cantors, it came as no surprise to most people. If women are already being ordained as rabbis, isn't it logical that they should be cantors as well? In secular terms it is a logical progression, but in religious terms it is a leap into the void. Certifying women as cantors is a far more radical step halachically than was the ordination of women as rabbis. Yet this step was taken almost casually, with no discussion even within the faculty of the seminary, let alone among our great rabbinic scholars or in the Jewish community at large.

When women were ordained as rabbis, they had a choice whether or not to breach Jewish law. Those who chose to sign divorce or wedding documents as official witnesses or serve as a sheliah tzibur prayer leader, would indeed be breaking Halachah. But those who chose to preach and teach without breaking Halachah could certainly do so. Women cantors, however, have no choice but to violate Jewish law, and this is why:

Men have an obligation to worship three times a day in minyan. They may not always do so, but the obligation is there from bar mitzvah onward. A

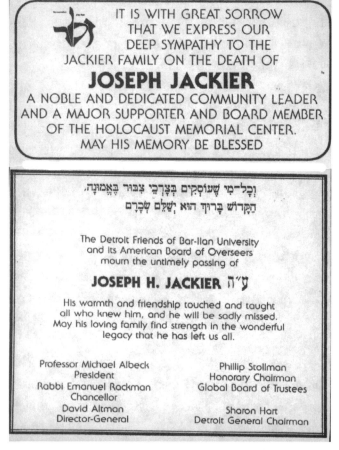

Several organizations placed ads in the *Jewish News* marking the passing of community leader Joseph Jackier.

woman is exempt from most time-bound mitzvot and does not have the obligation to pray in a minyan. In Jewish law, certain mitzvot can be fulfilled "vicariously," that is, through the actions of another. A woman could light the Chanukah candles for a man, for instance, because both have the obligation to do so. She could even say kiddush for him, though that is not traditionally done, since both have the obligation to sanctify the Sabbath. However, since women are exempt from prayer in a minyan, they cannot fulfill that obligation for men, which is part of a cantor's job. In a very real sense, unlike female rabbis, women cantors are being directed to violate Jewish law and tradition.

The worst part of this decision is that halachic jargon is being used to mislead the Jewish public into believing that this is permissible according to Jewish law. Just because one rabbi states his opinion that if a woman takes on the obligations of a man she can be allowed to lead the prayer service for men, does not make it Halachah. In fact, Dr. Israel Francus of the Jewish Theological Seminary Talmud faculty has ruled that should a woman take an oath to keep all of the mitzvot incumbent on men, she nonetheless does not have the same obligation.

Henry Ford II died in Detroit's Henry Ford Hospital at the age of 70. Unlike his grandfather, Ford was a longtime friend of the Jewish community. Ford defied an Arab boycott of Israel, which cost his company millions of dollars in sales, to maintain a plant in the Jewish state. Ford's friendship with Max Fisher led to an annual Ford donation of $100,000 to the United Jewish Appeal.

Alan E. Schwartz, a past president of the Jewish Welfare Federation, told the *Jewish News* that "Henry Ford was a man who had a keen interest in the Jewish community, Israel, and Jewish thought. He functioned on a national and international level. He was concerned about the problems of cities, countries, minorities. He was concerned about world forces and helped many. Not only the Jewish community."

Rabbi Allan S. Meyerowitz, who served a Spring Valley, New York, congregation, was hired by Congregation B'nai Moshe to replace Rabbi Stanley Rosenbaum. In December 1987, Daniel Schwartz, who served Temple Beth El for 14 years, the last six as senior rabbi, left his position a month earlier than the sabbatical portion of his extended contract began. Many Beth El members were upset with the Temple board for deciding not to renew Schwartz's contract.

In 1988, the once-elegant Michigan Central Depot near downtown was abandoned. The Fox Theatre building was restored to its former elegance by the Ilitch family, who were lured to Detroit by promises of tax-free years as they were planning a new headquarters in Farmington Hills for their Little Caesars corporate headquarters.

In 1988 the estimated population of Oak Park ranged from 31,500 to 34,000, down from a peak of 37,000 in the 1970s. Mayor Charlotte Rothstein claimed Oak Park had a 40 percent Jewish population, while blacks accounted for 12 percent of the city's

Advertisements placed in the *Jewish News* in 1987.

residents, and Chaldeans 10 percent. The other Oak Parkers were a mix of Europeans, Asians, and others.

Developers purchased eight homes east of the planned 13-acre shopping complex at 10 Mile and Coolidge to replace Oak Park's famous four-acre Farmer Jack/Dexter Davison Supermarket plaza. Farmer Jack, the food chain built by the Borman brothers, was sold to A&P in 1988.

Bill Davidson and partners David Hermelin and Robert Sosnick built the Palace of Auburn Hills. The 22,000-seat entertainment center housed the Davidson-owned Detroit Pistons basketball team. Sinai Hospital spread out to Farmington Hills, Livonia, and Southfield with satellite facilities. In 1988, there were only three strictly kosher eateries: Sperber's Cafeteria at the West Bloomfield Jewish Community Center, and two in Oak Park. Sara's, the kosher deli, was in the 10 Mile-Coolidge shopping center, and Cafe Katon, a small pizza parlor was operated by and next to Leo Mertz's bakery on Coolidge near 9 Mile Road.

Alvin Kushner, executive director of the Jewish Community Council of Metropolitan Detroit for almost 15 years, retired at 62. Samuel Lerner who served Jewish Family Service for the past 25 years as executive director, retired. Robert Naftaly, former state budget director and vice president of the Detroit Edison Company, became senior vice president and chief of finance for Blue Cross-Blue Shield of Michigan.

Frieda Stollman, who died at 76, was a founder of Akiva Hebrew Day School and Bar Ilan University in Ramat Gan, Israel. Besides her dedication to Jewish education, the Young Israel movement in Detroit, and the Mizrachi Orthodox Zionist movement, Mrs. Stollman was active in other areas of the community. She was a past president of the Women's Division of the Jewish Welfare Federation and was the first woman elected as vice president of the Federation. "Frieda was a tireless worker on behalf of all segments of the federated community," Federation president Dr. Conrad Giles told the *Jewish News*. "Her own dedication to the Orthodox movement significantly influenced Federation's role in broadening its own programming to that constituency."

Former disc jockey Mickey Shorr, who went on to operate an auto stereo business, died at 61. Harvey Deutch, who operated Paul's Cut Rate Drugs in downtown Detroit, died at 39. A member of Congregation Shaarey Zedek, Deutch was deeply interested in furthering Jewish education and helping the less fortunate.

Attorney M. Manuel Merzon, known throughout the community for his integrity, died at age 90. To help new immigrants, Merzon often waived his fees and was instrumental in helping Holocaust survivors obtain financial reparations from the German government. While Merzon, a small, slight man, may have cast the smallest shadow among the men of the community, he made the largest impression.

Merzon published the *Detroit Jewish Review* in the 1940s to help publicize the atrocities occurring in Europe. In a show of solidarity with European Jews, Merzon wore the yellow star of David armband around Detroit. Always seen in public wearing a yarmulke, Merzon once wrote, "the wearing of a yarmulke is a badge of honor, a mark of respect and self-respect, and above all an acknowledgment of the acceptance of the yoke of heaven."

After the elder Merzon's passing, his grandson, Gary Torgow, established the Bais Moshe Synagogue in his downtown law office (named after Mr. Merzon) to provide Jews working in the area with a place to

Bill Davidson (left) and David Hermelin built the Palace of Auburn Hills with partner Robert Sosnick.

(Courtesy of Leonard N. Simons Jewish Community Archives)

study and meet for afternoon prayers. Artscroll Publishers of New York published *Raising the Bar*, a book of Merzon's Torah writings and a sampling of articles from his *Detroit Jewish Review*.

Machon L'Torah, the Jewish Learning Network of Michigan, established in 1980 by Rabbi Avroham and Bayla Jacobovitz, opened its new learning center at 15221 West 10 Mile, Oak Park. Mrs. Esther Korman, a widow whose two children perished in a Nazi death camp, left half of the reparations money she received to help construct the building for Machon L'Torah. Befriended years earlier by Mr. and Mrs. M. Manuel Merzon, who helped her file a claim for reparations, Mrs. Korman lived in a one-room Oak Park apartment, and the Merzons kept in touch with visits. Mrs. Bertha Merzon brought her grandson, Gary Torgow, along to visit the woman who had no living relatives. On one visit Torgow helped feed Mrs. Korman, who was touched by the young attorney's values of Jewish education and decided to leave her reparation funds to institutions of Jewish learning.

After 38 years as executive director of the Hebrew Benevolent Society (Chesed Shel Emes), Rabbi Israel Rockove announced his retirement. Rabbi Bruce Aft became director of Midrasha and principal of the community high school, working with United Hebrew Schools Director Ofra Fisher. Congregation B'nai Israel of West Bloomfield planned a classroom wing for Hebrew school classes to become a full United Hebrew Schools branch. Because of reduced operating revenue, the United Hebrew Schools board voted to raise tuition by 10 percent, reduce the hours of Midrasha Library, and close the UHS branch at Congregation B'nai Moshe. The 63 B'nai Moshe students were merged with the classes at Congregation Beth Achim. Dr. Margaret Silverman Eichner became headmaster of the new Reform Jewish day school, located in the West Bloomfield Jewish Center, slated for an 1989 opening.

While enrollment at Yeshiva Beth Yehudah was a record-high 630 students at its day schools, Hillel Day School cancelled its ninth grade for the 1988-89 school year when only five students officially enrolled by the deadline. School officials said 10 was the minimum number of students needed to operate the class. Tuition at Hillel Day School for the 1988-89 school year was set at $3,950 per child. Akiva Hebrew Day School hired Rabbi Zvi Shimansky to replace Rabbi Sheldon Lopin as principal. The latter accepted a position in Seattle, while Shimansky, who led schools in Toronto and Houston, was teaching in Great Neck, New York, for the last year.

The Yeshiva Gedolah, formerly a division of the Beth Yehudah schools and an independent entity since 1985, had a student body of 100 led by a staff of ten instructors in 1988. The school building, formerly an

The Nathan and Esther Korman Building houses Machon L'Torah, the Jewish Learning Network of Michigan.

Oak Park public school a 24600 Greenfield a block south of 10 Mile, was within walking distance of most of its local students.

Debbie Schlussel, the 19-year-old University of Michigan student, Republican Party volunteer, and political activist, was invited to speak at the 1988 Republican National Convention representing National Teen Age Republicans. Judge Avern Cohn received the Fred M. Butzel Award at the Jewish Welfare Federation's 62nd annual meeting. It marked the first time the award was presented to a second generation of honorees. The late Irwin Cohn, the judge's father, received the Butzel Award in 1961.

At the Zionist Organization of America Balfour 55th Musical event at the Ford Auditorium, the father and son duo of Louis and Harold Berry were presented with the prestigious Justice Louis D. Brandeis Award "in recognition of their exemplary leadership on behalf of Israel and the Jewish community and their unflagging dedication to the advancement of Jewish values."

Temple Shir Shalom was founded with Rabbi Daniel Schwartz, who formerly served Temple Beth El as spiritual leader. Rabbi Daniel F. Polish was installed as senior rabbi at Temple Beth El by his father, Rabbi David Polish, a pioneer in Reform Zionist circles. Beth El's new spiritual leader was senior rabbi of a Hollywood, California, temple for seven years before accepting his new position.

Rabbi Arnold Sleuterberg, a recent graduate of Hebrew Union College, became the first spiritual leader of the five-year-old Troy Congregation. Later in the year, the Troy Jewish Congregation changed its name to Congregation Shir Tikvah (Song of Hope). Beth Abraham Hillel Moses, with 37 new members in the previous year, had a 600-plus family membership in 1988 and a Hebrew school enrollment of 170 youngsters.

With a membership decline from a peak of close to 800 families a decade earlier to 439 in 1988, Congregation B'nai Moshe eyed a West Bloomfield site in hopes of gaining more and younger members. The Oak Park synagogue had 283 member families led by persons over the age of 60.

After spending three years at the Chabad Lubavitch Yeshiva College in Melbourne, Australia, Rabbi Hershel Finman became the area's tallest rabbi when he accepted the position of outreach educational director for the State of Michigan Lubavitch Foundation. Bais Chabad of Birmingham-Bloomfield Hills was formed, with acting Rabbi Moshe Polter leading services at neighborhood homes.

In 1989 it was revealed that over 100,000 jobs were lost in Detroit in the 1980s, while the suburbs gained 250,000. Bill Davidson's suburban Detroit Pistons won their first National Basketball Association championship. Sara's Kosher Deli moved from the Dexter-Davison shopping center because its renovation translated into increased rent. Sara's owner, Morris Goodman, steered the Deli to the New Orleans Mall at 10 Mile and Greenfield.

Charles Buerger, publisher of the *Detroit Jewish News* and *Baltimore Jewish Times*, purchased the *Atlanta Jewish Times*. Arthur M. Horwitz, JN's associate publisher and the marketing director of Buerger's Baltimore publication, was given the same title of the Atlanta addition. Less than two years after his marriage to WJBK-TV anchorwoman Sherry Margolis, former Chicago-based *Wall Street Journal* reporter Jeff Zaslow took on the role of advice columnist by writing the nationally syndicated Ann Landers column.

Congregation B'nai David, in its Southfield location for the past 33 years, watched many of its members move farther north and its membership dwindle to less than 400. In 1989, its 47,000-square foot building and surrounding 10 acres were sold to the city of Southfield for $1.45 million as the congregation sought a West Bloomfield location. Because of its high intermarriage rate among member families, Trenton's Beth Isaac moved from Conservative to Reform as the congregation's board felt its membership would be better served with less traditional standards.

The new Huntington Woods Minyan meeting, one Saturday morning a month in the city's Burton Elementary School on Scotia, was put under the direction of Rabbi Yitschak Kagan of the Lubavitch Foundation. Cantor Gail Hirschenfang became Temple Beth El's first full-time cantor. The Young Israel of

Southfield doubled its membership in the past six years from 65 familes to 130.

While Yeshiva Gedolah Ateres Mordechai had an open house and formal name dedication in memory of Rabbi Mordechai Rogov, the new Yavneh Academy had an open house in the Maple/Drake Jewish Community Center. The Reform Jewish day school began with a kindergarten and first grade in 1989, with plans to add a grade every year. Akiva Hebrew Day School hired Rabbi Marc Volk as executive director and honored Dr Lawrence and Shirley Loewenthal at its 25th anniversary dinner.

Allen Juris, who served as associate executive director of the Jewish Welfare Federation for the past nine years, took a position on the other side of the Detroit River and became executive director of the Windsor Jewish Community Council. To replace Juris, Federation named Lawrence Ziffer, its planning director for the past four years, director of planning and agency relations. Susan Zaks became director of Camp Tamarack in Brighton. Former director Jeff Metz was named to head the newly created position of marketing director. Fresh Air Society restructured and cut its professional staff from 12 to 9 and eliminated two secretarial positions.

It was Detroit's 288th birthday, and Leonard Simons' 85th. The Detroit Historical Museum dedicated its most popular exhibit, the Streets of Detroit, to Simons. The plaque read:

In recognition of his major role in the development of Detroit's historical museums for over forty years under seven mayors as a founding Historical Commissioner on his 85th birthday and Detroit's 288th birthday July 24, 1989

Heinz Prechter, a native of West Germany who became internationally known as a custom installer of automobile sunroofs, was presented B'nai B'rith's highest honor; The Great American Traditions Award, at a dinner at the Westin Hotel. After the presentation by Max Fisher, former United States ambassador Jeane J. Kirkpatrick addressed the large audience. The Edward and Shirley Rosenberg Recreation Complex was dedicated in the Maple/Drake Jewish Community Center. Leon Warshay, sociology professor at Wayne State University, was installed as president of the Detroit Zionist Federation.

Actress comedienne Gilda Radner died at 42. An original cast member of "Saturday Night Live" from 1975 to 1980, Radner went on to appear on Broadway and in movies. Married to actor Gene Wilder since 1983, the Detroit native was survived by her mother, Henrietta, of Southfield, and a brother, Michael of Detroit. Jason Tickton, Temple Beth El's musical director for 55 years, died at age 74.

Dr. John Mames, who was given the first Holocaust Memorial Center leadership award at HMC's fifth anniversary dinner, died a few weeks later. Mames, a dentist, organized and served as president for 20 years of the Michigan Chapter of the Magen David Adom of Israel, the Jewish equivalent of the Red Cross. With the help of his wife, Eva, more than 70 ambulances were purchased, equipped, and sent to Israel. Dr. Mames pioneered the HMC oral history project, which numbered over 100 testimonial videotapes by survivors by the time of his death.

Tillie Brandwine, active in numerous community organizations, earned the Fred M. Butzel Memorial Award at the Federation's 63rd annual meeting. Mark

> WE AT THE HOLOCAUST MEMORIAL CENTER (HMC) ARE DEEPLY SADDENED AT THE UNTIMELY PASSING OF A NOBLE AND RIGHTEOUS HUMANITARIAN, A TRUE "TZADIK" IN OUR MIDST.
>
> **DR. JOHN J. MAMES.**
>
> HIS DEATH LEAVES AN UNFILLABLE VOID HERE AT THE HMC AND IN THIS COMMUNITY WHICH HE SERVED WITH UNIQUE LOVE AND COMMITMENT.
> HE DEDICATED MUCH OF HIS LIFE SO THAT THE MEMORIES OF THE SIX MILLION MARTYRS WILL NEVER BE FORGOTTEN. TO THIS END, DR. MAMES PIONEERED AND DEVELOPED THE CENTER'S ORAL HISTORY PROJECT, ENABLING SURVIVORS TO RECORD THEIR ANGUISHED STORIES OF THE HORRORS AND HEROISMS OF THE HOLOCAUST. IT WAS HIS FERVENT MISSION TO EDUCATE FUTURE GENERATIONS AND REMIND US OF MAN'S INHUMANITY TO MAN.
> OUT OF OUR DEEP AFFECTION AND ADMIRATION FOR DR. MAMES, WE AT THE HMC CHOOSE TO PERPETUATE HIS MEMORY BY NAMING THIS MONUMENTAL ENDEAVOR THE **DR. JOHN J. MAMES ORAL HISTORY PROJECT.** WE PRAY THAT HIS DREAM NEVER DIES AND HIS LEGACY CONTINUES TO ENRICH US ALL.
> TO HIS PARTNER, EVA, HIS BELOVED CHILDREN, ROBERT, ANDREA AND CRAIG AND HIS SISTER, MARY REM, WE EXPRESS OUR HEARTFELT SYMPATHIES.
> MAY YOU FIND COMFORT AMONG THE MOURNERS OF ZION AND JERUSALEM.
>
> **HOLOCAUST MEMORIAL CENTER**

From the obituary page of the *Jewish News*.

Schlussel, president and senior partner of the law firm Schlussel, Lifton, Simon, Rands, Kaufman, Galvin, and Jackier, was elected Federation president.

Robert Aronson, 38, left a similar title in Milwaukee to become executive vice president of the Jewish Welfare Federation of Metropolitan Detroit. Marty Kraar, who previously served Federation in that post, moved on to head the Council of Jewish Federations. As the Federation agencies were helping hundreds of Russian families adjust to their new surroundings, the 149-unit Harriet and Ben Teitel Building opened in late 1989, bringing the total of the four-building senior complex near the 10 Mile Jewish Community Center to 521 units.

As 1989 ended, interest given by local savings institutions averaged close to 7 percent. Southfield's Franklin Savings Bank boasted an annual return of over nine percent for 18-month certificates of deposits of $500 or more.

18

1990-1999
Century's End

Detroit's population kept plunging and stood at 1,027,974 in 1990, a loss of more than 486,000 in two decades. White flight continued, and many upper- and middle-class blacks stepped up their exodus from the reeling city, which now had a 76 percent black population.

According to a 1990 American Jewish census, the Detroit area had a Jewish population of 96,000—eleventh highest in the nation. More important, however, Jewish Detroit ranked fourth in per-capita fund raising.

The Federation, still headquartered at 163 Madison in downtown Detroit, was looking for a site closer to the Jewish population base and took an option to purchase five and a half acres of land in Farmington Hills on 13 Mile Road, west of Northwestern Highway. The Southfield city council passed a unanimous resolution asking the Federation to consider their city, as an estimated 28,000 Jews resided there—the largest Jewish population of any area suburban city.

While office buildings were under construction in the suburbs in 1990, *Crain's Detroit Business* reported that downtown Detroit had 46 vacant buildings of four stories or more, including such hulks as the Hudson's, the David Broderick Tower, and the United Artists buildings overlooking Grand Circus Park. Large, empty hotels also were eyesores as the Book-Cadillac, the Tuller, the Heritage (the old Statler), and the Hotel Fort Shelby were closed and rotting.

There were small pockets of hope as the Detroit Symphony Orchestra had moved to the renovated Orchestra Hall the previous September, and new buildings were planned for the Medical Center.

By June 1990, it was estimated that 60,000 Russian Jews entered the United States since January 1989. Almost 800 came to Detroit in that period and another 700 were expected to arrive in the area in the next 12 months. The growing Jewish population around the Grosse Pointes led to the formation of 90 east side families forming the Grosse Pointe Jewish Council. Several studies showed a high intermarriage rate among American Jews. Ranging from 40 to 52 percent in most studies, the Grosse Pointes, however, may have been double the national rate.

A sampling of a thousand Detroit area Jewish families, under the direction of Dr. Steven Cohen and Dr. Jack Ukeles, concluded that there were 13,000 youngsters between the ages of six and 17 in the area. In a front-page report on the study in the August 17, 1990, edition of the *Jewish News*, Alan Hitsky wrote:

> Three-fifths of the 13,000 attend Jewish schools and one-fifth are enrolled in Jewish day schools. "And over four-fifths have had some Jewish schooling between the age of 6 and 17," Dr. Cohen said.
>
> Most, however, complete their Jewish schooling by age 13. Less than one-third of the age group continue their schooling after bar or bat mitzvah.

The Beth Yehudah schools purchased the B'nai Moshe building on Church and 10 Mile Road in Oak Park, with the intention of remodeling it into the new home of the Sally Allan Alexander Beth Jacob School for Girls. Plans called for the girls' schools near Lahser and 14 Mile Road in Beverly Hills to be sold, providing part of the funds needed to reimburse United Jewish Charities, which recently had bought the building from Congregation B'nai Moshe for $1.6 million.

Nine classrooms on the Greenfield Road side of Yeshiva Gedolah Ateres Mordechai had been converted to 17 dormitory rooms that could accommodate 70 students. The dorm was an option for the 35 Detroit area students among the 98 enrolled in the yeshiva. Congregation B'nai Israel, which had moved from Pontiac to its West Bloomfield location 10 years earlier, merged its 135 families with Congregation Shaarey Zedek's 1,800 families. B'nai Israel's rabbi, Sherwin Kirshner, with three years left on his contract, told the *Jewish News* he was assured by Shaarey Zedek officials "that he will continue with the synagogue and services will continue to be held in the B'nai Israel building." Shaarey Zedek pledged funds to construct new classrooms for its Beth Hayeled nursery school and to refurbish the sanctuary and social hall at the West Bloomfield site.

Rabbi Milton Arm retired as spiritual leader of Congregation Beth Achim. Officials of the synagogue chose Rabbi Martin Berman as Arm's replacement to continue to lead the congregation on its path of traditional Conservatism. Temple Shir Shalom's rapid growth, from 30 families to 500 in two years of operation while in rented quarters in an Maple Road office building, led to the purchase of an 8.5-acre parcel at the corner of Orchard Lake and Walnut Lake Roads in West Bloomfield for a future building. After several delays due to zoning, Congregation B'nai Moshe held groundbreaking ceremonies on its West Bloomfield property at 6800 Drake Road.

Representatives of Moas Chitim, the organization that had distributed food for Passover for decades, met with like-minded people to start Yad Ezra. The new food pantry would provide nonperishable food complying with the kosher dietary laws. Wolf Blitzer, the Washington bureau chief for the *Jerusalem Post* since 1973, left his position to become an on-air reporter for CNN, the Cable News Network. After more than eight years with the *Baltimore Jewish Times,* Phil Jacobs joined the staff of the *Detroit Jewish News* as assistant editor.

There was some good news for downtown Detroit in 1991, as One Detroit Center—a 50-story office tower overlooking the Civic Center—opened. Several attorneys from the Jewish community interested in helping Detroit and seeking larger quarters relocated there, despite the long round-trip commute from their far-flung northern suburban homes.

Temple Israel celebrated its 50th anniversary during a festive weekend in April 1991. After 46 years of sketching his caricatures of celebrities at the eatery on Congress Street which evolved into the London Chop House, Hy Vogel, age 91, took his easel home as the famed restaurant closed. Fire destroyed the top half of the vacant former Shaarey Zedek Synagogue built in 1903 on Winder Street just east of what then was Hastings Street. The two-story gallery memorial-

The Yeshiva Beth Yehudah renovated the former home of Congregation B'nai Moshe on 10 Mile Road into a girls' school for its Beth Jacob division. The landmark Ten Commandments at the highest point of the building would remain.

izing artist Janice Charach Epstein, who died of cancer at age 39 two years earlier, opened in the West Bloomfield Jewish Community Center.

Parents of girls attending the Sally Allan Beth Jacob School for Girls of the Yeshiva Beth Yehudah were happy about the new location in the former B'nai Moshe Synagogue on 10 Mile Road in Oak Park. The former sanctuary was remodeled into six classrooms and the chapel into two preschool rooms.

As the students and staff were enjoying their new quarters, Congregation B'nai Moshe held services in the West Bloomfield Jewish Community Center, and some members wondered if their new site, a quarter mile south of the JCC on Drake Road would ever have a synagogue. Besides being without its own synagogue, B'nai Moshe did not have a spiritual leader, as Rabbi Allan Meyerowitz, who had served the congregation since 1987, was released from the remainder of his contract. Both sides called it an "amicable agreement."

The boards of Congregation Beth Achim and Congregation B'nai Moshe voted to merge. At the time, Beth Achim had 500 member families and B'nai Moshe had 300. However, a membership vote by each congregation several months later overwhelmingly defeated the proposal.

Congregation B'nai David, which sold its synagogue building to the City of Southfield and had two more years to vacate the premises under the sale agreements, voted to forge ahead with plans to construct a new synagogue in West Bloomfield, on the south side of Maple Road between Halsted and Haggerty.

Groundbreaking ceremonies took place for the Eugene and Marcia Applebaum Beth-Hayeled Building and Jewish Parenting Center adjacent to the Shaarey Zedek B'nai Israel Center in West Bloomfield. West Bloomfield had two Orthodox congregations on Farmington Road near Maple. Young Israel held services in rented quarters a 6450 Farmington Road, and Shomrey Emunah Ohel Moed had a new building at 6191 Farmington Road.

The girls' division of the Yeshiva Beth Yehudah moved into the former B'nai Moshe building on August 28, 1991.
(Photo by author)

The last remaining home of one of the original farm families in what is now Oak Park on 10 Mile Road was moved from in front of the Teitel Federation Apartments to a site in northern Macomb County. Several homes once dotted the farm landscape on what now belongs to Temple Emanu-El and the Jewish Center Campus. After almost 10 years of construction, the I-696 decks above the highway in Oak Park and Southfield officially opened.

Charlotte Rothstein, 66, who became Oak Park's first woman council member in 1973 and mayor in 1981, announced her retirement. Gerald E. Naftaly succeeded Rothstein, and Michael M. Seligson won a seat on the Oak Park council. Jeannie Weiner was elected president of the Jewish Community Council. She served as the council's vice president for the previous three years and became the second woman president of the organization. Leaders of the Jewish Welfare Federation voted to drop the word "welfare" and rename the organization the Jewish Federation of Metropolitan Detroit.

Jack A. Robinson was the recipient of the Fred M. Butzel Memorial Award by the Jewish Federation of Metropolitan Detroit. Robinson, the founder of Perry Drug Stores, had served on or headed numerous community charitable organizations for several years. Sam Fisher, executive director of Fresh Air Society, and his wife, Ofra, executive vice president for the Agency for Jewish Education, left their posts and moved to Washington to assume new career positions. Robert Steinberg, who was chief executive officer of Sinai Hospital, became executive director of Hillel Day School.

Yavneh, the Reform Jewish day school, decided it was not feasible to continue to operate for a third year. After much deliberation and a survey among its membership, Temple Israel nixed the idea of reopening and housing the school, which formerly used the West Bloomfield Jewish Community Center. The survey revealed that total enrollment of all classes would be under 20.

Going into the 1991-1992 school year, Yeshiva Beth Yehudah had 660 students; Hillel Day School, 650; and Akiva Hebrew Day School, 310. Darchei Torah had 150, and the Lubavitch Cheder had 145. After three years with the Agency for Jewish Education, Rabbi Bruce Aft took a position with a Washington

(Ad courtesy of Jewish News)

area Conservative congregation.

Yad Ezra, started through the efforts of Gary Dembs and Howard Zoller, who were active with the Food Bank of Oakland County, and Rabbi A. Irving Schnipper of Congregation Beth Abraham Hillel Moses, moved from its 700-square-foot basement office on 10 Mile Road in Southfield to a 4,200-square-foot building on Harding south of 11 Mile Road in Oak Park.

In the same year that Iraqi scuds fell on Israel, the axe fell on Pontiac's Temple Beth Jacob as officials voted to close Oakland County's oldest Reform congregation. The 68-year-old congregation once had 200 members, but had 60 when it entered into negotiations to sell the building to a local church. Pontiac had two Jewish congregations until 10 years ago when Congregation B'nai Israel, a Conservative synagogue, relocated to West Bloomfield.

In 1991 the Detroit Police Department had 10 Jewish officers, and Rabbi David Nelson of Congregation Beth Shalom became the first Jewish chaplain in the DPD, serving along with 49 other chaplains who volunteered each week.

Goldie Adler, widow of Shaarey Zedek's Rabbi Morris Adler, died at 83. Her civic and communal efforts and the passing out of candy to children in the synagogue endeared Mrs. Adler to people of all ages. Builder and developer Max Stollman also was well known in many facets of the community. A major supporter and leader in the Jewish day school and Zionist movement, Stollman was 87.

Early in 1992, the community mourned the death of Rabbi Leizer Levin at age 96. Regarded by the Orthodox community as "rosh ha'ir" ("the head of the city"), Rabbi Levin remained immersed in communal affairs and teaching a daily Talmud class despite failing health until he was hospitalized.

Rabbi Levin, who was born in Vaskay, Lithuania, came to Detroit in 1938 and was a disciple of the internationally known "Chofetz Chaim" in Radin, Poland. Jerusalem born Cantor Hyman Adler, who came to Detroit in 1945 and went on to serve Congregation B'nai David until he suffered a heart attack in 1983, died at 81.

Veteran Yiddish actress and singer Molly Picon died in New York at 94. Picon appeared in Detroit several times for Yiddish productions. She appeared in numerous Yiddish films, and younger members of the local Jewish community remembered Picon from her role of Frank Sinatra's mother in the Neil Simon

Rabbi Shmuel Irons, dean of the Kollel Institute of Greater Detroit, and Rabbi Levin, a few months before his death.

(Photo by author)

movie, *Come Blow Your Horn*, which had a long run at the Royal Theater in the 1960s.

A community-wide memorial service for Menachem Begin, the sixth Israeli prime minister who died at 78, was held in March at the Zionist Cultural Center on 10 Mile Road in Southfield. Miriam Starkman replaced Eli Finkelman as director of Hillel at Wayne State University. Beth Robinson left Beth Achim's executive director post for a similar position at Temple Emanu-El.

After 12 years with the Yeshiva Beth Yehudah, Rabbi E B. Bunny Freedman, 39, resigned to pursue other interests. For the third time in six months, the Yeshiva Beth Yehudah regrouped with a new, nine-member board. Poor local economic conditions, depleted funds, and educational differences on the amount of time allotted to English studies brought new leadership, including Gary Torgow, to the board, approved by leading local and national rabbis.

A Federation-sponsored, 10-member committee report, headed by Dr. Conrad Giles, recommended that the Federation withdraw its financial support of elementary Jewish education through the Agency for Jewish Education (AJE). No changes were proposed for 1992, but it was recommended that future AJE responsibility should cover only nursery school, the community high school, and adult and special education. Elementary education responsibility, according to the report, should fall to congregational schools, with the AJE providing curriculum and other advice, teacher training, and transportation for students. AJE's enrollment dropped from 3,500 students in 11 school branches in 1968, to 945 in three branches by 1992.

Howard Gelbard, former executive director of the San Francisco Bureau of Jewish Education, replaced Ofra Fisher as head of Detroit's Agency for Jewish Education. Phillip Schaengold left his position as CEO of Kansas City's Menorah Hospital to assume the post of president and chief executive officer of Sinai Hospital. The 43-year-old Schaengold hoped to turn the financially ailing hospital around, after Sinai dominated the news with employee layoffs and merger talks.

On March 27, 1992, as the *Jewish News* celebrated the 50th birthday of its inaugural issue, a defiant Coleman Young was serving in his 17th year as Detroit's mayor, and his deposed police chief, William Hart, was on trial for embezzlement.

Spring training was winding down and Sparky Anderson was shaping his roster for his 14th year as manager of the Detroit Tigers. Alan Trammell was getting in shape for his 16th season as Tigers shortstop.

The Dow closed at 3231.44 and the NASDAQ at 604.67. K-Mart skidded for the week, closing at 51

In 1992, the Jewish Federation of Metropolitan Detroit moved to Telegraph north of 14 Mile Road and honored Max Fisher by naming the building after the longtime community leader and philanthropist.

and five-eighths. Movie theaters in the northern suburbs offered *Beethoven, Bugsy, Fried Green Tomatoes,* and *My Cousin Vinny.*

Congregations Beth Abraham Hillel Moses and B'nai David were celebrating centennials, and the Hebrew Memorial Society—Chesed Shel Emes—founded to provide free burials to those who could not afford them, celebrated its 75th anniversary. After holding services in private homes, a Unitarian church, a Lutheran church, and using the Normister Presbyterian Church in 1992, the 200-member Troy Congregation Shir Tikvah celebrated its 10th anniversary.

In April 1991, Yad Ezra supplied food to 638 people. In April 1992, 1,034 people came to Yad Ezra for help as economic conditions also forced the Federal government to extend unemployment benefits from six to 10 months. After three years of negotiations and back and forth to the drawing board, the West Bloomfield Township Planning Commission finally approved Lubavitch's 40-acre Campus of Living Judaism proposal, to be located west of the Jewish Community Center on Maple Road.

The Max Fisher Building on Telegraph south of Maple was dedicated by the Federation on the first Sunday in May. An estimated 200 people braved the cool, windy day to honor Max Fisher. "To be honored by your own community is the highest tribute anyone could achieve," the 83-year-old Fisher said as he addressed those present. "I'll remember it all of my life."

West Bloomfield native Amy Bigman, 26, became the area's first woman full-time pulpit rabbi when she replaced Rabbi L. David Feder at Temple Emanu-El. Temple Beth El honored Rabbi Richard C. Hertz on his retirement as senior rabbi. The occasion also marked Rabbi Hertz's 40th anniversary of his rabbinical ordination. After 30 years of serving as senior rabbi, Hertz assumed the title of rabbi emeritus.

Rabbi Elliot Prachter was hired by Congregation B'nai Moshe to be its seventh rabbi in its 81-year history. Rabbi Prachter had been assistant rabbi at Adat Shalom for the past five years and was well known in the Conservative community. In addition to a new spiritual leader, B'nai Moshe finally had a home of its own, as its new synagogue was dedicated in August. From a high of 750 member families in the 1960s, B'nai Moshe sunk to a low of 270, but the anticipation and reality of a new rabbi and a new building brought in many new families. Leaders of the congregation hoped to have 400 families on the membership rolls in 1993.

As the 21,864 square-foot expansion and renovations for the Jimmy Prentis Morris Jewish Commu-

B'nai Moshe celebrated its 81st year with a new building on Drake Road and a new rabbi in 1992.

(Photo by author)

nity Center in Oak Park, begun the previous July, were making rapid progress in 1993, Detroit was still losing business and businesses. However, one downtown establishment was still thriving and celebrating its 100th year in business. "Henry the Hatter," opened by Henry Komrofsky in 1893 on Gratiot, was still topping off fashion-minded men at its store on Broadway a bit north of Gratiot.

As Sinai Hospital celebrated its 40th year of existence, Robert Steinberg, one of Hillel Day School's original financial backers in 1958, resigned his post of executive director after two years in that position. Phillip Slomovitz, who helped give birth to the *Jewish News* and became its editor and publisher, died at 96. Phil Jacobs, assistant editor of the *Jewish News* since 1990, became editor after Gary Rosenblatt left to assume the post of editor and publisher of the *New York Jewish Week*.

After its acreage served campers for 68 years, Brighton closed in 1993. It was a good year for Tamarack Camps as 1,650 children attended, the highest number in 15 years. Sixty years after Harry Mondry opened a small appliance repair shop in Highland Park, which evolved into Highland Superstores, the company declared bankruptcy and closed.

The changes continued at Yeshiva Beth Yehudah in 1993. Rabbi Raphael Skaist, principal for seven years, left for a position in his native New York, and Rabbi Eli Mayerfeld came from New York to assume the post of executive director.

Acting on the Federation-sponsored survey on education known as the Giles Report, which recommended the Agency for Jewish Education phase out the United Hebrew Schools and have the students placed into congregational schools, Beth Achim, Beth Abraham Hillel Moses, and B'nai David merged their schools and formed the Congregational Religious School.

In cost-cutting moves in 1994, the Federation shut down the United Hebrew Schools bus transportation system, and the Community Jewish High School was phased out, leaving education to the congregations.

Under the direction of its president Gary Torgow, the Yeshiva Beth Yehudah pulled itself out of debt and embarked on an extensive renovation, along with a new wing containing an office complex and gym. Because the student population exceeded building capacity, Hillel Day School had nearly 140 pupils learning in portable modules and announced plans for a 28,000 square-foot addition.

Close to 900 people gathered at the southeast corner of Orchard Lake and Walnut Lake Roads for groundbreaking ceremonies of Temple Shir Shalom. Started five years earlier by supporters of Rabbi Daniel Schwartz, the congregation boasted a membership of 650 families in 1994. Temple Israel planned the area's first Reform mikvah (ritual bath). Rabbis estimated the temple had 50 conversions each year, and on one morning, eight Temple Israel converts used the mikvah at Congregation Beth Achim.

The community welcomed three new rabbis in the summer of 1994. Rabbi Herbert Yoskowitz assumed the pulpit at Congregation Beth Achim, Rabbi Steven Weil became spiritual leader of Young Israel of Greenfield, and Rabbi Daniel Nevins became assistant rabbi at Adat Shalom. Later in the year, Rabbi Joshua L. Bennett was installed as the fifth rabbi of Temple Israel.

Friendship Circle was founded by Rabbi Levi Shemtov and his wife, Bassie, to provide assistance and support to families with children with special needs, in affiliation with the Lubavitch Foundation. Margot Parr became the fourth executive director of the Jewish Home for Aged in four years. Paul D. Borman was confirmed as a federal district judge for the Eastern District of Michigan. Borman, a past president of the Jewish Community Council and a past chairman of the Allied Jewish Campaign, taught at the law schools of Wayne State University and the University of Michigan and had an extensive background in law, including serving as federal defender for the Eastern District.

The huge, gray, generations-old federal courthouse downtown was dedicated as the Judge Theodore J. Levin United States Courthouse in 1995. Levin, who died in 1970, was appointed by President Harry S. Truman in 1946 and served as Chief Judge from 1959 until 1967. He was an uncle of Carl and Sander Levin.

The community lost two of its longtime favorites in 1995. Louis Berry, a founder of Sinai Hospital and past president of Congregation Shaarey Zedek, died at 93. Leonard Simons, like Berry, was honored numerous times for his civic and charitable work. Simons, also a founder of Sinai Hospital and a past president of Temple Beth El, was 91.

Twenty-two years after the Conservative movement's Rabbinical Assembly sanctioned the counting of women for a minyan (a group of at least 10 Jewish males over 13 years of age), Congregation Shaarey Zedek allowed women to be counted. Congregation Beth Shalom—under the direction of Rabbi David Nelson—had adopted the Assembly's decision almost immediately in 1973, but Shaarey Zedek was the first local Conservative congregation since that time to allow women part of a minyan.

In its January 20, 1995, edition, Ruth Littman, staff writer of the *Jewish News*, shed light on why some Conservative rabbis opposed counting of women in a minyan.

> *Some local Conservative rabbis contend the law is clear: no women. They explain that forming a minyan for prayer, which men are obligated to do at specific times during the day, falls into the category of "time-bound" commandments. Certain people are obligated to say certain prayers at certain times. Outside of lighting Shabbat candles, women are obligated to participate in few time-bound practices. Torah scholars reasoned that the obligation of daily communal prayer would interfere with women's other responsibilities, such as caring for the family.*
>
> *In Jewish law, where there is no obligation for an individual to take part in worship, there is no basis for counting that person in the minyan, some rabbis say.*

Trying to unify itself, Temple Beth El hired Rabbi Daniel Syme, son of Temple Israel's Rabbi M. Robert Syme. Controversy and divisiveness had reigned since the board of Beth El decided in January not to renew Rabbi Daniel Polish's contract. Polish, the congregation's rabbi since 1988, was placed on a sabbatical as of June 30, 1995. Cantor Gail Hirschenfang, wife of Rabbi Polish, whose contract also expired June 30, was told her contract would not be renewed.

After serving the Jewish Community Center for 30 years, Dr. Morton Plotnick left his top administrative post, and Leah Ann Kleinfeldt became executive director of the JCC. Later in the year, board members voted to offer membership to gentiles as health club or general members.

Troy's Congregation Shir Tikvah announced plans for a new building on Wattles between Coolidge and Crooks. Rabbi Arnie Sleuterberg said he hoped to be preaching and teaching in the new structure by 1997.

The Bais Menachem Academy, serving elementary-aged boys and girls, opened. Under Lubavitch auspices, the school planned to open a first grade every fall. There were already two Lubavitch-

The huge, block-filling downtown federal courthouse was dedicated as the Theodore Levin United States Courthouse in 1995.

sponsored schools operating. Boys were at Cheder Oholei Yosef Yitzchok Lubavitch in Oak Park, and girls attended Bais Chaya Mushka in Farmington Hills.

Hillel Day School decided to stay at its present location and expand, rather than to accept a $5 million dollar gift from real estate developer Jay Kogan toward construction of a new building on the grounds of the West Bloomfield Jewish Community Center Campus.

Later in the year, Kogan promised Hillel Day School $4 million if it would start a high school near the JCC, and a million dollar endowment for the present school, which went through the eighth grade.

Myron N. "Joe" Ginsberg, the catcher who spent 13 years in the major leagues including five with the Tigers, was inducted into the Michigan Jewish Sports Hall of Fame. In November, an estimated crowd of 4,500 jammed into Adat Shalom for a memorial service to slain Israeli Prime Minister Itzhak Rabin, organized by the Jewish Federation of Metropolitan Detroit.

In 1996, Ford Motor Land Development sold the Renaissance Center to General Motors and the Detroit Opera House opened on Broadway and Witherell in a 74-year-old theater built as a movie palace by George W. Trendle. Trendle gained nationwide fame in the 1930s as a creator of national radio programs, including "The Lone Ranger," "The Green Hornet," and "Sergeant Preston of the Yukon," beamed from the top of the Maccabees Building on Woodward.

Rubin "Rube" Weiss, the former Detroit public school teacher whose voice was known throughout the area through radio commercials, died at 76. Weiss also acted in radio productions of the Lone Ranger and appeared on Soupy Sales' Detroit television program.

Jewish News publisher and vice president of its parent company, Baltimore-based Waterspout Communications, Chuck Buerger died after heart surgery at the age of 57. Marla Feldman, a rabbi and attorney who directed the Jewish Community Relations Committee in Wilmington, Delaware, moved to Detroit as assistant director for domestic concerns at the Jewish Community Council. Lila Orbach, daughter of Temple Israel's Cantor Harold and Evelyn Orbach, returned to the area after 10 years to work as an on-air personality for WDIV (Channel 4).

David and Doreen Hermelin hosted President Bill Clinton at a $50,000-per-person private reception at their Bingham Farms home on the first Monday afternoon in March. The fund-raiser helped fill Clinton's re-election campaign treasury.

It was another try for a strictly kosher eatery as Classic Coney Island opened at the closed Sara's Glatt Kosher Deli 10 Mile and Greenfield location. Bagels Plus, offering fresh large bagels on a daily basis, opened in a small strip mall on Lincoln east of Greenfield in Oak Park. Jerusalem Pizza and One Stop Kosher Market also opened in 1996 on Southfield Road, in the same strip of stores just north of 10 Mile Road.

Machon L'Torah opened a learning center for Jewish students in Ann Arbor. Congregation Beth Shalom embarked on its renovations and classroom additions. Congregation T'chiyah, the Reconstructionist synagogue founded in 1977 by a group of Jewish professionals living in Lafayette Park just east of downtown Detroit, relocated from a church in Greektown to the Royal Oak Women's Club.

Young Israel of Oak Woods, the first Orthodox synagogue built in the suburb 42 years earlier, sold its Coolidge building to the De Por Montessori School Center. Funds from the sale would be merged into those of Young Israel of Greenfield to construct a larger synagogue and activities center on 10 Mile Road. After 20 years with Temple Emanu-El, Rabbi Lane Steinger took a position with the Union of American Hebrew Organizations. Rabbi A. Irving Schnipper, 69, retired from Congregation Beth Abraham Hillel Moses after 34 years as an area synagogue rabbi.

The 44-year-old Sinai Hospital was purchased in 1997 by the Detroit Medical Center. As part of the sale agreement, Sinai's name would continue at the current location. *Jewish News* editor Phil Jacobs returned to the *Baltimore Jewish Times* as editor.

Two new kosher take-out places were in operation in 1997. Taste of Israel opened between Zeman's Bakery and Borenstein's, and Ramatari Gourmet Vegetarian Cuisine was on Coolidge north of Lincoln in Oak Park. After 13 months of operation, the area's only sit-down meat restaurant, Classic Coney Island, closed due to lack of profits.

In 1973 partners Morry Mertz and Morris Weiss, who operated Weiss Bakery on Greenfield north of 10 Mile Road in Oak Park and the Country Corner Bakeshop on Southfield and 13 Mile Roads, bought out Zeman's Bakery on 7 Mile Road near Outer Drive and named all three bakeries Zeman's. An explosion destroyed the Detroit store in 1974, and Mertz operated the Southfield location, while Weiss handled the Oak Park bakery. In 1997 the Southfield bakery closed, sending a happy Mertz into retirement, while Weiss continued to handle the Oak Park Zeman's.

Established in 1981 in a converted house on West 10 Mile Road in Southfield, the Shirt Box relocated to Northwestern Highway in Farmington Hills. David Hermelin became United States Ambassador to Norway in 1997 and established a kosher kitchen in his Oslo residence. A. Alfred Taubman's firm built the Oak Park Jewish Community Center in 1956. In 1997, the JCC area was dedicated as the A. Alfred Taubman Jewish Community Center Campus.

While Congregation B'nai David was in rented quarters at 5642 West Maple Road in West Bloomfield, the city of Southfield opened the former B'nai David building on Southfield Road as the Centre for the Arts. Temple Emanu-El, built in 1955, began its renovation and expansion. Congregation B'nai Moshe completed its 4,500-square-foot addition to their building on Drake Read. The 10 new classrooms were put into immediate use as the student body grew from 30 in 1992 to 102 in 1997.

One of Michigan's greatest tennis players, Aaron Krickstein, who became the youngest man to be ranked among the top ten tennis players in the world in 1984, was inducted into the Michigan Jewish Sports Hall of Fame. Former Oak Park mayor Charlotte Rothstein died at 72, and former Detroit mayor Coleman Young died at 79.

Mark Schlussel, president of the Federation from 1989 to 1992, received the Federation's highest honor, the Fred M. Butzel Memorial Award. Under Schlussel's watch, the Federation relocated to Bloomfield Hills, Oak Park was solidified through the Neighborhood Project, and renovation of the former B'nai Moshe building into the girls' division of the Yeshiva Beth Yehudah was completed. Borman Hall was phased out, and Jewish day school education was boosted. Schlussel also was instrumental in facilitating the sale of Sinai Hospital.

In 1998, the Michigan Jewish Institute, a Lubavitch-sponsored college, received national ac-

Congregation B'nai Moshe had an expanded building in 1997.

creditation. A former Lutheran church on Coolidge south of Lincoln in Oak Park was converted into a Lubavitch girls' school. Rabbi Avrohom Fishman assumed the duties of principal of Yeshiva Beth Yehudah. At the time, enrollment at the yeshiva was 768, a gain of 193 students in five years.

Rabbi Craig Allen and Livonia's Conservative Congregation Beit Kodesh severed their eight-year relationship due to the synagogue's financial difficulties. Rabbi Sheila Goloby became Temple Beth El's first female rabbi. Robert Sklar became editor of the *Jewish News*, and Penny Blumenstein became the first female president of the Jewish Federation of Metropolitan Detroit.

As Israel was in its 50th anniversary year in 1998, Jane Sherman, considered by many as Detroit's ambassador to Israel, was honored by the Jewish Federation of Metropolitan Detroit with the Fred M. Butzel Memorial Award. Mrs. Sherman's father, Max Fisher, was the 1964 honoree.

The community bid farewell to several of its well-known members. Rabbi Benjamin Gorrelick, who came to Detroit in 1949 as spiritual leader of Congregation Beth Aaron, died at 91. After a merger with Congregation Ahavas Achim, Rabbi Gorrelick shared rabbinical duties with Rabbi Milton Arm at the renamed Congregation Beth Achim.

Alexander Roberg, who had a 37-year career with the United Hebrew Schools starting in 1940, died at 83. Joanne Zuroff, known for her volunteer work on behalf of the Jewish Home for the Aged, Jewish day schools, Jewish and civic causes, and active affiliation with Congregations Bais Chabad of Farmington Hills and Southfield's Shomrey Emunah, died at 56. Long associated in business and Jewish causes with his late brother Max, Phillip Stollman died at 92.

To pay back the kind treatment he received as a lonely 19-year-old from out of town on his visits to the old Jewish Community Center on Woodward and Holbrook, D. Dan Kahn and his wife, Betty, made a major gift to the JCC. In turn, the West Bloomfield Jewish Community Center was renamed the D. Dan and Betty Kahn Building. More than 3,600 athletes and coaches participated in the largest ever Maccabi Games competition, held on the grounds of the JCC in 1998.

Abe Pasternak, a survivor of the death camps who came to Detroit in 1947, was named a United Way Community Services Heart of Gold winner for his Sinai Hospital Guild volunteer work. Pasternak also was a volunteer for the National Council of Jewish

In 1998, the West Bloomfield Jewish Community Center was renamed the D. Dan and Betty Kahn Building.

Women/Kosher Meals on Wheels program.

As merger negotiations turned into reality, Congregation Beth Achim and Congregation Adat Shalom became a 1,200-member synagogue. As the agreement went into effect, Beth Achim's Rabbi Herbert Yoskowitz joined the spiritual staff of Rabbis Effy Spectre and Daniel Nevins. The former Beth Achim building on 12 Mile Road in Southfield was purchased by the United Jewish Foundation, the real estate endowment arm of the Jewish community. It would be renovated into the new home of Akiva Hebrew Day School.

Hundreds of camera-toters came downtown on October 24, 1998, to get as close as possible to the Hudson's block and click away at the implosion of the storied store. As the hulking building fell into history, debris damaged the People Mover and shut it down, and a gray coat of soot settled in the area.

Entrepreneur Eugene Applebaum, founder of Arbor Drugs, and his wife, Marcia, made a major gift, announced in 1999, for capital improvements to "agencies located on the northwest quadrant at Maple and Drake Roads in West Bloomfield." Even though the Applebaums didn't seek recognition, the result was that the 196-acre Jewish Community Campus at Maple and Drake became known as the Eugene and Marcia Applebaum Jewish Community Campus.

David Hermelin, 62, in the midst of a three-year term as ambassador to Norway, underwent 10 hours of surgery for a tumor near his brain. Later in 1999, Hermelin and friends donated $10 million to create the Hermelin Brain Tumor Center, as part of the Detroit-based Henry Ford Health System. Sinai Hospital, owned by the Detroit Medical Center, moved its base of operations to neighboring Grace Hospital.

The community lost several well-known members in 1999. A day after he conducted services at the Downtown Synagogue, where he had been the cantor for 19 years, Israel I. Idelsohn died at 85. Rabbi Richard C. Hertz, who served as Temple Beth El's senior rabbi from 1953 to 1982, died at 82. Rabbi

The implosion of the Hudson's building left acres of emptiness in what once was the heart of a thriving downtown.

(Courtesy of Michael Schupp)

Herbert Eskin, 88, was the first rabbi of Congregation Beth Shalom and conducted High Holiday service at Congregation Ahavas Achim in Detroit for over 20 years.

Isadore "Izzy" Malin, 82, a retired wholesale food salesman, was known as "Mr. Temple Beth El" for decades of cheerful work on behalf of groups. Billy Serman had a clothing store on Randolph in downtown Detroit for 56 years that bore his name. He was active in Congregation Shaarey Zedek and Jewish causes, and he was named Israel Bonds Man of the Year in 1987. Several women who made their mark also passed away in 1999. Among them were Jackie Gordon, widow of television personality Lou Gordon; Freida Fleischman; and Norma Jean Meer, who helped several Jewish organizations.

Besides Judge Victor Baum, the community lost businessmen Marvin Berlin, Stephen Levitz, and Stanley Winkelman. The latter, former chairman and chief executive officer of Winkelman's, the chain of women's fashion stores, played a leadership role in numerous civic and charitable causes. Berlin was a major supporter of Jewish day school education and several charities. He was known—along with his long time partner Irving Nusbaum—for building New York Carpet World into a national chain, and for providing jobs and a helping hand to Russian immigrants and others.

Stephen Levitz, only 48, was a builder who took pride in his projects and no profit for work he did for Jewish day schools. Under Levitz's direction, the former B'nai Moshe building in Oak Park was converted into the Sally Allan Alexander Beth Jacob School for Girls, and the Yeshiva Beth Yehudah building in Southfield was renovated and enlarged. Levitz was working to convert the former Beth Achim building in Southfield into the new home for Akiva Hebrew Day School when cancer claimed him. Levitz also donated his services to other organizations and hosted—along with his wife, Chayala—the annual National Conference of Synagogue Youth (NCSY) Sunday morning brunch.

Akiva Hebrew Day School began its 1999 fall term with rave reviews and 250 students in its new home, the former Beth Achim building on 12 Mile Road in Southfield. The Norma Jean and Edward Meer Early Childhood Development Center opened on the campus of the Yeshiva Beth Yehudah. The building housed nursery and kindergarten classrooms and expected to serve 150 children. Rabbi Lee Buckman left a Conservative pulpit in Milwaukee to become headmaster of the Jewish Academy of Metropolitan Detroit.

After much discussion and deliberation, the membership of Congregation T'chiyah split. The downtown congregation relocated to Royal Oak, and those who wanted to stay downtown formed the Reconstructionist congregation of Detroit and used space in the Wayne County Medical Society. Cantor Lori Corsin, a graduate of Southfield High, was brought back from a position with a New York synagogue by Temple Israel to become the temple's first female clergy member.

Tiger Stadium's final game took place on September 27, 1999, before an official attendance of 43,356 and an unofficial count of at least 10,000 cameras. The area's Jewish population was well represented at the old ballpark. Dr. Jack Belen, Dr. David Ungar, and David Wayntraub arranged for a Mincha (afternoon prayer) Minyan under the stands of the upper left field

Marvin Berlin helped raise the spiritual and educational level of the community while offering jobs to Russian immigrants and others in need.

(Photo by author)

corner.

As guest speaker George Stephanopoulos; former senior advisor to President Bill Clinton, and more than 2,000 other dinner guests watched, Fred and Miriam Ferber received Yeshiva Beth Yehudah's highest honor, the Golden Torah Award, for their devotion to Jewish education and Jewish survival.

As the century evolved into history, Sinai Hospital became history. The one Jewish hospital, purchased in 1997 by the Detroit Medical Center, closed its doors, and operations were moved down Outer Drive to Grace Hospital.

The sadness felt by the community was magnified by those who spent a major portion of their working lives there. Dr. Marcus Sugarman, 88, was a founding physician of Sinai in 1953 and was still serving patients there in 1999.

"Sinai was my home," Dr. Sugarman recalled. "It never occurred to me that I would outlast it. Everybody knew me at Sinai, and I knew everybody and where everything was."

Rabbi Steven Weil of the Young Israel of Oak Park (wearing jacket) checks out a souvenir stand prior to Tiger Stadium's last game.

(Photo by author)

19

THE NEW MILLENNIUM

On the first day of the new century, Congregation Beth Abraham Hillel Moses became Beth Ahm. Also in 2000, Beth Ahm installed new arrivals Rabbi Charles J. Popky and Cantor David Montefiore, and Temple Beth El celebrated its 150th year of existence.

Comerica Park, Detroit's new downtown home of the Tigers, opened. A century earlier, many Jewish families lived on where major league outfielders now roam. Less than two weeks after the Tigers opened their new home, Detroit saw another ray of hope, as Compuware broke ground for its new headquarters, which would overlook Campus Martius.

The new century also brought a new look to Congregation Beth Shalom. The foyer, lobby, social hall, and restrooms were renovated, and the sanctuary was freshly carpeted and painted. Oak Park's only Con-

A new century brought a new ballpark for the Tigers. A century earlier, many Jewish families lived on what today is the outfield of Comerica Park.

(Photo by author)

servative synagogue also opened a new school wing.

Lawrence Berry became the third generation member of his family to be president of Congregation Shaarey Zedek. Grandfather Louis held the position in 1958 and 1959, and again from 1965 to 1967. Lawrence's father, Harold, was president from 1975 to 1977. Rabbi M. Robert Syme celebrated his 80th birthday and retired after 47 years of service to Temple Israel. Rabbi Marla R. Hornstein made history as Temple Israel's first female rabbi and the sixth in its history.

The Jewish Academy of Metropolitan Detroit opened, with 53 freshmen and sophomores using facilities provided in the D. Dan and Betty Kahn Building in the West Bloomfield Jewish Community Center. The Agency for Jewish Education relocated from the former AJE (built as a United Hebrew School building) on 12 Mile Road in Southfield, to the Max M. Fisher Federation Building in Bloomfield Township. Darchei Torah, the 15-year-old Orthodox day school, quickly absorbed the space vacated by AJE.

Five years after the Friendship Circle began to match teen volunteers with children having special needs, more than 300 young people were involved, and plans proceeded for an all-inclusive facility for special needs children on the Meer Family Friendship Campus of the Lubavitch Foundation development, on Maple between Drake and Halsted.

Arthur Horwitz and New York philanthropist and Jewish community activist Michael Steinhardt partnered to form Jewish Renaissance Media, and to purchase the *Detroit Jewish News* and *Style* magazine, and the *Atlanta Jewish Times*. One Stop Kosher Food Market relocated from its cramped, 2,650-square-foot Southfield Road location to the former Hiller's Food Emporium in the New Orleans Mall, with 15,000 square feet. Matt Prentice opened Milk and Honey restaurant in the D. Dan and Betty Kahn Building in the West Bloomfield Jewish Community Center.

Most local Jews beamed with pride as Senator Joe Lieberman became the Democratic vice-presidential candidate. Many observant Jews, however, were cautious and worried how Lieberman would measure up in a crisis. Many non-observant Jews were concerned about Lieberman's religious practices being trumpeted by the media, leading to too many "how come you don't…?" queries.

They led full lives and saw the new century and left their mark on the community. Dr. Marcus Sugarman died at 89, a year after his beloved Sinai Hospital closed its doors. Besides time spent at Sinai since it opened in 1953, Sugarman maintained an office practice, made house calls, and visited patients in nursing homes, regardless of whether they could pay or not. He continued his practice until earlier in the year, when he suffered a stroke.

Judge Ira Kaufman, a Wayne County Probate judge for 27 years and a founder of Congregation Adat Shalom, died at 91. Harry Newman, who starred at quarterback at the University of Michigan and went on to play professional football with the New York Giants from 1933 to 1935, died at 90. After his football days, Newman returned to his native Detroit and operated a Lincoln-Mercury dealership at Outer Drive and Van Dyke for 20 years.

Saul Wineman, a.k.a. Paul Winter, died at 77. His voice was heard by generations of Detroiters, from 1952 to 1964 on WXYZ-AM radio, to Channel 56 television in the 1970s. He also was heard on WJR-AM and WQRS-FM, and he performed at the Jewish Ensemble Theater. Philanthropist Dr. Milton Shiffman, a staunch supporter of Jewish education, would live on through the many he helped receive knowledge and ethics to be part of the chain of Jewish leadership and continuity.

Sadie Cohn, wife of the late philanthropist Irwin I. Cohn, died at age 100. The Cohns were married in 1923, and as Mr. Cohn prospered in his law practice and real estate holdings, numerous Jewish organizations received generous donations.

Rabbi Irwin Groner of Congregation Shaarey Zedek told those present at the funeral how the parents of Mrs. Rita Haddow and United States District Judge Avern Cohn met. "She met her future husband at Ottawa Beach, Michigan, a resort on Lake Michigan," Rabbi Groner related. "Sadie went into the water and she couldn't swim. Irwin saw her begin to drown and jumped in, but he couldn't swim, either.

Just then, an unknown hero jumped in and saved both of them. That unknown hero helped shape the course of our Jewish community."

David Hermelin helped many people, causes, and organizations. He was a beloved, dynamic, and charismatic community leader with an engaging personality and an easy smile. His death on November 22, 2000, from brain cancer at age 63, affected many. Hermelin lent a helping hand to all segments of the community.

"He helped us to establish a charter for the Michigan Jewish Institute, which is a rare thing to get," Rabbi Yitschak M. Kagan, associate director of the Lubavitch Foundation of Michigan, told Shelli Liebman Dorfman of the *Jewish News*. "When things were going pretty much nowhere, David stepped in and it was done in a month."

Perhaps Gary Torgow best summed up what Hermelin meant to the community: "He was a man that could cross so many important parts of the communal spectrum and truly made you feel that your cause and your issue were the most critical issues of the day."

As Detroit celebrated its 300th birthday in 2001, the Jewish Community Center celebrated its 75th anniversary, and the JCC Annual Book Fair was 50 years old. Cantor Harold Orbach celebrated his 70th birthday, 50 years since his ordination as cantor and 40 years with Temple Israel. The Fisher Theatre marked its 40th year under the Nederlanders as Detroit's premier playhouse. Newsman Murray Feldman marked his 25th year in Detroit, and Hollywood producer Jerry Bruckheimer, who graduated from Mumford High 50 years earlier, put *Pearl Harbor* behind him and was working on his next movie.

2001 will always be remembered for 9-11, as Al Qaeda terrorists used passenger planes to attack the World Trade Center in New York City and the Pentagon in Arlington, Virginia, on that September date.

Besides feeling a deep sense of loss for those in other areas of the country it never knew, a few of the people the community mourned for in 2001 were: Martin Blanck (Wallside Windows); Barney Broner (Broner Glove Co.); Billy Jacobs (Buddy's Pizza); Henry Dorfman (Thorn Apple Valley); Murray Kahn (Kahn Coal Co.); Eugene Kraft (Serta-Restokraft Mattress Co.); Irving Pitt (Murray's Discount Auto Stores); Shalom Ralph (Sexton, B'nai Moshe); Abraham Selesny (Attorney); Lillian Sherman (co-founder Sherman Shoes); Sonia Syme (wife of Rabbi Syme and Temple Israel teacher), and Hy Vogel (caricaturist).

Perhaps "tragedy" best described the death of Rabbi Yitschak Meir Kagan. The dynamic Lubavitcher rabbi was only 59 when he was killed in an automo-

Detroit on its 300th birthday, July 24, 2001.

(Photo by author)

bile accident in New York after visiting the grave of the late Lubavitcher Rebbe, Rabbi Menachem M. Schneerson. Lubavitch smartly used Rabbi Kagan as their chief public relations professional in Michigan, endearing him to all segments of the community.

Noted philanthropist Alfred Deutsch, former president of Congregation B'nai Moshe who founded American Savings and Loan along with his father, died at 87. By 1982, the banking institution had 18 branches and merged with Erie Savings Bank of New York to form Empire of America. Earlier in 2001, the B'nai Moshe campus was named for Deutsch and his wife, Bernice.

Larry Gunsberg, great-grandson of Morris (Moshe) Gunsberg, for whom Congregation B'nai Moshe is named, became president of the synagogue in 2001. Young Israel of Oak Park chose Rabbi Reuven Spolter to replace Rabbi Steven Weil, who took a pulpit in Beverly Hills, California. Young Israel also dedicated its renovated and enlarged building.

David and Andrew Farbman purchased the Albert Kahn-designed Fisher Building. The young brothers planned to pump new life and residents into Detroit with renovated buildings downtown. After two and a half years of struggling to give the local community a top-notch kosher restaurant, Paul Kohn of Quality Kosher Catering closed the classy La Difference in the busy 14 Mile and Orchard Lake Roads area. Kohn succeeded as the restaurant received high marks for its food, service and class. However, the number of patrons fell short of expectations.

In 2001, the Michigan Jewish Sports Hall of Fame finally inducted one of the best all-around athletes the area ever turned out. Walter Godfrey starred in baseball and basketball at Cass Technical High School and Michigan State University, leading them to titles in both sports. Godfrey, who died in 1993 at age 51, went to spring training with the Detroit Tigers in 1956 and was offered a contract to pitch in their minor league system.

Penny Blumenstein completed her three-year term as president of the Jewish Federation of Metropolitan Detroit and received the Yeshiva Beth Yehudah's Golden Torah Award for her strong commitment to Jewish education and continuity.

The community felt the anguish of the *Jewish News* family as fire destroyed their offices on January's last Sunday in 2002. The staff and readers of JN felt more united than ever as the pages for the post fire edition were put together in a makeshift location and the issue arrived only a day later than usual.

In 2002, Congregation Shaarey Zedek, with about 2,100 member families including its branch in West Bloomfield, marked its 140th anniversary with a

In 2001, months before his passing at age 87, Congregation B'nai Moshe named their campus after Alfred L. Deutsch and his wife, Bernice.

musical program and tribute to Rabbi Groner, who celebrated his 70th birthday and more than 40 years of serving the congregation. The Fresh Air Society celebrated 100 years of camping, and Temple Emanu-El celebrated its 50th anniversary, as did the Great Lakes Yacht Club. The GLYC was founded in 1952 by Jewish sailors barred from membership elsewhere because of their ethnic and religious background. Rabbi A. Irving Schnipper celebrated his 75th birthday, and Bill Davidson marked his 80th.

David Tanzman was honored as one of eight local octogenarians for activism and volunteerism. Tanzman had a long career as a federal mediator and advised President Jimmy Carter during peace talks between Menachem Begin and Anwar Sadat. Carter sent Tanzman a letter of praise when he retired as a mediator in 1979.

Tanzman, also a cantor who attended services daily at the Young Israel of Oak Park, saw action in the Battle of the Bulge in Europe, became field chaplain for World War II concentration camp survivors, and conducted the first post war High Holiday ser-

Young Israel of Oak Park during construction and upon completion in 2001.

(Photos by author)

vices in Heidelburg, Germany.

Oakland County Commissioner Michelle Friedman Appel, daughter of Judge Benjamin Friedman, practiced law for 20 years and served as a public defender, mediator, guardian, and hearing panel member of the Attorney Grievance Commission. Friedman Appel won her campaign for judge of the 45B District Court, an opening created by the retirement of her father.

Jane Sherman, who had been an active member of the Jewish Agency for Israel Board of Governors since 1983, was named national chairperson of the United Jewish Appeal. Rabbi Marla Feldman left the Jewish Community Council of Metropolitan Detroit after six and a half years for a position in New York serving Reform congregations around the country. Michelle Faudem, rabbi-in-residence of Hillel Day School of Metropolitan Detroit and a former student of the school, celebrated her 10th anniversary of being the first woman Conservative rabbi to work in the community.

The Matt Prentice-operated Milk & Honey kosher restaurant opened in the West Bloomfield Jewish Community Center Kahn Building. Yad Ezra moved into its new food warehouse on 11 Mile Road in Berkley. Groundbreaking for the new Holocaust Memorial Center facility, on Orchard Lake Road north of 12 Mile, took place.

An anonymous $20 million endowment was granted to the Jewish Federation of Metropolitan Detroit for the purpose of supporting the Jewish Academy of Metropolitan Detroit. The Federation received a $2 million gift from the Ford Motor Company, which would help fund a 3,500-square-foot multimedia education center at the West Bloomfield JCC.

Rabbi Yechiel Morris became spiritual leader of the Young Israel of Southfield, replacing Rabbi Elimelech Goldberg, who was serving as the national director of Kids Kicking Cancer, the organization open to children of all ages and religions. Congregation B'nai David relocated to 634 Orchard Lake Road, Suite 100. The social hall at Adat Shalom Synagogue was named for former spiritual leader Rabbi Jacob E. Segal, who died in 1975. Chabad Jewish Center of Commerce-Walled Lake was formed using the Walled Lake home of Rabbi Schneor Greenberg and his wife, Estie. The long-awaited Shul opened on the 140-acre Chabad Lubavitch Campus of Living Judaism in in West Bloomfield.

The passing of Milton Berle and Ann Landers in 2002 was national news, but the notices carried by the *Jewish News* touched many segments of the community. Lois Sandberg, Mary Shapero, and Arlene Victor didn't live to a ripe old age but served many organizations for decades. Mrs. Lillian Cohen, 87, was a founder of the Yeshiva Beth Yehudah day school, PTA, and the Women's Orthodox League in the 1940s.

In the 1940s, Rabbis Avrohom Abba Freedman and Chaim Schloss began what would be a lifelong working association with the Yeshiva Beth Yehudah. While Freedman and Schloss were young rabbis at YBY, Rudy Newman, a young veteran of World War II, opted to leave Detroit, help Israel fight for its life, and mold what would become Israel's Air Force.

Robert Marwil had a bookstore serving the Wayne State University area and helped found the Jewish Book Fair, and Seymour Gretchko was preparing for a career as an educator. Gretchko was the Superintendent of the West Bloomfield School District at the time of his passing.

In 2003, Cheryl Chodun celebrated her 15th year with WXYZ-TV (Channel 7). The multi-talented reporter-anchorwoman grew up in Oak Park east of Scotia in the Ferndale School District. A cheerleader during her years at Ferndale High, Cheryl also had starring parts in variety shows and plays.

Her first TV appearance was as a cheerleader from Lansing's Jenison Fieldhouse when Ferndale won the state basketball championship. She met her future husband, Stan Chodun at Wayne State University, and their dates included movies at the Mercury and Royal theaters and eats at Darby's.

Mrs. Chodun majored in English at WSU, which led to doing press releases for her children's nursery. Writing for the Southfield *Eccentric* led to writing for Channel 7, which led to radio reporting for WWJ, then back to Channel 7 as an on-air anchor in 1988.

A winner of Emmys, UPI, and AP awards for both

Some Scenes from 2002

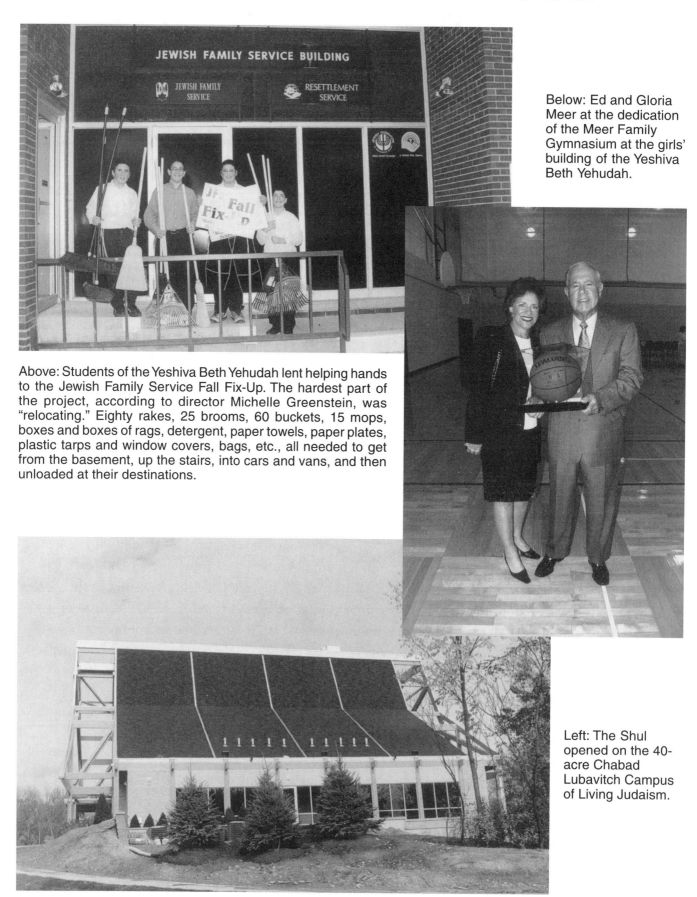

Above: Students of the Yeshiva Beth Yehudah lent helping hands to the Jewish Family Service Fall Fix-Up. The hardest part of the project, according to director Michelle Greenstein, was "relocating." Eighty rakes, 25 brooms, 60 buckets, 15 mops, boxes and boxes of rags, detergent, paper towels, paper plates, plastic tarps and window covers, bags, etc., all needed to get from the basement, up the stairs, into cars and vans, and then unloaded at their destinations.

Below: Ed and Gloria Meer at the dedication of the Meer Family Gymnasium at the girls' building of the Yeshiva Beth Yehudah.

Left: The Shul opened on the 40-acre Chabad Lubavitch Campus of Living Judaism.

ECHOES OF DETROIT'S JEWISH COMMUNITIES

Senator Carl Levin took time away from Washington to attend the Orthodox wedding of his cousin, Jack Baum. Levin showed Rabbi Yochanan Polter some moves on the dance floor.

The Sephardic Congregation Keter Torah had its first home of its own when their new synagogue opened in 2002 on Orchard Lake and Walnut Lake Roads in West Bloomfield.

(All photos by author)

radio and television work, Chodun, now a grandmother, is a major reason her station ranks high with local viewers in the all-important ratings game.

Television stations covered the space shuttle *Columbia* tragedy in February, sending the nation into mourning for the seven heroes. The Jewish community had special prayers and memorials for Israeli astronaut Ilan Ramon. Before the breakup of the space shuttle over Texas, Ilan, which means tree in Hebrew, sent a message back to Earth: "I call upon every Jew in the world to plant a tree in the land of Israel during the coming year. I would like to see at least 13 or 14 million new trees planted in Israel exactly one year from now, on the anniversary of the launching."

When she launched her career as an opera star, Emma Lazaroff Schaver had no idea that she would become world famous and plant the seeds of Jewish continuity through her compassion and support of Jewish causes. Mrs. Schaver, who died at 97, in 2003, had a deep love for Israel and the Jewish people that had enabled her to endure harsh travel conditions generations earlier to perform for the builders of Israel and the remnants of the Holocaust.

Detroit lost two of its veteran rabbis early in 2003. Rabbi Noah Gamze, who served the Downtown Synagogue for nearly 40 years, died at 78, and Rabbi M. Robert Syme, who had 47 years of service to Temple Israel, was 82.

Since it opened its doors in August 2000 to 53 freshmen and sophomores, the Jewish Academy had 112 students in four grades in 2003 and graduated its first high school class. The Alliance for Jewish Education and the Agency for Jewish Education were merged in one Federation department, creating a centralized agency for planning and implementation of educational services. Kadima, the Jewish mental health agency which provides psychological and residential care, employment, and social activities, marked its 20th anniversary.

Zeman's Bakery, operated by the Weiss family at its current location on Greenfield north of 10 Mile Road in Oak Park for 30 years, sold the business to computer whiz Jeff Abraham. Even though he had to lay out a lot of dough, Bill Davidson hired high-priced Larry Brown as Pistons head coach, giving the local basketball team the only Jewish head coach in the NBA.

Known as Dovy, Dov Efraim Gardin was a product of local Orthodox day schools and Hershel and Joy Gardin of Oak Park. Dovy, who became Dov. E., spent two years studying Torah and working in Israel before tackling college and graduating from the University of Michigan with honors and a fellowship to the graduate school of George Washington University in Washington, D.C.. However, days before he was to begin his graduate studies, Dov went to Washington to inform the university admissions office that he was withdrawing from the graduate program. A few weeks later he emigrated to Israel.

"Dov both attended an Ulpan (a program where

Legendary Tigers broadcaster Ernie Harwell (left) spoke at the 2002 Benefactors of the Jewish Home and Aging Services installation and dinner. Harwell was introduced by his longtime friend, author Irwin Cohen.
(Photo by Bob Benyas)

he studied to improve upon his command of the Hebrew language and attempted to enlist in the Israel Defense Forces," his proud father related. "The army was impressed with his enthusiasm but intended to give this "aged" youth of 24 years a simple desk job. The army expressed some concern about his command of the Hebrew language and his ability to withstand the rigors of field training experienced by the typical 18-year-old, native born draftees he would otherwise be grouped with. Dov was not to be deterred.

"Dov attended additional training in the Hebrew language and worked out on a near daily basis. The next time he presented his case to the army, he sailed through their language testing. They sent Dov on a two day field test of brutal physical exercises. They were convinced he would wash out. About 250 young men started the desert testing on a bright Sunday morning. By Monday night, only about 100 remained on their feet. Dov at 24 was the oldest of those who had passed the exercise. The second oldest young men still standing were 19 years old. The army had no choice but to permit Dov into regular service. Within months, Dov was at the Kotel (the Western or Wailing Wall, Judaism's holiest site) being inducted into the 101st Tzanchanim (Paratroopers), the elite infantry unit, before thirty of his closest friends and family."

Gardin trained as a team leader within his military unit and plans on continuing his graduate studies after his active service in defense of the Jewish people. This time, though, it will be in Israel.

Present community leaders realize our future leaders and protectors will come from the ranks of those attending day schools. Day school graduates are, for the most part, the ones who are going to serve, work, and study in and for Israel and Jewish causes.

Dov E. Gardin is only one of five young men from Detroit's Orthodox community serving with Israel's Defense Forces in 2003.

The Jewish Historical Society of Michigan consists of talented, interesting people on a mission. They want to "educate, celebrate and promote awareness of the contributions of the Jews of Michigan to our state, our nation and the world."

In 2003 they honored a remarkable woman who has made a decades-long career out of volunteering for the Jewish community. Matilda Brandwine was a past president of the Jewish Federation Women's Division and served on boards of several other organizations.

Her latest task was heading and organizing a statewide computerized Jewish cemetery index, a central registry of burials in southeastern Michigan to facilitate genealogical research.

Research led me to know of the community's unsung heroes in the Jewish Historical Society of Michi-

Dov E. Gardin is one of five young men who are products of local Orthodox day schools serving with the IDF in 2003.

Some Scenes from 2003

"We Were There," the permanent Jewish War Veterans of Michigan memorial, opened at the West Bloomfield Jewish Community Center.

Rabbis Leo Goldman (left) and Chaskel Grubner marked their 55th year of leading local congregations.

Mortgage maven Andy Jacob, a supporter of many charities, addresses the Friendship Circle dinner.

The Shul hosted its first wedding ever in 2003.

(All photos by author)

gan. Besides preserving history, their accomplishments make them candidates for induction into the Metropolitan Detroit Jewish Hall of Fame.

We honor local Jewish athletes with induction to the Michigan Jewish Sports Hall of Fame for performance during a relatively short athletic career. How about honoring those who work for decades on behalf of the community? The old Holocaust Memorial Center adjacent to the West Bloomfield Jewish Community Center would be an ideal place to house plaques, pictures, and information on worthy inductees.

Proceeds from an annual induction dinner should be split among all of the area's Jewish day schools according to student population.

After all, they're our future.

Civic leaders Peter Cummings (left) and Gary Torgow, whose projects are helping to rebuild Detroit, were part of the 2003 Jewish Historical Society of Michigan annual meeting and luncheon.

(Photo by Jim Grey)

Index

Aaron Moshe 96-97
Abraham, Chapman 5, 6
Abrams, Hillel 202
Adas Shalom 218, 269, 272, 276
Ahavas Achim 60, 142, 213, 220, 223, 236, 270
Adler, Dr. Liebman 11-13
Adler, Rabbi Morris 151, 167, 173, 260
Agree, Isaac Downtown Synagogue 76, 99, 102, 206, 234, 248
Ahavath Zion 74, 174
Aishishkin, Rabbi Ezekiel 42-43, 66, 69, 91-92, 101-102, 104, 137
Akiva Hebrew Day School 254, 256, 259, 275, 283, 288, 296, 303, 305, 327, 328
Ashinsky, Rabbi Aaron 26, 30, 91, 95, 101, 112, 118, 226
Avalon Theater 104-105, 201
Bais Chabad of Birmington-Bloomfield Hills 312
Bais Chabad of Farmington Hills 280, 307
Bais Chabad of West Bloomfield 298, 300
Ben-Gurion, David 152, 205, 213
Berlin, Marvin 280, 284, 328
Berman, Mandell L. 246
Berry, Harold 175, 284-285
Berry, Louis 175, 209, 248, 251, 281, 284, 323
Beth Abraham 28, 79, 96, 122, 131, 228-229, 276-278, 283, 290
Beth Abraham Hillel Moses (Beth Ahm) 290, 298, 300, 303, 312, 321, 330
Beth Aaron 186, 192, 210, 229, 238, 255, 270
Beth Achim 270, 272, 276, 280, 284, 316, 317
Beth Isaac 48, 251, 263
Beth Israel 88, 142, 215
Beth Itzchok 54, 110
Beth Jacob 23-24, 26, 30-32, 52, 262, 269
Beth Moses 70, 213-214, 269, 290
Beth Shalom 223, 229, 231, 240, 258, 291, 330
Beth Tefilo Emanuel Tikvah 50-52, 144, 173, 201, 210, 244, 255, 280-281
Beth Tephilath Moses 52, 70, 77, 237, 242, 290
Beth Tikvah 97
Beth Yehuda 55, 60, 102, 255, 269
Blumenstein, Penny 236, 333
B'nai David (Beth David) 28, 34-35, 41-42, 54, 60, 79, 88, 96, 102-104, 127, 137, 204, 215, 225, 229, 236, 258, 265, 271, 281, 283, 290, 312, 317, 321
B'nai Israel 21, 23-24, 26-28, 30, 32, 41, 43, 52, 84, 114, 142, 234, 240, 269
B'nai Jacob 88, 248, 251
B'nai Moshe 52, 55, 63-64, 80, 83, 98, 108, 136, 151, 177, 236, 238, 240, 243, 307, 309, 317, 321, 325, 333
B'nai Zion 258, 262
Boesky's Restaurants 75, 111-112, 116, 259
Borman, Al 97, 158, 228, 251, 285
Borman, Tom 97, 158, 196, 228, 232, 245, 256
Brandwine, Tillie 308
Butzel, Fred 92, 95, 98, 133, 134, 140, 143, 145, 199-200, 205, 209, 211
Chodun, Cheryl 335
Clemens, Clara 67, 118
Cohen, Marcus 8, 9, 11
Cohen, Reb Hersch 59, 179, 183
Cohn, Avern 169, 174, 189, 204, 208, 222, 235, 280, 281, 283, 294, 300-301, 304
Cohn, Irwin I. 172, 186, 204, 244
Cottler, Norman 61, 152, 213, 289
Cozens, Isaac and Sarah 8, 9, 38
Crescent Motor Company 43
Cunningham Drug Stores 62, 116-117, 141, 151, 216, 296
Davidson, Bill 89, 104, 120, 138, 176, 201, 206, 231, 271, 281, 283-284, 290, 296, 305, 310, 312
DeRoy, Aaron 137

Dexter-Davison Markets   61, 213, 239, 289
Dovid Ben Nuchim   203, 238, 242, 266, 286
Ehrlich, Dora   109, 134, 245, 267
Eisenman, Rabbi Joseph   50, 55, 88, 118, 167, 201, 279
Eliot, Sonny   104, 106, 169, 176, 181, 194, 298
Faudem, Frank   179-180, 203
Ferber, Fred   236, 307
Fine, Rabbi Samuel   121
First Hebrew Congregation of Delray   60, 88, 127
Fischer, Rabbi Moses   80, 83, 101, 167, 173, 233
Fisher, Max   120, 146, 223, 226, 232, 235, 237, 245, 254, 256, 263, 277, 283, 291, 301
Fram, Rabbi Leon   86, 142, 160, 167, 173, 185, 211, 213, 228, 275, 287, 290
Franklin, Rabbi Leo M.   33, 36-38, 49-54, 58, 62, 64, 78, 87, 91, 98, 120, 148, 151, 160, 167, 202-203
Freedman, Avrohom Abba   178, 179
Fresh Air Society and Camp   38, 44-47, 59, 66, 77, 83, 89, 96, 109, 125, 152, 173, 209, 230, 244, 246, 288, 334
Gabrilowitsch, Ossip   67, 103, 118, 125, 138
Gardin, Dov   339
Gemiluth Chassodim (Beth Hillel)   239, 243, 261
Glazer, Dr. B. Benedict   167, 168, 218
Goldman, H.L. and sons   43, 44
Gordon, Lou   126, 142, 288
Greenberg, Hank   127, 129-134, 138, 141, 147, 162-163, 176, 193-194, 222, 230, 234, 302, 307
Hadassah   57-58, 63, 87, 101, 116, 138, 216, 225, 238, 245, 258, 289, 307, 308
Hermelin, David   310, 332
Hershman, Rabbi Abraham   44, 46, 48-50, 57-58, 62, 69, 77, 90, 98, 101, 114-115, 167, 237
Hillel Day School   291, 311, 322, 324
Holocaust Memorial Center   303, 306, 313
Jackier, Edythe & Joseph   273, 280, 281, 293, 294, 306, 308
Jackier, Lawrence   287
Jewish American   36, , 47, 52
Jewish Chronicle   58, 65, 71, 101, 214-215

Jewish Community Center   124, 146, 150, 152-153, 157-158, 185, 213, 234, 238, 296, 300
Jewish Herald   99, 101
Jewish News   163-164, 188, 214-215, 222, 263, 273, 324
Jewish Welfare Federation   92-93, 112, 116, 125, 150, 165, 190, 195, 201, 209, 211, 227, 265, 296, 307, 314, 315, 320
Kahn, Albert   23, 27, 30, 39, 40, 47, 55, 60, 73, 77, 96, 105, 107, 146, 167-168
Kanter, Edward   11-12, 21, 32
Keidan, Harry B.   53, 70, 84, 95-96, 172-173
Kollel Institute   286
Levi, Benno   132, 149, 157, 162, 164, 169, 179-180
Levin, Abraham   60, 62, 121
Levin, Isadore   60, 62, 65-66, 297
Levin, Rabbi Judah   32, 37, 52-54, 58-60, 62, 69, 88, 90, 216
Levin, Rabbi Leizer   145-146, 167, 173, 238, 246, 259, 318-319
Littman People's Theater   99-100, 205
Loewenthal, Larry   252
Machon L'Torah   311
Marvel Motor Company   43, 44
Meer, Ed   172, 176, 195, 336
Meir, Golda   101, 121, 128, 141-142, 212, 265, 292
Mercury Paint Company   65, 89, 204, 265, 271, 290
Mercury Theater   241, 245
Merzon, Manuel   121, 164, 255, 310
Michelson, Larry   109
Milgrom, Max   65, 126
Milgrom, Myron   162, 265, 275, 300, 307
Mishkan Israel Nusach H'Ari Lubavitcher Center   54, 87-88, 235, 240, 269, 294
Mogen Abraham   52-53, 59, 70, 91-92, 159, 161, 174, 204, 262
Nederlander, David T.   54-55, 245
North End Clinic   77, 89-90, 109, 140, 186, 237
Nusbaum, Abe   97, 193, 202, 235, 297
Nusbaum, Irving   193, 287, 288, 290, 302
Nusbaum, Max   142, 186, 192, 297

Oriole Theater   104-105 , 110
Phoenix Club   21-22, 25, 43-45, 54, 62, 70, 76
Pipp, Edwin G.   74
Pisgah Lodge Community Center   91
Purple Gang   107, 113, 114, 128, 137, 267
Rabinowitz, Rabbi Joseph   92, 118, 127, 167, 203, 266
Radner, Gilda   121, 242, 313
Raskin, Danny   128, 143, 164, 195, 205, 214, 247, 273
Reliance Motor Company   43
Reshevsky, Samuel   85
Robinson & Cohen Co.   55-56, 244
Robinson, Jack A.   173, 232
Rosen, Abe, Dave and Sam   60
Rosenthal, Isaac   41, 42, 59, 112, 125, 140, 180, 189, 217, 219, 220
Royal Theater   241
Saltsman, Al   102
Sapiro, Aaron   98
Schaver, Emma Lazaroff   54, 74, 76, 83-84, 103, 105, 113, 121, 128, 184, 191, 194, 198, 200, 205, 226, 228, 234, 263, 265, 338
Schaver, Morris   83-84, 113, 174, 191, 221, 246
Schlussel, Mark   257, 280
Schneurson, Rabbi Joseph   114
Shaarey Shomayim   236, 238
Shaarey Zedek   13, 17-24, 26-27, 30, 32, 34, 36-37 39, 42, 44-48, 50, 52-54, 57-58, 60, 62, 64, 68, 84, 88, 90, 96, 103, 110, 114-115, 121-122, 142, 151, 158, 225, 234, 236, 246, 249, 265, 281, 299-300, 307, 333
Shapero, Nate S.   62, 116-117, 141, 151, 193, 216-217, 220, 232, 296
Sherman, Jane   235, 277, 304, 326, 335
Sholem Aleichem Folk Institute   178, 214, 225
Shomrey Emunah   234, 238-239, 279
Shul Chabad Lubavich   336
Simons, David W.   35, 38, 46, 53-54, 60, 62, 64, 68, 115, 120, 151, 205
Simons, Leonard   109, 227, 260, 273, 313, 323
Sinai Hospital   220-221, 237, 259, 322, 324, 329

Slomovitz, Phillip   71, 77, 99-101, 117, 119, 163, 215, 322
Soberman & Milgrom   89, 126, 151, 271
Soberman, Jacob   65
Stutz, George   112, 134, 149
Temple Beth El   10-30, 33, 36-40, 50, 53, 58, 64, 70, 77-78, 80, 86-88, 92, 151, 158, 160, 166, 168, 183, 195, 210, 218, 246, 272, 275, 277, 282, 283, 309, 323
Temple Emanu-El   226, 229, 231, 234, 240, 242, 272, 334
Temple Israel   161, 167, 173, 213-214, 246, 256, 261, 287, 290, 294, 296, 307, 316
Temple Shir Shalom   312, 322
Tifereth Israel   65
Torgow, Bob   183
Torgow, Gary   283, 301, 310, 332, 342
United Hebrew Schools   66, 70, 74, 76, 78, 83, 85, 87-88, 92, 101-102, 107-108, 112, 117, 140, 151, 158, 165, 178, 201, 214, 225-226, 231, 233, 247, 250, 268, 275, 311, 322
United Jewish Charities   33, 40
Warfield Theater   106
Warsaw Bakery   60, 89
Weil, Joseph and sons   8
Weingarden, Moses   94-95
Weizmann, Dr. Chaim   61, 73, 80, 101, 159, 205, 217
Wetsman, Joseph   69, 104, 142, 216
Winkelman's   103, 127, 235, 290, 293, 328
Wodic, Emanuel   28, 77, 87
Wohlgelernter, Rabbi M. J.   144, 166, 167, 179, 204, 210
Workmen's Circle Arbeter Ring   45, 60, 80. 178, 225
Yeshiva Beth Yehudah   95-96, 112, 121, 151, 158, 161, 165, 173-174, 178-179, 182, 192, 195, 202, 206, 216, 223, 226, 233, 234, 253, 261, 273, 275, 291, 226, 228-229, 233, 235, 245, 250, 253, 261, 265, 273, 289, 303, 305, 311, 315-317, 320, 322, 336
Yeshiva Gedolah   305, 311, 313, 316
Yeshivath Chachmey Lublin   165, 173, 178, 191

Young Israel of Detroit   84, 88, 91, 95-96, 127, 166, 183, 206

Young Israel of Greenfield   238, 240-241, 285-286

Young Israel of Northwest Detroit   210, 240, 247-248, 255

Young Israel of Oak Woods   223, 226, 231, 240, 268-269, 283, 324, 334

Young Israel of Southfield   283, 290, 307

Zussman, Raymond   177, 202

...and other doctors, rabbis, individuals, organizations, and synagogues listed within these pages but too numerous to index.